Spain, Portugal and the
Great Powers, 1931–1941

The Making of the 20th Century

Spain, Portugal and the Great Powers, 1931–1941

Glyn A. Stone

First published in 2005 by
PALGRAVE MACMILLAN
Houndmills, Basingstoke, Hampshire RG21 6XS and
175 Fifth Avenue, New York, N.Y. 10010
Companies and representatives throughout the world.

PALGRAVE MACMILLAN is the global academic imprint of the Palgrave
Macmillan division of St. Martin's Press, LLC and of Palgrave Macmillan
Ltd. Macmillan® is a registered trademark in the United States, United
Kingdom and other countries. Palgrave is a registered trademark in the
European Union and other countries.

ISBN-13: 978–0333–49559–9   hardback
ISBN-10: 0–333–49559–4   hardback
ISBN-13: 978–0333–49560–5   paperback
ISBN-10: 0–333–49560–8   paperback

This book is printed on paper suitable for recycling and made from fully
managed and sustained forest sources.

A catalogue record for this book is available from the British Library.

Library of Congress Cataloging-in-Publication Data

Stone, Glyn.
    Spain, Portugal, and the Great Powers, 1931–1941 / Glyn A. Stone.
        p. cm.—(The making of the 20th century)
    Includes bibliographical references and index.
        ISBN 0–333–49559–4 (cloth)—ISBN 0–333–49560–8 (pbk.)
        1. Spain – Foreign relations – 1931–1939. 2. Spain – History – Civil
War, 1936–1939 – Diplomatic history. 3. Spain – History – Civil War,
1936–1939 – Participation, Foreign. 4. Spain – Foreign relations –
1939–1975. 5. Portugal – Foreign relations – 1933–1974. 6. Portugal –
Foreign relations – 1910–1933. I. Title. II. Making of the 20th century
(Palgrave Macmillan (Firm))

DP257.S76 2005
327.46′009′041—dc22   2005049315

10 9 8 7 6 5 4 3 2 1
14 13 12 11 10 09 08 07 06 05

Printed in China

For Jane and Emma

Contents

Preface

Few subjects have had more written about them than the origins and development of the Spanish Civil War. Much of this historical work has focused on the domestic causes of the war and its impact on both sides in the struggle. The international dimension of the civil war – the intervention of some of the Great Powers and the non-intervention of others – has also attracted considerable attention from historians. It is therefore surprising that very few books have specifically focused on the role of all the Great Powers in the conflict, though many have focused on particular powers. Arnold Toynbee wrote a special edition of *The Survey of International Affairs* in 1938 which was devoted to exploring the motivations for intervention and non-intervention on the part of the Great Powers. Pamela van der Esch wrote her *Prelude to War: The International Repercussions of the Spanish Civil War, 1936–1939* in 1951 while in 1962 Dante Puzzo produced his *Spain and the Great Powers, 1936–1941*. These three works were written before the opening of many relevant archives and the publication of many relevant primary sources. Since then the number of books, articles and essays on specific aspects of the international dimension of the civil war has grown enormously and utilising many of these Michael Alpert wrote his *A New International History of the Spanish Civil War* in 1994. Since the publication of Alpert's book there has been no waning of interest as many more works have appeared including published documentary sources from archives, such as those of the former Soviet Union.

While this book focuses on the Great Powers and their respective intervention or non-intervention in the civil war, it also examines their attitudes and policies towards the Second Spanish Republic between it inception in April 1931 and the outbreak of the civil war on 18 July 1936. In addition, the relations of the Great Powers with Franco's Spain from the end of the Spanish conflict in March 1939 until the end of 1941, and the entry of the United States into the Second World War, are also explored. In this connection, advantage is taken of a growing number of recent studies on the

Second Spanish Republic and the early years of Franco's Spain. At the same time, the relations of the Great Powers with the Iberian Peninsula's lesser power, Portugal, are also given some attention and prominence both before and after the outbreak of the Second World War. By including Portugal an Iberian-wide perspective is achieved and, indeed, this book is the first general study of the significance of the whole of the Iberian Peninsula to the foreign relations of the Great Powers during the 1930s and early 1940s. By beginning in 1931 and including Portugal it is also intended to achieve a more comprehensive general account than has appeared hitherto.

Acknowledgements

In writing this book I am indebted to a large number of people. Those providing financial assistance, including the British Academy, the Twenty Seven Foundation (now the Scouloudi Foundation) and the University of the West of England, Bristol which also provided that precious commodity, time, in which to complete the manuscript. Those providing practical assistance in various libraries and archives, including The National Archives (formerly the Public Record Office), the Quai d'Orsay, the Vincennes Military Archives, the Archive Centre at Churchill College Cambridge, the British Library, the Bodleian Library, the Libraries of the Universities of Birmingham, Bristol, Cambridge and the West of England. Those colleagues and friends providing practical support and their insights and perspectives at the University of the West of England, Bristol and within the British International History Group. Above all, I am indebted to my wife Jane and daughter Emma for their love and support.

List of Abbreviations

AEF	Afrique Equitoriale Française
AGK	Ausführgemeinschaft für Kriegsgerät
AO	Auslandorganisation
AOF	Afrique Occidentale Française
CEDA	Confederación Española de Derechas Autónomas
CNT	Confederación Nacional del Trabajo
CTNE	Compañía Telefónica Nacional de España
CTV	Corpo di Truppe Voluntarie
DNB	Deutsches Nachrichten-Büro
FAI	Federación Anarquista Ibérica
GRU	Soviet Military Intelligence
Hisma	Sociedad Hispano-Maroquí de Transportes
ITT	International Telephone and Telegraph Company
NKVD	Soviet Secret Police
OKH	Oberkommando des Heeres
OKM	Oberkommando der Marine
OKW	Oberkommando der Wehrmacht
PCE	Partido Comunista de España
PCF	Parti Communiste Français
POUM	Partido Obrero de Unificacíon Marxista
PSOE	Partido Socialista Obrero Español
PSUC	Partido Socialista Unificado de Cataluña
PVDE	Policia de Vigilancia e Defesa do Estado
Rowak	Rohstoff–Waren–Kompensation Handelgesellachaft AG
SD	Sicherheitdienst
SIS	Secret Intelligence Service
SOE	Special Operations Executive
SS	Schutzstaffel
UGT	Union General de Trabajadores

Map of Spain and Portugal.

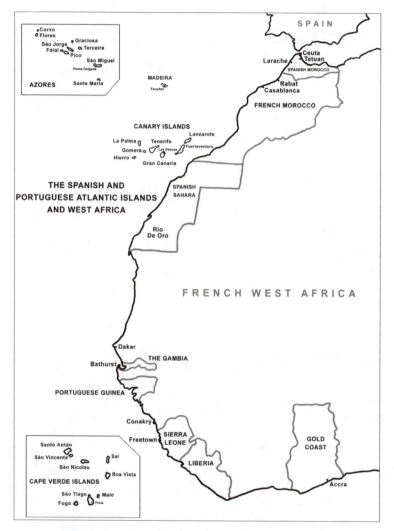

Map of the Spanish and Portuguese Atlantic Islands and West Africa.

Introduction

With the voyages of discovery and the establishment of global empires in the late fifteenth and sixteenth centuries the Iberian powers – Spain and Portugal – could properly be referred to as great powers. But the gradual decline of Spain and more rapid decline of Portugal in the seventeenth and eighteenth centuries relegated them to the ranks of the lesser European powers despite the persistence of their respective empires. Following the Peninsular War of the early nineteenth century, both powers appeared only intermittently on the radar of the great powers – the Spanish revolt of 1821–1823, the Portuguese succession crises of the 1820s and 1830s, the Carlist Wars of the 1830s, the Spanish Marriages of 1847–1848, the Spanish succession in 1870 which provided the pretext for the Franco-Prussian War, the Spanish–American War of 1898, the Moroccan Crises of 1905–1906 and 1911 and the Anglo-German machinations with regard to the Portuguese colonies of 1898–1899 and 1911–1914. During the First World War Spain remained neutral though leaning slightly towards the Central Powers, while Portugal belatedly joined the Allies in 1916 contributing 55,000 troops, of whom there were eventually 10,000 casualties.[1] As far as the Iberian Peninsula was concerned the 1920s scarcely registered a blip on the radar of the great powers regardless of the inception of the Primo de Rivera dictatorship in monarchist Spain in 1923, which lasted until 1930, or the overthrow of the Portuguese Parliamentary Republic and its replacement by a military dictatorship in 1926.

The Second Spanish Republic, which replaced the Alfonist Monarchy in April 1931 while the world was in the throes of the Great Depression, began to attract greater attention from the great powers for economic and commercial reasons but also in connection with international issues, such as disarmament, Mediterranean security and in 1935 the Ethiopian crisis. Above all, the internal politics of Spanish society, with its ideological polarisation between the forces of the Left and Right at a time when Europe itself was becoming more polarised ideologically, aroused growing interest and concern in the chancelleries of the European great powers and the United States. The Spanish Left was divided between anarchists (*Federación Anarquista Ibérica* – FAI) and their anarcho-syndicalist labour union the CNT (*Confederación Nacional del Trabajo*), socialists (*Partido Socialista Obrero Español* – PSOE) and their labour union the UGT (*Unión General de Trabajadores*), communists (*Partido Comunista de España* – PCE), the Left Republicans (*Izquierda Republicana*) and other smaller parties.[2] The Spanish Right was composed of monarchist parties, the Alfonist *Renovación Española* and the Carlist *Comunión Tradicionalista*, the nationwide mass Catholic party CEDA (*Confederación de Derechas Autónomas* – Spanish Confederation of Right Wing Groups), the much smaller Spanish Fascist party, the *Falange Española*, the Radical Republican Party (*Partido Republicano Radical*) and the Spanish military and church hierarchies. As Helen Graham has emphasised, it was the polarisation of these social and political forces and the inability of the Left Republicans and the PSOE to elaborate a strategy of mass mobilisation to counteract the mass mobilisation of conservative opinion in Spain which made the military rebellion of 18 July 1936 viable.[3] The great powers had virtually no part to play in the Generals' decision to issue a *pronunciamento* to overthrow the democratic Republic even though rumours of a coup had been circulating in Europe's capitals and also Washington since at least March 1936.

Had the attempted *coup d'état* succeeded it is almost certain that the great powers, with the exception of Soviet Russia, would probably have granted at least *de facto* recognition to the new military regime but it failed and instead provoked a civil war which was to last 33 months and cost the lives eventually of well over half a million Spaniards, including large numbers of Republican prisoners executed after the civil war, and the deaths of tens of thousands of foreign combatants.[4] It also brought the Iberian Peninsula to the centre stage of international politics for a time until at least the middle of 1938. Foreign influence on the outcome of the civil war was immense.

The intervention of Germany and Italy on the side of the Spanish rebels, who were increasingly referred to in diplomatic circles as the Nationalists, was extremely important from virtually the beginning of the civil war. Within days of the failed coup, the Spanish Army of North Africa consisting of 17,000 Moorish

Regulars, 17,000 Spanish conscripts and about 5000 soldiers of the Spanish Foreign Legion under the command of General Francisco Franco who would become the supreme leader of the Nationalist forces, was trapped by the Spanish Navy which had remained under Republican control as a result of treasonous officers being overwhelmed by their crews. As a result, German and Italian transport planes were used to ferry the African Army to the mainland during the last days of July and throughout August and September either directly or by escorting rebel troop ships. German and Italian aircraft also replenished the small rebel air force which helped drive the Republican Navy from the Straits of Gibraltar and provided air cover and support for the Nationalist drive north towards Madrid. German ships patrolling the Moroccan coastline were also used to harass the Republican Navy while Italian aircraft and ships were used to help the Nationalists seize Majorca where an Italian air base was established.[5] The arrival of the *Corpo di Truppe Voluntarie* (CTV) in Spain in early 1937 considerably reinforced the Nationalist forces contributing immediately to the capture of Málaga and while the Italian participation in the Battle of Guadalajara in March 1937 has been regarded as a disaster, Italian forces still occupied half the terrain they had initially seized. Although the Italian armies were held in reserve during the entire Bilbao offensive in April, May and June 1937 German and Italian aircraft were used to provide close air support to General Emilio Mola's attack on the Basque country. German bombers had also practised terror bombing on the civilian population of the small market town of Guernica in late April. In July 1937 German and Italian air personnel helped the Nationalists to repel the Republican Brunete offensive while in August the CTV contributed to the capture of Santander which was followed in September and October by the subjugation of the Asturias region.

The conquest of the Basque Country, Santander and Asturias gave Franco a decisive military and industrial advantage over his Republican enemies and German and Italian air support had by now delivered clear air superiority to the Nationalists which they never relinquished for the remainder of the war. Within a few more months and the end of the Aragón winter offensive of December 1937–February 1938 which had centred on Teruel, the Nationalists had achieved a 20 per cent advantage in terms of men and, thanks to German and Italian material assistance, an overwhelming one in terms of aircraft, artillery and other equipment.[6] The capture of Teruel was followed during March, April and May 1938 by a further massive offensive through Aragón aimed at cutting off Catalonia from Valencia and the central Republican zone. The CTV took part in this offensive which was supported by almost 1000 Italian and German aircraft and 200 tanks and when the offensive started to flag in June it was revived by further Italian aid, including 6000 new troops and large numbers of aircraft. When the Republican counter-offensive on the Ebro front created a stalemate between the two armies in late summer and autumn it was eventually broken with the help of further substantial arms deliveries from Germany which along with further Italian reinforcements contributed to the final offensive against Catalonia of December 1938–January 1939.

The Nationalist forces also received substantial assistance from the German and Italian Navies. They provided protection for the merchant vessels transporting illicit arms to the Iberian Peninsula and provided intelligence on Republican and Soviet maritime traffic. Italy was responsible for intelligence gathering in the Mediterranean except for the Moroccan coast which Germany was responsible for along with the region of Gibraltar and the Atlantic. The Axis Navies also participated in the war by direct clandestine combat operations involving the use of submarines. Most notably, in the summer of 1937 Italian submarines were responsible for an intensive campaign of submarine warfare aimed primarily against Republican warships and Republican and Soviet merchant ships but also including ships of other nationalities if they failed to display navigation lights within three miles of the Republican coast or were escorted by Republican warships. The effect of this campaign was to close off the Mediterranean as a direct route for Soviet arms supplies to the Spanish Republic.[7] During the civil war, Nationalist, Italian or German naval forces sank 44 foreign merchant ships, declared 23 war prizes, and confiscated the cargoes of 98 more. In contrast throughout the war it has been calculated that 180 German and approximately 290 Italian merchant ships carrying arms and munitions sailed to Spain under the cloak of deception and that except for the first two German vessels, all arrived without incident.[8]

In contrast with their Nationalist enemy, the Republicans never succeeded in securing consistent and sufficient material support from the great powers. The decision of the British, French and Americans not to intervene in the civil war and to impose an arms embargo on both sides irrespective of the legitimacy of the Government at Madrid and later Valencia, deprived the Republicans of the weapons and munitions they needed to stabilise their military fronts. Soviet assistance, while occasionally significant as in the defence of Madrid in October–November 1936, which transformed the Republican defence and made a long drawn out civil war inevitable, and the Ebro offensive in the summer and autumn of 1938, was never sufficient to enable the Republicans properly to fight an offensive war. Despite the considerable logistical difficulties of delivering war material through the Mediterranean in face of the covert Italian naval war on Republican and Soviet shipping which eventually forced the Soviets to reroute their arms deliveries via the Baltic, Atlantic and French territory, the Soviets continued to supply the Republican forces until the last arms shipment was dispatched in December 1938. But the effect of the non-intervention policy of the democratic powers was to condemn the Republic to a hand-to-mouth existence, dependent to some extent on the international black market in arms and vulnerable to the corrupt and deceitful practices of a whole succession of dubious arms dealers.[9] Moreover, because non-intervention forced the Republican authorities to spend a large proportion of their resources on arms procurement there was less available for sustaining the home front and the necessary priority given to providing food for the Republican armed forces contributed to internal instability and eroded the Republic's legitimacy in the minds of many facing increased hunger and hardship. The effect was to undermine the Republican war effort in face of Franco's determination to conduct a war of annihilation, to ruthlessly crush for the foreseeable and even distant future all and any remnants of Republican Spain.[10]

Foreign intervention and non-intervention in the Spanish Civil War was motivated by a range of ideological, political, economic and strategic considerations, some of which were immediate and others more long term but all have been debated at considerable length by historians from the end of the conflict onwards. New evidence has been revealed and emphases shifted over a period of time but what motivated the great powers remains a subject of some contention as does the significance of the civil war in the origins of the Second World War. In its focus on the civil war this study, which is concerned essentially to analyse the motivations of the Great Powers in the Spanish conflict rather than to engage in a detailed account of the actions and reactions to events as they developed, shares the assumptions of Willard Frank Jr that while it was not a dress rehearsal for, or a microcosm of the Second World War it contributed to both perceptions and misperceptions on the part of the great powers which were a crucial part of the process which led to war in September 1939. The civil war in Spain weakened the democratic societies, albeit to a limited extent, strengthened the dictators, and clarified the alignments but it also led Nazi Germany, Fascist Italy and Soviet Russia to seriously underestimate the determination of the western European democracies, Britain and France, to resist any further acts of aggression concerning Poland, despite the Nazi–Soviet Pact of August 1939.[11]

The Spanish conflict also brought Portugal within the radar of the great powers. Long regarded by the others as an ally firmly within Britain's orbit, German and Italian intervention on the same side as Portugal, a fervent supporter of, and contributor to the Nationalist cause, presented a golden opportunity to undermine the Anglo-Portuguese alliance and bring the Iberian lesser power within the Axis orbit alongside Franco's Spain. In seeking to exploit this opportunity the fascist powers forced the British to take a series of measures to counteract their influence so that before the Second World War the Portuguese remained committed to the alliance and after its outbreak prepared to pursue a neutralist policy which leaned benevolently towards the United Kingdom.

After the civil war ended in 1939, Spain and Portugal still maintained the interest and attention of the great powers though Iberian matters no longer occupied a significant position in their priorities and the decision of both countries to adopt a neutralist stance at the outbreak of the Second World War suited the purposes of the belligerent powers. At the outset of the war as far as the Iberian Peninsula was concerned, geographical realities undoubtedly favoured the Anglo-French Allies and it is entirely conceivable that had France not fallen so rapidly in the early summer of 1940 the influence of the Axis powers over Spain and Portugal would have been severely constrained. The French demise, however, left the British vulnerable to a sustained challenge from the

Axis powers which threatened serious military and strategic consequences for Britain's position in the Atlantic and Mediterranean
and provided Germany and Italy with a further opportunity to
strengthen their Iberian connections in pursuit of their wider
imperial ambitions. Accordingly, while ideological issues retained
some significance it was essentially economic and strategic considerations which were uppermost in Berlin, Rome, London and
eventually Washington. In contrast, Soviet Russia's interest in the
Iberian Peninsula had ceased in March 1939 and the influence it
continued to exert in Iberian affairs during the early years of the
Second World War was entirely negative and indirect. The degree
of hostility directed against Soviet communism within the authoritarian Right-wing regimes in Spain and Portugal was considerable and was certainly not underestimated by the Axis powers or
by Britain and the United States.

In retrospect, it is clear that the end of 1941 and America's
entry into the war following the German invasion of Soviet Russia
in June of that year marked a significant turning point in the
fortunes of the belligerent powers. Winston Churchill in his wartime memoirs referred to the entry of the United States as the
turning point which sealed Hitler's fate and Mussolini's fate and
also that of the Japanese: 'All the rest was merely the proper application of overwhelming force'.[12] After 1941 Spain and Portugal
would continue to attract the interest of both the Axis powers and
the western Allies but the opportunities for the former were again
constrained while the threats to the latter were beginning to
diminish. From 1942 onwards, Hitler's instructions and directives
concerning the Iberian Peninsula focused on measures to counter
allied actions rather than to initiate German offensive action and
Britain and the United States had no intention whatsoever of
threatening its neutrality. The end of 1941 therefore marks a
suitable termination date for this study.

1 The Great Powers and the Second Spanish Republic, 1931–1936

The Second Spanish Republic came into being in April 1931 with the end of the regime of Alfonso XIII who had fled Spain as a result of the successes of the Republicans and the reversals suffered by pro-monarchist parties in the municipal elections which had been intended to consolidate the Spanish Monarchy. According to one observer, the Permanent Under Secretary at the British Foreign Office, Sir Robert Vansittart, who reflected later, the Alfonist monarchy had become indefensible on account of the abuses which 'ran rife in army and administration' and because 'the navy was a fiction, education a joke, justice a mockery, Parliament absurd and violent'.[1] At the time the Foreign Office showed little enthusiasm for the new Republic and wanted the Great Powers to act together and 'merely recognise the [provisional] Republican Government *de facto* and transact business with it unofficially, deferring full *de jure* recognition until it had established itself in a constitutional manner'. They had in mind the precedent of the fall of King Manuel II of Portugal in 1910 when the British Government had declined to recognise the Portuguese Republicans until a constitution had been drawn up and ratified 18 months later.[2] Unfortunately for the Foreign Office, the French Government refused to wait and granted *de jure* recognition on 17 April and their political masters, the Labour Government, proved no less anxious to show goodwill towards the new provisional Spanish Government; accordingly, *de jure* recognition by Britain was granted on 22 April 1931 much earlier than intended by the Foreign Office.[3] By the end of April all of the Great Powers, with the exception of Soviet Russia which had not engaged in diplomatic relations with Monarchist Spain, had fully recognised the Spanish Republic; even neighbouring Portugal had done so despite the leftist character of the Spanish provisional Government.[4]

8

From the onset of the Spanish Republic to the outbreak of the civil war in July 1936 the Great Powers demonstrated varying degrees of interest in their relations with Spain; ranging from almost disinterest, if not indifference on the part of Germany and Soviet Russia, through the essentially commercially directed interest of the United States to the more concerned political and strategic interest of Italy, France and Britain.

The birth of the Spanish Republic was scarcely welcomed by Soviet Russia. According to the British Ambassador at Moscow, Sir Esmond Ovey, the Soviet press revealed little interest other than to express dissatisfaction at the Republic's bourgeois character and to accuse it of being just as imperialist as the former regime, while in Spain itself, the PCE, which had been taken completely by surprise by the fall of the Spanish monarchy, vainly campaigned for 'A Workers and Peasants Government' and a 'Soviet Spain'.[5] The Comintern, dominated more than ever by the Soviets, sent a representative to Spain, G. Péri, who reported pessimistically that 'eight days after the proclamation of the Republic the characteristic feature of the mood of the masses is the strength of their republican illusions'.[6] Such pessimism did not diminish the desire of the Comintern to promote a revolution in Republican Spain as was made clear in meetings of 17 and 19 May 1931 in Moscow with a Spanish Communist delegation led by José Bullejos.[7] Within a year the Comintern had become more optimistic declaring that the Government of liberal republicans and socialists, led by Prime Minister Manuel Azaña, all the republican parties and the Spanish Parliament (*Cortes*) itself had 'strikingly revealed their counter-revolutionary bourgeois class character' and that the 'workers' disappointment in the republican parties was growing steadily. Democratic illusions are being more rapidly dispelled.' In these changing circumstances, the Comintern leadership prognosticated a two-stage Spanish revolution – the first a bourgeois democratic revolution followed by the second, a proletarian one – consistent with Leninist theory. The task of the PCE meanwhile was to become a genuinely Bolshevik mass party.[8]

While the Comintern plotted Spain's communist future the Soviet Government sought to normalise relations with the Spanish Republic. At the end of July 1933 notes were exchanged between Madrid and Moscow by which each Government formally recognised the other, promising the immediate exchange of ambassadors and the opening of negotiations for the conclusion of a trade treaty between the two countries.[9] It was reported that Anatoli Lunarcharskii, a founder member of the Russian Bolshevik Party, was the Soviet Ambassador designate to Spain while the Socialist, Julio Alvarez del Vayo was the Spanish Ambassador designate to Moscow. But a change of Government in Spain following the elections in the autumn of 1933, which returned a rightist Spanish Government in which the Radicals, led by Alejandro Lerroux García, played the prominent role, and also one PCE parliamentary deputy to the *Cortes*, resulted in the suspension of diplomatic relations. At the same time, the Spanish authorities voted for the admission of Soviet Russia into the League of Nations in 1934 and did not oppose giving her a permanent seat on the Council. This surprising action by the Lerroux Government is accounted for by economic considerations, in recognition of the importance of Soviet oil and petroleum for the Spanish economy.[10] The Soviet response in October of the same year to failed riots and strikes in Madrid and Barcelona, organised by the PSOE, and the failed uprising in the Asturias mining region which attempted to establish a local 'Socialist Republic', organised by anarchists, communists and socialists, was relatively mild; despite the brutal suppression of the Asturias revolt by the Spanish military authorities, including the use of the Spanish Navy and Air Force and the deployment of Moroccan troops and the Spanish Foreign Legion. Thirty thousand people were imprisoned, many of them tortured.[11] These actions on the part of the Spanish Left were a response to the inclusion in the Government of ministers from the anti-republican, authoritarian Catholic party, CEDA, yet a leading article in *Izvestiya* on 17 October 1934 bordered on the anodyne when it declared that: 'If it should prove after all that the fighting of October 1934 is not to be Spain's "October Revolution", it is still possible to state with conviction that the Spanish proletariat, which is followed by the toiling peasantry, has made an important step on the road to its complete liberation.'[12]

The change in strategy announced at the Seventh Congress of Comintern in 1935 which required communist parties to collaborate with other progressive parties, including socialists, social democrats and liberals, in order to counter the growing threat of fascism in Europe, was endorsed by the Kremlin and its first major success was the victory of the Spanish Popular Front in the general election held in February 1936 in which the PCE secured 16 seats. Neither Comintern nor the Soviet Government anticipated the attempted military coup of the Spanish generals when it occurred in July 1936 and, despite accusations fostered by the extreme Right in Spain and elsewhere, neither were they plotting with the PCE, which was still far from being a mass party, to overthrow the Republic and establish a Soviet in Spain. Indeed, following the general elections of February 1936, Moscow, while acknowledging that Azaña's new Government was 'not a government of the popular front but a bourgeois government of the left' had instructed the PCE to support it against 'attacks and possible *coups d'état* from reactionaries, so that it may carry out the electoral programme of the popular front'. In April the Soviet authorities, referring to clashes between Left-wing revolutionaries and the armed forces of the Spanish Government, warned the PCE not to allow themselves 'on any account' to be provoked and not to precipitate events, as 'it would be harmful to the revolution at this moment and would only lead to the triumph of the anti-revolutionaries'. It was further emphasised that 'the creation of Soviet power [in Spain] is not in the order of the day'. Moscow wanted the PCE to stress their anti-fascist mission and even went so far in June as to urge them to convince the women of Spain that the party was not anti-Catholic.[13] The tardy and limited response of the Soviets to the civil war during its early weeks is a final repudiation of the charge that international communism was plotting to overthrow the Second Spanish Republic.

German interest in the Second Spanish Republic was certainly limited. According to Ángel Viñas, Germany was not especially interested in what Spanish diplomats did or did not do.[14] Interest in gathering intelligence with regard to Spain was also in short supply. The German Chancellor, Adolf Hitler, apparently spoke to the long serving German Ambassador at Madrid, Count Johannes von Welczeck, in the summer of 1933 and when the latter drew his attention to the danger of communism in Spain and requested that *Abwehr* (German Military Intelligence) agents be sent to observe such activities he seems to have agreed, but it is a matter of speculation whether this was followed up. Moreover, as Viñas and Carlos Seidel argue, there is no reason to believe that the *Abwehr* paid more than cursory attention to Spanish matters between January 1935 and July 1936 or that its head, Admiral

Wilhelm Canaris, made any visit to Spain during the period of the Second Republic.[15] In addition, when the Right-wing Spanish authorities approached the German Embassy towards the end of 1933 requesting the renewal of information exchange on subversive activities nothing came of it and so in early 1935 the Spanish Ambassador at Berlin, Francisco de Agramonte, tried again and underlined his Government's wish to engage cooperatively with the *Gestapo* (security police). By this time, the *Gestapo* was actively engaged in making secret arrangements against communist subversion with Hungary and Poland and so interest in Spain on the German side was raised with the involvement also of Canaris. On the Spanish side, the War Minister and leader of CEDA, José María Gil Robles who had visited Germany in August and September 1933, was involved, as was the Spanish Chief of Staff, General Franco. Although these contacts proved fruitless, after the success of the Spanish Popular Front in the elections of February 1936, *Oberinspektor* Paul Winzer of the SS (*Schutzstaffel* – Protection Squad) and SD (*Sicherheitsdienst* – Security Service) was sent to Spain to gather material about Left-wing activities but left immediately on the outbreak of the civil war.[16]

While, on the diplomatic front, relations between Germany and Spain remained low key, commercial relations were developed to the mutual satisfaction of both countries. Since the inception of the Nazi regime German imports from Spain had increased continuously and involved Spanish commodities essential for Germany's rearmament drive, such as iron ore and pyrites. Commercial arrangements were based on a strict compensation mechanism which obviated the expenditure on the German side of scarce foreign currency and were mutually satisfactory for both Germany and Spain. This satisfactory commercial relationship was evidenced at high level meetings held during May 1936, chaired by the leading Nazi and head of the Luftwaffe, Hermann Göring, which examined the possibilities of expanding imports of materials necessary for rearmament. Spain was acknowledged as one of the few countries where existing relations were good.[17]

Considerable interest was also shown by the Nazi regime in 1935 to Spanish requests for German armaments, with a total value of 60 million pesetas and which included heavy artillery, tanks, anti-aircraft guns and aircraft. According to Friedrich Freiherr von Lupin, Secretary General of the recently created cartel for German arms exports, the *Ausfuhrgemeinschaft für Kriegsgerät* (AGK), who was sent to Spain in September 1935, the Spanish Government had been galvanised into rearming the Spanish armed forces because of the developing Ethiopian crisis, which clearly had implications for security in the western Mediterranean, and because the increased striking power of the Spanish Army would prevent Left-wing internal subversion within Spain itself. With French competition for the arms orders seemingly compromised by an ongoing trade war between Paris and Madrid[18] the Germans were in a strong position, particularly as arms deliveries to Spain could without difficulty be fitted into the framework of the German–Spanish Trade and Payments Agreements of 1926 and 1934 respectively which could also enable the Third Reich to purchase greater quantities of Spanish raw materials, including iron ore and citrus fruit. Apart from the obvious commercial benefits, it was recognised that closer relations between the German and Spanish armies could contribute towards reviving and strengthening Spain's friendship which had proved itself during the First World War, and if an enduring link cemented by economic factors could be established with Spain's leading Catholic party, CEDA, anti-German feeling in Spain, caused by the ill treatment of religious groups within the Reich, could be ameliorated.[19]

By the end of 1935 Germany's hoped for monopoly in the provision of war material to Spain was proving elusive because the Spanish Government had concluded contracts with the British firm, Vickers, for field artillery and negotiations had been started with the French armaments manufacturer, Schneider-Creuzot.[20] Nevertheless, the giant German armaments firm, Friedrich Krupp AG, succeeded in concluding two deals with the War Ministry of the Spanish Popular Front Government in late April 1936 which involved an unspecified number of 10.5, 15.5, 24, and 30 cm guns and mortars as well as 8.8 cm anti-aircraft guns. The Left-wing character of the Spanish Government did not prevent the Nazi authorities from speedily issuing the requisite export permits.[21]

These arms deals with the Spanish Popular Front Government, which within the framework of the League of Nations had objected to the imposition of sanctions against Germany in retaliation for the remilitarisation of the Rhineland in March 1936, and the continuation of mutually satisfactory commercial relations provide evidence that Germany was not implicated in the conspiracy of the Spanish militarists which provoked the civil war in Spain, as argued by Left-wing contemporaries and subsequently by some historians.[22] German investment in the Spanish economy was insignificant and therefore the threat posed to foreign interests in Spain by Left-wing revolutionaries before July 1936 scarcely applied in the German case.[23] In addition, the German Embassy in late March 1936 expressed doubts as to whether the Army would suffice to crush a general revolution if called upon to do so by the Spanish Government and reminded the Foreign Ministry in Berlin that it took the military weeks to suppress the local revolt in the Asturias in October 1934 when they had to call in troops from Africa.[24] When it occurred in July 1936 the revolt of the generals came as a complete surprise to the German Foreign Ministry, the Nazi party organisation in Spain and German security and intelligence services, which explains why there was a delay in the German response to intervene in the civil war until Hitler himself was approached eight days later by intermediaries acting on behalf of General Franco.[25]

From the decision to recognise the Spanish Republic, only after Britain had done so, until the outbreak of the civil war the United States focused most of its attention on commercial and economic relations.[26] With a huge trade imbalance favouring the United States – 184 million pesetas in 1930 – it was hardly surprising that the new Republican regime would try to restore some balance in the Spanish–American commercial relationship. The first clear indication of this occurred in May 1931 when Madrid signed a three-year contract with the Soviets to supply 750,000 tons of gasoline at a price 18 per cent below that quoted by the American oil company, Cities Service Corporation, which had previously supplied much of Spain's petroleum needs.[27] While this decision was perfectly legitimate, Spanish discrimation against American exports was not. The sale of American automobiles in Spain, for example, had collapsed from almost 7500 in 1929 to less than 500 in early 1932. For their part, the Spaniards accused the Americans of their own trade discrimination, which included the protection of Californian fruit growers by an embargo on Spanish Almerian grapes. Washington was also concerned to compel the Spanish authorities to grant formal most-favoured-nation guarantees as they had previously to Britain. By the summer of 1933 and the end of the Azaña Government tough bargaining had produced few satisfactory results, with no formal trade agreement in sight and with American retaliatory action curtailed by concern for American investments in Spain and by the sheer size of their trading surplus which still amounted to 84 million pesétas, in contrast to the British deficit with Spain of almost 75 million pesetas.[28]

The succession of the Lerroux regime brought about an improvement in commercial relations but not before the American President, Franklin D. Roosevelt, acting on the advice of the American Ambassador at Madrid, Claude Bowers, intervened in early 1934 to persuade the State Department to become more amenable. As a result, in very quick time the United States tripled the Spanish wine quota to 1.1 million gallons while Spain agreed to purchase an additional 4 million pounds of American tobacco. Within months the dispute over Almerian grapes had also been settled and on 4 June 1934 the American Congress passed the Reciprocal Trade Agreements Act which opened the door to formal commercial relations between the United States and Spain. In the following year some progress was made with Spain eventually accepting that her trade deficit could be best improved by multilateral trade expansion as opposed to bilateral trade discrimination. Obstacles still remained, including Spanish quotas on American automobiles, but a 'full-fledged tariff war' between Spain and France in the summer and autumn of 1935 in which the Lerroux regime levied a 50 per cent surcharge on all French exports, concentrated American minds and in October 1935 a preliminary draft of the Spanish–American commercial treaty was initialled by the Secretary of State, Cordell Hull, and the Spanish Ambassador at Washington, Luis Calderón. The agreement provided tariff reductions on Spanish agricultural exports, including wine, while Spanish duties on American cotton, wheat and tobacco would be reduced and Spain guaranteed most-favoured-nation treatment on foreign exchange and import quotas to American exporters.[29]

Unfortunately, the provisional treaty remained unsigned following the demise of the Lerroux regime in late 1935 because of the *Straperlo* scandal which implicated the Prime Minister himself and forced his resignation on grounds of nepotism and corruption.[30] The victory of the Spanish Popular Front in the elections of February 1936 did nothing to improve US-Spanish commercial relations. Moreover, American investments in Spain, amounting to $90 million, were put at greater risk, including the assets of the International Telephone and Telegraph Company (ITT) which were held by its Spanish subsidiary, *the Compañía Telefónica Nacional de España* (CTNE) which was a consistent target for the Republican Left in Spain. As early as December 1931 Azaña's regime introduced a bill to revoke the ITT concession and the Americans responded by threatening to withhold financial aid and promising their unremitting hostility. As a result, the bill was withdrawn but in February 1932 an alternative one passed through the *Cortes* which regulated the CTNE more closely and included public scrutiny of its books for the first time. In the summer of 1932 the *Cortes* authorised the Spanish Government to create its own independent telecommunications system to challenge the CTNE monopoly and towards the end of the year the plan to expropriate this important ITT subsidiary was revived. This was clearly a dangerous precedent for American overseas investments which amounted to more than $14 billion worldwide and in December the State Department threatened to sever relations with Spain. Faced with this prospect, Azaña's Government retreated though in May 1933, to the great annoyance of the State Department and the White House, it rescinded the CTNE's contractual exemption from Spanish labour regulations.[31]

The Lerroux regime, which was mistakenly perceived in Washington as bringing a greater measure of stability to Spain, adopted a more conciliatory approach than its predecessor towards foreign capital and was rewarded with further American investment in the automobile industry, notably the expansion of the General Motors and Ford factories at Barcelona. For their part, the Americans were rewarded by higher profits as ITT, for example, free from Left-wing disruptions, increased its earnings on Spanish operations by almost 50 per cent during 1935. However, the reemergence of social and political instability in Spain in 1936 posed a considerable threat to American investments and reawakened fears of a Left-wing revolution in Spain.[32]

From the inception of the Spanish Republic the perception of the State Department and its representatives in Spain was deeply influenced by concerns that the liberal regime of Prime Minister Azaña was extremely vulnerable to a Soviet style takeover of the revolutionary Left encouraged by international communism. Azaña and President Alcalá-Zamora y Torres were perceived as

'Kerensky' figures and the liberal Republican regime as certain to share the fate of the Provisional Government in Russia which had succumbed to the Bolshevik Revolution of November 1917. By 1933 the State Department had been converted to the British view that the revolutionary threat in Spain was an indigenous one rather than international communism and came from anarchism, regional separatism and Left-wing socialism. But in the spring of 1936, with increasing social disorder in Spain, the fears of a 'Kerensky' scenario had reemerged leading Bowers to conclude that 'there are communistic elements in Spain that are working towards another French Revolution with its Terror'.[33] By July the Roosevelt Administration, influenced by its diplomats in France and Spain, had become convinced, along with the British Government, that, despite outward signs of restraint from both the Comintern and the PCE, Soviet agents were actively engaged in Spain and that the 'Kerensky' period of the Spanish Republic was drawing rapidly to a close.[34] This perception was to play a significant part in Washington's response to the outbreak of the civil war in late July and early August 1936.

For the Italian authorities the Second Spanish Republic was an unwelcome development because, ideologically, it was a blow to the anti-democratic and anti-parliamentary process which had been gathering momentum in Europe[35] and because it also presupposed a Franco-Spanish alliance which would, according to Dino Grandi, the Italian Foreign Minister, result in Italy 'losing a war in the Mediterranean without a fight'. For Grandi, however, the best outcome was a rapidly consolidated Republic because in his mind a strong Spain, capable of resisting French pressures, was in Italy's interest.[36] For the Italian dictator, Benito Mussolini, Republican Spain offered two political strategies which were not mutually exclusive – accentuate the ideological differences between the two regimes and support anti-Republican conspiracies and/or pursue an open good neighbour policy to reduce the Francophile tendencies of the Republican authorities in Madrid. In pursuing the second of these political strategies the Duce was mindful of the implications of a Franco-Spanish rapprochement for Italy's strategic position in the Mediterranean so that, for example, Italian naval manoeuvres were predicated on the assumption that in a Franco-Italian war the Balearic Islands would have been occupied by France with Spain's approval.[37]

In seeking to improve relations with Republican Spain the Italians took the initiative in 1932 to propose an early renewal of the Italo-Spanish Treaty of Friendship signed in 1926 at the time of the Primo de Rivera dictatorship in Spain. The Spanish Foreign Minister, Fernando de los Ríos, responded positively to this initiative and at the same time proposed negotiations for a Mediterranean pact between the principal powers with interests in the area – Italy, Spain, France and Britain. The Italian Government was favourably disposed in principle but the defeat of the Republican-Socialist Government in the elections of 1933 prevented negotiations from going further because, somewhat ironically, the victory of the Right-wing parties created greater political confusion and uncertainty in the perception of the Italian authorities so that it was thought inadvisable to raise the question of the 1926 treaty.[38] With the development of a Franco-Italian entente following the failed Nazi putsch in Austria in June 1934, the Rome accords of January 1935 and the formation of the Stresa Front in April 1935 Spain assumed a less significant place in Italian diplomacy. And when the Franco-Italian rapprochement was destroyed by Italy's war against Ethiopia the Spanish Government found themselves pressured by Britain to comply with their League obligations and impose sanctions against Italy. A divided Spanish Government, with CEDA leaning in favour of Italy, reluctantly complied but applied them in a manner most favourable to Italy. To all intents and purposes the Spaniards had adopted a neutralist position with regard to the Ethiopian war. The victory of the Spanish Popular Front in the elections of February 1936 did nothing to change this position. Indeed, Azaña and his Government opposed any stiffening or extension of sanctions against Italy from the start and as soon as Addis Ababa fell to the Italians in May 1936 it advocated the lifting of sanctions.[39]

From the point of view of its foreign policy the Spanish Republic gave no grounds to the Italians to conspire against it in concert with its internal enemies. Yet, within a year of its proclamation, the ideological side of Italian policy was being applied in Spain. Monarchist conspirators arrived in Rome from Spain in the spring of 1932 and persuaded the Italian Air Minister, Marshal Italo Balbo, to provide arms and munitions which, in the event, were issued but not collected owing to the rapid collapse of the *coup d'état* against the Spanish Republic, led by General José

Sanjurjo.[40] Balbo had promised support despite the risk that the Spanish Government would discover the extent of Italian collaboration with Sanjurjo.[41] Regardless of the victory of the Right-wing parties in the elections of 1933, Spanish conspirators continued to plot and to seek the assistance of the Italian authorities. In March 1934 Balbo received in Rome a small delegation from the two monarchist parties – the Alfonsian *Renovación Española* and the Carlist *Comunión Tradicionalista* – and agreed to provide a large quantity of arms, 1.5 million pesetas and military training to selected troops. In a secret pact signed by Balbo and the Spanish conspirators both parties agreed to conclude a treaty of neutrality and friendship guaranteeing the status quo in the western Mediterranean as far as Spanish interests were concerned while the new monarchist regime would reject any secret treaty which might exist with France. Apart from cementing close political relations with Spain, the Fascist regime was certainly motivated by ideological *animus* against the Spanish Republic. Yet, only a limited amount of assistance was provided and in March 1935 the agreement was cancelled because of the lack of initiative shown by the Spanish monarchists but more importantly because Mussolini preferred not to complicate his plans for the invasion of Ethiopia which required a calm and neutral Spain.[42]

The monarchist parties continued to receive financial support from Italy and earned it by supporting the Italian cause in the press and in the Spanish *Cortes*. The leader of *Renovación Española*, Antonio Goicoechea, for example, included in his speeches numerous suggestions from the Italian Embassy. The one genuine fascist party in Spain, the *Falange Española de las JONS*, and its leader, José Antonio Primo de Rivera, also received Italian support. From June 1935 until January 1936, he received 50,000 lire (*c.* $3500) per month paid through the Press Attaché of the Italian Embassy in Paris. Although Primo de Rivera drafted insurrectionary plans which were communicated to the Italians it appears they gave them little credence.[43]

It is somewhat ironic, as Ismael Saz has argued recently, that after supporting all the proposed insurrections presented to them until 1934 and financing the various groups on the Spanish extreme Right until 1936, the Italian authorities denied both forms of aid to precisely the conspiracy that would prove to be definitive – the generals' revolt of July 1936. Indeed, between March and July

1936 Mussolini rejected several approaches for support from Primo de Rivera, Goicoechea and another conspirator of 1934, the traditionalist Rafael Olazábal; the latter just three days before the military revolt.[44] Like his co-dictator, Adolf Hitler, Mussolini did not respond immediately to Spanish requests for support and delayed his decision until ten days after the beginning of the civil war.

Within two days of the proclamation of the Second Spanish Republic France had moved swiftly to become the first Great Power to grant *de jure* recognition to the provisional Republican Government. As a neighbouring country, Spain had immediate importance for French security but its geographical position and that of its remaining imperial possessions also held significance both for French defence and their imperial communications. As Jean Herbette, the French Ambassador at Madrid, reminded the French Foreign Minister, Pierre Laval, in December 1934: 'Its [Spain's] situation between France and North Africa, its long Mediterranean coastline, the Straits of Gibraltar and the Atlantic cannot be ignored by us or our eventual enemies. The Balearics, the Canaries, the Spanish zone of Morocco, the Rio de Oro, [the enclave of] Ifni, have an inescapable significance.'[45] Relations between the two countries during the period under review were sometimes strained because of differences relating to the Spanish and French zones of Morocco and French import controls on Spanish goods but generally they remained good and not only because of the ideological solidarity of the two republics.[46] Moreover, French investment in Spain, amounting to possibly $135 million, mainly in lead mines and railways, came second only to Britain. Until 1934, France provided the second largest market for Spanish exports, notably wine, lead, pyrites and bananas from the Canary Islands.[47]

French concerns with regard to Mediterranean security and the potential challenge posed by Italy were fully reciprocated in Madrid where, according to Herbette, the Spanish Government was 'far from closing its eyes to the consequences which could result from fascist policy'.[48] Following conversations in the spring of 1932 between Herbette and Luis de Zulueta, the Spanish Foreign Minister, the French authorities in the summer of 1932 proposed a 'Mediterranean Locarno' by which the interested powers, notably France, Britain, Italy and Spain would ensure the status quo and peace in the Mediterranean. Encouraged by the visit of Prime Minister Édouard Herriot to Spain at the end of October 1932 the Spanish Government was highly supportive because they saw the proposed pact as a means of reducing tension between France and Italy and thereby removing the danger of war in the western Mediterranean.[49] In the event, the British proved reluctant to discuss new commitments and the French initiative failed. However, the Herriot visit was judged a success even if it did create some consternation at Rome where it was believed, erroneously, that a secret agreement had been made concerning the possible movement of French colonial troops across Spanish soil. The visit was a success if for no other reason, as Saz argues, it showed that France and Spain had a similar perception of the great international problems of the time.[50]

The proposed *plan constructif* made by Herriot at the Geneva Disarmament Conference, two days before his visit to Spain, and the support given to it by the Spanish Government, also demonstrated the close cooperation that existed between the two countries even if the plan was eventually rejected by the conference because of German and Italian opposition and Britain's lukewarm response.[51] As a further example of this cooperation France offered her services as a mediator for the establishment of diplomatic relations between Madrid and Moscow.[52]Later, in the summer of 1933, the idea of a Mediterranean pact was revived on the initiative of the Spanish Government. The French Foreign Minister, Joseph Paul-Boncour, agreed with his Spanish counterpart, Fernando de los Ríos, that the Spaniards should take the initiative in proposing the pact which would focus on maintaining the status quo and peace in the western Mediterranean, on the basis of articles 10 and 16 of the League of Nations Covenant.[53] Unfortunately, the pact never materialised, partly because Azaña's Government fell when negotiations had barely begun and partly because the interested powers, including France, considered that a new project would only complicate matters at the Geneva disarmament talks. The growing rapprochement between France and Italy during 1934 rendered any further initiatives for a Mediterranean pact unnecessary.[54]

During 1934 and 1935 France's primary position in Spanish foreign policy was modified to a certain extent by the pro-British predilection of the Radicals in the governing coalition in Spain, led by Prime Minister Lerroux, and the anti-French, pro-Italian

CEDA, led by Robles, but the improvement in relations with both Italy and Britain made this change unproblematic for the authorities in Paris. The outbreak of the Ethiopian conflict in September 1935 was an entirely different matter because Mediterranean security for both France and Spain was now threatened by Italy's ambition and Britain's refusal to countenance any change in the existing status quo. In late September 1935, with war in Ethiopia imminent, Lerroux made it very clear that he wished to align Spain with France.[55] In fact, as mentioned previously, with CEDA adopting a pro-Italian stance Lerroux's Government imposed sanctions on Italy but did so reluctantly and with limited impact. Moreover, it was made abundantly clear that Spain would remain neutral in the event of an armed conflict between the western democratic powers – Britain and France – and Italy.[56]

For different reasons, in the French case because when compelled to choose between Britain or Italy as potential allies it was no contest, both France and Spain succumbed to British pressure to impose sanctions and did so reluctantly and like the Spanish Government when asked to consider extending sanctions in early 1936 the French authorities adamantly refused.[57] The victory of the Spanish Popular Front in February brought no fundamental change in Spain's relations with France. Both Prime Minister Azaña and his Foreign Minister, Augusto Barcía Trelles, were wary of unnecessarily alienating Italy and Germany and the trend towards neutralism in Spanish foreign policy continued in the months before the civil war. In this connection, on 11 May 1936, 11 days after the victory of the Popular Front in the French parliamentary elections, Herbette reported that Spain remained attached to the League of Nations and supported the maintenance of peace in Europe but if the great powers who belonged to the League ceased to fulfil their commitments she would consider herself released and would join the neutral powers. There was, perhaps, some comfort in Barcia's personal declaration to Herbette that in the event of a European war, in which France and Britain were on the same side, Spain would be benevolently neutral, and in the possibility of closer Franco-Spanish relations arising out of the victory of the French Left.[58]

The prospects for closer relations between the two ideologically compatible Popular Front Governments were certainly bright in the early summer of 1936 with no serious disagreements over foreign policy. But events within Spain were conspiring to destroy the relationship. The Quai d'Orsay were reassured by their Spanish counterparts that the possibility of a *coup d'état* in Spain was remote despite the deepening social and political crisis. Barcía, for example, told Herbette on 6 June that the Spanish military regarded the existing Government as the best possible protection for public order and it would only intervene if the Government were overthrown by a revolutionary movement.[59] When Azaña, as President of the Spanish Republic, saw Herbette on 10 July one week before the military coup, he spoke at length about the internal situation in Spain, vehemently criticising the anarchists for their subversive activities and, to a lesser extent, the Socialists for their disunity, but he made no mention whatever of any internal military threat to the Republican regime. The French Ambassador was less sanguine, warning Yvon Delbos, the French Foreign Minister, on 12 July that the outcome of the anarchic situation in Spain could be a regime which imitated those of Germany and Italy.[60] Within days the French Government would be confronted with a difficult and agonising decision, which would profoundly divide the French Popular Front Government less than two months after its famous victory.

Having shown an initial reticence in recognising the Second Spanish Republic, the British Foreign Office lost no time in consolidating their relationship with the Republican regime. Vansittart went out of his way to show friendliness to the Spanish Ambassador, Ramón Perez de Ayala, even supplying him on occasions with 'important and helpful secret information'.[61] In the early years of the Republic British policy was strongly influenced by the need to counter what was perceived in the Foreign Office as the growing entente between Paris and Madrid. The British Ambassador at Madrid, Sir George Grahame, counselled the Foreign Secretary, Sir John Simon, that while the Spanish authorities wished for 'a closer parallelism between British and Spanish policies in a general sense', they also suspected a residue of antagonism on the part of the British Government towards the Republican regime. He also warned Simon that if, owing to their attitude, 'a Franco-Spanish *Entente*, or quasi-alliance came into being, it would be hard to set a limit to its development. It might grow to quite unexpected proportions; and History shows that, whenever France and Spain have got together, trouble has ensued for England.'[62]

With Grahame's warning in mind, the Foreign Office remained committed to their policy of providing friendly encouragement to Spanish efforts to consolidate the Republic while applying 'firm but patient pressure' to secure 'fair treatment' for British interests in Spain.[63] These interests were essentially strategic and economic. At no time during the period of the Second Republic did the British authorities fear a threat to their strategic position in relation to Spain. The potential threats posed by a Franco-Spanish entente or even an Italo-Spanish alignment did not, at this time, translate into strategic ones and Britain's control of Gibraltar and, therefore, entry into and from the western Mediterranean appeared as firm as before 1931. Britain's economic interests in Spain, however, appeared more threatened from Left-wing regimes hostile to foreign capitalist enterprises or from Right-wing regimes inspired by economic nationalism. As by far the largest foreign investor in Spain with £40 million, representing some 40 per cent of total foreign investment in 1936, Britain had considerable interests to protect. A large part of British capital was concentrated in the mining industry: pyrite-mining companies in Huelva (Rio Tinto Company, Tharsis Sulphur and Copper Company etc.) accounted for 25 per cent of total British investment followed by companies quarrying iron ore, of which the largest was the Oconera Iron Ore Company in Vizcaya. British investments were also made in the electricity sector (the Barcelona Power, Light and Traction Company), railways and agriculture; the latter included: sherry, tomatoes and bananas from the Canary Islands. Finally, two-thirds of Spain's foreign trade was carried by foreign vessels and British shipping companies accounted for no less than 40 per cent while the British armaments company, Vickers-Armstrong, had a 25 per cent share in the Spanish company responsible for the construction and maintenance of the dockyards and naval ports of Spain.[64]

Before 1936, however, there was no fundamental challenge to British economic interests whether from Left-wing or Right-wing Republican regimes.[65] None the less, this did not prevent the Foreign Office from expressing great concern at internal political developments within Spain and the threat which they could pose to British interests. The Embassy at Madrid and the officials in London, including Vansittart, wished for strong and stable governments able to maintain law and order, and saw the alternatives as either a military coup which would restore the Monarchy or a Left-wing revolution. The former was attempted and thwarted in 1932, the latter, centred on Madrid, Barcelona, and most notably on the Asturias was crushed in October 1934. Despite the brutal suppression of the Asturias revolt by the Spanish military, the Foreign Office expressed considerable disquiet at its occurrence, even outrage in the case of Sir Orme Sargent, Assistant Superintending Under Secretary to the League of Nations and Western Department which oversaw Spanish matters. Sargent, in particular, condemned the Asturias rising for its anti-democratic character.[66]

Until the Ethiopian crisis deepened in the summer of 1935, the British had little to complain about with regard to Spain's foreign policy, not least Madrid's wish to see the status quo maintained in the western Mediterranean which suited British interests there, even if London was not prepared to commit to a Mediterranean pact. Spain was also a loyal member of the League of Nations but this commitment was severely tested by the outbreak of the Ethiopian war when, as noted previously, Lerroux's Government reluctantly imposed economic sanctions against Italy. According to French sources, the British had imposed pressure on Spain not only to impose sanctions but also to strengthen Mediterranean security. The British had apparently demanded from Spain guarantees involving her coasts and her island possessions so that no power (Italy) should utilise them as bases to attack British forces. Spain had responded by sending air squadrons to Algeciras, Cartagena, the Balearic Islands and Ceuta, by reinforcing the garrisons there and by sending units of the Spanish Navy.[67]

Spain's neutralist position should the Ethiopian crisis escalate into a war between Britain, France and Italy provoked little concern in London since the British Government, as shown by the Hoare-Laval fiasco in December 1935 and the failure to impose oil sanctions against Italy, had no intention of permitting such an escalation to take place. The victory of the Spanish Popular Front in February 1936 created more concern within the Foreign Office despite the fact that Foreign Minister Barcía confirmed that the foreign policy of the new regime was to follow Britain and France and in particular to continue with sanctions against Italy.[68] Senior Foreign Office officials, including Vansittart, remained sceptical about the Spanish Liberal Republicans, such as Azaña and Barcía, holding the political ring in face of the militant activities of their socialist, communist and anarchist allies on the one hand and, on the other, the forces of the Right, including Monarchists, CEDA, the *Falange* and the Generals themselves who were busy preparing a military coup. The Foreign Office, like the State Department, perceived the increasing social unrest in Spain in terms of revolutionary Russia in 1917. They regarded Azaña, who became President of the Spanish Republic in May 1936, as a Spanish Kerensky and his Government as the equivalent of the ill-fated Russian Provisional Government which eventually succumbed to the Bolshevik Revolution of November 1917. As in 1917, the options seemed to be either an extreme Left-wing revolution or a military coup.[69]

In the early summer of 1936, clearly aware of the deteriorating social and political situation in Spain, the Foreign Office focused its attention on the protection of British commercial interests which were threatened by new labour laws, by the threat of physical violence against British lives and property and by the imposition of heavy surcharges on nearly all imports into Spain which were contrary to a previous agreement of August 1935.[70] British representations at Madrid brought no material improvement so that on 24 June 1936 Vansittart advised the Foreign Secretary, Anthony Eden, to speak strongly to Barcía at Geneva.[71] When Eden spoke to the Spanish Foreign Minister on 29 June he was reassured but within days the situation relating to British companies in Spain worsened considerably with extensive strike action and disorders, with the murder of Joseph Mitchell, the British manager of a Barcelona factory, by Left-wing gunmen and with the apparent impotence of the Spanish Government to intervene and redress these grievances.[72]

The military coup, expected to resolve the crisis of order in Spain but which instead provoked revolution and civil war, followed within a matter of weeks and the British authorities, alienated by the impotence of the Republican Government and their faith in Spanish democracy severely diminished, determined to stand aside and let events take their course.

2 The Interventionist Powers and the Spanish Civil War, 1936–1939

The response of Germany and Italy to the failed insurrection of the Spanish military was neither spontaneous nor immediate. It was not until 25 July and Foreign Minister Galeazzo Ciano's meeting in Rome with Goicoechea that a favourable response was given to appeals for assistance from the Spanish rebels. However, Mussolini remained cautious about taking the final step to intervene, having previously, on 20 July, rejected a request from the Spanish rebels for aircraft. Only when he had assured himself, on the basis of reports from Italian diplomats, that neither France, nor Britain, nor Soviet Russia intended to intervene did the Italian dictator give the green light, on 27 July, for the despatch of aircraft to Spanish Morocco, to assist in the airlift of Spanish Moroccan forces to the Spanish mainland. At the same time, a cargo ship loaded with munitions and aviation fuel was sent to the rebels. The Duce's decision to intervene was made in the expectation that a small amount of Italian war material could be decisive for the rebellion. It was based, partly at least, on General Francisco Franco's personal assurances to the Italian Minister Plenipotentiary at Tangier, Pier Filippo de Rossi del Lion Nero, and his Military Attaché, Major Giuseppe Luccardi, that victory for the rebels would be certain and quick provided some outside assistance was forthcoming, and that with victory he intended to establish 'a republican government in the fascist style adapted for the Spanish people'.[1]

Adolf Hitler's decision to intervene was taken almost simultaneously, in the early hours of 26 July, independently of Italy. Like Mussolini his initial reaction to events in Spain had been a cautious one. Grand Admiral Erich Raeder, Chief of the Naval High Command (OKM – *Oberkommando der Marine*) recalled that he had had some difficulties in persuading the German Führer on 22 or

23 July to allow German ships to depart for Spain to repatriate German nationals there. Apparently, Hitler was afraid that some incident might occur.[2] Yet, within a few days and against the advice of his foreign and war ministries, he responded positively to a request from Franco for armaments and transport and fighter aircraft which had been presented to him personally at Bayreuth, where he was attending the Wagner festival, by a mission consisting of Joannes Bernhardt, a member of the Nazi *Auslandsorganisation* (AO) and formerly director in Morocco of its economics section, Adolf Langenheim, chief of the Nazi Party in Morocco, and Wolfgang Kraneck, head of the AO legal department.[3] Contrary to Bernhardt's account of events, in which he allocated himself a central role and which had become the accepted version, it is now clear that other individuals also played important roles in enabling the delegation to meet with Hitler, including Langenheim, Friedhelm Burbach, head of the department dealing with Spain and the Nazi Party in Morocco, and Alfred Hess, brother of Rudolf, the deputy Führer who convinced Hitler on the telephone to receive Franco's mission.[4] Under the Wagnerian code name *Unternehmen Feuerzauber* (Operation Magic Fire) the organisation of a support operation, known as *Sonderstab W*, was immediately set in motion.[5] Apart from the obvious significance of German and Italian intervention for the rebel forces, the decisions taken by Hitler and Mussolini in late July 1936 were in direct response to appeals from Franco rather than other Spanish generals and this connection undoubtedly contributed to his rapid rise to ascendancy as the pivotal figure on the rebel Nationalist side, as Generalísimo and Caudillo. In this context, it is notable that the individual responsible in Berlin for the actual despatch of arms and munitions to Spain, General Helmut Wilberg, personally reassured Franco about Hitler's decision to concentrate German assistance on him while Bernhardt was sent to inform General Emilio Mola, Franco's closest rival, that he would receive German weapons through Franco alone.[6]

For both Germany and Italy the limited commitment of July 1936 was to expand considerably by the end of the civil war. Throughout its duration more than 16,000 Germans helped the Nationalist forces, although the maximum in Spain at any one time was 10,000. These forces included the Condor Legion, despatched in December 1936, which consisted of 5000 tank and air personnel. At their maximum Italian forces in Spain numbered between 40,000 and 50,000 troops, including air personnel, though 80,000 actually went to Spain. German casualties were very slight, amounting to no more than 300 dead. Italian losses were far heavier with around 4000 dead and 11,000–12,000 wounded. German military hardware consisted essentially of tanks, aircraft and anti-aircraft guns plus a substantial quantity of small arms – machine guns, rifles and revolvers – transported via Portugal. Italy's contribution in this sphere was even more impressive including aircraft, tanks, motor vehicles, artillery and small arms including 319 million cartridges.[7] It has been variously estimated that the total cost of Italian war material amounted to between 6 billion and 8.5 billion lire (£64–£95 million) while for Germany the cost is variously estimated at between 412 million and 540 million reichmarks (£35 million and £46 million).[8]

The expenditure of such large resources was clearly a measure of the determination of the two dictator powers to ensure the victory of the Nationalist forces in Spain despite the risks of a further deterioration in their relations with Britain and France and even of a wider European conflagration. In the initial stages of the civil war ideological considerations figured prominently both in Rome and Berlin and continued to exert an influence throughout the conflict. Contrary to the views of certain historians, Italian claims that they were fighting against the forces of communism in Spain were not mere rhetoric but genuinely held.[9] Nor were Fascist fears of a red revolution in Spain and its possible effects misplaced, in view of the increasing popularisation of the Spanish Republican defence including the establishment of revolutionary committees. In this connection, the Italian Government was not inclined to make a distinction between libertarian anarchists in Spain, of whom there were many, and Soviet orientated communists of whom there were much fewer in July and August 1936. A victory for the Left in Spain held considerable dangers elsewhere since it might encourage revolutionaries in France and all of western Europe, including Italy. As Mussolini told his wife, Rachele: 'Bolshevism in Spain would mean Bolshevism in France, Bolshevism at Italy's back, and danger of [the] Bolshevisation of Europe.' The Duce and Ciano continued throughout the civil war to regard their intervention in Spain as safeguarding Fascism in Italy. However, the ideological motive remained essentially a negative one.

With the possible exception of the Farinacci mission to Spain early in 1937 there was no serious or sustained attempt to convert Franco's regime to Fascism during the civil war.[10]

Ideological considerations were also prominent in Germany's decision to intervene in Spain, and, as in the Italian case, essentially negative ones. Despite the involvement of the German Ambassador, General Wilhelm Faupel, with the one genuine Spanish fascist movement, the *Falange Española de las JONS*, there was no intention of seeking to establish a National Socialist regime in Spain; an objective which Hitler himself believed was impossible to achieve not to say 'superfluous and absurd'.[11] Indeed, any prospect of establishing a purely fascist regime in Spain was seriously undermined by Franco's action in April 1937 in forcibly fusing the *Falange Española de las JONS* with the Carlists and the rest of the Spanish Right to form a new political organisation under his leadership, the *Falange Española Tradicionalista y de las JONS*.[12] What mattered to Hitler and the Nazi leadership was the dangerous contagion of communism. As he told the British Prime Minister, Neville Chamberlain, at the Munich Conference on 30 September 1938, he had supported Franco only because of his abhorrence of communism. If he, Hitler, had failed to stop Bolshevism in Spain it could have spread to France, Holland and Belgium.[13] Referring to his decision to intervene later still, in 1941, the Führer explained that 'if there had not been the danger of the Red Peril's overwhelming Europe' he would not have intervened.[14] His memory was not at fault. When Vansittart visited Germany in August 1936, ostensibly to attend the Olympic Games but also to make contact, of a semi-official nature, with members of the German Government, including Hitler and his Foreign Minister, Konstantin Freiherr von Neurath, he found Nazi ruling circles obsessed with events in Spain and the threat of Bolshevism. According to the British Permanent Under Secretary at the Foreign Office: 'this is the constant theme of every man and woman in Berlin; indeed they can think and talk of little else. The obsession [with communism] is in any case endemic, but Spanish events have reinforced their thesis.'[15]

In fact, on 26 July Hitler had warned Joachim von Ribbentrop, before he went to London as Ambassador, that a victory for communism in Spain would in a short time result in the Bolshevisation of France in view of the current situation in that country; by which he probably meant the advent of the Popular Front Government of Léon Blum and their declared sympathy for the Spanish Republicans. Later, in October 1936 he told Ciano at Berchtesgaden that in Spain 'Italians and Germans have together dug the first trench against Bolshevism'. Neurath, was equally apprehensive about the Bolshevik contagion spreading from the Iberian Peninsula to the rest of western Europe.[16] Hitler, sharing the fears that arose from the civil war, also exploited them by extending conscription from one to two years and introducing the second Four Year Plan in August and September 1936.[17] Along with his propaganda chief, Joseph Goebbels, he also exploited the fear of communism in other European countries, including Right-wing circles in Britain and France. According to Robert Whealey, Hitler's stand against communism in Spain contributed to the successful outcome of German–Japanese negotiations for the Anti-Comintern Pact signed on 23 October 1936.[18]

This ideological preoccupation was linked in German minds with strategic considerations to produce what Denis Smyth refers to as 'a geo-ideological conception of the international system'.[19] Vansittart, for one, had no doubts but that it was the international strategic dimension of Bolshevism that concerned the Nazi leadership. They had little to fear from 'an internal [communist] recrudescence which would be ruthlessly crushed'. What they did fear was 'an external convergence, that Communism will extend in Europe and round on, if not encircle, Germany'.[20] The Nazis had no illusions concerning their strategic position. The possibility of a further strengthening of links between France, Soviet Russia and Czechoslovakia, following on from their mutual assistance pacts of 1935 and the victory of the Popular Front in France in the elections of May 1936, was all too real. No doubt they were also alarmed by the more than doubling of Soviet Russia's defence budget in 1936 from 6.5 billion to 14.8 billion roubles.[21] Apart from posing an external threat, the strategic consequences of a victory for communism in Spain would undermine the long term racial-imperialist ambitions of the Third Reich in eastern Europe and Soviet Russia; not least because, as Hitler himself revealed in April 1937, at a time when military cooperation between the French Popular Front and Soviet Russia arising from the Franco-Soviet Pact of 1935 still seemed a possibility, the establishment of a 'Bolshevik state' in Spain would 'constitute a land bridge for

France to North Africa' which would safeguard the passage of French colonial troops to the northern frontier of France.[22] On the other hand, a victory for the militarists in Spain would weaken Germany's potential adversaries, in particular the 'hate inspired enemy' France, improve the Reich's strategic defence and enhance its prospects for the conquest of *Lebensraum* in the East; whether as an end in itself or merely a staging post in a phased programme (*Stufenplan*) for world dominion.[23]

Both Germany and Italy recognised the strategic benefits, especially in the naval sphere, which might accrue to them as a consequence of cooperation with a grateful Nationalist Spain; benefits which would clearly be to the detriment of adversaries such as Britain and France. The latter was certainly aware of the potential strategic benefits to Germany as the French Naval Staff emphasised during September 1938: 'Germany obtained the friendship of Franco to have at its disposal the northwest coast of Spain, the coast along the Gibraltar Straits, the Canary islands, and the Spanish territories in Mauritania'.[24] In the summer of 1938 the Nazi General, later Field Marshal, Walter von Reichenau, emphasised the strategic benefits to an audience of National Socialist leaders at Leipzig: 'From the point of view of military strategy, we have got at the most vital lines both of England and France. Therein lies the paramount importance of our intervention in Spain.' Reichenau also advised that a victory for Franco in the civil war would provide the opportunity to transform Portugal into a willing satellite of the Axis and thereby secure considerable strategic benefits in the eastern Atlantic and western Mediterranean with dire consequences for British naval strategy. Significantly, at the time Reichenau made his speech, Hitler was planning a giant battlefleet (Plan Z) for war in the Atlantic where he needed bases.[25] Reichenau's observations on Portugal, although officially denied as authentic, were not isolated ones but reflected official thinking in Berlin and also Rome. Indeed, from the outset of the civil war in Spain the German and Italian governments sought to exploit Anglo-Portuguese differences over Spanish policy.[26]

Italy's intervention in Spain was certainly influenced by its strategic interest in the western Mediterranean. According to John Coverdale, from the outset of his regime in 1922, Mussolini thought of Spain primarily in terms of strengthening Italy's position *vis-à-vis* France by denying the latter the possibility of transporting troops across Spain from its North African empire, and that he might also have hoped to obtain bases in the Balearic Islands which intersected the routes between North Africa and France's Mediterranean ports.[27] In taking his decision to intervene Mussolini was aware that a Republican victory achieved with French support would result in closer Franco-Spanish relations and the loss of Italian influence in the western Mediterranean but that the reverse would be the case if the Spanish military succeeded in their rebellion. To ensure this outcome Ciano had insisted in his conversation with Goicoechea of 25 July that in return for Italian support the rebels would adhere to the terms of the 1934 agreement, signed by Mussolini and Spanish monarchists, which bound Spain to denounce any secret Hispano-French pact.[28]

Apart from acquiring the general support and collaboration of a victorious rebel government, the Italians hoped to establish naval and air bases in the Balearic Islands, which would weaken both the French and British strategic position in the western Mediterranean. Indeed, the British authorities were extremely concerned about the presence of increasingly large numbers of Italian air force personnel on Majorca between August and December 1936 and during 1937 the French considered seizing Minorca as a counter to the Italian presence on Majorca.[29] It is unlikely that in pursuing strategic objectives in the summer of 1936 Mussolini believed he could establish a complete Italian ascendancy in the Mediterranean basin and in the process revive the old Roman Empire. None the less, a successful intervention in Spain would strengthen Italy's security and that of its African empire while providing some scope for the further advance of imperial ambitions.[30]

The initial expectation of Hitler and Mussolini that the civil war would be of short duration precluded any expectation in the early stages of the civil war that intervention in Spain would yield actual military benefits, as opposed to strategic gains; though Göring at the Nuremberg Trials after the Second World War claimed that German intervention in Spain had been motivated by the need to test 'his Luftwaffe'.[31] However, as a by-product of the extension of the conflict from a matter of weeks to a matter of years, the Axis powers were able to test their weapons and to train personnel in their use under combat conditions. Indeed, many of Hitler's future wartime military commanders were present in Spain at various times including General Erwin Jaenecke, commander of the German forces in the Crimea in 1944, Generals Wolfram Freiherr von Richthofen and Hugo Sperrle of the Luftwaffe, Admiral Wilhelm Canaris, head of German Military Intelligence, General Wilhelm von Thoma of the future Afrika Korps and General Heinz Guderian the brilliant Panzer Commander promoted by Hitler in 1943 to Inspector General of Armoured Troops.[32] The Germans learned a number of valuable military lessons in Spain which were applied subsequently during the Second World War. In his address to National Socialist leaders Reichenau referred to some of these lessons which included the organisation of defence against air attacks; the superiority of the heavily armed tank as opposed to lighter models (such as the Italian Fiat Ansaldos or the German Panzer Mark I) which had proved ineffective against heavier Soviet tanks in 1936 and 1937; the use of motor vehicles in war; the vital importance of spare parts, oil and fuel; and the use of boldness in the conduct of operations in a war of movement. Reichenau also recognised the significance of the civil war for the development of tactical air strikes in support of ground forces. Later, General Karl Dunn of the Luftwaffe emphasised that the key experience gained by the Condor Legion in Spain was 'that pertaining to the methods of tactical air employment which was most significant and most far reaching in its effects'. In fact, the direct support of ground troops had been part of the Luftwaffe's mission before 1936 and army and air force units had practised the technique in field exercises but the success of close air support missions in Spain resulted in the Luftwaffe giving a higher priority to this aspect of aerial warfare. Arguably, the most effective weapon of the civil war was the German 88-mm anti-aircraft gun which was also used in an anti-tank role. The deployment of thirty German anti-tank gun companies in Spain also provided invaluable experience and lessons.[33] While many lessons were indeed learned, others were missed; not least the Luftwaffe's assumption that high-performance and well-armed bombers in mass formation could protect themselves against enemy fighters in daylight missions. The result was the very high losses sustained by Luftwaffe-trained bomber crews during 1940.[34]

Despite their substantial military involvement and investment in Spain, the Italians failed to apply many of the lessons of the Spanish conflict; possibly because the Second World War began before the Italian armed forces had digested them and acquired the resources to apply them. Several leading Italian Generals had commanded forces in Spain, including Mario Roatta, Ettore Bastico, Mario Berti, Gastone Gambara and Valentino Babini yet their performance during 1940–1941, in contrast with their German counterparts, was lamentable. The superiority of medium and heavy tanks had become quickly apparent in Spain yet as late as 1939 Italy manufactured only 194 tanks armed with cannon. The Italian Navy and Air Force provided prodigious service to the Spanish Nationalist cause but still failed to learn adequately from the experience. The limited success of Italian high level bombing against shipping in Republican ports, for example, helped convince Mussolini and the Navy and Air Force leadership that they did not need to develop torpedo bomber squadrons which were used so effectively against them by the British in 1940 and 1941. The experience of naval warfare during the civil war did not prevent the massacre of Italian submarines in June–July 1940 nor the Italian naval defeats at Punta Stilo, Cape Spada, Taranto and Matapan at the hands of the Royal Navy. The Italian Air Force continued to use biplane fighters beyond the civil war despite its awareness of the increasing superiority of monoplanes and the success achieved over Republican air forces served only to entrench tactical and operational methods suitable only for biplanes among both pilots and air staff, so that they continued to base air doctrine on Spanish combat experience well into 1941.[35]

Connected with their military operations in Spain was the prestige of the Italian and German governments. In the summer of 1936 neither Hitler nor Mussolini required a victory in Spain as a distraction from internal complications; a consideration which certainly figured prominently in Mussolini's decision a year earlier to wage war in Ethiopia.[36] None the less, having committed themselves to the cause of the Nationalists in Spain through their military and economic support and by their *de jure* recognition of Franco's administration in November 1936, it would have been difficult for the two dictators to save face in the event of defeat. Certainly, Italy's determination to maintain its forces in Spain until Franco's final victory, despite mounting costs and casualties, was connected to the prestige of the Fascist regime; and this was true particularly after the Italian defeat at Guadalajara in March 1937 which was contemptuously referred to as a 'Spanish Caporetto' by critics of the Fascist regime.[37]

While it is probably correct to regard actual military considerations as a by-product of Italian and German intervention, it is a mistake, at least in the German case, to view economic considerations in a similar light.[38] If Hitler's initial decision to intervene was motivated by geo-ideological considerations, it soon became clear that the war material provided from German sources would not be given *gratis* but that the Germans would exact a price in the form of Spanish raw materials in lieu of gold and foreign currency, which were in short supply on the rebels' side owing partly to the success of the Republican Government in maintaining control of Spain's gold reserves which ultimately ended up in Moscow and Paris to pay for arms supplies. In any case the Germans preferred the compensation to be paid in this form because these materials included iron ore, copper, pyrites and sulphur which were vital to Germany's second Four Year Plan, the inception of which coincided with the initial build-up of German aid to Franco's forces. The organisation charged with the task of obtaining and shipping these materials to Germany was the Hisma (*Sociedad Hispano-Maroquí de Transportes*) trading company which worked in concert with another company called Rowak (*Rohstoff-Waren-Kompensation Handelgesellschaft AG*) which was set up simultaneously in Berlin and which performed the task of distribution within Germany itself. Hermann Göring, as Plenipotentiary of the Four Year Plan, oversaw Hisma's economic activities which came to represent one facet of his control of economic planning in Germany.[39]

By exacting such compensation Germany was able to overcome the chronic shortage of foreign currency which limited her ability to purchase essential raw materials on the open market. Also, the Germans anticipated that in the event of a Nationalist victory supplies of such materials would be continued in the event of a general European war.[40] It was recognised that Britain was the leading foreign investor in Spain and that it was necessary to challenge this position by greater German direct investment in order to ensure continuity of supply of essential raw materials. As a result, in 1937 and 1938 the Reich Government sought to create a German owned network of enterprises to extract and acquire Spanish raw materials. However, the project, code-named 'Montana', was strenuously resisted by the Nationalist authorities. It was only in late autumn 1938 that they made grudging concessions to German demands and they did so because they desperately needed further

German war material to break the developing stalemate between their forces and those of the Spanish Republicans on the Ebro front. Alerted to the danger of being drawn too closely into the German economic orbit, Franco gave a more sympathetic reception to British and French economic requirements than might otherwise have been the case.[41]

In contrast to Germany, Italy made no concerted or sustained effort to advance her economic interests in Spain by exploiting Franco's dependence on Italian war material. While it is true that bilateral agreements were signed which provided for partial repayment in the form of Spanish raw materials – notably iron ore, pyrites, cocoa, olive oil, raw wool and coal – the Italians allowed postponement of repayment of a substantial proportion of Nationalist debts for the duration of the civil war. According to a leading authority on the finances of the Spanish Civil War, Ángel Viñas, the generosity of the Italians was 'the principal way in which the Burgos government could manage to make the international payments necessary to strengthen the war sector of its economy'. Indeed, the relatively harmonious nature of Italo-Nationalist economic and financial relations provided a stark contrast to the ruthless and opportunistic economic policies of the Third Reich in Spain. Later, the Italians lamented their generosity. On 26 August 1939 Mussolini complained to the German Ambassador, Hans Georg von Mackensen, that his country had been 'bled white' by the Spanish Civil War which had made enormous inroads on Italian foreign exchange reserves, thereby greatly increasing the problem of obtaining raw materials.[42]

It would appear then that ideological and strategic considerations were uppermost in the minds of Hitler and Mussolini when taking their respective decisions to intervene in Spain in July 1936, and with respect to their subsequent action. Early in the civil war economic considerations acted as a further incentive for German intervention which provided the opportunity to overcome problems of supply of important raw materials for the Four Year Plan. The decision to intervene by both Germany and Italy would have been taken even if the civil war had not provided the opportunity to test new weapons and to train personnel under wartime conditions. Military considerations of this kind should be regarded as a welcome by-product of the Spanish conflagration rather than as a motivation for intervention.

From the ideological standpoint the outcome of the Spanish Civil War, total victory for the Nationalist forces, represented a notable success for both Germany and Italy. Although Franco's Spain was not transformed into a Fascist state on the German or Italian model it was ardently anti-communist, as its adherence to the Anti-Comintern Pact on 27 March 1939 demonstrated. The threat of the Bolshevik contagion which figured so prominently in the calculations of Mussolini and Hitler in July and August 1936 was completely eradicated. The removal of this threat alone justified Axis intervention in Spain, as Ciano, for one, recognised: 'At Málaga, at Guadalajara, at Santander, we were fighting in defence of our civilisation and our Revolution.'[43] It was particularly important that the possible spread of the Bolshevik contagion to France should be neutralised. In fact, the Spanish Civil War contributed to the eclipse of the Popular Front. The ideological divisions within French society, so clearly apparent in February 1934 and June 1936, were, if anything, exacerbated by the civil war and this in itself probably weakened France's resolve for a time to resist Hitler's ambitions for European hegemony.

Aside from these unanticipated gains, the Axis powers benefited from the fact that France and Britain could no longer take for granted Spain's benevolent neutrality in any future European war, and more specifically that France would be preoccupied in making contingency plans for the defence of its Pyrenean frontier. No doubt they were relieved to find that the war had weakened rather than strengthened the Franco-Soviet relationship, and they also gained from the heightened fear of Bolshevism, engendered by the Comintern's involvement in Spain, which led Right-wing governments in the Baltic states and eastern Europe, Poland excepted, to look to Germany for deliverance.[44]

The economic benefits which Germany derived from its intervention in Spain continued after the civil war, and indeed after September 1939, in so far as the Third Reich was able to obtain a range of important minerals such as iron ore, copper, pyrites, wolfram, zinc, tin, mercury and lithium. At the same time, German imports of Spanish minerals during the civil war had fallen short of targets set under the Four Year Plan. Pyrites stocks, for example, were equal to only six months' consumption at the beginning of 1939. Moreover, no doubt with the experience of the Montana project in mind, Franco was determined to limit the amount of long-term economic concessions to the Axis powers and to control strictly the operations of foreign mining concern in Spain, including British ones, such as Rio Tinto.[45]

Despite their independent decisions to intervene in the conflict, there can be few doubts that the civil war in Spain, by providing an arena in which they could cooperate on a common project, contributed significantly to the rapprochement between Germany and Italy which had been set in train previously by Germany's benevolent neutrality in the later stages of the Italo-Ethiopian War and by Italy's decision to adopt a passive attitude to Hitler's remilitarisation of the Rhineland in March 1936. Significantly, it was after the outbreak of the civil war that Mussolini abandoned support for the Zionists and went over to a policy of anti-semitism.[46] At the same time, British efforts to improve relations with Italy after the Ethiopian débâcle foundered over the Spanish problem, not least because of the increasing hostility, arising from the civil war, in Franco-Italian relations.

That this benefited Nazi Germany cannot be denied. However, it does not follow, as some historians claim, that Hitler deliberately limited the extent of German intervention in Spain (in particular his refusal to send ground forces) in order to prolong the conflict and thereby keep alive the tensions engendered by it as a distraction from Nazi political and military expansion in central and eastern Europe.[47] Although the Führer told his military advisors at the Hossbach conference of 5 November 1937 that Germany was more interested in a continuation of the war with all the tensions arising from it between Italy and France in the Mediterranean,[48] his decision to limit the scale of German support for Franco was influenced by a more vital consideration. The dispatch of a large expeditionary force to Spain would have incurred the real risk of provoking a general conflagration. In December 1936 when Mussolini substantially increased his military commitment to Franco – within three months 50,000 Italian troops were sent to Spain – the Germans were much more circumspect. Canaris, reiterating the views of Hitler, the Wehrmacht and the Foreign Ministry, told the Duce and Ciano on 6 December that the possible international reaction to the dispatch of large numbers of troops to Spain could seriously affect Germany's rearmament plans. Field Marshal Werner von Blomberg, the German War Minister, and Raeder both feared being drawn into a protracted war not vital to German interests. Hitler agreed, confiding to his generals on 21 December that he would not emulate Mussolini by sending large numbers of German troops to Spain. The Führer's decision was reinforced by Delbos' warning two days later that if Germany sent further troop transports, in addition to the Condor Legion, such action 'would necessarily lead to war'. Moreover, the dispatch of such a force carried the further risk of fulfilling the primary objective of Soviet intervention in Spain, namely the crystallising of an anti-Nazi coalition comprising themselves and the western democracies. By limiting the scale of German intervention in Spain Hitler was able to contribute towards the neutralisation of Bolshevik influence without unduly antagonising Britain and France.[49]

Mussolini recognised that Italy was providing more aid to Franco than Germany but he did not attempt, for example on the occasion of Göring's visit to Rome in January 1937, to persuade his Axis partner to make a greater contribution to the Nationalist cause. The Duce did not wish to enhance Germany's influence in the Mediterranean because as Ciano explained to Roberto Cantalupo, briefly Italian Ambassador to Nationalist Spain: 'If we close the door of Spain to the Russians, only to open it to the Germans, we can kiss our Latin and Mediterranean policy goodbye.'[50] Towards the end of the civil war Italy's strategic ambitions had grown to unprecedented proportions with the Fascist Grand Council on 30 November calling for the expropriation of French territory, including Corsica and Nice, and Mussolini's memorandum of 4 February 1939, also for the Fascist Grand Council, proclaiming the necessity of a 'march to the oceans' at Gibraltar and Suez to break Italy's 'imprisonment in the Mediterranean' and achieve true great power status in the conflict with the western powers. Italy's successful contribution to Franco's victory probably encouraged the Duce to think that a break out into the Atlantic via the Straits of Gibraltar was now a real possibility.[51]

Unlike the German and Italian cases, it is not possible as yet to pinpoint precisely when Soviet Russia decided to intervene in Spain on behalf of the Spanish Republic. The initial response of the Soviets and the Comintern towards the outbreak of the war was to offer advice only to the PCE rather than provide assistance to the Republican Government, despite an appeal for war material made by Prime Minister José Giral on 25 July 1936.[52] The first instructions to the PCE from the Comintern, between 20–24 July 1936, emphasised the need for unity within the Republican side and, specifically, 'to create, in conjunction with the other parties of the Popular Front, alliances of workers and peasants, elected as mass organisations, to fight against the conspirators in defence of the Republic'. The Secretary General of the Comintern, Georgi Dimitrov, insisted that it would be a fateful mistake 'to assign the task of creating soviets and try to establish a dictatorship of the proletariat in Spain' and that it was necessary to create a people's Republican army and 'to attract to it all of the officers and generals who have remained loyal to the Republic'. With the approval of the Soviet dictator, Josef Stalin, the Comintern instructed the PCE to 'avoid any measures which might break up the unity of the Popular Front in its fight against the insurgents' and warned them 'not to run ahead, not to depart from the positions [in favour] of a democratic regime and not to go beyond the struggle for a genuine democratic republic'. Only in extraordinary circumstances were communists to participate in the Government.[53] False confidence as to the capacity of the Republicans to quell the military uprising was maintained for several weeks. In late July 1936 while individual communist parties, such as those in Britain, the United States, Poland and France declared their support and solidarity for the struggle against fascism in Spain, the Comintern remained as unmoved as its Soviet masters in Moscow to calls for intervention.[54]

During the first half of August the Soviet response was confined essentially to providing financial support derived from collections – in reality deductions from wages at source – amongst Soviet workers. Then, on 18 August Stalin informed Politbureau member Lazar Kaganovich that he considered it necessary 'to sell oil to the Spanish Republicans immediately on the most favourable terms for them at a discounted price, if need be' and if they needed 'grain and foodstuffs in general we should sell all that to them on favourable terms'. Kaganovich reported back immediately that 6000 tons of oil had already been sold and another tanker had been ordered to fill up.[55]

So far, no arms had been sent to Spain and on 22 August, the Soviet Government adhered to the Franco-British sponsored Non-Intervention Agreement. By this agreement the export of arms to the Republic was prohibited on 28 August and a Non-Intervention

Committee was established in London to ensure compliance. The same day, however, the first Soviet Ambassador to be accredited to a Spanish government, Marcel Rosenberg, arrived in Madrid accompanied by a Soviet military delegation headed by General Jan Berzin who prior to his arrival in Spain had been head of Soviet Military Intelligence (GRU). Berzin was assisted by Grigory Shtern, the chief military adviser, Vladimir Goriev, Military Attaché, Nicolai Veronov, the official in charge of artillery, Boris Sveshnikov, adviser for the air forces, and Semyon Krivoshein, the commander of the tank units. A few days previously Vladimir Antonov-Ovsëenko, a hero of the Russian Civil War, had been appointed as Soviet Consul-General in Barcelona. According to Walter Krivitsky, Chief of Soviet Military Intelligence in western Europe, who later defected to the West, Stalin called an extraordinary session of the Politbureau at the end of August and proposed cautious intervention in Spain while proclaiming neutrality. A plan for intervention in Spain, Operation X, was developed by the new head of the GRU, Semyon P. Uritskii and the head of the Foreign Department of the NKVD (Soviet secret police), Abram Slutskii, and presented to Kliment Voroshilov, Commisar for Defence, on 14 September. Daniel Kowalsky has argued recently that in view of the magnitude of the plan for Operation X Stalin almost certainly took the decision to intervene in Spain in late August presumably just before calling the extraordinary session of the Politbureau. Operation X was formally approved on 29 September at a meeting of the Central Committee chaired jointly by Kaganovich and Vyacheslav Molotov in Stalin's absence. Three days earlier, on 26 September, Voroshilov had telephoned Stalin who was on holiday in Sochi to tell him about the first massive despatch of military material to Spain. On 7 October the Soviet representative, Samuel Cahan, warned the Non-Intervention Committee in London that unless breaches of the Non-Intervention Agreement by Germany, Italy and Portugal ceased immediately the Soviet Government would 'consider itself free from the obligations arising out of the [non-intervention] agreement'. The first consignment of Soviet armaments on board the Soviet vessel *Komsomol* arrived at Cartagena, Republican Spain's main naval base, on 15 October. The Soviet Naval Attaché, Nikolai Kuznetsov, was instructed officially to meet the vessel on arrival, and the same day an exchange of telegrams took place and was reported in *Izvestia*.[56]

From October 1936 until the summer of 1938 Soviet military aid to the Republicans was extensive, and included aircraft, tanks, armoured cars, artillery pieces, lorries, machine guns, rifles and mortars. According to one military historian, the Red Army supplied enough armoured vehicles and artillery pieces to equip four Soviet rifle divisions and more than enough rifles and machine guns to arm thirty more.[57] The Soviets also provided most of the Spanish Government's imports of oil. During the civil war between 2000 and 3000 Russians were present in Spain with 700 as the maximum at any one time. Soviet personnel, with the exception of some pilots and tank crews, did not engage directly in combat; rather they acted in the capacity of specialist advisors and included amongst their number agents of the Soviet secret police, the NKVD, who were active late in 1936 and during 1937 in helping their Republican counterparts to expose and liquidate anarchist and Trotskyist 'subversives'.[58] Unlike Germany, and particularly Italy, Soviet Russia did not send combat troops to Spain but the Comintern organised an extensive volunteer force, the International Brigades, variously estimated as numbering between 39,000 and 60,000 in the course of the civil war, which began to arrive in Spain in October 1936 providing the Republic with a core of experienced fighters – especially German and Italian brigaders – who could be utilised quickly for the defence of Madrid.[59]

As a direct consequence of Soviet aid, and in contrast to the limited influence which Germany and Italy wielded within the political counsels of the Francoist authorities, Soviet influence on the political and military organisation of Republican Spain was profound. Increasingly, Republican policies were subordinated to directives emanating from Moscow. Moreover, while Soviet advisors were penetrating many institutions of the Spanish government the membership of the PCE expanded rapidly. In April 1936 it claimed 50,000 members, by the end of the year its General Secretary, José Díaz, estimated its membership at 250,000. The increase in numbers was accompanied by a rapid extension of the PCE's prestige and authority.[60] However, the change in the fortunes of the PCE, as a direct consequence of Soviet aid, did not presage a Soviet revolution within Republican Spain. Contrary to German and Italian expectations, the Soviet authorities from the beginning of the civil war had no intention of 'Bolshevising' the Iberian Peninsula or western Europe for that matter; not least because they recognised that a Spanish Soviet State was unviable since it would be isolated, more than a thousand miles from Russia, and its existence would confirm fascist propaganda and isolate Moscow from potential allies in the west. As Marcelino Pascua, Republican Spain's Ambassador at Moscow, reported early in 1937, Stalin and the Soviet leadership realised that Spain was not suitable for communism, was not prepared to adopt it and even less to have it imposed on her. Moreover, even if Spain did adopt communism or permitted it to be imposed on her, a Soviet state could not last because it would be surrounded by hostile bourgeois regimes.[61] In this connection, the replacement in May 1937 of the Spanish Prime Minister, Largo Caballero, by Juan Negrín, another Socialist leader, was not the result, as some commentators have suggested, of Soviet and PCE pressure and machinations, but a consequence of the former's incompetence in the vital task of state building on the Republican side, including the creation of viable, conventional armed forces to counter Franco's war of annihilation.[62] On the defensive, the Soviets also approached the conflict from a 'geo-ideological' perspective, which had led them to pursue collective security and, through the Comintern, a Popular Front strategy in the mid-1930s.

Prior to 1933 Soviet foreign policy, reflecting the triumph of the doctrine of 'socialism in one country' over that of 'world revolution', was essentially isolationist. The only communist state in the world, the bastion and supposed hope for further communist advance at a distant date, the Soviet Union needed time to develop the fundamental industrial and technological capacity so essential for its security in a hostile capitalist world. From 1928 to 1933 rapid and forced industrialisation at home was accompanied by a Soviet search for security through 'the exploitation of friction and antagonism within the capitalist camp'; an approach which ruled out entangling alliances.[63] In 1933 the advent of the Nazi regime in Germany, with its virulent anti-communist rhetoric, its suppression of the German Communist Party, its exit from the Geneva Disarmament Conference and League of Nations and its rapprochement with Poland towards the end of the year, created considerable apprehension in Moscow and encouraged the alternative foreign policy approach of collective security, which was favoured by the Soviet Foreign Minister, Maxim Litvinov, and the *Narkomindel* (Russian Foreign Ministry). To this end, Soviet Russia entered the League of Nations in 1934 and in 1935 signed separate pacts with France and Czechoslovakia.[64]

The adoption of collective security by the Soviet Government was not followed immediately by a change in direction on the part of the Comintern, many of whose members remained critical of the change in Soviet policy. At its seventh and final congress during July–August 1935, however, the Comintern adopted a Popular Front strategy which involved cooperation and collaboration between communists, socialists (the former social fascists of the sixth congress), and liberal progressives.[65] The Popular Front was intended to facilitate and complement the policy of collective security. Unfortunately for the Soviets, the very governments earmarked for collaboration in an alliance against German fascism, namely Britain and France, viewed the Popular Front with alarm and suspicion. These apprehensions appeared to be borne out by the decisive election victories of Popular Front coalitions in Spain and France in February and May 1936 respectively and by the sit-ins and demonstrations of French factory workers in June.

This contradiction notwithstanding, Soviet leaders continued to pin their faith on collective security and the Popular Front strategy after the intervention of Germany and Italy in Spain in July 1936. They recognised that a victory for the militarists in Spain, backed by Hitler and Mussolini, would leave France, Soviet Russia's new partner, surrounded on three sides by hostile neighbours, while the collapse of the Popular Front in Madrid would have serious consequences for its French counterpart, but they faced an acute dilemma when the French Popular Front Government proved reluctant to intervene. Soviet intervention was required to save France from encirclement, but any attempt to intervene would upset the delicate balance in France and jeopardise the prospects of transforming the Franco-Soviet Pact into an alliance with military conversations taking place at that time between the French and Soviet military authorities. Moscow had hoped that the French Communist Party (*Parti Communiste Français* – PCF) could influence the French Popular Front Government to intervene. On 29 July the PCF was instructed to help the Republicans materially, 'for the defeat of the Spanish Republic would mean the defeat of the Popular Front in France'. With no improvement, on 7 August, the PCF leader Maurice Thorez was told in no uncertain terms from Moscow that: 'There must be no hesitation even for a minute in giving real assistance. We insist on urgent measures on your part. We immediately await news of what has concretely been done.'[66]

The Soviets waited in vain and in the absence of French or British intervention in Spain during August 1936 they restricted their activities largely to propaganda support for the Republic accompanied by demonstrations and collections in the cities of Russia. In order to keep in step with the development of Anglo-French policy the Soviets reluctantly acceded to the French proposal for a Non-Intervention Agreement on Spain and accepted membership of the Non-Intervention Committee. However, continued intervention by Italy, Germany and Portugal, despite their adherence to the Non-Intervention Agreement, and the uproar this created in Left-wing circles in Europe, including Britain and France, along with the rapidly deteriorating position of the Spanish Republican forces and the realisation that France was too paralysed by internal dissent over Spain to take action herself, compelled Moscow to alter its policy during late August, September and October to one of covert intervention in Spain combined with active participation in the work of the Non-Intervention Committee.[67]

Soviet intervention helped to reinforce the Italo-German relationship, which was consolidated in the declaration of the Rome–Berlin Axis during October 1936, and encouraged Germany to sign the Anti-Comintern Pact with Japan the same month. Relations with France and Britain were also impaired. However, with Soviet assistance Madrid was saved from Franco's forces and the Spanish struggle prolonged. Soviet leaders still hoped to persuade the western democracies to help save the Spanish Republic and themselves from the consequences of fascist aggression. To this end, they used their increasingly vital intervention to pressure the Spanish authorities into creating a conventional Republican army in place of the FAI and POUM militia system and to suppress radical social experiments within the Republican territories. The Soviets were only too aware of the hostility of Britain and France towards revolutionary activity in Republican Spain. In late November and early December 1936, for example, the French Ambassador at Moscow, Robert Coulondre, explicitly warned Soviet officials that a success for the anarchists and communists in Spain could have adverse effects on Franco-Soviet relations.[68] In order to strengthen the Republic's military resistance, to neutralise the possibility of a bourgeois secession to the Spanish fascists and to make the French and British Governments more amenable the Soviet leaders were prepared to sacrifice the Spanish revolution. Indeed, at their insistence the Spanish Government espoused the cause of bourgeois parliamentary democracy and tended to condemn 'any action against the property rights and legitimate interests of those foreigners in Spain who were citizens of states which did not support the rebels'.[69] The events in Barcelona in May 1937 when revolutionary Anarchists, Left-wing Socialists and dissident Communists, including the POUM, were crushed by Government forces supported by the PCE and its Catalan ally, the PSUC (Partido Socialista Unificado de Cataluña) were an inevitable part of this counter-revolutionary process.

From October 1936 until the summer of 1938 the Soviets, in their pursuit of collective security, sought in vain to use the Spanish conflagration as a means of persuading the British and French governments to forsake their appeasement of the fascist dictators. Moscow's patient commitment to collective security during this period was not a product of illusion but of the absence of a viable alternative policy other than a return to isolationism. A rapprochement with Berlin, despite tentative feelers on the Soviet side, was ruled out by Hitler's continued hostility and his ambitions in central Europe.[70] Meanwhile, Japanese aggression in northern China, especially in August 1938, imposed further problems for Soviet defence in the Far East .[71] The exclusion of Soviet Russia from the Munich Conference in September 1938 signalled the collapse of the policy of collective security and a return to isolationism. It was now clear, if it had not been before, that Republican Spain could not expect a concerted Anglo-French–Soviet intervention on its behalf. As E. H. Carr notes, the Munich agreement showed that Spain had been relegated 'to an insignificant place' in the preoccupations of the European powers and that 'no future efforts to sustain the democratic cause in Spain could be expected from those who had so easily abandoned it elsewhere'.[72] The Soviets, however, continued to provide assistance to the Spanish Republic, sending a further large consignment of arms in December 1938 in spite of Spain's relegation in their foreign policy concerns, and in spite of the logistical problems of transportation and the risks of the arms falling into enemy hands. In Moscow's perception after Munich, maintaining Republican resistance for as long as possible was a means of staving off fascist aggression in the east directed against Soviet Russia herself.[73]

The Soviet failure to win the western powers to collective security through Spain did not mean that Soviet intervention was entirely fruitless from the point of Soviet interests. As with Germany and Italy, as a by-product of her intervention Soviet Russia was able, in the words of the Spanish socialist Indalecio Prieto, to use Spain as 'a real life military academy' to test some of its latest weapons and to provide battle experience for ground and air personnel. Many of the leading Soviet Army commanders of the Second World War visited Spain including Marshals Georgi Zhukov, Nikolai Voronov, Rodion Malinovskii who later became Defence Minister under Nikita Khrushchev, Ivan Konev, Kiril Meretskov and Konstantin Rokossovskii, Generals Semen Krivoshein, P. I. Batov and Mikhail Yakushin, and Admiral Nikolai Kuznetsov, commander of the Soviet fleet throughout the Second World War. Other ex-Spanish veterans such as Rosenberg, Berzin, Antonov-Ovsëenko, Mikhail Koltsov, Arthur Stashevskii and Vladimir Goriev were not so fortunate, suffering execution or slow death in concentration camps on their return to Russia.[74] The Soviet military decimated as it was by the purges of the High Command of the Red Army in 1937–1938 failed to learn one of the key lessons of the Spanish Civil War, namely the superiority of heavy armoured formations. Prior to 1938, the Red Army under the leadership of Marshal Mikhail Tukhachevsky had vigorously embraced mechanisation and had produced a complete tank corps. But in the aftermath of the purges with the emergence of a less proficient Stalinist officer corps incorrect lessons were drawn from the civil war in Spain and the Soviet armoured corps was disbanded in favour of infantry and anti-tank dominated formations.[75] At the same time, the experience of Soviet pilots and aircraft during the civil war added urgency to the need for a Soviet aviation reform programme. Soviet fighters, notably the I-16 and I-153, were outgunned and outmaneuvred by German aircraft, even by German bombers. About 90 per cent of Soviet fighters had only machine guns whereas German aircraft had both guns and cannons. It was certainly no coincidence that the end of the civil war in Spain was followed by a Soviet construction programme for newer modern fighters.[76]

Finally, although Soviet Russia failed to obtain short-term or long-term economic concessions in Spain, the financial cost of its intervention was defrayed to a large extent by the deposit of Spanish gold, amounting to $518 million, in Moscow early in 1937. At least $340 million of it was reexported to the *Banque Commerciale pour L'Europe du Nord* in Paris to cover expenditure on the activities of the International Brigades, sponsored by successive war ministries and the Republic's state purchasing agency, *Campsa-Gentibus*, which was responsible for directing purchasing abroad.[77] Non-intervention by the western democracies had deprived the Spanish Government of any prospect of cash credits which forced them to utilise their gold reserves and also to purchase arms at extortionate prices on the black market. Moreover, because there was a considerable risk that their financial resources would be frozen if they were deposited in western banks, the Republican authorities chose the safer option of sending them to Soviet Russia.[78]

Recent research by Gerald Howson has revealed that in providing armed assistance to the Spanish Republicans the Soviets indulged in a massive swindle operation which, by deliberately inflating the prices of Soviet arms, cheated their Spanish allies out of millions of dollars. He also claims that many of the items supplied were obsolete.[79] While Howson presents a convincing case, it cannot be denied that without Soviet armed assistance the Spanish Republic would have succumbed much earlier to Franco's forces, that modern weapons were supplied on a large scale, including tanks and aircraft, if only to enable Moscow to test them on the battlefield. Indeed, according to Helen Graham, in 1936 the Soviet Government dispatched at least 50 per cent of its total annual production of military aircraft to Republican Spain.[80] Apart from casualties in Spain, the Russians lost a large number of merchant ships to German and Italian bombing and submarine raids while in the process of transporting arms and munitions to the Republican forces, even if the bulk of Soviet arms shipments were transported in Spanish merchant ships.[81] Indeed, it has been estimated that even before the Italian submarine offensive in the Mediterranean in the summer of 1937, 96 Soviet (or Spanish) merchant ships were captured and three sunk.[82] Moreover, later in the war in 1938 the Soviets provided substantial credits to the Republic when the prospects for recouping them had seriously diminished and it is probable that without them the Republican war effort could not have been sustained through the second half of 1938.[83] The effect of Soviet support in raising the morale of the Spanish people in Republican Spain, reiterated constantly in Government propaganda, should also not be discounted nor the degree of humanitarian aid provided by Moscow, including the treatment of 3000 Spanish refugee children during the course of the civil war;[84] a humane approach denied to tens of millions of Soviet citizens.

Finally, a brief mention should be made of the Spanish Republic's only other ally, Mexico. Under President Lázaro Cárdenas' leadership, Mexico sent approximately 300 volunteers to Republican Spain of whom only 20 per cent returned home, supplied arms between September 1936 and September 1937 to the value of $2.2 million, including artillery pieces and anti-aircraft guns, trans-shipped arms to Spain from other countries, notably Soviet Russia, provided diplomatic support in the League of Nations, where the Mexican delegate, Isidro Fabela, attacked the non-intervention policies of the democratic powers, and also in Latin America, offered asylum to Spanish diplomats who backed the Republic, and tried unsuccessfully to protect Republican interests in Germany, Italy and Portugal.[85] Cardenas' Government took the decision to support the Spanish Republic because they saw it was carrying out a revolution similar to the Mexican Revolution which had been underway for decades, including agrarian reform, the rights of industrial workers, and the elevation of popular culture through secular, progressive education. In addition, for the Cardenistas Franco's rebellion threatened the Iberian Peninsula with a takeover by international fascism which would enable it to prepare a bridge head for a future infiltration of Latin America.[86]

3 The Non-Interventionist Powers and the Spanish Civil War, 1936–1939

In contrast to Germany, Italy and Soviet Russia, the western European democratic powers, Britain and France, deliberately sought not to become directly involved in the civil war in Spain. The policy of non-intervention was the invention of the French authorities. The British Government, however, was already committed in thought and deed to non-intervention before the French made their proposal for a non-intervention agreement on 1 August 1936, and adhered strictly to the agreement throughout the 33 months of the civil war. Yet France was not entirely strict in its neutrality, while Britain chose to interpret non-intervention in politico-military terms which did not preclude economic intervention. During the civil war the French sold between 100 and 150 aircraft to the Republicans. Facilities were provided for the export of gold from the Bank of Madrid between July 1936 and March 1937 while the Soviet *Banque Commerciale pour l'Europe du Nord*, operating in Paris under French laws, was able to facilitate international payments for war material on behalf of the Spanish Republic. At various times during the war the French Pyrenean frontier was opened for the transportation of arms to Spain, notably during July and August 1936, October 1937–January 1938, March–June 1938, and January–February 1939. The largest contingent of foreign combatants in the International Brigades was composed of Frenchmen, some 10,000 in all.[1] In the economic sphere the British authorities deliberately sought to curry favour with the Spanish Nationalists in order to counter German influence which threatened established British economic interests in Spain, notably those of the Rio Tinto and Tharsis Sulphur and Copper companies. In November 1937 they went so far as to concede *de facto* recognition by appointing a special agent, Sir Robert Hodgson, to the Nationalist authorities and receiving the Anglophile

51

Duke of Alba in return. The French Government studiously avoided following the British example despite their own economic interests in Nationalist Spain which were, admittedly, less extensive.[2]

Ideological considerations certainly influenced the French and British decisions to pursue non-intervention in Spain. The initial, and natural response of the French Popular Front Government was to provide military assistance to its Popular Front counterpart in Spain. But fears of a Right-wing backlash in France creating further civil disorder and ideological division and possibly civil war, following the workers' occupation of the factories in June, prompted a more cautious response, not least to preserve the social reform programme of the Popular Front as enshrined in the Matignon agreements which had brought the occupations to an end.[3] The French Government itself was divided over allowing the export of French arms and aircraft, though not entirely along Radical and Socialist party lines. As a compromise, the Government proposed a non-intervention agreement in the hope that, starved of outside assistance, the rebellion would be short-lived. For most members of the Government and the Quai d'Orsay there appeared to be little alternative since it was clear within days of the Generals' revolt that Britain intended to pursue a strictly neutral policy which would leave France dangerously isolated if she intervened in the Spanish conflagration. French efforts to persuade the British to change their position, such as the visit to London of Jules Moch, assistant to the French leader, Léon Blum, on 30 July and the mission of the Chief of the French Naval Staff, Admiral François Darlan, to London on 5 August, proved unavailing despite growing evidence of Italian and German intervention in Spain.[4] The Quai d'Orsay was also convinced that French intervention in Spain would alienate fervently anti-communist East European allies, notably Yugoslavia and Romania.[5]

In order to overcome the increasing opposition to non-intervention within the Popular Front, which resulted from an increased awareness of German and Italian intervention, Yvon Delbos, the Foreign Minister, and his officials at the Quai d'Orsay, deemed it essential to win full backing from Britain for their non-intervention proposals. Eden, Lord Halifax, who deputised for the Foreign Secretary during the first two weeks of August, and the Foreign Office proved only too willing to support French requests for assistance. This collaboration between the two foreign ministries ensured the survival of the non-intervention policy. Without Britain's full backing it is probable that the moderates in the Popular Front, including Delbos, Edouard Daladier, the Minister of War and Blum himself, would have been unable to restrain those elements which incessantly demanded French intervention on behalf of the Spanish Republic.[6]

In contrast with the French Government, the ideological predilections of the British Government in July and August 1936 were clearly anti-Republican and pro-insurgent. Within days of the rebellion Conservative politicians such as Sir Henry Channon and the Government Chief Whip, David Margesson, were lamenting its failure while the Prime Minister, Stanley Baldwin, was adamant that 'on no account French or other' should the Government enter the civil war 'on the side of the Russians'.[7] The expropriation by armed workers of British companies in Republican Spain, such as the Barcelona Power, Light and Traction Company, in late July and early August 1936 strengthened the anti-Republican sentiment in Whitehall. In addition, the failure of the Madrid authorities to control the extreme elements in the Spanish Popular Front and to restore law and order within their territory earned the contempt of senior Foreign Office officials, including Vansittart and his deputy as Permanent Under Secretary, Sir Alexander Cadogan. These same officials remained convinced that Soviet-Comintern influence had been active in Spain long before the revolt of 17 July and had compared Azaña's Popular Front Government after February 1936 with the Russian Provisional Government after March 1917 which eventually succumbed to the Bolshevik Revolution in November that year. Within this perception Azaña, who had become President of the Spanish Republic in May 1936, was viewed as a potential Kerensky, the ill-fated leader of the Russian Provisional Government. During the early weeks of the civil war, in spiritual unison with Hitler and Mussolini, they continued to fear the spread of the Bolshevik contagion to France. The only dissentient voice at the Foreign Office was Lawrence Collier, the Head of the Northern Department.[8]

The British Admiralty shared these misgivings. At various times during 1936 and 1937 senior naval officers, such as Admiral Sir Ernle Chatfield, the First Sea Lord, his successor, Sir Roger Backhouse, and Admiral Geoffrey Blake, Commander of the Home Fleet, expressed strong anti-Republican and pro-Franco sentiments.

After May 1937 Alfred Duff Cooper, as First Lord of the Admiralty, was no less sympathetic to Franco than his senior naval advisors or his predecessor, Sir Samuel Hoare. All, with Invergordon probably in mind, continued to condemn unreservedly the killing of Spanish naval officers by Republican sailors during the early weeks of the civil war despite the fact that these officers were in open revolt against the democratically elected government of Spain.[9] Although Eden and Vansittart were converted during 1937 to the view that the survival of Republican Spain was in Britain's best political and strategic interests, the passage of time converted few others.[10] Indeed, Neville Chamberlain, the Prime Minister, was compelled to warn his Cabinet colleagues in January 1939 that the Government 'should avoid showing any satisfaction at the prospect of a Franco victory'. As for the Prime Minister himself, according to Eden's admission to the Spanish Prime Minister, Juan Negrín, in September 1937, he feared that 'Communism would get its clutches into western Europe' through the Spanish Civil War.[11]

While there was a strong ideological antipathy towards the Spanish Republic and sympathy for Franco's cause in British ruling circles, it was hardly possible for the British Government to assist actively and openly a rebellion against a legitimate and democratically elected government, particularly when such action would alienate the French and arouse the fury of the political opposition at home. British statesmen recognised that the best means of containing the Bolshevik contagion was to support Blum's non-intervention proposals. Failure to provide such support, they were convinced, would undermine the moderate elements in the French Government and make French intervention a certainty.[12] Moreover, non-intervention would serve to contain any further polarisation than was necessary of British society.[13]

The French Government's persistence in pursuing non-intervention in the face of increasing hostility within the Popular Front cannot be explained merely in terms of their fear of civil disturbances at home and the need to keep in step with London. Blum, Delbos, Daladier and other ministers genuinely feared a general European war if intervention in Spain proceeded unchecked. Nor could this danger be discounted. When Blum referred to the possibility in a major speech at Luna Park in Paris on 6 September 1936, and urged that non-intervention was the best means of preventing such a calamity, there was little dissent, and he was able to maintain Socialist party support for the non-intervention policy.[14] During July and August 1936 Eden and his Foreign Office advisers, who had a horror of a European war based on ideological divisions, similarly insisted that it was essential to confine the conflict to Spain.[15] Like Blum, they also feared that any intervention in Spain by either Britain or France might irretrievably jeopardise their efforts to reach a general European settlement, based on a new Locarno, which had been proceeding since Hitler's reoccupation of the Rhineland in March.[16] Indeed, especially after Chamberlain became Prime Minister in May 1937, the British Government was determined not to allow the civil war to interfere with its efforts to appease both Hitler and Mussolini despite their constant breaches of non-intervention.[17]

Both Paris and London recognised that the civil war held serious strategic consequences. As early as 24 August 1936 the British Chiefs of Staff advised that in a war with a European power it would be essential for British interests that Spain should be friendly or at worst strictly neutral. A hostile Spain or the occupation of Spanish territory by a hostile power would make Britain's control of the Straits of Gibraltar and the use of Gibraltar itself as a naval and air base extremely difficult if not impossible, and would accordingly endanger imperial communications through the Mediterranean. Similarly, the possession by a hostile power of the harbours of the Spanish Atlantic seaboard would imperil Britain's communications across the Atlantic. The Chiefs emphasised that Britain's interests in the Spanish crisis were first, the maintenance of the territorial integrity of Spain and its possessions (Balearics, Morocco, Canaries and Rio de Oro); and second, to secure the benevolent neutrality of a future Spanish government in the event of Britain being engaged in any European war. They shared the Foreign Office view that the best means of securing these objectives was by promoting non-intervention. They repeated this advice in July 1938, and in the course of a major appreciation of Britain's strategic position during February 1939 they could not emphasise too strongly 'the strategic need of pursuing a policy which will ensure at least the neutrality of Spain, whatever the outcome of the civil war'.[18] The decision to exchange agents with Franco in November 1937 was due as much to the need to safeguard Britain's strategic position in the western Mediterranean and eastern Atlantic as to the concern for British economic interests in

Spain, since his regime controlled all Spanish territory in proximity to Gibraltar and the Straits.[19]

The French High Command regarded the strategic implications of a Franco victory in cooperation with Germany and Italy as extremely serious for France. In that case the Iberian Peninsula would become a third unsympathetic if not hostile front which could only be defended at the expense of the Rhine and Alpine theatres. A Franco victory might also result in a tightening of Spain's stranglehold on the Straits of Gibraltar by means of Italian and German air and naval bases on the Spanish coast or in the Balearics or Canaries which could seriously impair the coordination of Franco-British naval operations in the western Mediterranean and eastern Atlantic. The exploitation of Spanish bases by pro-rebel forces, whether Nationalist or foreign, could jeopardise troop and munition transports between France and North Africa with grave consequences for the operation of the French mobilisation plan. The dilemma was that these strategic dangers could come to pass if France intervened unsuccessfully in the civil war just as much, if not more than, if it remained neutral. In particular there was a risk of escalating the war into a major European conflict, which might have as one of its theatres the Pyrenees, the least fortified of French frontiers. Moreover, intervention might prejudice Franco's supposed resolve to remove his civil war partners once his victory was assured. At the same time, any military intervention was certain to be expensive in financial, material and human resources which would necessarily be diverted from the more acute dangers on the Rhine and Alpine frontiers.

The French High Command therefore favoured non-intervention, but to understand fully this preference it is important to recognise that they expected the rebels to win in Spain and that their sympathies, as General Maurice Gamelin, Chief of the General Staff, later admitted, were always with Franco.[20] According to both army and naval intelligence summaries in the summer of 1936 Franco was 'a dedicated and clear-headed professional' and a 'Francophile' possessed of 'immense intelligence and energy'. In contrast, the Republican Government was characterised as a revolutionary cabal dominated first by anarchist and later communist extremists. The intensity of the military's views was such that Blum feared that France was 'on the eve of a military *coup d'état*' in the summer of 1936.[21] Certainly, the civil war in Spain had heightened the military's concern over France's volatile situation in the summer of 1936; a concern which the Germans sought to exploit, including the preaching of anti-Bolshevism to Gamelin's staff by the German Military Attaché in Paris and Hitler's deliberate query to the French Ambassador at Berlin, André François-Poncet, as to whether French troops would fire on the '[French] revolutionary masses'.[22]

For the French Governments of the period intervention in Spain was considered an extremely high risk policy and both the Army High Command and the Quai d'Orsay counselled against such a venture. As late as March 1938, in the immediate aftermath of the *Anschluss*, during the short-lived second ministry of Léon Blum, Gamelin advised against intervention on the grounds that France had insufficient forces to risk war, while the Secretary General of the Quai d'Orsay, Alexis Léger, expressed his conviction that both Italy and Germany would regard French intervention in Spain as a *casus belli*.[23] In view of these risks the Blum, Chautemps, and Daladier administrations, at various times between August 1936 and February 1939, used non-intervention as a cover for assisting the Republican forces in Spain, though on nothing like the same scale as Soviet aid to the Republic or Italian and German assistance to the rebels. In this way their consciences were eased to some degree and the non-intervention policy was made more palatable to the rank and file of the Popular Front.[24]

The British authorities were not prepared at any point during the civil war to risk a European conflagration by intervening in Spain, and especially not on the side of the Spanish Republic. None the less, they recognised that despite the exchange of agents there was a clear danger that British influence in Spain might be eclipsed in the event of an Axis-backed victory for Franco, which seemed increasingly likely as time went by. In order to justify this risk, which was inherent in non-intervention, the British Government fell back on two superficially attractive arguments. The first was that by pursuing a politically non-partisan policy Britain would receive favourable treatment from whichever side emerged victorious because it alone among the European powers had not intervened to kill Spaniards. The second argument emphasised the financial superiority of Britain in that whoever won in Spain would have to seek British financial assistance in the task of reconstruction, particularly as it was widely believed that neither Germany nor Italy could provide such assistance.[25] The aftermath of the civil war was to demonstrate the emptiness of these assertions.

There can be little doubt that the defeat of the Spanish Republic was a painful and bitter experience for the Popular Front including the Radical Socialists as well as the Socialist and Communist parties, when they found that they could not save their Spanish comrades. Nevertheless, the adoption of non-intervention probably prevented a socio-political crisis in France. Despite occasional breaches of the Non-Intervention Agreement by the French authorities, the French Right was mollified by the policy of nonintervention, especially as it appeared to benefit Franco rather than the Republicans and because it was consistent with British policy. Although sympathetic to the Spanish Republicans, when their cause appeared hopeless in February 1939 French political leaders were quick to repair relations with the victorious Nationalists through the granting of *de jure* recognition to the Franco regime and the signing of the Bérard-Jordana Agreement.[26] Clearly, from the ideological point of view, Franco's victory was satisfactory for the British Government and their official advisers: but while, unlike the Labour and Liberal parties, they did not mourn the passing of the Spanish Republic it is to their credit that in February 1939 they tried, albeit unsuccessfully, to achieve safeguards against reprisals as a condition for granting *de jure* recognition to Franco's regime.[27]

Contrary to some historians who see a British-led conspiracy against the Spanish Republic during the civil war, the Baldwin and Chamberlain Governments were motivated above all by strategic and political realities, as they perceived them, and less by their ideological prejudices. As the detailed minutes of the meetings of the Cabinet and the Cabinet Foreign Policy Committee confirm, nonintervention in Spain was regarded as essential if the policy of seeking general European appeasement was to be sustained and a general conflict avoided. Moreover, despite their anti-Republican prejudices British Ministers, Chamberlain included, made several genuine attempts to bring about mediation in the civil war, even as late as the autumn and winter of 1938 when the fortunes of war had again turned against the Spanish Republic, for the last time. Until virtually the end of the conflict, the British Government had steadfastly refused to grant belligerent rights unconditionally to the Franco authorities despite their constant complaints.

The decision of Britain and France to adhere to a policy of non-intervention did not safeguard their strategic position in the western Mediterranean and along the eastern Atlantic seaboard. British military authorities had hoped at best to secure a benevolently neutral Spain in any future European conflict; at worst a strictly neutral Spain. In March 1939 the British Joint Planning Staff were compelled to recognise that, in view of German and Italian armed assistance Franco's Spain might be hostile or at any rate afford facilities to the Axis powers.[28] A year earlier, as a Franco victory aided and abetted by Germany and Italy appeared increasingly likely, the French military authorities had been compelled to face up to the consequences for their own strategic position. They anticipated that a victorious Franco regime would provide strategic naval and air bases to the Axis powers including: Ferrol and Vigo on the Cantabrian coast, Cádiz and Ceuta at the entrance to the Straits of Gibraltar, Cartagena and the Balearic Islands which intersected French lines of communication in the western Mediterranean, and the Canary Islands and Rio de Oro which lay along the route Dakar-Fernando Po-French Guinea. It was recognised that a Franco victory was particularly dangerous for French communications in the Mediterranean with North Africa and the Levant but also that it would affect French Atlantic communications (Morocco to America) and imperial communications to the French oversea empire, notably the *Afrique Occidentale Française* (AOF – Senegal, Mauritania, French Guinea, French Sudan, Ivory Coast, Niger and Dahomey) and the *Afrique Équatoriale Française* (AEF – French Congo, Cameroon, Gabon, Chad and Ubangi Shari).[29] As Peter Jackson stresses, the civil war played an important role in the evolution of French strategic policy, magnifying as it did concerns about France's strategic vulnerability and intensifying the ideological dimension to French military planning.[30]

The gloomy prospects for British and French strategy arising out of Franco's victory contrasted sharply with Britain's success in protecting her economic interests in Spain, and thereby limiting the success of German economic policy in Spain. Neville Chamberlain's Government, after he became Prime Minister in 1937, went out of its way to curry favour with the Spanish Nationalists in order to counter German influence with Franco and safeguard their economic interests in Spain. Agents were exchanged with the Nationalists in November 1937 and although there was no formal recognition of the Franco regime until the virtual end of the civil war the agents – in the British case, Sir Robert Hodgson, and in the Nationalist case, the Duke of Alba – in effect were accorded full diplomatic status.[31] As a result of such measures, the independence of British companies in Spain, in the pyrites trade for example, was preserved: supplies to Britain were not restricted during or after the civil war while as early as May 1939 the Rio Tinto Company was not penalised by the Spanish authorities for refusing to supply Germany. According to Charles Harvey, Franco's determination to pursue a strongly nationalistic economic strategy only constrained the activities of British companies in Spain at a later date.[32]

As non-participants in the civil war, the British and French armed forces did not acquire battlefield experience or experience of aerial warfare as did their German, Italian and Soviet counterparts. They did not, however, remain entirely ignorant of military developments in the war. The French military authorities were active in gathering intelligence on German, Italian and Soviet participation. A lengthy study produced by the Army *Deuxième Bureau* in March 1938, for example, focused on tank and anti-tank warfare and on the effectiveness of anti-aircraft activity. The superiority of Soviet armour over Italian tanks and German light tanks was clearly recognised as was the effectiveness of German and Italian anti-tank weapons. German anti-aircraft fire was also deemed to be effective. The coordination of ground and air forces was also emphasised and the role of aircraft in all active phases of battle.[33] Unfortunately, the effect of this intelligence was to merely reinforce the French belief in the superiority of firepower over speed and mobility. As Peter Jackson emphasises with reference to lessons taken from the Spanish Civil War: 'Whenever artillery, anti-tank, and anti-aircraft weapons proved effective these successes were consistently interpreted as confirmation of the inherent superiority of defensive fire. When armoured formations or aircraft achieved decisive success in frontal assaults without the benefit of infantry support, this was attributed to inadequate defensive preparations or insufficient firepower.'[34]

It would appear that British military observers in Spain, including the military historian and theorist Major-General J. C. Fuller, learned little from the conflict, which in view of the way in which other powers misread the lessons of the civil war was perhaps a blessing. Their reports, which were received by the Army's Directorate of Military Operations and Intelligence, were critical of the use of tank tactics by both the Nationalists and the Republicans and emphasised that aircraft played a more important role than tanks, including aerial attacks on ground troops. The motorisation of the Nationalist Army was also singled out for praise.[35] In the one area where Britain participated in the Spanish struggle, the Non-Intervention-sponsored naval patrol, the Royal Navy benefited from its observation at length of Italian naval operations in the Mediterranean. Certainly, this contributed to British successes against the Italian Navy in 1940–1941.[36]

Historians tend to characterise French foreign policy in the late 1930s as being subservient to that of Britain; that at least France obeyed its 'English governess'. In this version France's invention of, and commitment to non-intervention in Spain in August 1936 was a direct response to British pressure: without it French intervention would have been inevitable. By the same token the decision of the French Government in June 1938 to close their frontier with Spain which had been open since March was purportedly a consequence of British pressure.[37] French policy towards the Spanish Civil War tends to bear out Anthony Adamthwaite's view that 'in practice French policy was much more assertive and independent than supposed'.[38] Yvon Delbos and the Quai d'Orsay initiated the policy of non-intervention then sought British support since otherwise, they feared, the more extreme elements in the Popular Front would succeed in forcing France to intervene in Spain. Accordingly, throughout August and September 1936 they covertly solicited British pressure, which admittedly the British authorities willingly provided.[39] Similarly, in June 1938 the British Ambassador, Sir Eric Phipps, strongly advised the French Government to close their frontier with Spain, but the French needed little persuasion. As Georges Bonnet, the Foreign Minister, later told Phipps, his Government were convinced that if they did not close the frontier the risk of war would have been increased by 100 per cent because they had heard that a large shipment of war material had left or was about to leave Soviet Russia for Le Havre and Bordeaux for trans-shipment to Spain. Bonnet deplored 'Russia's renewed and unhealthy wish to fish in troubled Spanish waters far removed from her own territory, which would therefore be immune from the disturbances and damage she wished to cause others'.[40]

Earlier in the civil war, in October 1937, the French Government had agreed to keep the Pyrenean frontier closed, partly in deference to British wishes but largely because apart from some Socialists there were few Frenchmen who wanted to open it. Senior officials at the Quai d'Orsay, notably René Massigli and Léger, were opposed to opening the frontier because they believed it would be completely ineffective in so far as it was intended to help the Republican Government to free Spain from the 'Italian stranglehold'. As an alternative to opening the frontier the Quai d'Orsay favoured the occupation of Minorca as a *gage*.[41] The French authorities also demonstrated their independence by refusing to follow London's lead in exchanging agents with the Nationalist authorities in Spain. For their part, the British Government were often irritated by French attempts to disregard non-intervention. Early in September 1936, for example, Britain strongly reprimanded France for allowing several hundred Republican militiamen who had fled from Irun into France, to return rearmed in special trains to the Pyrenean frontier where they were able to rejoin the Catalan anarchist militias. When in October 1937, the French suggested a temporary authorisation of the transit of arms to the Spanish Government unless the Italians desisted from further armed intervention in Spain, the British Cabinet rejected the suggestion out of hand, deploring it for 'casting doubts on Italian pledges and good faith'.[42] While in these cases the British view tended to prevail, it can hardly be claimed that the French were passive or supine. It is also clear that differences with regard to the Spanish issue were never substantial and did not prevent Anglo-French cooperation at the Non-Intervention Committee or on matters elsewhere, such as Czechoslovakia and the colonial appeasement of Germany. The meetings of British and French Ministers in November 1937, April 1938, September 1938 and November 1938 and the eventual emergence of a military alliance in February–March 1939, provide solid testimony to this fact. Consequently, when Enrique Moradiellos emphasises the 'paralysing and debilitating' division of the Franco-British entente and their respective public opinions caused by the Spanish Civil War, there is an element of exaggeration.[43]

Most probably during the late 1930s the greatest divergence in the respective policies of France and Britain occurred in respect of their relations with Italy. As far as successive French Governments were concerned, and also the French Navy, Italy's extensive intervention in the Spanish Civil War made it impossible to consider seriously a rapprochement with Rome, although the Army High Command continued until the end of 1938 to cling to the vain hope of reviving a military alliance with Italy to deter German aggression. The British authorities who, since the summer of 1936, had made strenuous efforts to repair their relations with Mussolini expressed dissatisfaction at the French attitude. The French were equally annoyed with Britain's appeasement of Italy and particularly the Anglo-Italian Agreement of April 1938. Daladier on a visit to London at the end of that month expressed his displeasure at Britain's lack of firmness and her refusal to collaborate with France in dealing with Italy and he attempted to enlighten Chamberlain about the problems for French security caused by German and Italian intervention in Spain. For his part, the British Prime Minister acknowledged the civil war as a major obstacle to the appeasement of Italy when he informed George VI that Spain was the 'nigger in the woodpile' and that 'unless and until that affair is settled there will always be the danger of an open quarrel with France and always the road to appeasement will be blocked'.[44] Unfortunately for Chamberlain, the end of the Spanish conflict did not herald an improvement in Franco-Italian relations. While Daladier was prepared, eventually, to make some concessions to Franco's Spain, he was not prepared, despite the urgings of Chamberlain, Halifax and even Bonnet, to do the same for Mussolini's Italy before September 1939.[45]

The deterioration of Franco-Italian relations was not matched by an improvement in Franco-Soviet relations even though the Soviet Union had intervened on the side of the Spanish Republic. During 1937 the French authorities refused to consider military conversations as a means of strengthening and consolidating the Franco-Soviet Pact of 1935. The reluctance of the French General Staff to seriously consider a military convention was partly influenced by the Spanish Civil War and Soviet Russia's involvement in it. The Deputy Chief of Staff, General Victor Schweisguth, who attended the Red Army manoeuvres in September 1936, remained convinced that the Soviets were 'exploiting events in Spain, pushing France towards dangerous provocations vis-à-vis Germany' with the hope that another world war would erupt from which they could stand aside and eventually emerge as 'the arbiter of a drained and exhausted Europe'.[46] The French authorities, like their British counterparts, saw no virtue in the pact other than as a means of preventing a Nazi–Soviet rapprochement, and the purges in the Red Army during the middle of 1937 ended any lingering thought that conversations might be possible or desirable.[47] The Soviet failure to win over Britain and France to collective security through Spain and Czechoslovakia reinforced Moscow's isolationism after September 1938 and increased fear and suspicion that the western powers intended to direct Germany eastwards. In view of these apprehensions, made worse in November 1938 by Moscow's awareness that German–Japanese–Italian negotiations for a tripartite pact had progressed to a new and active stage after Munich, it was clearly prudent for the Soviet authorities to withdraw completely from their involvement in Spain.[48] Stalin's warning in his report to the eighteenth Communist Party Congress on 10 March 1939, with the end of the Spanish Republic in clear sight, 'to be cautious and not allow our country to be drawn into conflicts by warmongers who are accustomed to have others pull the chestnuts out of the fire for them', was almost certainly directed at Britain and France and influenced by the Soviet experience of the Spanish Civil War and the failure of the western powers to become involved.[49] Yet, seemingly undeterred by their previous failures to involve Britain and France in a genuine collective security against the tide of Fascism, the Soviets initiated negotiations for a triple alliance with these powers during April 1939. But, as Geoffrey Roberts rightly emphasises, the experience of appeasement in action, Spain included, dominated Soviet perceptions of their erstwhile allies so that Moscow feared that London and Paris would be tempted by another non-intervention policy, one of standing by while Soviet Russia alone engaged Germany on the Eastern front.[50]

In view of the refusal of the British authorities to take advantage of the opportunity provided by the Spanish conflict to achieve an Anglo-French–Soviet rapprochement, it is surely ironic that the British Chiefs of Staff should advise in May 1939 that 'the possibility of antagonising Franco's Spain should not from the military point of view be allowed to stand in the way of the conclusion of a pact with Soviet Russia'.[51] The alliance with Soviet Russia, advocated by the British Chiefs of Staff, was not to materialise until more than two years later in the context of a much greater conflagration than the civil war in Spain.

Although 3000 miles from the conflict in Spain, the United States Government was compelled to make a clear statement of its position when at the beginning of August 1936 it became apparent that the Spanish Republicans intended to purchase American weapons and munitions. Secretary of State Cordell Hull informed the press on 5 August that the United States would pursue a course of total non-involvement in the Spanish Civil War. The following day Under Secretary William Phillips told the Spanish Ambassador, Luis Calderón, that his Government had no intention of aiding either the Republicans or Franco's rebels. On 7 August all American officials in Spain were informed by circular telegram that although the Neutrality Law had no application in the case of civil wars it was intended to 'scrupulously refrain from any interference whatsoever in the unfortunate Spanish situation'. This statement, which amounted to a moral embargo, was published by the State Department on 11 August, one day after receiving a request from the Glenn Martin Company to sanction the sale of eight bombers to the Spanish Government. On instructions from President Roosevelt and Hull the company was sent a copy of the circular telegram of 7 August and advised that the proposed sale of aircraft 'would not follow the spirit of the Government's policy'; advice that was repeated to other companies enquiring about the export of war material to Spain. The message was also reinforced on 14 August when Roosevelt, in a speech at Chautanqua (New York), declared that war might profit individual Americans who sold armaments but it would be disastrous for the United States itself. As Hull later recalled, the moral embargo evoked widespread approval from isolationists because it was a safeguard against American involvement in Spain while internationalists approved it as a measure of cooperation with the Franco-British effort to contain the civil war.[52] In this last connection, according to the French Ambassador at Berlin, André François-Poncet, the fascist powers were persuaded to accept the French proposal for a Non-Intervention agreement by America's moral embargo of war material to Spain.[53]

The moral embargo was upheld for the most part until the end of 1936; one notable exception being the despatch of 19 aircraft to Le Havre for onward trans-shipment to Spain, including Vultee airliners which could be converted into bombers and Lockheed Orions.[54] However, in December Robert Cuse, President of the Vilamert Company in New Jersey which had received large sums of money from the Soviet trade organisation, *Amtorg*, applied for a licence to export aeroplanes and engines valued at almost $3 million to the Spanish Republican Government. The State Department had no alternative but to issue a licence and a second, highly suspect applicant, Richard Dinley, who headed Consolidated Industries Inc., a dummy company in San Francisco through which arms and munitions manufacturers conducted sales with which they did not want their names to be publicly associated, was also seeking licences for an even larger shipment of aircraft and war material for the Spanish Republic, amounting to $4.5 million. While Roosevelt admitted to a press conference that Cuse's request was perfectly legal, he believed it was a 'thoroughly unpatriotic act'. Encouraged by the President, Senator Key Pittman of Nevada, Chairman of the Senate Foreign Relations Committee, introduced a joint resolution into Congress proposing an embargo on the sale and export of all arms, munitions and implements of war to either side in Spain thereby equating the legitimate Spanish Government with the rebel Nationalists. The resolution also banned the sale of munitions to neutrals for trans-shipment to Spain and existing licences issued by the State Department were invalidated, and it was binding until the President declared the emergency in Spain ended. The Senate approved the resolution by a vote of 81 to 0, with 12 not voting. The House of Representatives approved the embargo 400 to 1. The lone negative vote was cast by Minnesota's Farm-Labor Congressman, John T. Bernard.[55]

The arms embargo stayed operative for the remainder of the civil war despite a number of attempts to modify its impact. In March 1937 the arch isolationist Senator Gerald Nye, North Dakota, introduced a resolution suggesting that the Spanish embargo be extended to include other nations participating in the civil war but in early May Hull opposed on the grounds that it would undermine Franco-British efforts at non-intervention by revealing widespread breaches of the Non-Intervention Agreement by Germany, Italy and Soviet Russia. As a result of the Secretary of State's intervention the resolution was not even put in the Senate. Roosevelt then announced that his Administration's policy towards the Spanish Civil War remained unchanged but when challenged by the American Socialist leader, Norman Thomas, that the embargo policy was 'a kind of left-handed aid to Franco, and the dictators who are supporting him', the President instructed Hull to enquire of US diplomats in Europe on the extent of German and Italian involvement in Spain. The diplomats advised against any extension of the embargo; in particular, Robert Bingham, Ambassador at London, had reported the British view, which was strongly held, that any extension of the American embargo would complicate their main objective which was 'to foster a withdrawal of foreign interference in Spain so as to eliminate the danger of an extension of the conflict beyond the confines of Spain'. As a result, Roosevelt maintained the existing policy.[56]

Nye tried again to repeal the Spanish embargo in May 1938 when he introduced Senate Joint Resolution 288. This resolution would have raised the embargo against the Spanish Republican Government while continuing it against Franco's Nationalists provided all sales and shipments to Spain were conducted on a cash-and-carry basis. But the intervention of Hull, which was approved by Roosevelt, persuaded the Foreign Relations Committee to postpone consideration indefinitely. In a letter to Pittman, which was circulated to all members of the Committee, the Secretary of State had warned that in view of the continued danger of international conflict arising from the civil war 'any proposal which at this juncture contemplates a reversal of our policy of strict non-interference which we have thus far so scrupulously followed, and under the operation of which we have kept out of involvements, would offer a real possibility of complications'.[57]

While Roosevelt was not prepared to challenge his Secretary of State, he conspired with the Secretary to the Treasury, Henry Morgenthau, to sustain the Spanish Republicans by purchasing $14 million of Spanish silver in 1938. Morgenthau told Ambassador de los Rios in June, 'We can give you cash ... and you could do whatever you wanted with the cash'.[58] In this connection, a compelling case has been presented recently which personally implicates the President in a covert scheme in June 1938 to send to France large numbers of American aircraft which would be quietly shipped across the border into Republican Spain. The scheme never materialised owing to the strong opposition of the State Department and, in particular, the Ambassador at Paris, William Bullitt.[59] Roosevelt continued to be concerned about the fortunes of the Spanish Republic and his concerns were reinforced in the summer of 1938 by reports of Germany's military build-up in contrast with the military unpreparedness of France and Britain and the German success at Munich made him even more reluctant to see Spain's Republic become a fascist regime. Encouraged by the stalemate on the Ebro front in September and October 1938 and by British and French conviction that an armistice in Spain was possible, the President attempted to achieve a mediated settlement involving the Vatican and Latin American states through the Lima Conference. Although Hull raised the suggestion in Lima, divisions among the Latin Americans killed the idea.[60] In November 1938 Roosevelt also considered recommending that Congress lift the embargo when it reconvened in January 1939 but, in the event, there was no resolution partly because Republican gains in the November congressional elections had strengthened the coalition of Republicans and conservative Democrats which had blocked his demands before November, and partly because it was clear from organisational lobbying, opinion polls, thousands of letters, telegrams and petitions containing millions of signatures which bombarded Congress and the White House during January 1939, that American society was still deeply divided between supporters of the Spanish Republic and Franco.[61]

By this time, with the rapidly deteriorating position of the Spanish Republic in face of Franco's final offensive, Roosevelt for the first time confessed that the embargo had been a great mistake. According to Harold Ickes, Secretary of the Interior, the President told his Cabinet on 27 January 1939 that 'the policy we should have adopted was to forbid transportation of munitions of war in American bottoms. This could have been done and Loyalist Spain would still have been able to come to us for what she needed to fight for her life against Franco.'[62]

If the American President had belatedly come to regret the decision to remain uninvolved in the civil war in Spain and to impose an arms embargo on the Spanish Republic as well as Franco's forces, the reasons for taking such a stand certainly appeared compelling in the early weeks and months of the conflict and served to reinforce it thereafter. As in the case of the other great powers, the United States was influenced by ideological and political considerations though strategic issues hardly applied in view of the 3000 miles of ocean between the American mainland and the Iberian Peninsula. In late July and early August 1936 the State Department and its diplomats in Spain grew increasingly alarmed at developments in the Republican zone and they had little faith that the regime of Prime Minister José Giral would succeed in restraining the revolutionary Left. Like their Foreign Office counterparts in Britain, State Department officials were appalled by the Spanish Republic's decision to arm the working population. On 24 July Hull emphasised this disquiet to Roosevelt himself, complaining that 'the Spanish Government has distributed large quantities of arms and ammunition into the hands of irresponsible members of Left-wing political organisations' and on 27 July he privately warned the President that many observers feared that 'in the event military authority should fail, mob rule and anarchy would follow'.[63] While the Secretary of State was making these observations armed workers seized control of the Ford and General Motors assembly plants in Barcelona and these developments were greeted with alarm on Wall Street where the price of shares in these companies and other American concerns in Spain collapsed by as much as 25 per cent.[64] When discussing the 'embarrassing' possibility that the Spanish Republicans would turn to the United States for military assistance on 4 August, the day before Hull's public statement announcing his country's intention to maintain total non-involvement in the civil war, Under Secretary Phillips, echoing the fears of Hitler and Mussolini, expressed his concern to Hull that 'the critical part of the situation is that if the [Spanish] Government wins, as now seems likely, communism throughout Europe will be immensely stimulated'. On the basis of such evidence Douglas Little has concluded that 'the overpowering fear that Bolshevik subversion in Spain would endanger American interests and contaminate Western Europe was the crucial ingredient in the making of the moral embargo of 11 August 1936'.[65]

The tendency to perceive the struggle in Spain as one between nationalism and communism persisted in US official circles long after the summer of 1936. Ambassador Bowers was almost alone in seeing the civil war as a struggle between authoritarianism and democracy with the Republican side championing the latter. Few in official circles would have agreed with Dante Puzzo's judgement that 'it [the Spanish Republican Government] was certainly not communistic; nor even moderately socialistic; it was Azañan. Its spirit was not that of Stalin and the Dictatorship of the Proletariat but rather of Roosevelt and the New Deal.'[66] Even Bowers remained convinced that the interests of Spain and global democracy could best be served, as he advised Hull on 10 December 1936, by 'the

United States setting an example to the other great powers and maintaining its position of absolute neutrality and non-interference in this wretched war'.[67] Indeed, the Ambassador waited almost two years, until June 1938, before he finally advocated an end to the embargo in order 'to grant the Spanish Government the right to buy planes and guns necessary for the protection of its people'.[68]

As in the case of France and Britain, United States society was divided between those who were indifferent, those who were supporters of the Republic, including many American intellectuals, and supporters of the Nationalists. Among the latter was the Roman Catholic Church and while it is probable that many Catholics were not imbued by strong pro-Franco sentiments the hierarchy of the Church certainly were, even to the point of portraying the Generalísimo as a latter day George Washington fighting to save Spanish democracy from communism and anarchism. The Catholic vote provided substantial support for the Democratic Party and the New Deal and as a result Roosevelt hesitated to give offence with the presidential election of 1936 particularly in mind, and later the congressional elections of 1938. Certainly, the Administration's neutralist position with regard to Spain represented the safe option from the point of view of electoral politics.[69]

Hull and his State Department officials also shared the same concerns about the civil war escalating into a general conflict as the British Foreign Office and the Quai d'Orsay and as a result it was to be expected that they would support the Non-Intervention Agreement and the Non-Intervention Committee in its early days since it seemed to offer the best means of avoiding escalation; and the corollary to the Non-Intervention Agreement for the United States was the moral and then legal arms embargo. In supporting British and French efforts to contain the civil war, the State Department was anxious to avoid unduly complicating the non-intervention process and they remained convinced that repealing the arms embargo or extending it to include the interventionist powers, which would result in open American recognition of German and Italian aid to Franco, would be taking an enormous risk which could provoke a general conflict. Roosevelt concurred in this view and, as Richard Traina argues, Britain, France and the United States were neither 'militarily nor psychologically prepared to abandon their efforts towards maintaining peace and embark on a general preventive war'.[70] By pursuing a neutralist role the State Department was also able to keep its option open in the Latin American context and maintain American credibility while it sought to challenge the menace of both fascism and communism in the Western Hemisphere.[71] In addition, the United States Military Attachés in Spain were able to provide extensive reports on the conduct of the civil war and innovations in weapons and tactics, including the effective use of airpower against ground forces, the need for anti-aircraft artillery and the failure of light tanks. This intelligence was disseminated within the War Department, including the Army War College.[72]

If Roosevelt and his colleagues eventually regretted the embargo policy it is certain that Franco was very appreciative, declaring that the American President in promoting the embargo had behaved like a 'true gentleman'.[73] The Generalísimo had even more for which to be grateful to the United States because, as Robert Whealey has demonstrated, American business made a substantial contribution to the Nationalist war effort. The Texas Oil Company, for example, provided the rebels with oil on credit in July 1936 and Texaco, Shell, Standard of New Jersey and the Atlantic Refining Company conducted about $20 million worth of business with Franco during the civil war at a time when Germany and Italy were also dependent on Anglo-American oil companies for their supply.[74] As far as the Spanish Republic was concerned, such activities reinforced the view that American neutralism was in practice malevolent.

4 The Great Powers and Spanish Civil War Diplomacy, 1936–1939

Although the war in Spain appeared on the agenda of the meetings between the great powers, such as the Anglo-French conversations of December 1937, April 1938 and November 1938, the meetings between Hitler and Mussolini in September 1937 and the Duce and Neville Chamberlain in January 1939, and the Four Power conference at Munich in September 1938, Spanish Civil war diplomacy after August 1936 was largely conducted within and around the Non-Intervention Committee in London. Despite a number of appeals made to it by the Spanish Republican Government, and apart from providing a forum for the occasional debate, the League of Nations remained largely on the sidelines of diplomatic activity between the powers. Britain, as the power most responsible for the organisation and operation of the Non-Intervention Committee, took an essentially negative attitude towards the participation of the League other than to persuade it to adhere to the non-intervention policy.[1]

The Non-Intervention Agreement of August 1936 which, it was claimed, formed the legal basis of international non-intervention in Spain, was based an exchange of diplomatic notes with the French Government who originated it, beginning with an Anglo-French exchange of notes on 15 August and concluding with the reply of the Estonian Government on 3 September. In all, 28 European countries adhered to the Non-Intervention Agreement.[2] In essence, it was no more than a moral commitment on the part of the participating powers not to intervene in the Spanish Civil War. As Norman Padelford observed in 1939, it was not a formal treaty in the sense that it was signed and ratified by the interested parties in one written agreement. Departures could not be condemned as violations of international law or of treaties. Moreover, the notes exchanged with the French Government were by no means identical and several, including those of Germany, Italy and Portugal, contained reservations which seriously weakened the Agreement and provided unlimited opportunities for interpretation and deviation. The lack of a binding commitment meant that from the outset the Non-Intervention Committee was vulnerable to threats of withdrawal.[3]

Historians have long debated the issue of responsibility for the non-intervention policy. Until the archives were opened in the late 1960s many remained convinced that Britain was the originator of non-intervention rather than France.[4] It is now conclusive that it was the French who invented the policy by proposing a non-intervention agreement. While the British Government did not invent the policy they were already committed, in thought and deed, to non-intervention before the French made their proposal for a non-intervention agreement on 1 August 1936. During the early weeks of August, faced with the prospect of a collapse of French resolve to maintain non-intervention in the face of escalating German and Italian intervention on the side of the rebel forces, the Foreign Office offered full support to the urgent requests for diplomatic assistance from the Quai d'Orsay; notably, in persuading other powers, such as Germany and Portugal, to adhere to the proposed non-intervention agreement. This close collaboration between the two foreign ministries ensured the survival of the non-intervention policy.[5]

The idea of an international committee to supervise non-intervention was first broached by the French authorities on 24 August. Charles Corbin, the Ambassador at London, told the British Foreign Secretary, Anthony Eden, that the French Government were convinced that if non-intervention was to work it was essential that some committee should be established to deal with the many technical details which would inevitably arise; and the best place for such a committee was London. The French Government attached great importance to the committee's location in London because in Eden's words: 'to be frank, they felt that our capital was more neutral than the capitals of any of the other Great Powers in this difficult business'.[6] The British Government raised no objection to the committee's location in London and as a preliminary to its creation decided to set up its own interdepartmental technical committee under the chairmanship of a minister to deal 'with any questions which may arise here as to the interpretation of the agreement, and to be ready to deal with any questions raised by the international committee if it is established'. W. S. Morrison, Financial Secretary to the Treasury, was invited to act as chairman of this technical committee.[7]

At the beginning of September 1936 the International Committee for the Application of the Agreement for Non-Intervention in Spain was established under the temporary chairmanship of Morrison, and the overwhelming majority of those countries which had previously adhered to the Non-Intervention Agreement were represented. By the time of the first meeting of the Committee on 9 September 1936 only Portugal had failed to become a member and she subsequently joined, following intense British and French pressure, on 28 September.[8]

The Non-Intervention Committee met on 30 separate occasions during the Spanish Civil War and 14 of these meetings had been held by the end of 1936. After November 1937 only two further meetings were held, one in July 1938 and the final meeting to terminate its existence in March 1939. From the Committee's third meeting onwards, the Earl of Plymouth, British Parliamentary Under Secretary of State for Foreign Affairs, acted as chairman with Francis Hemming, Secretary of the Economic Advisory Council, acting as permanent secretary. From its inception, it was clear that the Non-Intervention Committee was too large to be an effective agency for upholding the Non-Intervention Agreement. Consequently, after the first meeting on 9 September Eden suggested to his officials that it would be advisable to work through sub-committees. Acting upon his suggestion the Foreign Office proposed the setting up of a chairman's sub-committee to consist of representatives of nine countries, that is, the six 'closely interested powers' – the United Kingdom, France, Germany, Italy, Soviet Russia and Portugal – plus Belgium, Sweden and Czechoslovakia.[9] The second meeting of the Non-Intervention Committee on 14 September agreed to the setting up of the proposed sub-committee to assist the chairman in the day-to-day work of the Committee. The Chairman's Sub-Committee, as it was called, met more frequently than the full Committee, some 93 meetings in all. By 22 December 1936 the Chairman's Sub-Committee had met on 17 occasions and by 11 January 1938, 77 times. While during the last 12 months of the civil war in Spain, April 1938 to March 1939, the Chairman's Sub-Committee met more frequently than the Non-Intervention Committee itself, it still only registered a total of ten further meetings, indicating that the Spanish crisis was ceasing to be a significant factor in European international relations.

In addition to the two main committees, there were seven *ad hoc* advisory sub-committees; six of these to advise on technical matters and the seventh, a Committee of Jurists, to report on the European destination of capital assets. The six technical advisory sub-committees provided support on a range of issues in some cases with very limited effect. For instance, Technical Advisory Sub-Committee No. 1, established in November 1936, was required to report on the supervision of aircraft flown directly to Spain; an intention which proved not to be feasible. The Technical Advisory Committee No. 5 was charged to report on the grant, in certain circumstances, of belligerent rights to the two contending parties in Spain; belligerent rights were not granted during the period of the civil war.[10] The complete committee structure was supported by Hemming's Secretariat and the cost of the whole enterprise was met by individual and proportionate contributions from the member countries with the European great powers contributing the lion's share.

In view of the weaknesses and contradictions of the Non-Intervention Agreement, it could not be said that the Non-Intervention Committee was established on firm foundations, yet it would be judged precisely on its ability to effectively confine the Spanish struggle to the two contending parties and perhaps ultimately to the achievement of a successful mediation in the civil war in Spain. Unlike their German, Italian, Soviet and even French counterparts, there could be no doubt as to the commitment of the British Government in achieving a successful outcome of the work of the Non-Intervention Committee. As Eden declared in his welcoming address which, owing to ill health, was read out on his behalf at the first meeting of the Non-Intervention Committee on 9 September 1936:

His Majesty's Government in the United Kingdom will contribute by all the means at their command to ensure a successful outcome of the work of the Committee. His Majesty's Government attach the greatest importance to the effective application of measures which have been or may be agreed internationally with regard to non-intervention in the conflict in Spain. For their own part His Majesty's Government are prepared to take every step in their power to secure the rigid enforcement in this country of any measures which may be agreed upon by the Committee.[11]

As the next two and a half years were to demonstrate, Britain's intention to ensure effective non-intervention was no substitute for the absence of a consensus which proved impossible to achieve, except for a brief period of time, owing to the interventionist policies of the Germans, Italians and Portuguese on one side of the conflict and of the Soviets, and occasionally the French, on the other. Ultimately, the Non-Intervention Committee failed to resolve any of the key elements of foreign intervention in Spain – the continuing supply of war material and the flow of foreign volunteers – or to mediate successfully in the conflict, or to deal with the thorny question of the grant of belligerent rights to the contending Spanish parties.

The first major issue to confront the Non-Intervention Committee occurred in October and November 1936 and consisted of allegations and counter-allegations of breaches of the Non-Intervention Agreement, involving Germany, Italy, Portugal and Soviet Russia. While the allegations were numerous, firm and conclusive evidence was in short supply. For instance, according to a secret report from the British Foreign Office's own sources, Italy had consciously broken the Non-Intervention Agreement but that while it was at least doubtful whether Germany had kept her undertaking the evidence did not establish a case against her; and the evidence against Portugal was not sufficient to convict her of a breach of the Agreement.[12] During October the Soviet Government, aided by their Spanish Republican allies, waged an all out assault on Portuguese infractions of the Non-Intervention Agreement, apparently with the intention of knocking out the weakest of those powers supporting the Spanish insurgent forces within the Non-Intervention Committee, and thereby setting a successful precedent for further assaults on Germany and Italy.[13]

The Soviet (and Spanish Republican) charges against Portugal were eventually examined in some detail at the eighth meeting of the Non-Intervention Committee on 28 October and then dismissed on the grounds of inconclusive proof; newspaper sources being dismissed as providing inadequate evidence.[14] Meanwhile, the Foreign Office had been accumulating evidence, obtained from British consular sources, of large-scale Soviet intervention in Spain on behalf of the Spanish Republicans. This evidence and evidence received earlier relating to Italian infractions was placed before the Non-Intervention Committee. On 28 October, with the approval of the British Cabinet, Plymouth submitted particulars of the evidence to the Italian and Soviet Governments with a request that they furnish the Committee with a response.[15] At its meeting the same day, Ivan Maiskii, the Soviet Ambassador at London, announced that his Government were no more bound by the Non-Intervention Agreement ' to any greater extent than any of the remaining participants'.[16] In retrospect, the fact of large scale Soviet and Italian intervention in Spain during the autumn of 1936 cannot be disputed, yet on 4 November during the course of two meetings of the Non-Intervention Committee neither Italian nor Soviet intervention could be demonstrated to every member's satisfaction.[17]

In the light of the Committee's inability to demonstrate conclusively foreign intervention on either side in the Spanish conflagration, the British Government proposed a scheme, first mooted in the Chairman's Sub-Committee on 24 October, for the establishment of a system of supervision in Spanish territory to enable the Committee to obtain reliable evidence of breaches of the Non-Intervention Agreement.[18] The scheme, which envisaged the establishment of 'two impartial bodies of persons' stationed at the principal points of entry (by sea and land) in Spain and the Spanish dependencies, was introduced at the Chairman's Sub-Committee on 2 November and approved at the twelfth plenary session of the Non-Intervention Committee on 12 November.[19] The proposals were then forwarded to the contending parties in Spain only to be rendered inoperable by their negative responses.[20] At the same time, an Anglo-French proposal for mediation in the civil war, of 4 December, announced by Eden in the House of Commons on 5 December, was allowed to lapse in view of German, Italian, Portuguese and Soviet reservations and their continued intervention in Spain.[21]

At the end of 1936, at the same time as the 5000 men of the Condor Legion arrived in Spain from Hamburg and a further 6000 Italian 'volunteers' were embarking at Italian ports,[22] the British and French Governments, undeterred by their failures so far, appealed to the other 'closely interested powers', outside the procedures of the Non-Intervention Committee, to prohibit the participation of foreign volunteers in the fighting in Spain. In addition, they proposed a revised scheme for the supervision of the sea and land frontiers of Spain and the Spanish dependencies to control the entry of arms and munitions of war. The proposal was developed by the technical advisers of the Non-Intervention Committee and, following the fourteenth meeting on 23 December, it was communicated to the contending parties in Spain.[23] This revised control scheme provided the main focus of discussion and diplomacy within the Non-Intervention Committee during the early months of 1937.

Apart from the urgent need to establish an effective scheme to control the entry of arms and munitions into the Spanish arena, the British Foreign Office realised that something would also have to be done about the alarming increase in the number of foreign combatants engaged on both sides. The sending of thousands of so-called 'volunteers' from Italy and Germany at this time, combined with the arrival previously in Republican Spain of tens of thousands of volunteers organised in international brigades, was testimony to the complete ineffectiveness of the appeal to curb foreign intervention in Spain. It was apparent to Eden and some of his officials that if nothing was done, in particular about German intervention in Spain, there would be little chance of the moderating influences in the Third Reich – the Army and Foreign Ministry – checking similar aggressive tendencies in respect of Memel, Danzig and Czechoslovakia. Within the British Cabinet the Foreign Secretary argued forcibly that Britain should take action in the form of Royal Navy supervision of 'all approaches to Spanish ports both in Spain and in the Spanish overseas possessions with a view to preventing the access to these territories either of volunteers from foreign countries or of war material which is subject to prohibition under the agreement of the Non-Intervention Committee established in London'.[24] The Cabinet, however, rejected Eden's proposals on the grounds that it amounted to nothing less than a unilateral blockade of the whole Spanish coast.[25] As a result, there was no alternative other than to return responsibility for producing a control scheme to the Non-Intervention Committee. Discussions within the committee concentrated during January and February upon the task of prohibiting the entry of arms and munitions into the Spanish arena, while the question of extending the scheme to include volunteers was conveniently put to one side.

Although the Axis powers and Soviet Russia raised a number of objections, the greatest stumbling bloc proved to be Portugal who rejected any supervision by the Non-Intervention Committee of its land frontier with Spain.[26] After several weeks delay following the submission of a detailed scheme of international supervision (prepared by Technical Advisory Sub-Committee No. 3, comprising military and naval experts of several countries) to the Chairman's Sub-Committee on 28 January 1937, the Non-Intervention Committee appeared to achieve its first major success when, on 8 March, by a unanimous resolution, the complete scheme of supervision by land and sea was adopted. The scheme included the supervision of the Franco-Spanish frontier by a team of international observers, the Portuguese–Spanish frontier by a separate team of British observers, and a four power naval patrol of Britain, France, Germany and Italy, with the Soviets excluded.[27]

Having achieved a major diplomatic success with the establishment of the naval and land schemes the British Government was certainly not prepared to consider an attempt by the Spanish Republicans to solicit British and French intervention in the Civil War. The Republicans had sent a memorandum to both the British and French Governments on 9 February 1937 offering an 'entente' with both and an end to Spain's traditional neutrality in international affairs in return for an end to non-intervention.[28] Instead, the authorities in London were encouraged to explore other initiatives. The intensification of the civil war with the terror bombing of towns in the Basque region of Spain by units of the Luftwaffe in April 1937, including Bilbao and Guernica, influenced them to have another go at mediation in the civil war with a view to procuring an armistice and also to devise proposals to humanise the vicious nature of the struggle. In this last connection, British ministers were anxious to establish an international enquiry to investigate the bombing of Guernica and other Basque towns. The Foreign Office, however, advised Eden not to take the lead in establishing such an enquiry though there was no objection to cooperating with other powers.[29] In the event, it proved impossible to persuade all of the powers to agree to the establishment of an international enquiry; the Soviets responded favourably, the

Italians and Portuguese were opposed while the French and Germans failed to reply and the suggestion was dropped.[30]

The British Cabinet's intention to pursue mediation in Spain in late April, early May produced an equally lukewarm response in the Foreign Office where officials believed that such action was premature by several months. However, Eden believed that the interventionist powers were 'dissatisfied with the results so far achieved' in the civil war and that there was, accordingly, grounds for some optimism. Moreover, in conversation on 11 May 1937 with Julián Besteiro, the Republican representative at the coronation of George VI, the Foreign Secretary appeared well disposed to the Republican cause. But he conceded that British representatives in Paris, Berlin, Rome, Lisbon and Moscow should be sounded as to the prospects for mediation in Spain.[31] Unsurprisingly, the responses of the accredited British diplomats in these capitals were essentially pessimistic and the mediation proposal was not pursued.[32]

By the early summer of 1937, in terms of positive achievement, non-intervention diplomacy had only the naval and land supervision scheme to show for its endeavours. In June even this one achievement was undermined with the withdrawal of Germany and Italy from the naval patrol and Portugal's suspension of land observation on the Hispano-Portuguese frontier. The withdrawal of Germany and Italy from the naval patrol followed the bombing, by unidentified aircraft on 29 May, of the German battleship *Deutschland* while laying at anchor off Ibiza. Thirty one German sailors were killed and sixty seven wounded.[33] Germany's withdrawal from the patrol represented the absolute minimum response by the Nazi Government. After considerable persuasion by his Foreign Minister, Neurath, Hitler, who favoured a declaration of war on the Spanish Republicans, opted reluctantly for withdrawal accompanied by the bombardment, by the German battleship, *Admiral Scheer*, of the undefended port of Almería in which 19 civilians were killed.[34] The Italians immediately followed the Germans and withdrew from the patrol. Both announced that they would no longer participate in the business of the Non-Intervention Committee.[35] At the same time, the Soviets and their Republican allies attempted to convene a meeting of the League of Nations Council in London to discuss the shelling of Almería but were rebuffed by a joint Anglo-French refusal.[36]

After a period of intense diplomacy Eden, who believed that the *Deutschland* incident might have been provoked by the Republican authorities at the urging of Moscow, succeeded, on 12 June, in persuading the Italian and German Governments to resume their places on the Non-Intervention Committee and to participate in the naval patrol.[37] On 19 June, however, the Germans claimed that their cruiser *Leipzig* had been attacked by Spanish Republican submarines, north of Oran on the African coast. While no submarines were actually observed by those on board the *Leipzig* the captain had reported that at least four torpedoes had been fired at his ship and that their course had been tracked by sound detectors.[38] Supported by the Italians the German Government, at a four-power meeting in London which excluded the Soviets, demanded a firm response, including an immediate joint naval demonstration by the four naval powers before Valencia, the seat of the Spanish Republican Government, and the surrender of all Republican submarines.[39] The sympathies of senior ministers, including the Prime Minister, Neville Chamberlain, and the Secretary of State for Air, Lord Swinton, clearly lay with the Germans. Indeed, as a new Prime Minister anxious to make progress in the pursuit of general European appeasement, Chamberlain went out of his way in the House of Commons on 25 June 1937 to express sympathy for German losses on the *Deutschland* and, oblivious of the bombardment of Almería, not to speak of German complicity in the bombing of Guernica, Bilbao and other Republican held towns, to praise the German Government for 'showing a degree of restraint which we all ought to recognise'.[40] However, it was recognised in London that the French would not countenance any demonstration before Valencia without a prior enquiry as to what had happened to the *Leipzig*.[41] As a result, and despite further four-power meetings and the pro-German inclinations of the Prime Minister, the German demands were refused and they retaliated by withdrawing completely from the naval patrol and cancelling the proposed visit to London of Neurath which had been hurriedly arranged following the *Deutschland* incident.[42] According to Ribbentrop, in conversation with Eden, Hitler was 'extremely wrought' that there had been no immediate agreement on the 'very mild' German proposals.[43] Needless to say, the Italians also withdrew from the patrol while on 25 June the Portuguese informed the British Foreign Office of their decision to withdraw from the scheme of maritime control and to suspend the facilities granted to the British observers in Portugal.[44]

As a result of the withdrawal of Germany and Italy from the naval patrol, Republican ships and ports were able to escape supervision while those of Franco remained under the effective control of British and French forces. To restore a position of equality the British and French governments proposed to extend their patrol so that the whole of the Republican coast and a small part of the Nationalist coast would be patrolled by the Royal Navy and the remainder of the Nationalist coast by the French fleet. At the Chairman's Sub-Committee on 29 June Germany, Italy and Portugal rejected this joint Franco-British proposal.[45] Berlin and Rome believed that an exclusive Anglo-French patrol was unacceptable because it 'made possible a blockade of Franco' while Lisbon declared that it had little confidence in French supervision of the coasts of Barcelona and Valencia.[46] As a compromise, Britain and France proposed that German and Italian observers should be allowed on their ships but this was also rejected. As a result, the French determined on a firm course of action to the effect that they and the British should take neutral observers on board regardless of German, Italian or Portuguese abstention. If Germany, Italy and Portugal continued to abstain Britain and France should then publicly declare a resumption of 'complete freedom of action' leaving the responsibility for the breakdown of non-intervention on those powers. In that case the control plan on the Franco-Spanish frontier would also cease.[47]

Although they stood firm initially with regard to the revised joint proposal for a Franco-British naval control scheme, by 9 July and the twenty fourth and twenty fifth meetings of the Non-Intervention Committee the British Government had shifted its position from full cooperation with the French to one 'midway between France on the one hand and Germany and Italy on the other'.[48] At the Non-Intervention Committee the British accepted responsibility for formulating proposals which would close the gap in the control scheme and enable the policy of non-intervention to be continued.[49] Inevitably, the previous Franco-British cooperation was sacrificed to some degree to enable a compromise with Germany, Italy and Portugal to be achieved. To this end, on 14 July the British authorities proposed a scheme which explicitly linked naval observation with the withdrawal of volunteers and the recognition of belligerent rights to the contending parties in Spain. Under these proposals the naval patrol was to be withdrawn and replaced by the establishment of international officers in Spanish ports; commissions were to be established in Spain to arrange and supervise the withdrawal of volunteers; and recognition of belligerent rights to both sides was to become effective when the Non-Intervention Committee confirmed that the withdrawal of foreign nationals had in fact made substantial progress.[50] The decision of the British authorities to distance themselves from the French was only partly based on the need to achieve a workable compromise amongst the international powers in the Non-Intervention Committee. They did not believe that this shift in policy would involve a real breach with France because the essential interests of both countries were too closely bound up.[51] Moreover, the deadlock in the Committee provided an opportunity to deal effectively with the long-standing and important questions of foreign volunteers and belligerent rights. The French did not disguise their disappointment at the shift in Britain's position but they confined their response to the suspension of international observation on the Franco-Spanish frontier, which meant that it was once more open as an entry point into and escape route from the Spanish arena.

The question of foreign volunteers had been on the agenda of the Non-Intervention Committee since November 1936 yet, despite a number of attempts to effect their withdrawal, agreement on the issue remained elusive. Indeed, in March 1937 the Italians had informed the Committee that Italy would not withdraw any 'volunteers' from Spain until Franco had defeated the Republicans.[52] The last attempt to make some headway had occurred during May 1937 when the British Foreign Office suggested a temporary cessation of hostilities in Spain for a period 'sufficient to enable the withdrawals to be arranged'.[53] Apart from the French Government the suggestion had been received with little enthusiasm by the 'closely interested powers', even before it was rendered out of court by the *Deutschland* incident.[54]

As to granting belligerent rights to the two contending parties, it was clear that neither the French nor the Soviets wished to legitimize the actions of Franco's Navy in stopping and searching ships suspected of supplying the Spanish Republicans or in carrying out a blockade. The Germans and Italians having officially recognised Franco's Nationalist administration as the legitimate authority in Spain in November 1936 wished to deny belligerent rights to the Spanish Republicans.[55] The British for their part had considered granting belligerent rights to Franco in November 1936 when the fall of Madrid appeared imminent, despite their knowledge that France would not follow suit and that Dominion opinion, especially that of New Zealand, would be lukewarm.[56] Although the opportunity had receded with the successful Republican defence of Madrid during November 1936, the issue revived momentarily as a result of the Nationalist siege of Bilbao in April 1937 which included a naval blockade by Franco's Navy. In the event, the British Cabinet, acting on the advice of its Foreign Office, had agreed that 'they cannot recognise or concede belligerent rights and cannot tolerate any interference with British shipping'.[57] By the beginning of July, however, both the Foreign Office and the Admiralty were more inclined towards conceding Franco's wish for belligerent rights.[58] The change of heart was largely based on a recognition of the realities of the war – the recent Nationalist conquest of Basque territory – and a growing conviction that Franco was by no means irrevocably wedded to the Axis powers.

This conviction was based on three sources. The first was a message of 14 June from Franco's brother, Nicolás Franco, to the effect that the Generalísimo was anxious for closer relations with Britain. The second, received soon after the first, was the assurance of the Duke of Alba, acting on Franco's personal instructions, that 'there was nothing that the General desired so much as good relations with England'. The final source was the Portuguese Government who, having instituted an enquiry at Salamanca as to Franco's intentions, assured their British ally that in his response he had made it clear that his indebtedness to Germany and Italy would be paid only in the commercial sphere; that no territorial concession was contemplated or would be granted; and that as to the future it was his desire that the nations of the Iberian Peninsula should work together within the orbit of British foreign policy. Franco was also willing to accept the withdrawal of volunteers from his side provided that the Moors were not included, that the Republican withdrawal at Valencia was properly supervised and that no assistance should be granted while the withdrawal took place.[59]

The problems connected with the proposal for the withdrawal of foreign volunteers, upon which the granting of belligerent rights was made contingent, proved far more intractable than those concerned with the naval patrol. The naval part of the 'British Plan', as it was referred to, was in fact accomplished reasonably smoothly and quickly, not by the Non-Intervention Committee but rather by means of the Nyon Conference, held on the initiative of the French Foreign Minister, Delbos, between 10–14 September to deal with the growing menace of submarine attacks, mainly by Italy, in the Mediterranean.[60] After refusing initially to attend the Nyon Conference the Italians relented and agreed to participate in the revised patrol scheme. They were allotted patrol zones in the central and western Mediterranean, between the Balearics and Sardinia and inside the Tyrrehenian Sea which enabled the Italians to continue sending supplies to the Nationalists without detection. The British and French navies together patrolled the main Mediterranean trade routes from Suez to Gibraltar, from the Dardanelles to Gibraltar and from North African ports to Marseilles. The Soviet Navy was excluded from the revised naval patrol duties in the Aegean Sea in deference to the wishes of Greece and Turkey and to the great satisfaction of the Italians.[61] The Germans who also refused to attend at Nyon ceased to be involved in the patrol while the French agreed once more to close their frontier with Spain.[62] Unfortunately, the impact of the Nyon Conference was lessened by the British Admiralty's categorical rejection of the French suggestion that the Mediterranean patrol should be extended to hostile surface ships and aircraft threatening merchant ships as well as taking action against submerged submarines.[63] In addition, after Nyon the Italians changed their tactics. Italian submarines were handed over to Franco's forces and Italian aircraft on Majorca flew with Spanish markings. According to Michael Alpert, from this time onwards the bombing of all Republican ports and cargo ships bound for them could be carried out with virtual impunity for the rest of the war.[64]

Throughout August and September no progress whatever was made on the issue of volunteers within the Non-Intervention Committee. Indeed, the difficulties of making any progress were thrown into sharp focus at the end of August with Mussolini's public congratulations to Franco on the capture of Santander (on the Bay of Biscay) in which he laid great stress on the contribution made by Italian forces to the Nationalist victory.[65] At the end of September the British Government, already seeking to open separate conversations with Italy as part of their general appeasement strategy, and two months after Chamberlain's personal intervention with Mussolini aimed at kick-starting such talks, reluctantly agreed to a French proposal for a joint Anglo-French approach to Rome with a view to tripartite negotiations on the non-intervention policy in Spain and, in particular, the withdrawal of volunteers.[66] On 2 October a joint Anglo-French note was sent to Mussolini and a reply received on 9 October which rejected tripartite negotiations and which advised that the question of the withdrawal of volunteers should continue to be dealt with at the Non-Intervention Committee.[67]

While they insisted on their involvement in the negotiations with the Italians, the French Government, which had become increasingly alarmed by the build up of Italian bombers on Majorca and with it an increase in the scale of aerial attacks on Republican ports and shipping in the Balearic Sea, had also attempted to persuade the British to take firmer action over Italian intervention in Spain, such as consenting to the opening of the Franco-Spanish frontier for the transit of arms to the Spanish Republicans or by stationing a joint Anglo-French naval force at Port Mahon on Minorca. But even Eden, who had privately expressed some sympathy for such action, was opposed to this and the rest of the British Cabinet along with the Admiralty were positively hostile in their rejection. At the same time, senior officials in the Quai d'Orsay, notably Léger and René Massigli, were opposed to opening the frontier on the grounds that it could make matters worse for the Spanish Republic if Mussolini retaliated by sending additional troops to Spain.[68] As a compromise the decision was taken to open the frontier at night only and this was maintained until January 1938 when it was closed completely following the withdrawal of the Socialists from the Chautemps Government.

In an attempt to force the issue of volunteers the French insisted, at a meeting of the Chairman's Sub-Committee on 16 October, that there should not be man-for-man withdrawals but that instead account should be taken of the disproportion which existed between the number of foreign combatants serving on either side in Spain. On this occasion Plymouth announced British support for the French proposal.[69] The question of proportionate withdrawals proved an immediate stumbling block to progress on the whole volunteers issue within the Non-Intervention Committee. At the next meeting of the Chairman's Sub-Committee, the Italian and Portuguese representatives, Ambassadors Dino Grandi and Armindo Monteiro, protested vehemently against proportionate withdrawals in the clear knowledge that Franco had far more foreign volunteers serving on his side than did his Republican enemies. As a result, Maiskii announced the Soviet Government's firm refusal to consider the grant of belligerent rights.[70] The Soviets were no longer opposed in principle to granting belligerent rights provided there was agreement on all aspects of the 'British Plan'. By October 1937 Stalin was prepared to concede belligerent rights in return for an agreement on the withdrawal of foreign troops because it would have enabled the Republic to effectively defend its war material en route to Spain. Less wastage in arms and munitions exports through sinkings and impoundings would have been clearly in Soviet interests, and there were sufficient Republican warships to serve as escorts in the Mediterranean.[71]

Through November and December 1937 the Non-Intervention Committee made slight progress in terms of preparing the separate commissions which would oversee the withdrawal of volunteers within Republican and Nationalist territory in Spain. It was also agreed that international observation would be restored on the land frontiers of Spain shortly before the withdrawal of volunteers.[72] The problem of acceptable numbers, however, became even more intractable. Eden and Maxim Litvinov, the Soviet Foreign Minister, agreed informally at Brussels, during the Nine Power Conference convened to respond to the Sino-Japanese War which had started in July 1937, that something more than 50 per cent of foreign volunteers in Spain would have to be withdrawn before belligerent rights were accorded to Franco. The Generalísimo had other ideas, arguing that belligerent rights should be granted simultaneously with the withdrawal of a mere 3000 volunteers.[73] Clearly, his proposal was unacceptable since it bore no relation to the 'substantial progress' which was the condition within the 'British Plan' for the granting of belligerent rights; substantial progress meaning that the residue of volunteers left in Spain following withdrawal would have no appreciable influence on the outcome of the civil war. In December 1937 the appropriate figure for withdrawal was considered by the British authorities to be something in the ratio of three quarters.[74]

The German, Italian and Portuguese Governments, however, remained unimpressed by the suggestion of a 75 per cent withdrawal, even though Plymouth reiterated it once more at the seventy seventh meeting of the Chairman's Sub-Committee on 11 January 1938.[75] A compromise proposal was eventually worked out which involved a complicated if ingenious formula for withdrawals. According to this, a basic figure would be fixed in advance by the Non-Intervention Committee sufficient to confirm substantial progress and this figure would represent the number of volunteers to be evacuated from the side found by the commissions to have less. The other side would have to evacuate a proportionately larger number in accordance with figures produced by the commissions.[76] By the end of March 1938 the principle of the formula had been accepted by the six 'closely interested powers'; and with the exception of the Soviet Government a basic figure of 10,000 volunteers was agreed.[77]

Unfortunately, by the time the numbers problem had been resolved other difficulties had already emerged with regard to the restoration of observation on the land frontiers of Spain. At the end of February the Axis powers and Portugal had insisted that observation should be restored at the moment the commissions commenced their work in Spain whereas the French wished to defer until they had sent their report on the number of volunteers and the management of withdrawal to the Non-Intervention Committee. The British favoured an early closing of the land frontiers and warned Paris that, in order to prevent the complete collapse of the whole non-intervention policy, it was essential that as soon as the commissions left for Spain, France should close her frontier and permit the restoration of international observation for 60 days on the strict understanding that it would be automatically suspended unless within the period the withdrawal scheme had begun to operate effectively.[78]

Far from agreeing the new, Socialist led, second Popular Front Government of Léon Blum, responding to a personal appeal from Juan Negrín and concerned that the *Anschluss* which had taken place only days before would encourage the Italians to extend their intervention in Spain, threw open the Pyrenees frontier for the transit of arms and munitions to the Republican forces who were facing a ferocious Nationalist assault on the Aragón front which threatened to engulf the territory along the Franco-Spanish frontier. This assault was also accompanied by Italian terror-bombing on the inhabited parts of Barcelona and increasing air raids on Republican ports and shipping. In the Barcelona raids delayed-fuse and lateral-force bombs were used and intended to inflict maximum civilian casualties. As always, diplomatic protests by the Republican authorities proved futile. The French Foreign Minister, Joseph Paul-Boncour, intending but without success to influence the Anglo-Italian talks proceeding in Rome, explained to the British authorities that the maintenance of the Italian base in the Balearics as well as those existing south of the Pyrenees would eventually 'constitute the most grave menace' to French territory and France's Mediterranean communications.[79] By this time, the French frontier had become crucial to the Republican capacity to wage war because the successful quarantining of the Republic's Mediterranean ports and the control of the Straits of Gibraltar by the Nationalists forced the Soviets to reroute the export of war material via the Baltic and the Atlantic which was substantially longer and dependent on French cooperation in allowing transportation across France to the Spanish frontier.[80] The fall of Blum's short-lived Government early in April did not halt the supply of arms over the French frontier. On the contrary, his successor, Édouard Daladier, kept the frontier open during April, May and the first part of June allowing the transit of 25,000 tons of war material and 300 Russian aircraft, transported in large lorries. Meanwhile, Mussolini proclaimed in Genoa on 14 May that Italy and France were on 'opposite sides of the barricade' in the Spanish conflict, thereby ruling out any prospect of a Franco-Italian rapprochement to complement the Anglo-Italian accords of Easter 1938.[81]

At a meeting of British and French Ministers in London on 28–29 April 1938 Daladier, having complained strongly about Italy's terror-bombing of Barcelona in March and the Italian offensive across Aragón in April, was persuaded to agree to the closing of the Franco-Spanish frontier on the day on which the commissions were reported to be in position to commence counting.[82] Otherwise, during April and May no substantial progress was made within the Non-Intervention Committee either in relation to the withdrawal of volunteers or the restoration of international observation on the land frontiers of Spain. Unsurprisingly, a resolution presented by the Republican Foreign Minister, Julio Alvarez del Vayo, at the Council of the League of Nations on 13 May 1938, calling for an end to non-intervention, was overwhelmingly defeated with only Soviet Russia voting in favour.[83] Faced with the impasse at the Non-Intervention Committee the British Government took the initiative and Lord Halifax, who had succeeded Eden as Foreign Secretary in February, addressed a personal appeal to Paris, Berlin, Rome, Lisbon and Moscow 'to assist His Majesty's Government in a joint effort to lift the Committee's plan out of the morass of technical and detailed discussion in which it has become embedded, and to start it again on a more profitable course'.[84]

The closing of the French frontier with Spain in mid-June – done partly in deference to British pressure, partly because it was feared in Paris that further large consignments of Russian war material transported across the frontier entailed a serious risk of escalation of the civil war, and partly to appease Franco who refused to resume pyrite exports to France until the frontier was closed[85] – helped pave the way for agreement on the revised 'British Plan' which was endorsed by the penultimate meeting of the Non-Intervention Committee on 5 July 1938.[86] The French Government agreed but also warned the Foreign Office that France would not hesitate to reopen the Pyrenees frontier if non-intervention did not take hold or if Britain succumbed to Italian pressure and ratified the Anglo-Italian Agreement without a Spanish armistice and the evacuation of Italian troops from Spain.[87] The Soviets, who had previously expressed grave reservations, were persuaded to agree on the condition that permanent observing officials would also be stationed in the principal Spanish ports; a condition which was consistent with the original 'British Plan', which had included international observation at all the ports in Spain where the unloading of war material or the landing of volunteers was possible.[88] One year after its creation the revised 'British Plan' was forwarded for approval to the belligerent parties in Spain.

Although the 'British Plan' had finally received the endorsement of the Non-Intervention Committee, the belligerent parties in Spain, and especially Franco, remained unconvinced so that rapid progress would be difficult to achieve. To expedite acceptance of the plan the British authorities, at the end of July, suggested that

Hemming, in view of his 'unrivalled knowledge of the details of the plan', should proceed to Spain and provide both parties with additional information not contained in the resolution of the Non-Intervention Committee of 5 July and the benefit of his advice on administrative matters.[89] With the growing crisis over Czechoslovakia, it was not until the beginning of September that the British formally requested the Non-Intervention Committee to authorise an approach to the Spanish parties 'with a view to making the necessary arrangements to enable Hemming to proceed to Spain as soon as possible'.[90] A further delay was encountered during September owing to the objections of the Soviet Government and in the event the visit was arranged to take place in October 1938 without the unanimous approval of the six 'closely interested powers' in the Non-Intervention Committee'.[91] Meanwhile, on 12 September as the Czechoslovak crisis gathered pace, the Foreign Office issued instructions to their Embassy in Republican Spain that the Republicans should not hope for British mediation.[92]

Buoyed by the apparent success of the Munich Conference, Chamberlain announced, during the last week of October, that he intended to visit Mussolini in Rome in January 1939 and that one of his objectives was to secure the Duce's help in bringing about an armistice in Spain; during the Munich Conference the Prime Minister had taken the opportunity to solicit Mussolini's support for an armistice and he had promised to think about it.[93] Despite Chamberlain's optimism, there could be few illusions that the dual approach – proceeding with the revised 'British Plan' while simultaneously seeking an armistice in Spain – would prove extremely difficult, if not impossible to achieve. The extent of the difficulties was revealed during November 1938 on Hemming's return from Nationalist Spain. Although the withdrawal of all foreign volunteers from the Republican side had been completed by November, Franco would not consider, let alone accept, any further withdrawal of volunteers – other than the 10,000 Italians recently withdrawn by Mussolini as the price to be paid for the ratification of the Anglo-Italian Agreement held over since April 1938 and ratified on 2 November – unless belligerent rights were conceded in advance. Previously, in the second week of September in secret talks between Negrín and the Duke of Alba in Zurich, it had become clear, if it had not before, that Franco would accept nothing less than unconditional surrender. It was also clear that Germany,

Italy and Portugal supported Franco's position and also his rejection of the 'British Plan'.[94] Indeed, by the end of 1938, far from endorsing further withdrawals Franco was receiving additional support in the form of German war material and the recruitment of volunteers in Portugal.[95] Moreover, while Italian shipments of aircraft, arms and other war material declined during the last quarter of 1938, in January 1939 Mussolini ordered the despatch of several thousand Italian troops to Spain.[96]

The British Government continued to insist that belligerent rights could not be granted to Franco unless progress was made on the withdrawal issue and they refused to accept that the withdrawal of 10,000 Italians in November 1938 constituted sufficient grounds. The Foreign Office was convinced that in face of Franco's intransigence British opinion would not countenance the granting of belligerent rights. Moreover, as Corbin told Halifax on 5 January 1939, opinion had hardened considerably in France in favour of the Spanish Republicans and his Government had information that the Italians had been sending considerable reinforcements of men and material for Franco's offensive in Catalonia. Halifax agreed that a similar shift in opinion had taken place in the United Kingdom which put the issue of the immediate grant of belligerent rights out of the question as practical politics.[97] However, both governments recognised that the 'British Plan' was doomed unless Mussolini was prepared to make a positive response in its favour. In the event, during the Rome conversations the Italian dictator made no positive response to Chamberlain. Even if he did not say so directly, it was apparent that he had no intention of withdrawing any further troops and remained committed to a Franco victory in Spain.[98] The prospects for an armistice had evaporated despite British urgings and strong support from French Ministers and ex-Ministers, including Bonnet, Paul Reynaud, Vincent Auriol, Georges Mandel, Blum and Herriot, and to all intents and purposes the 'British Plan' was doomed.[99] At the same time, the British Government stuck resolutely to its non-intervention policy, refusing the advice of the Chief Diplomatic Adviser, Vansittart, to encourage the French to supply arms and munitions to the Republican forces.[100] Within a matter of weeks, following the fall of Barcelona on 26 January, the British and French Governments bowed to the inevitable and granted *de jure* recognition to the Franco regime.[101]

The Non-Intervention Committee, which was highly dependent on British and, to a lesser extent French initiatives in the absence of any positive proposals by the interventionist powers – Germany, Italy, Portugal and Soviet Russia – had failed to deal positively with accusations of breaches of the Non-Intervention Agreement, to establish a permanent and effective system of control on the land and sea frontiers of Spain, and to effect the complete withdrawal of foreign volunteers from the Spanish arena; the withdrawal of Republican volunteers in the autumn of 1938 was a unilateral act unaffected by the deliberations of the Non-Intervention Committee. The flow of volunteers and arms and munitons continued unabated throughout the civil war, especially to the Nationalist side. The British were fully aware of this from their quite excellent intelligence sources. The struggle was, however, confined essentially to the two contending parties; it did not become, as Britain, France and the United States feared in August 1936, a European-wide conflagration. From that perspective it was a success for British and French diplomacy. At a meeting of ministers in London, in late November 1937, the French Prime Minister, Camille Chautemps, thought their two countries 'could congratulate themselves that their Spanish [non-intervention] policy had undoubtedly helped them to pass a very difficult year without a breach of the peace'.[102] The same could have been said at the end of 1938. Halifax later recalled that the non-intervention policy was essential to 'prevent Spain from becoming the opening campaign of a general European war' and after making 'every allowance for the unreality and make-believe and discredit that came to attach to the Non-Intervention Committee' he insisted that 'this device for lowering the temperature caused by the Spanish fever justified itself'.[103] At the same time, while the work of the Non-Intervention Committee may have contributed to the containment of the civil war in Spain it was also the case that none of the powers wished to push it to the point of provoking a general conflict and there is some substance in the view that from its inception the Committee was a face-saving device for Britain and France.[104]

It suited German and Italian purposes, in particular, to maintain the Non-Intervention Committee because, as the German Foreign Ministry recognised as late as December 1938, it provided an instrument for giving Franco diplomatic support while tying down French

and British policy with regard to Spain.[105] Throughout its existence, as Christian Leitz has observed, both Germany and Italy
had reacted in almost identical fashion to the efforts of
the Committee, in rarely letting it disturb their interventionist
activities.[106] Surprisingly, Soviet Russia persisted with her participation in the Non-Intervention Committee until the very end of
the civil war in March 1939. But as Litvinov explained to the Soviet
leadership in October 1937 'our participation in the London
Committee has from the very beginning caused France, and
especially England, much embarrassment, preventing them from
deceiving public opinion and making difficult an internal deal
with Germany and Italy'. Similarly, in March 1938 Maiskii
warned that if Soviet Russia left the Non-Intervention Committee
it would leave the way open for a four-power agreement on Spain
excluding the Soviets.[107] More significantly, such an agreement,
as Stalin continued to fear, could be extended beyond Spain to isolate Soviet Russia completely within the European great power
system.[108]

Certainly, British and French diplomacy conducted through the
Non-Intervention Committee had done little to prevent Axis or
Soviet intervention throughout the civil war. The latter had failed
to prevent the collapse of the democratic Spanish Republic and
Moscow's interest in Spanish matters receded rapidly after March
1939. The short-term benefits for Germany and Italy were considerable but it was still an open question whether their successful
intervention in Spain would be so beneficial in the longer term.

5 The Great Powers and the Aftermath of the Spanish Civil War, March–August 1939

Germany and Italy had derived a number of significant benefits from their intervention on the winning side in the Spanish Civil War. Afterwards, they clearly intended to consolidate and further exploit their relations with the new regime in Spain to draw it inexorably into a Rome–Berlin–Madrid Axis. The first substantial test of this relationship had taken place during the civil war at the height of the Czechoslovak crisis in September 1938 when Franco declared his neutrality in the event of a European war. The Caudillo, who was encouraged by his fellow dictator in the Iberian Peninsula, António Oliveira Salazar, to declare neutrality, had every reason to avoid being drawn into a conflict which would result in the hostility of Britain and France and their inevitable support for his Republican enemies. He was particularly concerned about French actions in such circumstances being convinced that France would occupy the entire eastern coast of Spain, including the railway lines leading to it, in order to safeguard her troop transports from North Africa. In addition, it was to be expected that Spain's overseas possessions would be lost immediately and that France would occupy Minorca. Franco was also compelled to acknowledge his powerlessness in the face of Anglo-French military action which would cut his supply lines through Portugal when he had only six weeks ammunition left with only a remote prospect of Germany, confronted by an allied blockade, continuing to supply.[1] On this occasion, and despite Göring's annoyance with the ungrateful Franco, even Hitler had to admit that in view of the continuing civil war in Spain the Spanish leader was left with little choice.[2]

As the civil war reached its end in late March 1939 Franco secretly committed Spain to the Anti-Comintern Pact and under pressure from both the Italian and German Governments made her adhesion public on 6 April.[3] Both the German Foreign Ministry and Franco had studiously avoided such a step during the civil war for fear of provoking British and French intervention on the side of the Spanish Republic.[4] For his part, Mussolini had originally called for Spain's adhesion in November 1937 but agreed to its postponement until the war was over.[5] While Spain's adhesion to the Pact fell short of an actual alliance with Italy and Germany, it did signify Franco's determination to maintain intimate relations with his civil war partners; in his brother, Nicolás Franco's words it was 'a political confession of faith and a clear statement of future policy'.[6] No doubt to allay British suspicions, the Caudillo told the Portuguese Ambassador at Madrid, Theotónio Pereira, that the Anti-Comintern Pact was merely 'rose water' and that Spain was not unconditionally tied to the Axis.[7] However, on 31 March 1939, at Burgos, he also signed a Treaty of Friendship with Germany in which both sides pledged to avoid 'anything in the political, military and economic fields that might be disadvantageous to its treaty partner or of advantage to its opponent' and on 8 May he took Spain out of the League of Nations.[8]

The Treaty of Friendship also emphasised Germany and Spain's 'desire to intensify economic relations between their countries as much as possible' and affirmed their intention to 'supplement each other and cooperate in economic matters in every way'. As noted previously, during the civil war both the Germans and Italians had sought to increase their economic influence in Nationalist held territory with the former achieving greater success than the latter, notably through the Montana project. Franco's dependence on German arms supplies compelled him to make concessions to reduce his debt but he succeeded in setting limits to German economic expansion before the Second World War.[9] While his reluctance to allow unrestricted German ownership and investment in the Spanish economy annoyed the German leadership, in particular Göring, the crucial factor in the economic sphere was for Germany, in its preparations for war, to have access to Spain's mineral wealth through a trading partnership, including bartering armaments for raw materials. Indeed, a German delegation, led by Helmuth Wohlthat, a permanent secretary in the Four-Year Plan Office, visited Spain in June 1939 with the intention of normalising trade relations by modifying and eventually abolishing the Hisma–Rowak system and of persuading Franco to increase the proportion of Spanish exports allocated to raw materials vital for German rearmament.[10] In this connection, in August 1939, the *Reichsstelle für Wirtschaftsausbau* (Reich Office of Economic Expansion) concluded that Spain's wealth of pyrites, iron ore, zinc, copper, lead and bismuth made her 'an especially valuable partner' and that she formed 'a natural addition to south-eastern Europe, indispensable to the *Grossraumwehrwirtschaft* [Greater War Economy]'. According to Chritian Leitz , Spain's iron reserves, not including those in Spanish Morocco, were estimated at 711 million metric tons, and the Huelva region alone contained over 200 million metric tons of pyrites; and German attention was also focused on copper, lead and wolfram production.[11]

The relative failure of the Italians to exploit their economic opportunities in Spain was blamed on their participation in the civil war. In this context, on 26 August 1939 Mussolini complained to the German Ambassador, Hans Georg von Mackensen, that his country had been 'bled white' by the war which had made enormous inroads on Italian foreign exchange reserves, thereby greatly increasing the problem of obtaining raw materials.[12] Italy's lack of military hardware when she entered the Second World War in June 1940 was also attributed to the war in Spain but it has been argued that this was an excuse to cover Italian inefficiency because over half of the material sent to Spain had arrived by the summer of 1937 and this allowed almost three years for its replacement and, in any case, most of the arms sent to Spain were antiquated and needed to be replaced anyway.[13] However, this argument has been challenged on the grounds that, while these arms were outmoded by the standards of 1940–1941, they were still useful. For instance, the Italian artillery, tanks and trucks consumed by the civil war were sufficient to equip four of five motorised divisions suitable for mobile operations in North Africa and had the 373 Fiat C.R. 32 fighters left in Spain, condemned as obsolete, been available in North Africa they would have dominated the even more antiquated aircraft of the British forces there.[14]

Either way, while the Spanish conflict continued, for Mussolini and Ciano economic considerations were always secondary compared with the ideological, political and strategic benefits to be gained. Certainly, the Duce was convinced that Franco's victory had put additional pressure on France and Ciano believed that

Italy's relations with Spain were so advanced as to allow her 'at one stroke a breathing space and access to the Atlantic ocean' because 'Gibraltar's importance was reduced and France's overland route to Africa cut'.[15] In this connection, at a meeting with Göring on 16 April, Ciano revealed the existence of a secret treaty with Franco, presumably the Italo-Spanish Agreement of 28 November 1936, under which, in the event of war, Italy would be granted air bases in the Balearics and in other parts of Spain.[16] In early May, Ribbentrop, the Reich Foreign Minister, confirmed that it was necessary for Germany to work together with Italy to 'strengthen still further the bonds between the Axis and Spain' and that it might even be necessary 'to reach a proper alliance' since 'it would be very useful to us to pin down some French Army Corps for the defence of the Pyrenean frontier'.[17]

After the civil war with these strategic considerations clearly in mind, for Germany and Italy the acid test of their relations with Franco's Spain was the latter's commitment to their side in the event of a general European war. Would she repeat her neutrality decision of September 1938? The early indications were not promising when Franco told General Gastone Gambara, Commander of the Italian forces in Spain and head of the Italian Military Mission, on 10 March 1939 with the end of the civil war imminent, that if an armed conflict should develop in Europe in the near future Spain would have to remain neutral but that he anticipated that Germany and Italy would assist 'in building up a strong [Spanish] defence force'.[18] Immediate support was forthcoming when, following the victory parade in Madrid on 19 May which, in Paul Preston's words, 'clearly projected Franco as a full-scale military partner of the Axis',[19] German and Italian troops were withdrawn but left behind a considerable supply of aeroplanes, tanks, artillery and other military equipment for use by the Spanish Army and Italian and German personnel remained to supervise its use.[20] Three days later, Germany and Italy signed the Pact of Steel which represented for Mussolini 'a unity of ideological and geopolitical purpose';[21] a unity which had been forged during the recent Spanish conflict. The Pact brought with it military obligations for Italy which were soon clarified in Italo-German naval talks held at Friedrichshaven in late June when Grand Admiral Raeder emphasised that, in the event of war, the Germans expected the Italians would plan for operations in the western

Mediterranean against France, taking advantage of Spain, the Balearics and Sardinia to prevent the transfer of French North African troops to the European continent.[22]

Rome and Berlin were left in no doubt as to Franco's military ambitions which were closely linked to his declared intention to create a new colonial empire in Africa.[23] While the Spanish Army was reduced by about a half in the summer of 1939, there remained more than 500,000 men under arms, albeit poorly armed. The primary purpose of this still large army, which was to be divided between the Pyrenees and Gibraltar, was, as he told the Italian Ambassador, Count Guido Viola di Campalto, to counter the 'impositions' of Britain and France.[24] At the same time, the Caudillo planned a considerable increase in the Spanish Navy. Responding to the suggestion made by Mussolini to Ramón Serrano Suñer, his brother-in-law and Spanish Minister of the Interior, that Spain should construct four battleships of 35,000 tons each, Franco told Ciano on 19 July at San Sebastián that he intended to order the construction at Ferrol of two battleships immediately and requested the Italians to provide him with the plans of the *Vittorio Veneto* class and the assistance of Italian engineers. He also confirmed that he intended to develop the Spanish Air Force.[25] Within days of the Second World War, on 8 September 1939, the Spanish Government announced a ten-year naval armament programme of four battleships, two heavy and two light cruisers, 54 destroyers, 36 torpedo boats and 50 submarines.[26] All of this was wildly unrealistic given Spain's desperate economic condition after the civil war and the Second World War soon put an end to such grandiose schemes.

Indeed, the only means of fulfilling Francoist ambitions was to secure the support of Germany and Italy. The latter was hardly in a position to offer yet more war material before September 1939 since it was the deficiencies in this area which helped prevent her from entering the Second World War on Germany's side.[27] However, the former was prepared to discuss the supply of arms with the Spanish authorities. In May 1939 about 150 Spanish officers and technicians accompanied the returning Condor Legion to Germany and there visited a number of German arms producers, including Krupp, and conducted talks with German military leaders. In addition, the Wohlthat delegation offered 15 million reichmarks worth of war material as part of the general exchange of goods between Germany and Spain; it is not clear what proportion of this material ever arrived in Spain.[28]

Rome and Berlin were left under no illusions by Franco, Serrano Suñer, Foreign Minister General Francisco Gómez Jordana y Sousa and others in the Spanish Government and armed forces, concerning the huge amount of reconstruction needed in Spain to repair the damage to the Spanish economy caused by the civil war and that, accordingly, the Spanish armed forces would not be ready to fight another war for at least three years and probably five.[29] For a while Mussolini, encouraged by Serrano Suñer, continued to believe that Franco would make an alliance at least with Italy. The Spanish Minister of the Interior, who declared himself to be offended by the anti-Catholic excesses of the Nazis, apparently advocated such an alliance in order 'to raise a dike against the German flood' but in June 1939 he believed it would be premature 'to put it in a protocol' though he acknowledged it 'a fact in our minds'.[30] As soon as Serrano Suñer left Italy on 14 June, the Duce expressed his desire to Ciano that they 'begin to define with Spain the future programme for the western Mediterranean'. According to this programme, at the expense of France, Morocco would go completely to Spain while Tunisia and Algeria would go to Italy. Mussolini, with his memorandum to the Fascist Grand Council in February 1939 still in mind, was convinced that 'an agreement with Spain should insure our permanent outlet to the Atlantic Ocean through Morocco'. However, it was not felt appropriate at this stage to broach with Franco the strengthening of the fortifications on the Balearics, as recommended by the Italian Naval Staff.[31]

At this stage, of course, only Germany was preparing for war, though Hitler intended and anticipated that it should be a localised one to solve the Reich's Polish problem. He did not expect Spain to participate in it but he had every reason to believe that if the Polish crisis escalated into a general war Franco would adopt a policy of benevolent neutrality, not least because, as he told his senior military advisers on 14 August, Spain would 'look with disfavour upon any victory of the democratic nations' since the democracies would 'introduce a monarchy dependent on [the] western Powers'. In a further meeting with senior military personnel on 22 August he referred to Franco as 'the champion of centralized, progressive leadership and of [a] pro-German policy in Spain'.[32] In this connection, the German Ambassador in Spain, Eberhard von Stohrer, had reported on 13 July that Ciano in his meeting with Franco at San Sebastián the previous day had told him that Spain could not remain neutral in a possible European war, as the victory of the Axis powers could alone guarantee Spain's future and freedom, but that in present circumstances Italy like the German Government at least expected Spanish benevolent neutrality in the event of war. The Caudillo, taking to heart Mussolini's personal warning to place no hopes on France and Britain who by definition were 'irreconcilable enemies of *your* Spain,'[33] had replied that the Axis powers could count on more, namely, 'the most extreme degree of friendly neutrality from Spain'.[34] At the same time, as von Stohrer told Jordana at the end of June, the German Government attached 'the greatest importance to Spain's attitude in a future war remaining a completely unknown quantity for France and Britain' in order to tie down French forces on the Pyrenean frontier and to discourage those countries from armed intervention 'in problems which were no concerns of theirs', obviously, Poland.[35]

Franco was only too ready to comply and, to demonstrate his attachment to the Axis cause, in early August 1939 he ordered troop movements and the building of fortifications near the French border and on the frontier between Spanish and French Morocco and later set up a new Gibraltar command of one division. In addition, in late July he told Canaris, head of the *Abwehr*, that he intended to assist the German Navy in its Atlantic operations by means of logistical support points for refuelling and crew replacements at Santander, Vigo, Cádiz and possibly Barcelona. According to Canaris, Franco also suggested that a midget submarine base might be established at Tarifa in order to threaten the Straits of Gibraltar.[36] When confronted by von Stohrer in late August with rumours emanating from the French press that the French Foreign Minister, Georges Bonnet, and/or the French Ambassador in Spain, Marshal Philippe Pétain, had received official reassurances of Spain's intention to remain neutral in the event of war, the new Spanish Foreign Minister, Colonel Juan Beigbeder, insisted that despite French protests the fortifications in the Pyrenees would continue to be built along with troop reinforcements. He claimed that France had been compelled to take counter measures in the Pyrenees and that she would not be able to withdraw any French troops from Morocco as 87,000 Spanish soldiers were concentrated in the Spanish zone, which was more than the peace time strength of the French zone.[37] The Germans were also reassured to learn that the Spanish Government had warned Salazar that if his country did not maintain her neutrality Spain would be compelled to revise her policy towards Portugal.[38]

In view of the unremitting hostility of the Franco regime towards international communism, it was to be anticipated that the news of the Nazi-Soviet Non-Aggression Pact of 23 August 1939 would be a hammer blow. Indeed, a number of senior Spanish military figures, including the Air Chief, General Alfredo Kindelán, and the Chief of the Navy, Admiral Salvador Moreno, expressed their outrage as did Beigbeder. Franco, however, was more relaxed. He told the Portuguese Ambassador, Theotónio Pereira, on 25 August, that he found nothing scandalous about the German understanding with Soviet Russia. On 30 August Serrano Suñer provided the Ambassador with a full-scale justification of the German move.[39] If anything demonstrated the attachment of Franco to the Axis powers it was this response to the Nazi-Soviet Pact and he underlined his commitment when he refused Bonnet's request to mediate over Poland, having first checked with Mussolini.[40] When a European conflict became certain, with the declaration of war by Britain and France on 3 September 1939, the Spanish Government issued their own declaration of neutrality. It would, however, be a benevolent neutrality towards Germany for, as Beigbeder explained to von Stohrer on 1 September, reasons both of self-interest and honour; self-interest because it was considered that a victory for the democratic powers would render in vain the sacrifices made by Nationalist Spain in the civil war and honour because of the support rendered by the Third Reich to the Nationalist cause in the same war.[41]

With the end of the civil war imminent in late February 1939 the British and French Governments granted *de jure* recognition to the Franco regime and French recognition was accompanied by the Bérard–Jordana Agreement which was intended to improve Franco-Spanish relations as was the deliberate appointment of Marshal Philippe Pétain as Ambassador at Burgos.[42] The Foreign Office and the British Cabinet sought also to improve relations with Franco and the military chiefs in both France and Britain concurred in this objective.[43] In February 1939 the British Chiefs of Staff could not emphasise too strongly 'the strategic need of pursuing a policy which will ensure at least the neutrality of Spain whatever the outcome of the civil war' and in March the Joint Planning Staff warned of 'the possibility of Nationalist Spain being hostile or at any rate affording facilities to German and Italian naval and air forces' which, apart from its effects on Gibraltar, would also threaten Portuguese territory and thereby involve Britain in further commitments in the area.[44] The French High Command were just as anxious to secure Spain's neutrality. During the second stage of the Anglo-French military conversations in late April–early May, the French military authorities admitted the vulnerability of south and south-western France to air attack from aerodromes in Spanish territory and the grave disadvantage of having a third frontier to defend. At the same time, they acknowledged Spain as a significant supplier of key materials for war production; in particular, iron ore, copper, pyrites, mercury, lead and zinc.[45]

As the Foreign Office realised in late August 1939, the fundamental factor influencing Franco's neutrality was the slow economic recovery of Spain.[46] Throughout the civil war the British Government had remained confident that whatever the outcome Spain would need financial assistance to reconstruct her shattered economy which only Britain could provide – certainly not Germany and Italy. According to Charles Corbin, the French Ambassador at London, the British took the long view that time and money would dissipate Spanish gratitude towards Germany and Italy.[47] British optimism, however, was to be seriously disappointed in the months after the civil war. Rather than seeking to enter the liberal-capitalist world economy, Franco's Government was inclined to adopt a more autarchic approach on the model of the Axis powers. As an ardent nationalist he was determined to counter any foreign economic penetration in Spain, particularly by Britain and France. In a public speech, on the occasion of the victory parade in Madrid on 19 May, he warned 'certain nations', almost certainly Britain and France, not to try to use economic pressure to control Spanish policy.[48] Over several months the Foreign Office, despite the reservations of the Chief Diplomatic Adviser, Sir Robert Vansittart, sought but failed to persuade the Spanish authorities to engage in negotiations involving new commercial arrangements.[49] In view of this experience they concluded that there was nothing to hope for from official approaches; the Franco regime was not strong enough *vis-à-vis* Germany and Italy to engage openly in any negotiations with Britain and France.[50] It was also somewhat ironic, in view of the official optimism concerning Spain's need of British financial assistance, that the Government was unable in the summer of 1939 to consider providing a guarantee for a loan in the open market owing to the enormous call on its financial resources in consequence of rearmament and war preparations.[51]

Without its economic lever the British Government had an uphill task in the search for improved relations with Franco's Spain. The task was made even more difficult owing to the serious rift in Franco-Spanish relations caused by the refusal of the French Government to fulfil the Bérard–Jordana Agreement of February 1939.[52] The Agreement, along with Pétain's appointment as Ambassador to Spain, was intended to be the start of a new 'good neighbour' relationship between France and Spain, to put behind them the considerable animosities of the civil war. Apart from both Governments affirming their resolve to maintain friendly relations as good neighbours and to collaborate frankly and honestly in Morocco, the French Government undertook 'to use all means in its power' to secure the return of Spanish property found in France to the Spanish nation without delay. The property included: gold deposited as security and loaned to the Bank of France at Mont-de-Marsan; arms and war material of the former Republican regime; merchant and fishing vessels; all Spanish works of art exported after 18 July 1936; and motor vehicles.[53] On paper it seemed as if the French had made all the concessions but during the negotiations Jordana had provided a number of verbal assurances including pledges to remain neutral in the event of a general war and to receive back without distinction all the Spanish refugees who had fled across the French frontiers during the last days of the Spanish Republic, some 500,000 in total. The Spanish Foreign Minister also reassured the French authorities on 23 February, three days after Franco had taken his decision to join the Anti-Comintern Pact and one week before the signing of the German–Spanish Treaty of Friendship, that his Government was not bound by any engagement with regard to other powers.[54]

With regard to Franco's adhesion to the Anti-Comintern Pact, the British Government was prepared even before its announcement to accept that it was an ideological gesture and not a confirmation of Spanish intentions to ally with Germany and Italy.[55] The French also proved amenable when, on 26 March, they followed the British example of releasing a Spanish warship detained at Gibraltar and released Spanish warships held at Bizerta.[56] The Quai d'Orsay was less sanguine about Franco's adhesion to the Anti-Comintern Pact. The Secretary General, Alexis Léger, believed it was only a façade for something more extensive and he was particularly concerned about Italian troop movements in Spain in the neighbourhood of Gibraltar and Spanish reinforcements numbering more than 30,000 men in the Spanish zone of Morocco.[57] The British Government was dismissive of French fears and accepted Mussolini's assurances that all Italian troops would be withdrawn from Spain immediately after the victory parade in Madrid. Indeed, British Ministers regarded the action of the Italian Government over Spain as the ultimate test of whether it intended to abide by the terms of the Anglo-Italian Agreement of November 1938, and Halifax was hopeful that if Italian troops left Spain within a short time it would be possible to recognise Italy as at least the *de facto* ruler of Albania.[58] In the event, all Italian troops were withdrawn from Spain after the victory parade. By that time, the French authorities, reassured by Pétain and the reports of the French Naval and Military Attachés in Spain, had reached the conclusion that the Italian threat was much exaggerated. At the same time, they were prepared to accept Jordana's assurances that his Government had not entered into engagements which permitted the utilisation of Spanish air and naval bases by Germany and Italy. Equally, they accepted Pétain's advice that in the case of international conflict the Spanish authorities would genuinely seek to remain neutral, although, in view of Axis support during the civil war, he did not discount the possibility that in the event of such a conflict the Spaniards would cause concern in France by the movement of troops designed to pin down French forces on the Pyrenees.[59]

French concerns about Spanish reinforcements in the Spanish zone of Morocco originated with the warnings of their Resident-General in Rabat, General Charles-Auguste Noguès, who emphasised that they would create an occupation force in the zone of more than 60,000. These forces, once installed in the region where fortifications had recently been constructed, would prohibit French penetration into the Spanish zone and also control access to the ports of disembarkation of Larache and Melilla.[60] Franco's Government moved quickly to dispel French concerns. The Spanish Ambassador at Paris, José Felix Lequerica, assured Bonnet that it was inevitable during the period of demobilisation after the civil war that Moroccan troops would be repatriated to Morocco and that there should be troop movements, but they should not be interpreted as being hostile towards France and he added that his Government intended to maintain a friendly collaboration with France in Morocco.[61] In the event, unlike Noguès, the French Government was prepared to give the benefit of the doubt to Spain with regard to Morocco.[62]

While the French Government was prepared to fulfil the more minor requirements of the Bérard–Jordana Agreement, it would not return either the gold or the war material without substantial progress on the return of the 500,000 Spanish refugees interned in France. The flood of refugees during January and February 1939 had created an immense social and political problem. Apart from the obvious and immediate strain which such an exodus imposed on the French communities who inhabited the region bordering on the Pyrenees, in particular the Département des Pyrénées-Orientales, the French nation was divided between those on the Left who supported a safe haven for Spanish refugees on French soil and those on the Right who demanded immediate and forced repatriation.[63] Having acquiesced in the Spanish exodus, the French authorities, confronted with this division and the escalating costs of maintaining the refugee camps, wished to achieve full-scale repatriation within as short a timescale as possible. As a result, and despite the pleas of Bonnet, Pétain and the British and Portuguese Governments, Daladier, supported by Finance Minister Paul Reynaud and Léger, insisted on making the fulfilment of the Bérard–Jordana Agreement conditional upon a resolution of the refugee problem.

In early May, aware from both Portuguese official sources and from their Ambassador at Burgos, Sir Maurice Peterson, that the Spanish authorities were very bitter about the failure of the French to implement the Bérard–Jordana Agreement in full and their endeavour to link this with the liquidation of the refugee problem,[64] the Foreign Office applied pressure in Paris but failed to move the French Government. Bonnet evidently feared the effect on French public opinion of conceding to Spain without progress on the refugee problem.[65] However, Daladier, Reynaud and Léger insisted on the explicit linkage of the refugees with the fulfilment of the terms of the Bérard–Jordana Agreement largely because they distrusted the motives of the Franco regime. The French Prime Minister confirmed his suspicions to Phipps on 19 April. While he did not go so far as to say that the Spanish Government was completely in the pocket of the Germans and Italians, Daladier thought an impression of strength and decision on the part of France and Britain would turn the scale. Moreover, be believed that in the last resort 'an openly hostile Spain would be preferable in case of war to a Spain hypocritically lending its ports and islands to the German and Italians for their submarines, etc.'.[66] The Foreign Office was critical of Daladier's views on Franco's Spain and when Halifax saw him in Paris on 20 May he sought to persuade him to adopt a more conciliatory position. The British Foreign Secretary emphasised his conviction that Franco would wish to remain neutral in any war and that it was important 'to get on to as friendly terms as possible with him'. He told Daladier that he had been particularly impressed by what the Portuguese Ambassador in London had told him, especially Monteiro's view 'that Franco was annoyed with His Majesty's Government but still more with the French Government: but he wished, if we could play our cards well, to establish friendly relations with both governments'.[67]

The slow progress in implementing the Bérard–Jordana Agreement was a source of considerable exasperation for Neville Chamberlain. The Prime Minister, already vexed by French refusals to woo Mussolini, told his Cabinet on 7 June that Britain had a strong interest in seeing that relations between France and Spain did not deteriorate and that it was essential to continue to bring pressure to bear on the French authorities.[68] The need to do so was underlined by Portuguese warnings that the lack of progress in fulfilling the Bérard–Jordana Agreement was undermining the position of the Spanish Foreign Minister and that Franco was contemplating removing his Ambassador from Paris. According to Salazar, Jordana was a member of the moderate group within the

Spanish Government which had sympathetic inclinations towards France, and if he ceased to maintain his influence in Spanish politics the pro-Axis clique, headed by Serrano Suñer would achieve complete ascendancy.[69] When Chamberlain met the French Ambassador, Charles Corbin, on 12 June the latter asked him to consider the worth of Spanish neutrality in the light of recent pro-Axis speeches by Serrano Suñer, notably his effusive toast on the occasion of his recent visit to Rome, and by Franco himself.[70] While the Prime Minister apparently nodded his assent and did not demur, he certainly shared the Foreign Office view that improved relations between Britain and France on the one hand, and Italy and Spain on the other represented the best hope of renewing a means of approach between the democracies and Berlin, stalled by the German destruction of Czechoslovakia in March 1939.[71]

Despite British pressure and the urgings of Pétain, Daladier and Reynaud continued to refuse to return the gold, valued at between £7 million and £9.5 million, to Franco's Spain without real progress on the repatriation of the Spanish refugees which they defined as the immediate return of 50,000 followed by an increased tempo, so that all would be returned within three months.[72] At the end of June, however, the French Government received intelligence via their embassy in Spain which indicated that many in the Spanish ruling elite, including high ranking officers, were alienated by Nazi German culture based on paganism and racism.[73] Moreover, on 4 July Pétain reported that according to a diplomat in Jordana's immediate circle the restoration of the gold would strengthen the argument of those in government circles, and they were numerous, who supported neutrality in case of a European war.[74] Whether the French Government was entirely convinced about Spain's intention to remain neutral, they decided to concede and the gold was returned to Spain on 28 July. Large numbers of refugees were repatriated following this decision but more than 200,000 claimed asylum in France and were absorbed into the French economy and armed forces, thereby supplementing the nation's war resources.[75]

Although the French authorities returned the gold, they had no intention of returning all of the captured Republican war material, such as brand new Czech anti-aircraft guns and motor equipment, which had been redistributed among the French armed forces. In this connection, a French eye witness told Peterson in early July that: 'Our officers had never seen such stuff nor dreamed that things could be. Their eyes popped out of their heads: and in a twinkling the material was being hurried off in all directions'.[76] In late August the French sought to defray its loss to the Spanish Government by reducing the financial claim for the maintenance of the refuges in Spain. The result was estimated to be a credit balance in favour of France of some 150 million francs; a sum which France, as Pétain admitted to Peterson, had no great hope of ever receiving.[77] The outbreak of war in Europe at the beginning of September ensured this would be the case.

With the outbreak of war the British and French governments declared their firm intention to respect Spanish neutrality.[78] Franco's neutrality, which in practice was benevolent towards the Axis powers, owed little to British and French efforts to improve relations with Spain in the aftermath of the civil war and to the eventual fulfilment of much of the Bérard–Jordana Agreement. The dire condition of the Spanish economy was the deciding factor in Spain's decision to adopt neutrality and ultimately it would be economic realities which would limit the degree to which Franco would support Germany and Italy in the ensuing war years and which would also set considerable limits to his own international and imperial ambitions.

6 The Great Powers and Portugal, 1931–1939

The Iberian Peninsula's lesser power, Portugal, had for centuries held a tenuous hold on her national integrity and independence in the face of Spain's irredentist ambitions. Serrano Suñer's declaration in September 1940 that 'geographically speaking, Portugal really had no right to exist; she had only a moral and political justification for independence',[1] was a view shared by Spanish statesmen since at least 1640 when, after 60 years, Portugal had finally broken free from Spanish rule. The possession of a global empire in Africa and the Far East and the maintenance of its long-standing alliance with Britain played a considerable part in the continuity of Portuguese independence. Portugal's participation on the victorious Allied side in the First World War, compared with Spain's neutrality, reinforced her independent position in the Iberian Peninsula. In addition, by the early 1930s the political and financial instability which had threatened to undermine the Portuguese state had been overcome, albeit at the expense of parliamentary democracy, with the advent of a military dictatorship in 1926.[2] The authoritarian nature of Portuguese politics was developed further with the establishment of the *Estado Novo* in 1933 under the leadership of Prime Minister António Oliveira Salazar, a former professor of economics at Coimbra University and Finance Minister. The Portuguese New State, with its Catholic corporatist structure, shared certain similarities with Mussolini's Italy and, after 1934, Austria.[3] The head of state and President of the Republic was General Oscar António de Fragoso Carmona who remained in office until 1951.[4]

These changes in Portugal barely registered among the concerns of the great powers. Nazi Germany, while having an ideological affinity with the Salazar regime, traded little with Portugal and could acquire no strategic benefits because of the existence of the Anglo-Portuguese alliance;[5] the same was true for Fascist Italy. Soviet Russia was *persona non grata* at Lisbon and had no official relations with Portugal[6] and France placed her close to the bottom of its long list of priorities in Europe. The United States seemed concerned only with Portugal's commercial policies, in particular discriminatory charges against American goods in Portuguese ports.[7]

The exception among the great powers was Britain who alone had an embassy in Lisbon, the others choosing to maintain only legations. As recently as 1927, the British Government, while originally having doubts as to its benefit, had confirmed in the House of Commons their intention of maintaining in force the Anglo-Portuguese alliance which dated back to 1373. This decision followed a substantial reappraisal by the Foreign Office which stressed the great strategic benefits accruing to the United Kingdom by means of the alliance, including the use of the Tagus (Lisbon) and the Portuguese Atlantic Islands (the Azores, Madeira and the Cape Verde Islands) as bases for warships, submarines and aircraft in time of war. It was stressed that Britain's situation in 1914 would have been rendered 'immeasurably more dangerous and difficult' if the Portuguese had been in alliance with the Germans or had been neutral in the sense that the Swedes were neutral and that it 'might indeed have cost Britain the war'. It was also recognised that Britain could usually count on Portuguese diplomatic support at international conferences and on bodies, such as, the Committee of Control at Tangier. A second appraisal by the Foreign Office in 1930 confirmed the economic advantages which Britain derived from the alliance, notably, it gave her a certain standing in pressing for equitable treatment for the very large British financial and commercial interests in Portugal and her African colonies, particularly Mozambique and Angola.[8] Within six years, in early 1936, the Foreign Office again debated at length the value of the Portuguese alliance and concluded that it remained a vital part of British strategic and foreign policy. It also noted that Portugal's small, but new fleet had been largely built in British shipyards and that the Salazar Government intended in future, wherever possible, to purchase arms and equipment for their armed forces from the United Kingdom.[9]

Although the British recognised the value to them of the alliance, prior to the outbreak of the civil war in Spain the Portuguese Government had frequently complained of their neglect of Portuguese interests and concerns. Events in Spain from the inception of the Spanish Republic had raised considerable concern in Lisbon.

The Salazar regime was quite capable of putting down purely internal revolts as it demonstrated in the Azores and Madeira in April 1931 and in Portugal itself in the following August but Portuguese revolutionaries acting in concert with Spanish Left-wing organisations were another matter entirely. In this connection, the Portuguese Foreign Minister, Commander Fernando Branco, told the British Ambassador at Lisbon, Sir Claude Russell, at the end of August 1931 that, confronted by official Spanish indifference, he feared organised attacks and raids on Portuguese territory from across the Spanish frontier. He was concerned for the future and thought the time had come when Portugal and Britain would be forced to act together to save the whole peninsula from falling under communist rule.[10] Fear of Spanish developments encouraged this tendency on the part of the Portuguese to lay stress on the alliance with Britain, as the British Chargé d'Affaires, Frederick Adam, noted in October 1931: 'But the whole population is keenly alive to the fact that ... it is the existence of the Alliance which at the moment prevents the neighbouring republic or its Communist demagogues from attempting by peaceful penetration or propaganda the absorption of Portugal into an Iberian federation'.[11]

Relations between Portugal and Spain were strained throughout the period of the Liberal Republican regime of Prime Minister Azaña, who had actively collaborated with Portuguese revolutionaries by providing them with arms,[12] but the election victory of the Spanish Republican Right in 1933 and its aftermath, especially during the period of Lerroux's ascendancy, brought about a noticeable rapprochement between the two countries. However, following the victory of the Spanish Popular Front in February 1936 Portuguese concerns for their security and independence were greatly accentuated. On 21 March the Portuguese Foreign Minister, Armindo Monteiro, who was visiting London, told Foreign Secretary Eden that the Portuguese authorities were seriously concerned about the relations which existed 'between the present Spanish Government with its communist tendencies, and the Communist party in Portugal' which he claimed had 20,000 members and was well organised.[13] He emphasised that there had in the past been instances of arms-running between Spain and the Portuguese communists and his Government were afraid that with the return of Azaña to power this might begin again.[14] There was little the

British Government could do despite the alliance as Eden candidly admitted to the British Ambassador at Lisbon, Sir Charles Wingfield, at the end of April: 'I doubt whether in the event of any Communist movement in Portugal, even if encouraged or supported from Spain, His Majesty's Government would, in fact, be in a position to take effective action.' The Ambassador was warned that it would be unwise to make any declaration which might raise expectations in Portugal which might later have to be disappointed.[15] Indeed, during the early weeks of the civil war in Spain the Foreign Office were extremely careful not to encourage the Portuguese to believe that in the event of a Spanish invasion of their country arising out of the conflict they could expect or rely upon British assistance. Salazar was told in no uncertain terms that the best guarantee for his country's integrity and independence lay in the successful implementation of the Non-Intervention Agreement which had been proposed by the French and supported by the British Government.[16] The French authorities were also quick to disillusion the Portuguese of any expectation of French support outside of their obligations under the Covenant of the League of Nations.[17]

The French authorities were also aware of Portuguese apprehensions and fears before the outbreak of the civil war. According to the Minister at Lisbon, Amé Leroy, the Salazar regime was apprehensive about the possibility of a communist *coup de main*, sustained financially by Spanish extremists and supported by certain Portuguese political exiles. The regime was also uncertain as to the loyalty of its Navy and feared, in the event of a coup, defectors within the Lisbon garrison.[18] With the failure of the Spanish military coup in July 1936 and the onset of civil war in Spain the Portuguese authorities feared, with some justification in view of their declarations and statements, that a victory for the Spanish Republicans would soon be followed by the invasion of Portugal and the establishment of a Portuguese communist republic as part of an Iberian federation of soviet republics; and in such an eventuality the Portuguese empire would cease to exist.[19] While Salazar clearly recognised that a victory for the Nationalists in Spain could encourage them to attempt to reincorporate Portugal into one Iberian state, he hoped that by actively supporting their cause the threat from the Left would be destroyed and Portuguese integrity and independence would be maintained. Hence, for the

33 months of the civil war Portugal provided material and moral assistance, on an impressive scale for such a small country, including the despatch of some 10,000 men who suffered heavy casualties – estimated at 6000 killed or wounded – and facilities to transport German and Italian arms into the Spanish arena.[20] Salazar's reward was the signing of the *Pacto del Bloque Ibérico*, a treaty of Hispano-Portuguese Friendship and Non-Aggression in March 1939.

In supporting the Nationalist cause in Spain the Portuguese found themselves on the same side as Germany and Italy and opposed to Soviet Russia. They collaborated closely with the Axis powers in the Non-Intervention Committee and often came into conflict with the Franco-British policy of non-intervention, for example, by withholding cooperation with regard to international observation of the Portuguese frontier after July 1937. As a result, an opportunity developed for the Fascist powers who, in their Iberian ambitions, were not unmindful of Portugal. The German Minister at Lisbon, Baron von Hoyningen-Huene, recognised this opportunity when he reported to the German Foreign Ministry in early March 1937: 'In the fight against Communism Portugal stands in full agreement with us. Thanks to the policy of the Führer and the support given to Spain, we have gained much ground in the country, not least among the government. Scarcely any other country is at present as strongly opposed to Bolshevism as Portugal.'[21]

In the circumstances of the civil war, both Italy and Germany anticipated the break-up of the Anglo-Portuguese alliance and the inclusion of Lisbon in the Rome–Berlin–Madrid Axis. Certainly, they were aware of the significance of the Portuguese connection for Britain. The Nazi General, Walter von Reichenau, Commander of the Fourth Army Group, stressed its significance before an audience of National Socialist leaders at Leipzig in the summer of 1938:

> The most important of sea and latterly also air routes lead along Portuguese coasts and can be either defended or attacked from it. Portugal's bridge-like position towards Africa is obvious. So is its close connexion with the Mediterranean basin. Madeira is ideal as an observation post on the entrance to the Mediterranean. The Azores ... are bound to play a big part in international aerial intercourse over the Atlantic. The right to make use of them would free England from many a care regarding supplies of food and raw

materials in war time. Together with the Cape Verde Islands, the Azores are strung out along the first half of the seaway to South Africa; the southern half of that route leads past Portuguese Guinea, São Tomé, Príncipe and the long coast of Angola. The mere thought that these positions might some day fall into the hands of an enemy is irreconcilable with the existence of the British Empire.

Reichenau also stressed the potential significance of southern Portugal for the air defence of Gibraltar and concluded that it was in German and Spanish Nationalist interests that Portugal should 'cease being consciously or unconsciously a pawn on the Anglo-French chessboard'. The General was certain that Portugal could be won to the Axis cause through either diplomacy or Spanish military intervention.[22]

Although officially denied,[23] Reichenau's observations on Portugal were not isolated; they reflected official thinking in Berlin. From the outset of the civil war in Spain the Axis powers sought to exploit Anglo-Portuguese differences. Italian propaganda, for example, tried to exploit Portugal's exclusion from the British inspired Nyon Conference in September 1937.[24] The Italian press fomented rumours and invented stories damaging to British standing in Portugal, such as claiming that the British intended to annex the Azores or that the British secret service were culpable in the abortive attempt to assassinate Salazar in July 1937.[25] By virtue of their support for Franco, the Italians worked closely with the Portuguese propaganda department and as a result articles appeared in the Portuguese press which expressed common Latin sympathies and extolled common corporative structures and objectives.[26] The extent of Italy's success could be measured by her complete rehabilitation in Portugal after the nadir of 1935 when the *Estado Novo* imposed sanctions and supported Britain and the League of Nations. The British Embassy appreciated that the decline in the influence and authority of the League after the close of the Ethiopian war was a measure of Italy's return to favour.[27]

For their part, the Germans were even more active in their Portuguese policy. By the end of 1938 they had virtually ousted the pro-British Reuters and Havas news agencies and replaced them with the *Deutsches Nachrichten-Büro* (DNB) in Portugal.[28] In the previous year active centres of Portuguese culture were established in Berlin, Hamburg and Cologne and Portuguese was put on the same level as French as an optional romance language in the German gymnasia. German vied with English in Portuguese secondary schools and was taught jointly with English in their universities, and German centres of culture were well established in Lisbon and Coimbra.[29] Both the Germans and the Italians increased their influence with the youth movement in Portugal, the *Mocidade Portuguesa*, and with the Portuguese Legion (*Legião Portuguesa*).[30] Contacts between the *Mocidade* and the Hitler Youth were established in August 1936 when contingents of the former visited Berlin for the Olympic Games.[31] The Germans also strengthened their contacts with other movements similar to their own, such as, the Portuguese 'National Foundation for Delight in Work', established in 1935. The visit of the German 'Strength through Joy' movement in April 1938 was observed personally by the Editor of *The Times*, Geoffrey Dawson:

> As it happened, Lisbon was infested that morning with a party of 4,500 Germans brought in four liners as part of the 'Strength through Joy' movement. They swarmed in Cintra, where we spent the morning – whitecloth caps, open-necked shirts, Kodaks, and the rest, with Swastikas in their buttonholes and little flags to distribute to the Portuguese … there is no doubt about German propaganda, and the German Embassy (sic) dominates the diplomatic quarter of Lisbon in striking contrast to our own inconspicuous edifice.[32]

As a means of undermining Britain's political preponderance with Portugal, the Germans sought to weaken Britain's leading position as Portugal's most important trading partner. By the end of 1938, using the weapon of export subsidy, they had succeeded in acquiring a larger share of the Portuguese market, notably in coal, tin-plate and motor vehicles at Britain's expense. Moreover, a German company, *Siemens Schuckert*, dominated the electricity supply industry in Portugal at a time when she was poised to substantially expand the electrical grid system.[33] German business received encouragement from the Nazi regime which expressed an interest in increasing its purchases in Portugal, particularly as the Portuguese military authorities continued to demonstrate an interest in acquiring German arms which Salazar hoped could partly be paid for from Portuguese and Portuguese colonial products.[34]

In view of the military dictatorship in Portugal, the Germans worked assiduously to cultivate good relations with the Portuguese military and police authorities. German (and Italian) instructors contributed to the training of the Portuguese secret police, the PVDE (*Polícia de Vigilancia e Defesa do Estado*) while the regular Portuguese police attended an international police conference, held in Berlin under Heinrich Himmler's direction, during August 1937.[35] In the same year, a number of German warships visited Lisbon – the *Admiral Scheer* in September and the light cruiser *Köln* in October. Early in February 1938 the German flagship *Deutschland* visited Lisbon accompanied by two submarines, U33 and U36.[36] During 1937 the Germans also succeeded in installing a wireless air station at Sintra and secured accommodation for the *Lufthansa* airline next door to the Portuguese naval air station in Lisbon, despite the strong opposition of several members of the Portuguese Air Council.[37] The German Army also cultivated closer relations with the Portuguese military. In October 1937 Field Marshal Werner von Blomberg, German Minister of War, visited Madeira and the Azores and his visit was followed on 5 November by the presentation to Salazar, 'as a symbol of the cordial spirit of camaraderie which now exists between our two armies', of the standard of the 10th Portuguese infantry battalion which was captured at Ferre du Bois during the battle of Lys on 9 April 1918.[38]

Above all, from mid-1936 onwards the Germans made strenuous efforts to supply the Portuguese armed forces with war material and presented formidable competition to British armaments man-ufacturers. One month after the outbreak of the Spanish Civil War the German Legation at Lisbon advised that advantage ought to be taken of increasing pro-German sentiment in Portugal by 'prompt and generous action with regard to participating in the rearmament programme of the Portuguese armed forces'.[39] This advice was repeated on numerous occasions by officials in the German Government. In May 1938, for example, Dr Karl Schwendemann, a Foreign Ministry official, was adamant that 'we have an interest in not letting the English take such positions of economic and potentially military importance in Portugal' and that 'Conversely, we should use this kind of co-operation as a foundation for our economic and political relationship [with Portugal]'.[40] German arms missions regularly visited Portugal headed by Hans Elze, Deputy Chairman of the AGK, and by the end of the war in Spain negotiations were under way for Germany to supply arms to Portugal, notably field artillery and anti-aircraft guns, in return for Portuguese goods. Moreover, arms contracts amounting to 28 million reichmarks, were exchanged during 1937 and 1938. The Italians had also made efforts to supply the Portuguese armed forces but with the exception of mountain artillery supplied in 1939 they were relatively unsuccessful.[41]

Confronted by the Axis challenge to their predominant position in Portuguese affairs the British Government sought to undo some of the damage caused by their championing of non-intervention which Salazar and his Ministers clearly interpreted as benefiting the Republicans in Spain rather than Franco's Government which they formally recognised in April 1938. In meeting the fascist challenge the British could not rely upon French support because in the minds of the Portuguese leadership France was too closely associated with Republican Spain.[42] For their part, successive French governments adopted a critical and at times hostile attitude towards Portuguese support for Franco, and in particular to the suspension of international observation on the Hispano-Portuguese frontier after June 1937 only three months after it had been established in March. Previously, the frontier had been completely open to the transit of arms from Portugal across the frontier into Spain where all the territory bordering it was under Nationalist control. Portugal's open frontier after June 1937 was a source of constant irritation and anger in Paris though it served as a reason to suspend international control on the Franco-Spanish frontier at various times, such as, between July and September 1937 and March and June 1938.[43]

Faced with the intensification of Italian and German propaganda in Portugal, the British authorities responded in a number of ways. The News Department of the Foreign Office persuaded *The Times* to publish articles and editorials favourable to the Salazar regime. Between September 1937 and August 1939, having previously paid little attention to Portugal, *The Times* published nine editorials and seven leading articles on Portuguese affairs and on 2 August 1939 a 36-page special on Mozambique.[44] In addition, several important British journals, including *International Affairs*, the *Quarterly Review*, *Nineteenth Century and After*, the *Fortnightly Review* and the *Contemporary Review* published articles on Portugal during

1938 and 1939 which usually praised Salazar's achievements, notably in financial affairs.[45] At the same time, the British Council was active in improving Anglo-Portuguese cultural relations during 1937 and 1938. Representatives of British universities attended the Historical Congress of the Portuguese empire, held in Lisbon in July 1937 and also the celebrations held at Coimbra University to commemorate its fourth centenary in December. Eminent British academics, including Professor Lionel Robins and Sir Charles Webster, delivered lectures at Lisbon and Coimbra between 1937 and 1939. In May 1938 the Anglo-Portuguese Society was founded in London, followed in November by the inauguration of the British Institute in Lisbon. In January 1939 a Portuguese fortnight was held in London which included lectures, receptions and a Queens Hall concert. Later in 1939, the BBC news service to Portugal commenced broadcasting in the Portuguese language and included a broadcast of short talks by prominent British figures organised in conjunction with the Portuguese broadcasting corporation, the *Emissora Nacional*. The talks included those by Lord Baldwin, Lord Hailsham, Lord Stamp and the Bishop of London which generally praised Salazar.[46] In addition, the decline of the Reuters and Havas news agencies in Portugal and the rise of the DNB compelled the British Government to take action and establish a British news service in Portugal in the summer of 1939 along with the appointment for the first time of a permanent Press Attaché to the British Embassy.[47] Despite these measures, the British were not entirely successful in countering German and Italian activity in Portugal in the cultural sphere but by taking them they were able to limit the damage which it may have caused to Anglo-Portuguese relations before the Second World War.

With regard to combating Germany's economic offensive in Portugal, the British Government were made aware of Portuguese dissatisfaction at what they believed was British disinterest in important developments in their economy. They contrasted the British attitude unfavourably with German willingness to exploit opportunities, such as the development of the Portuguese electrical grid system. Considerable discussion between the Embassy, the British community in Lisbon, the Foreign Office, the Department of Overseas Trade and the Board of Trade took place during 1938 and 1939 but the end result was inconclusive. Despite the fact that the overall balance of payments between the two countries was in approximate equilibrium, the Board of Trade could see no possibility of obtaining concessions for British exports to Portugal unless and until steps had been taken to increase British purchases of Portuguese products; there were no tariff or other concessions the Government could offer which the Portuguese would regard as being of any practical advantage. In the event, shortly before the outbreak of the Second World War the two Governments came to the conclusion that private initiative on both sides, without official intervention, was the best way forward.[48] Unfortunately, the new set of circumstances created by the war demanded a radically different approach to Anglo-Portuguese economic relations.[49]

Before the war, in complete contrast to other economic and commercial considerations, the British Government adopted an extremely interventionist policy when it came to the export of arms to Portugal. The Foreign Office was under no illusions as to the importance of the Portuguese rearmament programme which had become even more urgent for Portugal in view of the civil war raging over her border. As the Permanent Under Secretary at the Foreign Office, Vansittart, told the Labour MP, Hugh Dalton, in June 1937, Germany and Italy were trying to take Britain's place in Portugal. As well as political influence, the supply of arms generally carried with it a supply of manpower, such as trained instructors. Vansittart believed that if Britain ceased to supply Portugal, her political influence, already much diminished, would vanish altogether.[50] In July 1937, acting on the advice of the Chiefs of Staff, the Committee of Imperial Defence and the Cabinet itself reaffirmed the great importance of the Anglo-Portuguese alliance to British air and naval strategy[51] and stressed the need to counter the competition of Germany and Italy for arms contracts. As a result, they endorsed the sending of a military mission to Portugal which spent six months in 1938 in advising the Portuguese Government and its armed forces.[52]

The mission arrived in Portugal towards the end of February 1938 and was preceded by the visit of 14 units of the British home fleet, including the battleships HMS *Nelson* and HMS *Rodney*; the largest number of warships to visit Lisbon since 1931.[53] The naval demonstration was intended to counteract the smaller German naval visit headed by the battleship *Deutschland* and to prepare the way for the arrival of the mission. Support for the mission also came from the United States Naval Attaché in Lisbon and from the French Government: Leroy provided regular reports for it on the activities of the mission in Portugal, and it was, in fact, discussed by the French Army Staff during April 1938.[54] In the event, the visit made a considerable contribution to the Government's efforts to persuade Salazar to seriously consider purchasing British arms comprising modern fighter aircraft, mobile anti-aircraft guns, submarines, motor torpedo boats, and a coastal defence system for the port of Lisbon. Export credits of £1 million were provided to Portugal to smooth the transactions. Unfortunately, it proved extremely difficult to fulfil these orders in view of the United Kingdom's own considerable defence requirements on land, sea and air, despite the repeated urgings of the Foreign Office and armaments companies, such as, Vickers Armstrong.[55] However, this failure to supply Portugal's demands for modern armaments did not prove fatal to Anglo-Portuguese relations before September 1939. In this connection, the appointment in the early summer of 1939 of permanent service attachés (military, naval, air) for the first time to the British Embassy in Lisbon did much to mitigate criticism in Portugal that Britain was disinterested in Portuguese rearmament.[56] Despite the advantages which Germany and Italy possessed in terms of their ability to supply Portuguese needs, Salazar did not sign any substantial contracts for artillery, aircraft, or naval vessels other than with Italy for mountain artillery during 1939.[57]

Apart from their respective positions in relation to the civil war in Spain, the absence of an ideological affinity between Britain and Portugal – the former a liberal parliamentary democracy, the latter an authoritarian corporatist dictatorship which was utterly disdainful of democracy – made it more difficult to counter the Italian and German challenge. However, the increasing aggressiveness of German foreign policy in the later 1930s created as much apprehension in Lisbon as it did in London and Paris and therefore helped to neutralise the German challenge in Portugal. The German annexation of Austria in March 1938 was a hammer blow to Salazar not only because Austria shared certain characteristics with the *Estado Novo*, such as a Catholic corporatist structure, but also because of the presence of Italian and German forces on the other side of the Portuguese frontier. The successful prosecution of the civil war by Franco's forces, aided and abetted by Germany and Italy, raised the spectre of Spanish nationalism's traditional ambition for a united Iberian state and in this connection the *Anschluss* had set a dangerous precedent. It was hardly surprising in these circumstances that Lisbon should grant *de jure* recognition to the Spanish nationalist administration at Burgos in April 1938.[58] The Portuguese dictator revealed his concerns at developments in central Europe in June 1938 when he publicly criticised the dangerous tendency of 'patriotism becoming daily more exclusive'. According to the Papal Nuncio, Salazar had gone as far as he had ever gone in suggesting that he did not endorse German extremism; the reason for his change of attitude was the demise of Austria.[59] At the same time, he welcomed the Anglo-Italian Agreement of April 1938 and endorsed Neville Chamberlain's pursuit of a peaceful solution to the growing crisis over Czechoslovakia. For their part the British Government encouraged Portuguese efforts in September 1938 to secure Franco's neutrality in the event of a European war and on 29 September, the first day of the Munich Conference, Lord Halifax sent a personal message of goodwill to Salazar as a demonstration of British faith in the alliance.[60]

The end of the civil war in Spain in March 1939 and British and French *de jure* recognition of the Franco regime a month earlier removed a serious obstacle in the way of improved relations for both countries with Portugal. Aware of Portuguese fears of an attack from Spain and the poor condition of Portuguese defences, the Foreign Office supported Portugal's Treaty of Friendship and Non-Aggression with Franco's Spain, signed on 17 March 1939, regarding it as 'welcome evidence of the desire of the Portuguese and Spanish Governments to place their future relations on a sure foundation, thus contributing to the re-establishment of peaceful conditions and stability in the Iberian Peninsula'.[61] From the Portuguese point of view it was an important step towards the neutralisation of the Iberian Peninsula in case of a future European war; which, they believed, would be favourable to Britain's strategic interests.[62]

During April 1939 the Spanish authorities, prompted no doubt by Berlin and Rome, sounded Salazar on the possibility of Portugal joining the Anti-Comintern Pact, to which Spain had given her adhesion at the end of the previous month, but were met with a blank refusal. Spain's membership of the pact also sharpened fears in Lisbon, Paris and London at the continued presence in Spain of Axis, particularly Italian, troops. Unsubstantiated rumours, emanating from the French Legation, claimed that fresh contingents of Italian troops, having landed at Cádiz, were concentrated close to the frontier with Portugal where, it was believed, their presence was intended to intimidate Portugal to adopt a policy of benevolent neutrality in the event of a European war. On 17 April the Italian Minister at Lisbon, Francesco Giorgi Mameli, provided a written statement to the Portuguese Government which denied the presence of Italian troops near the Portuguese frontier. The following day Franco's Foreign Minister, Jordana, assured the Portuguese Ambassador at Madrid, Theotónio Pereira, that all foreign troops would leave Spain immediately after the victory parade in Madrid, due to take place in May.[63]

While Italian and German troops were eventually withdrawn from Spain, the Portuguese shared British and French concerns that Franco might irrevocably align his country with the Axis powers and believed in that event Portugal would be compelled to follow. Indeed, on a visit to Italy in early June 1939 Serrano Suñer told Ciano that he considered it fundamental to Spanish and to Axis policy 'to take Portugal out of the British sphere of influence'. The Spanish Minister of the Interior recognised the difficulties but he intended to exert his efforts in that direction and he invited Italy's collaboration.[64] Salazar's fears were not assuaged by Franco's claim in an interview with the Portuguese official newspaper, the *Diário de Notícias*, in July that in the event of war Spain would remain neutral if her territory, honour and independence were not affected and Ciano's visit to Spain the same month only increased them so that by early August he became concerned that Spain would irretrievably commit herself to the Rome–Berlin Axis.[65]

The British Government saw their opportunity and Halifax instructed Selby to try to establish closer contacts with Portugal on the Spanish question. Salazar reciprocated and declared his intention to keep his British ally informed on Spanish developments.[66] In the event, on 31 August, at the height of the Polish crisis, Monteiro informed the Foreign Office of Franco's intention to adopt a neutral position should war break out, in advance of the official declaration. The following day Salazar emphasised to Selby that the maintenance of Spanish neutrality was essential for Portugal and assured him that Britain could rely upon her to continue to exercise all her influence in this direction.[67]

At the same time, and despite the announcement of the Nazi-Soviet Non-Aggression Pact on 23 August 1939 which was ill received in Portugal, Salazar was still not inclined towards a policy of unconditional support for Britain in the event of a general conflict. His reticence was undoubtedly influenced by strong German pressure. On the day before the German invasion of Poland the German Legation in Lisbon was asked by Ribbentrop to enquire whether Berlin might count on 'impeccable neutrality' from Portugal should war break out between Germany and Great Britain, and to stress, in the event of the Portuguese Government raising their treaty obligations under the Anglo-Portuguese alliance, that the German Government would be unable to admit such an appeal. In response Salazar told Hoyningen-Huene, on 1 September, that his country's alliance with Britain placed her 'under no obligation whatever to render assistance, not even in the case of a defensive war' and he could not see 'the slightest reason which might compel Portugal in the future to render assistance'. He believed that the most welcome outcome for Britain would be for the whole of the Iberian Peninsula to constitute a neutral zone.[68] Salazar's belief was prescient and his British ally required no more of Portugal than that she should maintain a benevolent neutrality. The British Chiefs of Staff were extremely wary of taking on an additional commitment to defend Portugal, which would require considerable assistance in view of the poor state of her armed forces, and they feared that her entry into the war might convert Spanish neutrality into Spanish hostility and, paradoxically, it was only in the event of Spanish hostility that Portuguese facilities, such as Lisbon and the Atlantic Islands, became attractive.[69]

Despite the strain in Anglo-Portuguese relations caused essentially by the civil war in Spain and the readiness of the Axis powers to exploit this, the British succeeded in maintaining the alliance and subsequently ensuring a neutrality on the part of Portugal that increasingly leaned towards benevolent neutrality as the Second World War proceeded. Yet, it was not the Italo-German challenge which presented the greatest danger to the British predominant position in Portuguese foreign relations before September

1939 but the willingness of the Chamberlain Government to consider sacrificing virtually the entire Portuguese empire in Africa to achieve a general settlement in Europe, and in particular Angola which was coveted by many in the Nazi leadership, including Hermann Göring and his predecessor as Reich Economics Minister, Hjalmar Schacht, though not Hitler. Certainly, with the pre-1914 negotiations between Britain and Germany to partition their colonial empire in mind, the Portuguese were only too aware of the vulnerability of their colonial possessions at a time when, in 1936 and 1937, colonial revision was openly discussed in the international press. They constantly sought reassurance from the British authorities that no arrangement existed or would be concluded between Britain and Germany to partition the Portuguese empire. In fact, reassurances were provided through diplomatic channels but also by statements in the House of Commons, notably that by Eden on 21 December 1937 when he repudiated suggestions that the British Government was 'thinking of reviving certain pre-war negotiations, in regard to Portuguese territories' and emphasised that, 'so far as we are concerned, those pre-war proposals are dead and we have not the least intention of endeavouring to revive them'.[70]

As Sir Eyre Crowe recognised before the First World War, the essence of the alliance for Portugal was British assistance to preserve not only her own independence and territorial integrity but also that of her empire.[71] Only Hitler's refusal to consider colonial retrocession as an immediate practical issue in March 1938, when the British Ambassador, Sir Nevile Henderson, presented proposals for an African settlement, spared the British Government the considerable embarrassment of explaining to their oldest ally, less than three months after Eden's public denial, that whereas most of the British empire in Africa would remain firmly under British sovereign control an overwhelming proportion of the Portuguese African empire would be subject to limitations of sovereignty and part, at least, would be placed under German control.[72] With their confidence in their ancient ally profoundly shaken and faced with a considerable diminution in their imperial standing it is probable that the Portuguese would have decided that closer cooperation with Germany would be the only means of avoiding further humiliation and ultimate absorption into Franco's Spain. In that event, and assuming a German appetite unsatisfied by colonial appeasement, Britain's strategic difficulties in any future war, as the Chiefs of Staff reminded Cabinet during 1937, would have been seriously compounded. Indeed, the early period of the Second World War, especially after the fall of France, was to bear solid testimony to the importance of maintaining the Portuguese connection. By his disinterest in colonial appeasement, the German Führer let the British off a considerable hook.

7 The Axis Powers and Franco's Spain, 1939–1941

The outbreak of the Second World War posed serious problems for Nazi Germany in relation to Spain. Apart from the Nazi–Soviet rapprochment which displeased the Spanish generals, the Germans also lost much of their leverage with the Franco regime owing to the physical barrier of a belligerent France and the effectiveness of the allied blockade. If Spain entered the war on Germany's side it was probable that the allies would seize the Atlantic islands and attack Spanish Moroccco even if they desisted from invading Spain itself.[1] In the economic sphere, in particular, relations remained dormant before the fall of France in June 1940. Moreover, Franco was compelled from sheer necessity to maintain trading relations with Britain and France, especially the latter. As Christian Leitz emphasises: 'if Franco's Spain had remained totally committed to the Axis, widespread starvation and total economic collapse would have ensued'.[2] At the same time, German contacts with Spanish officials and businessmen were kept alive and a number of schemes were enacted to beat the British blockade such as those involving the transportation of German goods by rail to Italy where they were flown to Spain in Italian planes or carried in Italian ships.[3]

During the Phoney War it was estimated that there were 80,000 Germans in Spain, including a large number of personnel in the German Embassy and German consulates in the provinces. German intelligence agents were active throughout the country and Germans were also employed in the Spanish secret police.[4] Indeed, Spain became the most developed area abroad for the *Abwehr* with about 250 of its agents active in Spain by 1943–1944. According to British intelligence, who had succeeded in decoding the secret radio communications between the *Abwehr* and its outposts and branches abroad, including German missions, German agents, who had been recruited and trained to penetrate the United Kingdom and the Americas, were sent to their destinations via Spain and Portugal.[5] Moreover, Spanish officials were actively engaged in gathering information, albeit not always reliable, for the Germans and Italians. Most importantly, in September 1940 the Spanish Ambassador at London, the Duke of Alba, was instructed to include in his reports information on the targets and effects of German air attacks, their effects on factories, harbours, ships and airfields, on the morale of the British population, and the morale generally of the Royal Navy and Royal Air Force.[6] From the outset of the war the Spanish press, encouraged by the Franco regime, was studiously pro-Axis and remained so for most of its duration. The German Press Attaché was reputed to have more than 400 Spaniards on his extensive payroll and such was the effectiveness of German propaganda that Hitler was moved to remark that the Spanish press was 'the best in the world'.[7]

The Spanish authorities also lost no time after the outbreak of war in fulfilling Franco's promise to Canaris to establish logistical support stations at Cádiz, Vigo and Santander, notably the refuelling, restocking and repairing of German ships and submarines in Spanish coastal waters. Cartagena on the Mediterranean coastline and Las Palmas in the Canary Islands also provided support. Until at least 1942 the German Navy made use of these facilities to replenish U boats, and for a time during late 1940 and 1941, even its destroyers. In this connection, a United Nations Security Council investigation immediately after the war revealed that German aircraft had attacked Allied shipping using Spanish airfields as their bases of operations, that the Spanish radio stations had provided important information to the German Air Force and that German reconnaissance aircraft had been permitted to fly utilising Spanish markings as camouflage. In addition, German observation posts on the Mediterranean coast of Spain were able to closely monitor Allied shipping which was subsequently attacked. In the summer of 1943, for example, these posts were directly responsible for damage caused to a British convoy consisting of 50,000 tons of shipping.[8]

Germany's economic relations with Spain, which had begun to expand considerably during the civil war and its aftermath, were seriously disrupted by the blockading strategy of the Anglo-French allies before the fall of France. The extent of the decline in

Germany's trading relations with Spain can be seen by the sharp fall in Spanish exports to the Third Reich, which even in 1935 before the civil war were 12.7 per cent of all Spain's exports but which in 1940 accounted for just 5 per cent and Spain's imports from Germany amounted to only 3.7 per cent. After the French collapse trading relations recovered with increasing momentum so that in 1941 Spain was conducting 28 per cent of her foreign trade with the Third Reich.[9]

From 1941 onwards, Spanish workers were sent to Germany to help alleviate in a small way the Third Reich's labour shortage. At the highest point in the summer of 1943 about 8000 Spanish workers were employed in Germany. Spanish exports to Germany included skins and hides, cork, oranges, mercury, fluorspar, amblygonite, lead and iron ore. The supply of clothing hides contributed to the provision of warm clothing for the German forces on the eastern front from the end of 1941 onwards following the catastrophic shortages of November and December. Indeed, during 1942, 35 per cent of the Wehrmacht's requirements of clothing hides depended on supplies from Spain.[10] The most important export, however, was that of Spanish wolfram. As a tungsten ore, its application in war was extremely varied and significant; for example, as a core for armour piercing projectiles, as an alloy in stellite used for engine valve sealing and as a catalyst for synthetic oil production. The Iberian Peninsula accounted for virtually all European production and the large reserves of tungsten ore in China, Korea and Burma were inaccessible owing to the closing of the Trans Siberian route following the invasion of Soviet Russia in June 1941. Franco (and Salazar) continued to supply wolfram to Germany until the last months of the war.[11]

In return for Spanish raw materials the Germans exported armaments vital for the rearmament of the Spanish armed forces, including aircraft, artillery, anti-aircraft guns, anti-tank weapons and small arms. The arms negotiations with the Spanish authorities were often protracted with hard bargaining on both sides between 1941 and 1944. According to Christian Leitz, the value of German war material contracts peaked in 1943 when at 258 million reichmarks (of a total of 1304 million reichmarks) Spain had become Germany's biggest customer, just ahead of Italy.[12]

While economic relations acquired increasing importance, they were overshadowed during 1940 and 1941 by political and strategic issues which threatened to bring about Spain's entry as a belligerent ally of the Axis powers. With the battle of France looming, the German Embassy in Madrid began to anticipate Spain's eventual intervention in the war. According to Stohrer, events in Spain and Italian rearmament made Spain's entry more likely and he reported that both Franco and his Minister of the Interior, Serrano Suñer, had complete confidence in a German victory.[13] However, Ribbentrop and Göring remained unconvinced and expressed concern at the Spanish tendency to plead economic difficulties as justification for Spain's continuing neutrality. Indeed, the Reichsmarschall told the German Air Attaché at Madrid, Colonel Eckart Krahmer, that he was not certain whether 'Spain believed in a German victory' and he felt her conduct 'to be super-neutral'.[14] Beigbeder's assertion to Stohrer, on 20 May 1940, that even Italy's expected entry into the war would not necessarily draw Spain into the conflict, was scarcely reassuring to the German Government.[15] At the same time, apart from the economic problems confronting Spain, the Germans were aware that the Franco regime harboured territorial ambitions which in the right circumstances would persuade it to become involved in the conflict against Britain and France. Beigbeder told Stohrer on 4 June that Spain wanted Gibraltar, Tangier, French Morocco and frontier rectification in Spanish Guinea. The Spanish Foreign Minister emphasised that his Government would regret it if Italy established herself in these regions; 'Morocco in Spanish hands would be, for a friendly Italy, a sufficient guarantee that Italian interests would be respected'.[16] Mussolini was more generous when on 9 June, the day before Italy declared war, he requested Spain's 'moral and economic solidarity' with Italy and promised her Gibraltar as part of the new reorganisation of the Mediterranean which would result from the war.[17] On 13 June, clearly impressed by Germany's stunning victories in western Europe and three days after Italy's entry into the war, Franco's Spain discarded its neutrality in favour of non-belligerency. The following day Paris fell to the Germans and the Spaniards occupied Tangier on the pretext of ensuring its neutrality, but in reality as the first positive step towards a full-scale African empire. The Spanish military authorities, however, were deterred from invading French Morocco by the presence of French air power in North Africa, French aircraft having been sent there prior to the armistice.[18] The fall of France brought German troops to the Pyrenees where they remained as a constant reminder of German power.

The French surrender and the installation of the Vichy regime of Marshal Philippe Pétain created three potential rivals for Hitler's support regarding North Africa and the western Mediterranean, not to speak of Germany's own ambitions in the region. On 16 June, shortly before the armistice with France, on his visit to the Château Acoz in Belgium, the Führer assured General Juan Vigón, Director of Procurement for the Spanish Army, that if any attempts were made by enemy powers (Britain or the United States) to land in Portugal or Morocco 'all Germany's forces would be at Spain's side'. He also approved of Spanish intentions to take over Gibraltar and suggested a meeting between himself, Mussolini and Franco to discuss Spain's claims in Morocco, though he stressed that Germany's interests were solely economic ones.[19] Three days later, the Spanish Government denied the continued existence of the French empire in North Africa and reiterated their demands, including 'the territory of Oran, the unification of Morocco under a Spanish Protectorate, the extension of Spanish territory in the Sahara to the 20th parallel and the extension of Spain's coastal territories situated in the area of the coast between the mouth of the Niger and Cape Lopez'. If Britain continued the struggle after France had surrendered, the Spaniards promised to enter the war, following a short period devoted to preparing the Spanish public, provided Germany could supply war material in the form of heavy artillery, aircraft for the attack on Gibraltar and submarine protection for the Canary Islands, and also foodstuffs, ammunition, motor fuels and equipment which could be drawn from captured French stocks.[20]

Britain's refusal to surrender, however, compelled Hitler to include Vichy France in his calculations to ensure its continued support and prevent the growth of an anti-Axis front in France's North African territories and Vichy exercised at least nominal authority over the greater part of the French empire and French fleet.[21] Apart from Spain's demands, the Germans were aware of the extent of Italian claims which were not insubstantial. Ciano outlined Italian interests to Ribbentrop on 19 June; these included as a minimum Nice, Corsica, Tunisia and French Somaliland. The Italian Foreign Minister also hinted at Italy's need for access to the Atlantic via Morocco and Algeria. Ribbentrop expressed reservations about these last two French colonies and reminded Ciano of Germany's historical ambitions with regard to Morocco and the satisfaction of Spain's claims in North Africa as an incentive to her to join in policing the post-war settlement.[22]

It is conceivable that had Britain chosen to surrender in the summer of 1940 Hitler would have maintained his long-held promise to guarantee the British Empire. On his visit to Munich on 18 and 19 June 1940 Ciano observed that the Führer 'makes many reservations on the desirability of demolishing the British Empire, which he considers, even to-day, to be an important factor in world equilibrium'.[23] In this case Franco's Spain would almost certainly have been left in the cold with her territorial ambitions unsatisfied. Britain, however, chose to continue the struggle against the Axis powers with the result that Spain became a serious factor in Hitler's world policy.

The Führer's greatest strategic priority was unquestionably the conquest of living space in the east, entailing the destruction of Soviet Russia, to ensure for the Third Reich an unassailable political, economic and military position of hegemony on the Continent, but with Britain refusing to surrender in the summer of 1940 he needed to develop a peripheral strategy, involving the Mediterranean and North Africa, to bring about her defeat, particularly after the failure of Operation 'Sealion', for the invasion of Britain, in September 1940. The invasion and conquest of Soviet Russia, first mooted in the late summer of 1940 and planned to commence in the early summer of 1941, was intended to compel Britain to surrender by removing her one remaining hope of a continental ally but, meanwhile, measures, such as the capture of Gibraltar, the establishment of German bases along the Northwest African coast and in the Atlantic islands of Spain and Portugal, would immeasurably strengthen Germany's strategic position. Apart from the necessity of defeating Britain, Hitler's Mediterranean and North African strategy would provide the basis for the acquisition of a future colonial empire in Africa and beyond which would follow the achievement of continental hegemony. That such ambitions would lead sooner or later to an armed clash with the United States was fully understood by Hitler and his military advisers and commanders who recognised that this would entail Germany becoming a first class oceanic naval power. To that end in July 1940 Hitler approved a naval construction programme which was largely based on the Z plan of 1938–1939. The plan's objective had been to create a large ocean going navy with aircraft carriers and 56,000 ton battleships as its nucleus. In the light of these ambitions it is hardly surprising that Spain, with its important geo-strategic position, became a significant factor in Hitler's world policy.[24]

With the peripheral strategy and wider ambitions in mind, the Führer told General Franz Halder, Chief of the General Staff of the Army High Command (OKH – *Oberkommando des Heeres*), on 13 July, that he intended 'to draw Spain into the game in order to build up a hostile front against England from the North Cape [of Norway] to Morocco'.[25] Having set up a 'Gibraltar reconnaissance staff', the Armed Forces High Command (OKW – *Oberkommando der Wehrmacht*) sent the head of German Military Intelligence, Admiral Wilhelm Canaris, and several other officers to Spain between 20 and 23 July in order to examine on the spot the prospects of success of an operation against the Rock. At the same time, according to British sources, Mussolini appealed to Franco to enter the war immediately because as long as Gibraltar remained in British hands it was impossible for Italy to operate successfully in the Mediterranean.[26] Although Franco resisted Mussolini's invitation, on 18 July he declared that Spain's 'duty and mission' was to regain mastery over Gibraltar and to deepen Spanish influence there.[27]

While Hitler's mind was already focusing on Soviet Russia,[28] he charged Ribbentrop to achieve Spain's early entry into the war and the Foreign Minister, accordingly, recalled Stohrer to Berlin. On 8 August the Ambassador reminded Ribbentrop of the Spanish Government's intention, as communicated on 19 June, to enter the war provided Spain received territorial acquisitions and military and economic aid. The former included Gibraltar, French Morocco, part of Algeria around Oran, the enlargement of Rio de Oro and the colonies in the Gulf of Guinea. Stohrer emphasised that Spanish entry would benefit Germany by further undermining Britain's prestige and prospects for victory, by cutting off her trade with and destroying her economic influence in Spain, including access to vital strategic minerals, and by ensuring control of the Straits of Gibraltar by the Axis powers. At the same time, he warned that if Britain intervened preemptively in anticipation of

Spain's entry she could consolidate her position at Gibraltar, occupy the Canary Islands, Tangier and the Spanish colonies, and even the Balearic Islands. Moreover, a British invasion of Spain from Portugal or a Franco-British Moroccan campaign against Spain in North Africa could not be ruled out and Spain's ability to sustain a war for any length of time without German and Italian support, in view of the chronic economic problems arising from the civil war, was very problematic.[29] These reservations were reinforced on 10 August by the OKH which emphasised the poor condition of Spanish artillery, inadequate spare parts for the 200 light tanks still fit for war use and extremely limited stocks of ammunition. Criticism was also expressed of Spain's field fortifications on the Pyrenees frontier, the absence of fortifications on the Portuguese frontier and the limited utility of the installations around Gibraltar. While the Spanish army was fully capable of defending Spain itself and its possessions, it was incapable of fighting a war other than one of very short duration without foreign support. Accordingly, the OKH, with considerable prescience, predicted that non-belligerent Spain would enter the war 'only if German–Italian successes should permit the expectation of a quick, certain, and riskless attainment of Spanish aims'.[30] In other words, until Britain was clearly on the point of defeat Spain would not become a belligerent power. Moreover, the fact that Spain could not sustain anything other than a very short war was confirmed in mid-August when the Embassy at Madrid sent a long list of Spain's economic requirements, including: an absolute minimum of 300,000 tons of grain and 400,000 tons of gasoline, 200,000 tons of coal, 200,000 tons of fuel oil, 40,000 tons of lubricating oil, 20,000 tons of manganese, 100,000 tons of cotton, 25,000 tons of raw rubber, 625,000 tons of nitrogen fertiliser and a range of other commodities.[31]

There were, however, some indications that Spain would participate in the war sooner rather than later because of the closer cooperation between Portugal and Spain with the signing in late July of a protocol to the Treaty of Friendship and Non-Aggression of March 1939, the diminution of the danger of Anglo-Spanish cooperation over Morocco, the coordination of military matters between Vigón and Canaris, and the strong attacks on Britain of the Spanish press encouraged by Serrano Suñer and intended to prepare the Spanish public for war. Further encouragement was provided by Vigón who told Canaris that Franco was considering an early entry into the war because Britain was already conducting economic warfare against Spain and was possibly reconciling himself 'even to a war of longer duration'.[32] Apart from German pressure to enter the war, Franco was also encouraged to abandon non-belligerency by Mussolini who regarded Spain's entry as inevitable. The Duce was convinced that Franco would not 'let this opportunity go by of giving Spain her African vital space'.[33] Canaris was less sanguine because he had reservations about Spain's entry as he told General Franz Halder on 27 August: 'The consequences of having this unpredictable nation as a partner cannot be calculated. We shall get an ally who will cost us dearly.'[34]

By early September, as part of the struggle with Britain, and also to forestall any American intervention in North Africa, Hitler decided that it was essential to capture Gibraltar by means of an armed land assault with Spanish approval and support. He also agreed with the Chief of the OKM, Grand Admiral Erich Raeder, that Germany would need to occupy the Canary Islands on Spain's entry into the war because the British would seek a new base there and possibly also the United States.[35] As a result, planning for Operation 'Felix' duly commenced. Meanwhile, on 17 September, the day when Operation 'Sealion' (the invasion of Britain) was indefinitely postponed, Hitler expressed his conviction to Mussolini that it was 'important to make it possible for Spain to enter the war' despite her excessive economic requirements.[36] The following day, the Führer appealed to Franco for joint action to expel the British from Gibraltar and transform the strategic position in the western Mediterranean to the advantage of the Axis and thereby 'help to show England even more emphatically the hopelessness of continuing the war and force her to give up once and for all her unjustified claims'. He also underlined the strategic significance of the Canary Islands for the German war effort and advised Franco to strengthen the defence forces there, and offered to transfer to Las Palmas German dive bombers and long range fighters either before or at the same time as Spain's entry into the war.[37] Mussolini also recognised the strategic advantages of Spain's entry and he suggested to Ribbentrop, during his visit to Rome on 19 September, a real tripartite alliance between Germany, Italy and Spain.[38]

While Franco ruled out any prospect of British landings in the Iberian Peninsula within the immediate future, and expressed his optimism concerning operations against Gibraltar which, he believed, could achieve success within a matter of days, he also issued a discouraging reply with regard to German bases in Morocco.[39] Serrano Suñer's visit to Berlin between 16 and 27 September was equally discouraging as far as German demands for bases in Spanish territory, including the Canaries, were concerned.[40] At the same time, he told Mussolini and Ciano on 1 October that 'Spain – which from the beginning of the struggle has always given the Axis Powers moral support – is preparing to take up arms to settle its centuries old account with Great Britain'. For his part, the Duce ruled out any Italian economic aid to Spain but promised 'a concentration of air strength'.[41]

Spain's position was made abundantly clear when Serrano Suñer handed an unsigned memorandum to Stohrer on 27 September in which the Spanish Government declared its solidarity with the policy of the Axis and its readiness to conclude 'in the form of a tripartite pact a military alliance for ten years with Germany and Italy'. The declaration of solidarity assumed recognition of the reincorporation of Gibraltar into Spanish sovereign territory and the annexation by Spain of the province of Oran and of the whole of Morocco, and extension of the Spanish frontier to the desert.[42] Little wonder that Hitler should remark to Ciano on the occasion of the signing of the Tripartite Pact in Berlin on 27 September 1940 that he was opposed to Spanish intervention because 'it would cost more than it is worth'.[43] By this time, as Hitler's meeting with Mussolini at the Brenner Pass on 4 October revealed, Vichy France had been elevated to a position of importance at least equal to Spain in German calculations. The postponement of Operation 'Sealion' and Vichy's spirited defence against Anglo-Gaullist forces at Dakar were responsible for this promotion.[44] The Führer was adamant that the Spanish claims for territory were too high and that Oran could not be awarded to Spain.[45] In the event, this scarcely mattered because while the Führer wanted the support of both against the British and their potential American allies – he was particularly concerned that a part of the French empire would desert Vichy and go over to the Free French led by General Charles de Gaulle[46] – it was his intention that North West Africa should be dominated by neither but by Germany herself. Hence, his meetings with Franco at Hendaye on 23 October and Pétain at Montoire on 24 October were, as

Norman Goda argues, essentially exercises in the use of 'smoke and mirrors' by which he sought the commitment of both to the Axis cause without making any substantive concessions.[47] In the absence of a firm and clear commitment to cede French Morocco to Spain, Franco withheld her immediate entry into the war.[48] This had been predictable from the start. As Franz Halder noted in his diary, in early October, Hitler already realised that the reconciliation of conflicting French, Italian and Spanish interests would be possible only by 'a gigantic fraud'.[49]

Despite the fraud he wished to perpetrate, Hitler's meeting with the Generalísimo was particularly galling. He told Mussolini five days later that he would prefer to have three or four teeth pulled rather than suffer another interview with Franco and Halder noted on 1 November the Führer's reference to Franco as that 'Jesuit swine'. The passage of time did not mellow the experience for he wrote in his testament in February 1945 that at Hendaye he had to submit to receiving honours at the hands of a false friend.[50] Franco and Serrano Suñer were equally bitter about the outcome of the Hendaye meeting. A secret protocol, which had been drafted by the Germans prior to the meeting and which was signed by the Foreign Ministers of Germany, Italy and eventually Spain 'in the greatest secrecy' was a particular source of grievance at Madrid. Article five of the protocol stated clearly that Spain would receive territories in Africa 'in the same measure as that in which France may be compensated, by having assigned to her in Africa other territories of equal value while German and Italian claims against France continued to be maintained'. Franco and Serrano Suñer had attempted unsuccessfully to amend this article with the intention of achieving a more explicit commitment from the Axis powers to Spain's ambition to acquire territory at France's expense. However, article four of the protocol provided a get-out which left Franco complete freedom of decision because Spain's entry into the war was made conditional on Germany and Italy providing Spain with the assistance necessary to complete her preparations for war, including economic assistance in the form of foodstuffs and raw materials sufficient to meet the needs of the Spanish people and the requirements of war.[51]

Undeterred by Spain's failure to enter the war immediately after Hendaye, Hitler proposed to Mussolini in Florence on 28 October that all necessary preparations should be made with

Spain for her entry into the war and that a meeting should then take place in Florence 'between the Führer, the Duce, and Franco, at which the participation of Spain in the Tripartite Pact [signed between Germany, Italy and Japan on 27 September 1940] and the German–Italian Alliance could be announced with full publicity'. At the same time, because it was essential to hold out some inducement to the French to defend their North African territories themselves, he insisted that the most Spain could expect by way of territorial acquisition was 'a substantial enlargement of Spanish Morocco'. The Führer also reiterated that Germany had to have bases on the African coast and that he would prefer 'to lay claim to one of the islands off the coast of Africa for this purpose'.[52] Soon after, on 12 November, Hitler issued his directive for intervention in the Iberian Peninsula – Operation 'Felix'. The aim was abundantly clear, to drive the British out of the western Mediterranean. To this end, Gibraltar was to be captured and the Straits closed and the British were to be prevented 'from gaining a foothold at any other point on the Iberian peninsula or in the Atlantic islands'. It was envisaged that while there would be collaboration with the Spanish authorities the actual attack on Gibraltar would be made by German troops. At the same time, German forces would also be assembled to invade Portugal in case the British gained a foothold there. The directive also envisaged German air and naval support for Spain's defence of the Canaries against a possible British occupation.[53] Hitler remained concerned that the French colonies in North and West Africa would detach themselves from Vichy and offer the British dangerous bases of operations and in such circumstances, as he informed Mussolini on 5 December, the possession of Gibraltar was of the greatest importance: 'From that moment only can the situation in Northwest Africa be considered as definitively resolved in our favour'.[54]

The signs of Spanish cooperation were not good, however, with Serrano Suñer complaining bitterly to Hitler at the Berghof on 18 November about article five of the Hendaye Protocol which, he argued, could only be interpreted as Germany sacrificing Spanish friendship for a rapprochement with the hereditary enemy, France. The Spanish Foreign Minister also rebuffed Hitler's offer of artillery and aircraft for the defence of the Canaries, claiming that Spanish defences were sufficient and advising that each individual island would defend itself 'as the Alcázar did at the time of the Civil

War'.[55] Spanish reticence was further revealed to Canaris, who was well acquainted with Franco since the civil war days, when he saw the Caudillo on 7 December and informed him of Germany's wish to undertake the attack on Gibraltar and that German troops would enter Spain on 10 January 1941. Canaris emphasised that there was a brief window of opportunity to carry out the operation but it would soon be closed because the available troops were required for other operations. As soon as the entry of troops had begun, German economic assistance would also commence. However, Franco, confronted with increasing Anglo-American pressure on the economic front which sought to exploit Spain's dependence on grain imports from North America and Argentina, concerned by possible opposition from some of his more influential generals[56] and still extremely disappointed about the lack of German support for his ambitions in North West Africa, continued to prevaricate about the timing of Spain's intervention. He told Canaris that it would be impossible for Spain to enter the war in January because her military preparations were incomplete, including the reinforcement of the Canaries which were vulnerable to British naval operations, the food crisis continued with a deficit of 1 million tons of grain, and transportation was inadequate owing to the lack of railway rolling stock. He expressed the opinion that in the case of a long drawn-out war, the 'weakening of Spain was sure to become a disadvantage and burden for Germany'. According to Canaris, Franco also made it clear that Spain could enter the war only when Britain was about to collapse.[57]

Hitler ordered the postponement of Operation 'Felix' on 10 December, and although reconnaissance missions in Spain and the Canary Islands continued all other elements of the operation were discontinued and German artillery destined for the Canaries remained undelivered.[58] However, the hope that Spain might soon enter the war lingered on. In discussion with Raeder on 27 December the Führer expressed his opinion that the seizure of Gibraltar was necessary. The Grand Admiral agreed because apart from securing the western Mediterranean and the French colonial empire, the Navy was also interested in using El Ferrol and Cádiz as bases for battleships and U boats. He stressed that the recent developments in the Mediterranean situation had increased the significance of a German occupation of Gibraltar because it would protect Italy; safeguard the western Mediterranean; secure the supply line from the North African area, important for Spain, France and Germany; eliminate an important link in the British Atlantic convoy system; close the British sea route through the Mediterranean to Malta and Alexandria; restrict the freedom of the British Mediterranean fleet; complicate British offensive action in Cyrenaica and Greece; relieve the Italians; and make possible German penetration into the Atlantic area via Spanish Morocco. Hitler agreed to try to persuade Spain to enter the war because he realised the precarious situation in North Africa could not be resolved without the capture of Gibraltar.[59] Soon after, on 31 December 1940, he informed Mussolini that he believed that Franco had committed 'the greatest mistake of his life' but he hoped that the Generalísimo would become aware, even at the last minute, of the 'catastrophic nature of his own actions' and enter the war.[60] He told his military leaders at the Berghof on 8 January 1941 that while Spain's attitude had become hesitant and it seemed 'scarcely promising', a further effort would be made to induce her to enter the war. The Führer recognised the strategic value of Gibraltar which had often been emphasised by the Naval Staff and revealed that Franco had intimated that he would not take part in the war until Britain was at the point of collapse and even the promise of grain had had little effect in changing his mind.[61]

When Hitler met Mussolini at the Berghof on 19 January 1941 he sought the Duce's support to persuade Franco to intervene and at a further meeting the following day stressed that what was at stake was not only the occupation of Gibraltar and the strategic advantages of the African territory across from it, but also the possibility of establishing German submarine bases on the Spanish Atlantic coast, which would be less exposed to British air attacks than the French submarine ports.[62] Accordingly, Franco was invited to Italy but before the Italian and Spanish leaders met Hitler tried again to commit Franco to a date for Spain's entry into the war. Following a number of strong and forceful but ultimately counter-productive interventions by Stohrer in Madrid, who was acting on personal instructions from Ribbentrop, Hitler wrote to Franco on 6 February and warned him that only in the event of an Axis victory would his regime survive and that if Germany and Italy lost the war, there would be 'no future whatever for a truly national and independent Spain'. He also dismissed Spanish arguments for refusing to enter the war immediately, including economic factors.[63] Franco remained unconvinced and when he saw Mussolini at Bordighera, on the Italian Riviera, on 12 February he reiterated that it was Spain's continuing economic crisis that prevented an early entry into the war and that her requirements, not only in food but also war material and transport, needed to be fulfilled in order to prepare for war. At the same time, the Caudillo was adamant that Spain should receive French Morocco as well as Gibraltar and he insisted that the eventual operation to capture the latter would be carried out as an exclusively Spanish operation and not as a German one, since other troops would not be allowed to replace Spanish forces.[64]

Mussolini had been sceptical about the value of the meeting before it took place, telling King Victor Emmanuel III on 9 February that he regarded his journey to Bordighera as 'perfectly useless' and that he would 'willingly have avoided it' because 'Franco will not say to me anything different from what he has already told the Führer'.[65] When he reported to Berlin on the meeting, the Duce emphasised that Spain was in no condition to enter the war within the near future and that their endeavours should be restricted to keeping her 'in the political sphere of the Axis Powers'. This would, he stressed, provide Spain with a necessary breathing space to overcome the present grave food crisis and improve the 'entirely inadequate condition of her armaments'.[66] Time, however, was no longer on the side of the Gibraltar operation. Even if preparations for 'Felix' were resumed immediately the OKH advised Field Marshal Wilhelm Keitel, Chief of the OKW, that the attack on Gibraltar was not possible before the middle of April and that the forces earmarked for this operation would not be available in time for 'Barbarossa'. When Keitel passed on this advice to Hitler on 28 January the Führer gave instructions that 'Operation Felix will have to be dropped because it was impossible to create the political prerequisites'.[67]

The Germans drew the conclusion from Spanish responses that they 'had not the least intention of entering the war' because their prior conditions made postponement inevitable or, alternatively, they made 'the entry into the war completely problematical' since Spanish troops alone would never succeed in capturing Gibraltar.[68] As a result, on 22 February 1941, Ribbentrop instructed

Stohrer not to take 'any more steps whatever in the question of Spain's entry into the war, and [to] refrain from any initiative in this respect'.[69] Franco's eventual response to Hitler's letter of 6 February did nothing to change the cooling of relations between Madrid and Berlin. The Caudillo shared Hitler's view that the position of Spain on both sides of the Straits forced them to look upon Britain, who aspired to maintain her domination there, as their greatest enemy, but he also insisted that it was essential to close the Suez Canal at the same time as the operation against Gibraltar, otherwise the war would be prolonged and Spain's position would become extremely difficult.[70] Although he did not say so at the time, but as he made clear later in December 1944, Hitler attributed Franco's caution partly to Italy's failed invasion of Greece in the winter of 1940–1941. He told Mussolini that if, rather than attacking Greece, Italy had resolved the Spanish problem together with Germany, the development of the war could have taken a different course.[71] While Serrano Suñer continued to insist that Spain was ready to enter the war as soon as the food situation improved and the Spanish people were adequately prepared, and the Spanish military favoured the continuation of military and economic preparations for war, there was no decisive move on Madrid's side to bring this about during the spring and early summer of 1941.[72] Indeed, rather than Spain entering the war as a matter of choice there was a greater prospect at this time of the Iberian Peninsula itself becoming another theatre of operations.

Hitler was clearly exercised by what he perceived as British intentions with regard to the Iberian Peninsula and North Africa. On 28 April he told the Spanish Ambassador, Major General Eugenio Espinosa de los Monteros, that he could not escape the impression that 'the English had the intention of establishing themselves on Spanish territory' and that the current objective of the British was 'to establish themselves in North Africa, to occupy the Portuguese islands, and overthrow Franco'.[73] As part of the programme for securing Western Europe while carrying out Operation 'Barbarossa', the OKH drew up plans – Operation 'Isabella' – involving both Spain and Portugal. It was assumed that Britain might take advantage of the mass of the German Army being tied down in the eastern theatre of war in the summer of 1941 to 'create for herself a new continental position on the Iberian Peninsula' with the aim of preventing Spain from joining the Axis powers, restoring some lost prestige and offering the United States promising conditions for her entry into the war, enhancing her strategic position for naval and aerial warfare, and improving the defences of Gibraltar. According to 'Isabella', in the event of a landing in either Portugal or northern Spain or an advance from Gibraltar by British troops, German military forces would destroy or at least force them out and in so doing take possession of the most important ports on the Spanish and Portuguese Atlantic coast and create favourable conditions for a later attack against Gibraltar.[74] In the event, Operation 'Isabella' was not activated because Britain had no intention of invading the Iberian Peninsula, whether via Portugal, northern Spanish ports or Gibraltar.

Spain was discussed briefly between Hitler and Mussolini at their meeting on the Brenner on 2 June 1941. The Führer continued to lament the missed opportunity of January–February when Gibraltar could have been taken with far less difficulty than the present because the British had since reinforced it with first class troops and installed new improvements for its defence. As far as the western Mediterranean was concerned, he believed an attempt would have to be made to try to bring the Spanish to adopt 'at least a friendly attitude towards the Axis'.[75] The following day Ciano, who had been present at the Brenner meeting, wrote to Serrano Suñer to request Spain's official accession to the Tripartite Pact even if she was not yet ready to enter the war. From the Spanish point of view, as related by Serrano Suñer in his reply, the advantage of such a move lay in making it clear where Spain stood, namely that the final objective of her foreign policy was entry into the war on the side of the Axis powers. Spain's accession would also result in a further loss of prestige for Britain and it was also possible that it would have a deterrent effect on a decision of the United States to enter the war. On the other hand, the reverse could be the case and Roosevelt might interpret Spain's accession as a threat to the Western Hemisphere and accelerate American entry into the war. In addition, the surprise factor would be lost when it came to Spain's eventual entry into the war, but above all imports of grain, maize and petroleum amounting to 300,000 tons which were en route would be lost and a total blockade would be immediately imposed on Spain.[76] The end result was that Spain remained outside the Tripartite Pact.

Spain's refusal to accede to the Tripartite Pact made no difference to either Hitler or his generals in their consideration of the preparations to be made for the period after 'Barbarossa' had been completed. In a draft directive of 11 June, Hitler asserted that after the destruction of the Soviet armed forces, Germany and Italy would be masters of the European Continent, with the temporary exception of the Iberian Peninsula. He insisted that in the near future Spain would have to decide whether she was prepared to cooperate in driving the British from Gibraltar or not. The preparations for undertaking 'Felix', already planned, would be resumed to the fullest extent even during the course of operations in the East. After the capture of Gibraltar only such forces would be moved to Spanish Morocco as were necessary to protect the Straits. The control of the Straits would also facilitate the use of West African bases by German aerial and naval forces and possibly also the occupation of the Atlantic Islands.[77]

Although the Spanish authorities had chosen not to be linked directly with the Tripartite Pact, the German invasion of the Soviet Union on 22 June 1941 created a further opportunity for serious consideration about entering the war. As early as 25 June Stohrer suggested to Serrano Suñer that 'a public declaration that Spain was in a state of war with the Soviet Union would be appropriate and desirable' but the Spanish Foreign Minister demurred because he believed that Britain and possibly the United States would react if not by a declaration of war on Spain then undoubtedly by the imposition of a blockade, including the seizure of Spanish assets abroad.[78] The Francoist authorities were prepared, however, to declare on 1 July that Spain's position was one of 'moral belligerence'.[79] Moreover, Franco, urged on by Serrano Suñer, and in a further gesture of ideological solidarity, agreed to the despatch of a division of Spanish volunteers to fight with the Axis forces on the eastern front. This 'Blue Division' consisted of more than 18,000 men – 642 officers, 2272 non-commissioned officers and sergeants, and 15,780 troops – and was led by General Augustín Muñoz Grandes. By the time it was finally withdrawn in February 1944, a total of 47,000 Spanish troops had fought with the German Army on the eastern front, approximately 10 per cent of whom lost their lives.[80] In addition, clearly encouraged by the early stunning victories of the German forces on the eastern front, the Caudillo on 17 July, in a speech to mark the fifth anniversary of the military insurrection against the Second Spanish Republic, declared publicly that Britain had lost the war.[81] According to the German Chargé d'Affaires at Madrid, Erich Heberlein, Franco's speech was the most open declaration to date of his position on the side of the Axis powers against communism and democracy and of his faith in the final victory of Germany and Italy.[82]

Hitler declared himself to be encouraged by these developments but Mussolini was less sanguine. He did not believe that Spain could do more than send the Blue Division and although Franco had burned his bridges behind him in his speech he had not moved from 'the sphere of words into action'.[83] The Duce's view was insightful and Hitler was soon again expressing his 'genuine and profound disappointment' with Spain when he met Mussolini at the Führer Headquarters, the so called Wolf's Lair (*Wolfsschanze*), at Rastenberg in East Prussia on 25 August 1941.[84] At the same time, the OKH, in a memorandum approved by Hitler himself on the strategic situation in late summer 1941 as the basis for further political and military plans, predicted that while Spain would not weaken in her moral support for the German conduct of the war she would defer entering the war until she considered the German–Italian power position in the Mediterranean fully secured or until she herself was attacked. It was recognised that if Spain entered the war she would impose a heavy material burden on the Third Reich but she would also provide the naval bases of El Ferrol and Cádiz, the elimination of the British base at Gibraltar and perhaps even the seizure of the Rock itself and therewith the domination of the entrance into the Mediterranean. For the German military authorities, therefore, the military value of Spain's entry into the war would be very great but only provided the French colonial empire in North Africa did not shift its attitude; in particular, the possession of Gibraltar would lose its essential significance if North Africa fell into Anglo-French hands. Moreover, unless German ground and air forces were available to reinforce the French and Spanish positions or to exploit them offensively, the value of the entry into the war of either of these countries, but especially by Spain, remained problematical. And owing to continuing operations in Soviet Russia it was anticipated that the forces of the Army and the Luftwaffe would scarcely be available before the spring of 1942 for decisive operations in the Mediterranean, in the Atlantic and on the Spanish mainland. Accordingly, it was important not to let the political and military relations with France and Spain be severed, but rather to increase them.[85] As a result, the OKW issued a further order which emphasised that branches of the Wehrmacht were not authorised to carry out reconnaissance in Spain or to undertake military discussions with the Spanish authorities, and the service attachés were also required to adopt a reserved attitude to the question of Gibraltar.[86]

Having failed earlier in the year in persuading the Franco regime to adhere to the Tripartite Pact or even formally to declare war upon Soviet Russia, the Germans had more success in late November 1941 when Spain joined Germany, Italy, Japan, Manchukuo and Hungary in signing a protocol, in Berlin, to extend by five years the period of validity of the Anti-Comintern Pact. Serrano Suñer represented the Spanish Government and four days after the signing ceremony on 29 November he met Hitler, Ribbentrop and Ciano and presented the usual litany of reasons as to why Spain could not be more assertive on behalf of the Axis powers in her foreign policy: her economic dependence upon foreign countries, notably the United States; the lack of grain and petroleum which made every thought of participation in the war unpopular; internal enemies, including a 'tremendous number of Reds' who were directed by foreign agents; and insufficient anti-aircraft artillery and coastal batteries to defend herself against a possible enemy. Hitler was clearly unimpressed and repeated his regret that the Gibraltar action had not been carried out earlier owing to the Spanish attitude.[87] When General José Moscardó, head of Franco's Military Household, on his way to visit the Blue Division, saw Hitler at the Wolf's Lair on 7 December 1941 he received a similar response. Moscardó stressed that Spain was very interested in eliminating the British base at Gibraltar which would always be like a dagger in the heart for Spaniards but the Führer riposted that the time was not yet appropriate and he regretted that Franco had not seized the opportunity in the spring of 1941.[88]

Hitler's meeting with Moscardó coincided exactly with the Japanese attack on Pearl Harbor. The entry into the Second World War of the United States in December 1941 transformed the prospects of the anti-Axis forces, particularly Britain. For Franco it was certain that the war would now be one of long duration and attrition with no clear sign of the inevitable Axis victory claimed by Hitler and Mussolini since June 1940. As a result, he was forced to postpone Spain's entry into the war indefinitely.[89]

8 The Allies and Franco's Spain, 1939–1941

The British and French Governments held no illusions as to Spain's sympathy for the Axis cause during the period before the fall of France in June 1940. As early as 26 September 1939, for example, Pétain, as Ambassador to Spain, expressed his astonishment to Foreign Minister Beigbeder at the lack of sympathy shown by the Spanish press towards Catholic Poland in its failed struggle against Soviet atheism and German paganism.[1] At the same time, the Allied powers recognised that Spain needed peace at any price in order to carry through its programme of consolidation and economic reconstruction.[2] They had gone to war in September 1939 to challenge Nazi Germany's intention to dominate the European continent rather than to create a new democratic order in Europe and, accordingly, as long as Spain maintained its neutrality Franco's regime had nothing to fear from either despite the warnings of Hitler and Mussolini to the contrary.

Even if they had wished to do so, the Allies had no effective contingency plans in 1939 to wage war against the Spanish mainland. It is true that the French had created a mobilisation *Plan E* in early 1938 which considered a possible offensive into northern Spain but it was never taken seriously by the French High Command. Before *Plan E* was even in place the operations bureau of the General Staff had concluded that such an operation was unfeasible because it would require troops and equipment already earmarked for the German and Italian fronts. Detailed French plans did exist for a move into Spanish Morocco and attacks against the Balearic and Canary Islands but were never implemented.[3] The British, however, did wage an intelligence war in Spain where they established two SIS (Secret Intelligence Service) stations. One was busy 'keeping an eye on Franco, second guessing German intentions towards the Iberian Peninsula and tracking the comings and goings of German U-boats which used Spanish ports to replenish their stores'. The other used Ultra intelligence from decrypted

German Enigma messages to track down German agents, some of whom became double agents feeding the Germans with disinformation as part of successful deception operations.[4]

Despite the considerable reservations of their own labour movement, incensed by Franco's repression of hundreds of thousands of Republicans, the British authorities signed a trade treaty with Spain in April 1940 which included the export of vital Spanish raw materials, notably pyrites, to Britain and a loan to Spain of £2 million for expenditure in the sterling area. The Franco regime had also agreed that goods exported to Spain through Allied controls would not be reexported except with Allied approval.[5] The French Government had already concluded its own trade agreement with Spain in January 1940 and before the German invasion in May it was engaged in exploring a commercial exchange of 100,000 tons of French wheat for Spanish minerals, including iron ore, tungsten, zinc and mercury.[6] During this period the British Embassy in Spain and the Foreign Office continuously argued against holding an anti-Franco debate in Parliament because it could benefit no one but Germany and Italy.[7] They took a similar view with regard to anti-Franco articles in the British press. At the same time, the French authorities received numerous assurances that Spain would not abandon its neutrality in favour of the Axis powers, notably from Foreign Minister Beigbeder on 22 May 1940 when he stressed that no advantage would be taken of French misfortunes in the Battle of France. When Spain declared its non-belligerency on 14 June Beigbeder assured Pétain's successor as Ambassador, Renom de la Baume, that it signified the absence of 'active or passive participation in the conflict' and that Spain would not imitate Italy and would guarantee French security along the Pyrenees.[8] However, according to Rafael Pérez, before the French defeat Spain was hostile towards France with the intention of gaining concessions in North Africa to permit Spanish expansion there.[9]

The fall of France – which ironically concluded with Pétain as Prime Minister seeking to use Franco's Spain as an intermediary for armistices with both Germany and Italy[10] – brought no change in British policy concerning Spain. After June 1940 there was no question of Britain, or the United States, threatening to intervene in Spain or conspire to overthrow the Franco regime which, despite its Falangist tendencies and overt support for the Axis powers, retained the Allies tacit support; tacit because although they grew to despise the regime, they could not and would not contemplate an alternative in case this resulted in either Spain's intervention on the Axis side or a German invasion of the Iberian Peninsula from their base in the Pyrenees which would destroy not only Spain but Portugal as well and result in the loss of Gibraltar.[11]

While the outcome of the war remained in the balance, the British Government preferred to avoid a leap in the dark as far as Franco's Spain was concerned. That Britain had no intention of intervening in the internal affairs of Spain was made abundantly clear by Sir Samuel Hoare, sent to Spain as Ambassador 'on special mission', in May 1940. Following Spain's declaration of non-belligerency Hoare saw Beigbeder on 22 June to deny rumours spread about Madrid that the British were plotting to overthrow the Franco regime. The exact opposite was the truth because the British Government was convinced that a regime change in Spain 'would only lead to greater confusion and danger' and Hoare had been appointed to do what he could 'to help the present [Spanish] Government in the much needed work of reconstruction and in its efforts to keep out of the war'.[12] Denial of any intention to intervene in Spain's internal politics accompanied by reassurances to that effect became a constant theme of Hoare's tenure as Ambassador at Madrid and these were reinforced by public statements in London, notably by the Prime Minister, Winston Churchill, in the House of Commons on 8 October 1940.[13] Another constant theme was the Embassy's criticism of anti-Franco articles in the British press and their wish that they be curbed. Churchill and his Foreign Secretary, Lord Halifax, intervened often in press circles in 1940 to prevent or, at least, moderate press attacks on the Franco regime but with indifferent success and the latter was compelled to warn Hoare that the Government could not legally prevent the publication of anti-Franco material.[14] Accordingly, anti-Franco attacks continued to appear in the British press to the continued chagrin of the Foreign Office and the Madrid Embassy.[15]

Official British concerns about being identified as anti-Franco were extended to the area of asylum policy with the presence of Spanish Republican exiles in the United Kingdom. The Foreign Office and the Madrid Embassy argued strongly that the presence of these exiles undermined the assurances they made to the Spanish authorities of British disinterest in Spain's internal politics and gave credibility to Axis propaganda that the British Government wished to overthrow the Franco regime. With Labour and Liberal members of the War Cabinet, notably the Deputy Prime Minister, Clement Attlee, and the Secretary of State for Air, Sir Archibald Sinclair, opposed to applying pressure to remove the Republican exiles Churchill and Halifax were resigned, as the attempt to remove the former Spanish Republican Prime Minister, Juan Negrín, from Britain in the autumn of 1940 demonstrated, to allowing Republican exiles to stay as long as they did not actively engage in anti-Francoist politics.[16]

Despite the lack of a favourable reaction to their reassurances in Madrid, the Spanish press had not even reported Churchill's friendly references to Spain in his speech of 8 October 1940, the British Government, understandably in view of the great crisis they were facing with invasion of the United Kingdom still a possibility, continued to appease the Franco regime. In February 1941 Hoare was instructed to give a personal assurance from both Churchill and Eden, who had succeeded Halifax as Foreign Secretary, that the last thing they wanted to do was 'to interfere in Spanish internal affairs nor would we countenance such action for a moment'.[17] The German invasion of Soviet Russia in June and the despatch of the Spanish Blue Division made no difference as far as the British authorities were concerned except to endorse Hoare's stricture that from the point of view of the Iberian Peninsula it was most important to avoid any actions or statements that seemed to identify the British empire with the communists.[18] Indeed, so successful were they in distancing themselves from their Soviet ally that Hoare was able to report late in July 1941 that the effect of Britain's alliance with Soviet Russia had been much less hostile than expected in Spanish military circles in which there was an appreciation that 'our alliance with the U.S.S.R. was dictated for purely military reasons and was not a step towards communism in spite of German propaganda to the contrary'.[19]

Even Franco's hostile anti-British and anti-American speech of 17 July 1941 provoked no change in the official attitude. Outraged by the speech, Sir Auckland Geddes, chairman of the Rio Tinto Company, which had the largest foreign holdings in Spain, and a fervent supporter of the Nationalists during the Spanish Civil War, urged the Government to encourage a wide resistance movement to the Falangist-dominated Franco regime. He suggested that Negrín and other Republican leaders in Britain and France should be approached to organise such resistance against what he considered to be the weakest of the fascist governments in Europe. According to Geddes, the time was ripe because the German Army was fully engaged in Soviet Russia and there was probably no German armoured division in France.[20] In the circumstances, the Government's response, one more of regret than anger, reflected their policy of measured caution in Spanish matters; certainly, there would be no *volte face* involving encouragement and support for an anti-Francoist movement. The public response, revealed in Eden's speech to the House of Commons on 24 July, was merely to question whether the Franco regime really desired economic assistance from Britain and the United States.[21] Moreover, by mid-August Churchill had convinced himself that Franco's speech was not so hostile after all. In this respect, he agreed with Hoare that far from giving himself over to the Axis, Franco was trying to put himself at the head of his own movement and to reconcile Germany in advance to some arrangement by which Serrano Suñer would be restrained or excluded.[22]

The pro-Axis Spanish Foreign Minister's position was by no means secure during the later months of 1941. Intelligence received by the British Embassy indicated that the Spanish generals had completed plans for an early *coup d'état* designed to get rid of Serrano Suñer and of the *Falange* and possibly Franco himself. The Foreign Office, however, remained sceptical that a new military junta in Spain would be any less influenced by Germany than Franco's regime. Eden advised his Cabinet colleagues that the German preoccupation with the Russian campaign did not alter the strategic fact that Germany was in a position at relatively short notice to dispose of any Spanish resistance and that, accordingly, 'the substitution of a less unpopular regime, which would still find itself compelled to bow to German pressure, might not benefit us to any important extent'. The Foreign Secretary remained sceptical of the likehood of a *coup d'état* by the Spanish generals in the near future and reiterated his doubts whether regime change in Spain would produce a genuinely independent policy while German influence remained strong.[23] As a result, the decision was taken in early December 1941 to maintain an attitude of non-intervention in Spanish internal affairs.[24]

Along with their determination to avoid interfering in Spanish internal affairs, the British authorities from the early summer of 1940 adopted a strategy of controlled economic assistance to Spain which aimed at keeping the Iberian Peninsula out of the war. In this they were supported by the United States and Salazar's Portugal. The Foreign Office was convinced that the key to keeping Spain out of the war was to be found in consolidating Franco's regime and the chief danger to his regime came from economic distress, exploited by Axis agents. While, immediately after the fall of France, the Foreign Office decided that Germany was to be deprived by means of preemptive purchases of important supplies from Spain, particularly fats and foodstuffs, steel hardening materials, textile fibres and non-ferrous metals, arrangements were also made for Spain to receive 100,000 tons of wheat and to buy Portuguese colonial products – including castor oil seeds, copra, maize, groundnut oil, coffee and sisal – subject to a guarantee on non re-export, payment to be made through the sterling area account of the Anglo-Spanish clearing which had a large balance in favour of Spain, representing the underspent portion of the recent British loan of £2 million.[25] An exchange of notes (constituting a tripartite agreement) on 24 July between the British, Portuguese and Spanish Governments provided the necessary credit facilities in the Anglo-Spanish clearing for the Portuguese colonial products. Although the total at this stage was £600,000, further negotiations ensued with various alterations and extensions so that by the end of September a payment of up to £728,00 had been authorised. As his contribution, Salazar secured an agreement with Franco, on 29 July 1940, in the form of the Hispano-Portuguese Protocol under which both Spain and Portugal declared their intention to remain at peace and to keep the war from the Iberian Peninsula.

With German troops on the Pyrenean frontier threatening possible invasion, anti-British demonstrations in Spain demanding the return of Gibraltar, Spanish troops occupying Tangier and Franco's declaration of non-belligerency, the British authorities were seriously concerned that the Iberian Peninsula would become embroiled in the war and the Protocol, in their mind, made this less likely. While the Germans publicly described the Protocol as 'a link in the chain of British diplomatic defeats and the end of the Anglo-Portuguese alliance', Halifax expressed his personal appreciation of Salazar's contribution to the Portuguese Ambassador and former Foreign Minister, Armindo Monteiro. Hoare believed the Protocol was significant because it was 'a very substantial factor on the side of Spanish peace and the more definitely this view was stated the less likelihood there was of German exploitation of the agreement by attempts to estrange Portugal from the British alliance.[26] In contrast, the Italians, according to the Portuguese Historian, António Telo, saw the Protocol as Salazar's first strike against the 'English alliance' and confirmation of Lisbon's capacity to resist British pressure. Telo also argues that Serrano Suñer, Beigbeder and Franco interpreted the Protocol as facilitating the entry of Spain into the war and not the contrary.[27]

The United States authorities had indicated their willingness to provide further credits to the Franco regime before the fall of France, provided it agreed to maintain and develop friendly commercial and political relations, and they were prepared to negotiate a trade agreement.[28] By the late summer of 1940 Washington was ready to support the British policy of controlled economic assistance to keep Franco's Spain out of the war. At this time, there could be no doubt that Spain's economic crisis was deepening. Despite the latest harvest and the purchase of 200,000 tons of Australian wheat, it was estimated by the Spanish Ministry of Industry and Commerce that there would be a deficit of at least 1.3 million tons. Spain required substantial credits which it was hoped the Americans would provide.[29] As Secretary of State Cordell Hull indicated to the Ambassador at Madrid, Alexander Weddell, the Roosevelt Administration was prepared to consider providing further credits to Spain to enable her to purchase foodstuffs and raw materials in the United States, such as wheat, cotton and gasoline but would require public assurances as to the future direction of Spanish policy.[30]

From the outset the Americans took a firmer line with regard to their negotiations with the Spanish authorities than the British who were more inclined to give the benefit of the doubt concerning the sincerity of Franco and his Ministers. On the British side, the exception was the Labour Minister of Economic Warfare, Hugh Dalton, who was particularly disconcerted by Spain's refusal to apply for navicerts, which were intended to prevent the reexport and transit of Spanish and Portuguese colonial produce to the Axis powers and countries occupied by them, and by the 'anti-British orgies' of the Spanish press. He was also anxious not to build up Spain's war potential lest she followed Italy's example. However, he was overruled by both Churchill and Halifax and the policy of controlled economic assistance continued throughout the autumn and winter months of 1940–1941 though admittedly in difficult and trying circumstances.[31]

The dismissal of Beigbeder, who had increasingly adopted a pro-Allied attitude, and the accession of Serrano Suñer as Foreign Minister during October 1940, while also retaining the post of Minister of the Interior, and Franco's meting with Hitler at Hendaye the same month created concern in both London and Washington and produced a stiffening in attitude with regard to Spain; and this was reinforced on 3 November when, without warning, the Spaniards annexed the international zone of Tangier, opposite Gibraltar.[32] Serrano Suñer's reassurance to Weddell on 31 October that 'there had been no pressure not even an insinuation on the part either of Hitler or Mussolini that Spain should enter the war' failed to convince Washington; not least because he had also affirmed Spain's 'political solidarity' with the programme and aims of Germany and Italy.[33] The Spanish Foreign Minister's visit to Berchtesgaden on 18 November was also badly received in Washington. As a result, the American Government was inclined to drag its heels in sending relief ships under the auspices of the American Red Cross to Spain where famine was imminent. Hull was adamant that it would not be possible to justify to American public opinion the provision of such relief if Spain gave practical assistance, direct or indirect, to the Axis powers. The Secretary of State insisted that the only remedy would be a clear cut and public declaration of policy on behalf of the Franco regime that it not only intended to remain neutral but would also not undertake any kind of assistance to Germany and Italy which would aid them in their war against the British Empire.[34]

In return for the grant of additional credits up to a limit of £2 million the British Government required the Franco regime to remove obstacles which impeded Anglo-Spanish trade, to adopt a fairer attitude in the Spanish press and to provide just treatment of their nationals in Spain. At the same time, they were not inclined to press Franco to make a public statement affirming non-belligerency because they recognised that it was not practical for Spain to make such a declaration with German divisions on the

Pyrenees. The strong American stance on this issue worried Halifax and Churchill who feared it might provoke Franco to join the Axis powers. Indeed, the policy of controlled economic assistance was dictated by the clearly and frequently expressed opinion of the Chiefs of Staff that it was essential to keep Spain out of the war and that, if it was necessary for the purpose, the blockade must be worked gently.[35] Accordingly, a number of appeals were made during November 1940 to the Americans to soften their attitude with regard to the export of foodstuffs and raw materials on credit to Spain, including a personal telegram from Churchill to the President, Franklin Delano Roosevelt.[36]

When Weddell saw Franco on 29 November the Caudillo agreed to provide a personal and private guarantee to Roosevelt that Spain did not envisage any departure from her present international attitude and that it did not contemplate any aid to the Axis powers[37] The State Department regarded this as sufficient but the negotiations for extending credits and the wheat shipment continued to be delayed as a result of a hostile Spanish propaganda campaign which had been proceeding since the Pan American Conference in Havana in July 1940 and was directed against the United States in Latin America, including accusations of imperialist designs. The State Department had also become increasingly concerned about the recent appointment of Falangist agents to important Spanish diplomatic and consular posts in some of the Latin American republics and the Philippines and to indications of German interest and collaboration in the anti-American propaganda campaign.[38] Hull continued to insist that the extension of credits was contingent as before upon Spain remaining outside the war and refusing aid to the Axis powers but now also upon the cessation of 'press attacks and other manifestations of hostility towards this country in Spain and through Spanish sources in the Spanish-speaking countries of this Hemisphere'.[39]

Consistent with their softer approach the British Government decided to proceed with a loan of £2 million to the Spanish Government with the provision of a further £2 million should the political situation improve, and the Ministry of Economic Warfare was prepared to grant navicerts for wheat imports up to a million tons for the next 12 months. These offers were made conditional upon being given full publicity in the Spanish press and broadcasts. Following an appeal by the Dominions Office, Canada agreed

on 5 December to supply wheat to Spain.[40] However, the decision
of the Spanish authorities, on 1 December 1940, to incorporate
the international zone of Tangier into Spanish Morocco and subsequently to dismiss British nationals employed in the zone administration, coupled with the prolonged stay by Italian submarines in
Tangier, compelled Britain to issue a warning, on 14 December,
that unless the Franco regime showed goodwill in the matter of
Tangier it would be impossible to secure the offer of economic
assistance and to implement the arrangements for the delivery
of wheat.[41] The warning was issued despite Halifax's view
that the Spanish move into Tangier was not 'an Axis plot' and
that any British counterstroke 'would put Spain definitely into the
Axis camp'.[42]

In view of their own difficulties with the Franco regime, it was
no surprise that the United States Government should support
Britain's decision to hold up its economic assistance to Spain until
the Tangier crisis was satisfactorily resolved. As Hull explained to
Weddell, who had been urging the State Department to expedite
their assistance to Spain irrespective of the Tangier crisis, the
whole question of such assistance was based on the policy of
'furnishing all possible assistance short of war to Great Britain in
her defence against aggression' and that the delays in the shipment of food to Spain would have been 'obviated if the Spanish
Government in recent weeks had followed a policy clearly indicating a desire to develop closer and more friendly relations with us,
rather than a policy of increasing collaboration with the Axis'.[43]
In the event, in early February 1941 the British Government, supported by Salazar's Portugal, succeeded in negotiating a solution
to the Tangier problem. Although not entirely to their satisfaction,
they accepted Spain's assurances with regard to their *desiderata*
which included the maintenance of the existing rights of British
nationals and institutions in the zone and full compensation
for displaced officials.[44] The British decision to compromise was
almost certainly influenced by the knowledge of increased German
and Italian pressure on Franco to enter the war on the Axis side.[45]
London was also aware that the Germans had approached the
Portuguese during January 1941 to ascertain if the passage of
German troops, through Spain to Gibraltar, ran counter to the
Protocol. Salazar had delivered a strong affirmative answer. When
the Portuguese Ambassador at Madrid, Pedro Theotónio Pereira,

saw Franco on 29 January, he emphasised that any decision to allow the passage of German troops through Spain would be a breach of both the Protocol's letter and spirit. The Caudillo, somewhat disingenuously, insisted that his only commitment was the Protocol which was the basis of his policy.[46]

Even before the resolution of the Tangier crisis the Ministry of Economic Warfare had given the go ahead to begin shipments of wheat to Spain from Canada and Argentina and had granted the necessary navicerts for the shipment of an additional 400,000 tons of Argentine wheat. Following Churchill's personal intervention, on 12 February 1941, in opposition to Eden, it was agreed to grant navicerts for 200,000 tons of wheat a month during February and March in addition to the wheat already coming from Canada and Argentina. Eden, who believed a well-supplied Spain would offer a tempting target to Hitler, reluctantly accepted the new initiative following discussions in Gibraltar with Hoare and the Chief of the Imperial General Staff, General Sir John Dill, on 17 February. The Foreign Secretary recognised the force of the arguments that by taking a tough line Serrano Suñer would be presented with the opportunity to blame Britain for the starvation of the Spanish people which would facilitate his efforts to bring Spain in on the side of the Axis powers and that Salazar would certainly not appreciate a change in policy.[47]

Accordingly, the British continued to pursue an agreement with the Spanish Government involving credits totalling more than £4 million to be spent in the sterling area, as proposed in December 1940 before the Tangier crisis developed. At the same time, they approached the Americans with a proposal which aimed to undermine the influence of Serrano Suñer and to create 'an economic bloc in the Western Mediterranean independent of the German continental system'. The proposal envisaged American loans to Spain of at least £4.5 million, to be spent in the United States on commodities such as oil, sulphate of ammonia and cotton. In addition, it was proposed that American experts and businessmen should visit Spain to counteract German influence there.[48]

Despite these plans to conciliate Spain, the Franco regime continued to maintain an outwardly hostile attitude towards Britain and the United States. When Colonel William Donovan, personal representative of the Secretary of the Navy on special mission in Europe, saw Serrano Suñer on 28 February 1941 the

Spanish Foreign Minister told him that 'we hope and believe in the victory of Germany in the present conflict'. Spain, he explained, owed a debt of gratitude to the Third Reich for its support in the civil war and equally resented British and French attitudes during that struggle. In addition, he frankly admitted that Spain's legitimate aspirations based on her 'natural rights' – Gibraltar and Africa – would be safeguarded in the event of a German victory. While being somewhat ambiguous, Serrano Suñer also stated that Spain would remain outside of the war until her 'honour or interests or dignity' were in question. In his response Donovan was certainly unambiguous when he emphasised the 'gigantic' scale of rearmament in the United States, the huge growth and development of its armed forces and other 'significant points' and what these meant in the 'scales of victory for Britain'.[49] Following the announcement of Lend Lease in March 1941 the State Department adopted a more forceful and strident note in its instructions to heads of American missions in Europe, including Italy, Finland, Sweden, Romania, Portugal and Spain stressing the determination of the United States Government to play its part in resisting the forces of aggression. As part of this diplomatic offensive, Weddell was urged to make clear to the civil and military leaders of Spain the scope of America's national effort and determination to resist aggression and her absolute conviction that the forces of aggression would be checked and defeated.[50]

While he was able to carry out his instructions in conversation with Serrano Suñer on 19 April 1941, Weddell was unconvinced that the Foreign Minister would communicate the American position to Franco and if he did it would probably be in a diluted or garbled form.[51] Unfortunately, the Ambassador was having great difficulty in arranging an appointment to see the Caudillo who had been unavailable to see Donovan when he visited Spain at the end of February. Apart from the uncertainty as to whether Franco had been kept fully informed as to the American attitude towards the war, Weddell needed to see him in order to tell him that he was authorised by Washington to initiate discussions with a view 'to broadening and liberalizing the basis of mutual trade between Spain and the United States', including the supply of wheat, corn and cotton and possibly sulphate of ammonia, some machine tools and moderate amounts of tin plate.[52] It seemed to Weddell and the State Department that Serrano Suñer was deliberately blocking access to Franco and that this was explained in part by a simmering row between the Ambassador and Foreign Minister arising from their meeting on 19 April. Subsequently, Serrano Suñer accused Weddell of insensitive and offensive behaviour and of impugning Spain's loss of sovereignty while the Ambassador, supported by the State Department, protested at being denied access to the Spanish Chief of State. The result was a suspension of top-level diplomatic contacts between the United States and Spain in Madrid from mid-June until the following autumn.[53] Franco's refusal to see Weddell cannot be explained entirely by reference to a personal row between the Ambassador and Serrano Suñer. The German victories in the eastern Mediterranean, North Africa and the Balkans in April–May 1941 and Axis pressure on Franco to adhere to the Tripartite Pact in early June doubtless contributed to the reluctance of the Caudillo to see Weddell, though he did see Hoare on 28 June when the British Ambassador asked him directly whether he and his Government 'really wished for friendly relations with His Majesty's Government and the United States Government' and whether he wanted the plans for economic assistance to succeed. Franco replied that he wished the economic plans to succeed.[54]

The dispatch of the Spanish Blue Division to Soviet Russia and Franco's anti-British and anti-American speech of 17 July 1941 failed to deter the British from continuing with their controlled economic strategy. Eden recognised that the Iberian Peninsula was indivisible and that the maintenance of Portugal's benevolent neutrality required the maintenance of Spanish non-belligerency. As a result, following consultation with Hoare during August and September 1941, the Foreign Secretary appealed to Washington for an improvement in economic cooperation between the United Kingdom, the United States, Portugal and Spain. In making this appeal Eden recognised that the first steps had been taken towards ending the impasse in Hispano–American relations. He regarded this as significant because Britain's own means of action in the economic sphere were nearly exhausted and further developments were dependent on American cooperation.[55] The Americans, however, were disinclined to cooperate despite Weddell's appeal to ease recent restrictions on gasoline exports in order to meet Spain's desperate shortage. With the rift in Hispano–American diplomatic relations slowly being repaired, the Ambassador felt it appropriate to remind Hull and Welles that the policy with regard to Spain was based on the avoidance of steps which would result in pushing her into the arms of the Axis powers, create strategic dangers for Britain and the United States and cause complications for American interests in Latin America. While he considered that America's ability to supply and withhold petroleum products represented the trump card in their political and economic relations he did not think the moment had arrived when it should be played. Hull remained unimpressed and pointed to the fact that while the United States had cooperated with Spain in the solution of its economic problems the Franco regime had shown no desire to reciprocate and had furnished 'no evidence of any wish to extend or improve relations'.[56] The need for petroleum certainly concentrated the minds of the Franco regime and in late September even Serrano Suñer was compelled to adopt a more positive attitude, even arranging a meeting for Weddell with Franco for 6 October 1941. Both the Caudillo and Serrano Suñer, who also attended, stressed Spain's need for petroleum and the former acknowledged that his regime was interested in improving commercial relations with the United States.[57]

Washington, however, remained reticent about meeting Spanish shortages of petroleum, partly because they suspected, from reports they had received, that American supplies were being transferred from Spanish tankers at sea to Axis ships or reexported to Axis destinations from Spain. Roosevelt and Hull accepted British assurances that while there were probably isolated cases of small quantities of petroleum products disposed of clandestinely the aggregate amounts would be insignificant and there was no systematic shipment of petroleum products to the Axis powers from Spain.[58] Yet, domestic pressures in the form of critical press commentary persuaded the State Department to develop a new system to control the use of oil by Spain by establishing supervisory control, using United States agents, over the distribution and use of oil inside Spanish territory. The Spanish Government conceded the principle of supervision by the Americans of their distribution and employment of oil imports from the United States but there was no genuine progress in negotiations and by the end of 1941 Washington had suspended, in practice, all oil shipments to Spain. This decision was partly a response to the enthusiastic accounts which appeared in the Spanish press of early Japanese victories in the Pacific and partly a result of Hull's anxiety over a possible German move in the Iberian Peninsula.[59]

America's entry into the war following Pearl Harbor, the reports of increased German pressure and activities in the Iberian Peninsula and Morocco and Washington's decision to suspend oil exports to Spain created an even greater sense of urgency in London with regard to improving economic relations with Spain. On 19 December the Washington Embassy was instructed to emphasise to the State Department that the British Chiefs of Staff remained convinced that it was most important, on strategic grounds, to maintain the neutrality of the Iberian Peninsula for as long as possible. It was not to be expected that either Portugal or Spain would offer organised resistance to a German invasion but there was still some hope that the Spanish Government could be dissuaded from joining the Axis powers and the Portuguese Government persuaded to continue to resist overseas. In these circumstances, the British hoped that the United States authorities might be persuaded of the paramount strategic importance of keeping the Iberian Peninsula out of the war; that with this object in mind they would send supplies to Spain; and they would not be 'too exigent in the negotiations which they have now begun with the Spanish Government'.[60] Further interventions by the Washington Embassy made little impression on the State Department as did Churchill's personal appeal to Roosevelt of 5 January 1942 to 'kindly consider giving a few rationed carrots to the Dons to help stave off trouble at Gibraltar'.[61] The United States attitude was encapsulated in Hull's directive to Weddell of 12 January 1942 that in future decisions concerning exports to Spain would be based on whether 'a valuable and tangible *quid pro quo* could be obtained from Spain'. Negotiations with regard to both oil exports and other commercial deals were protracted and it was only in July 1942 that the United States agreed to allow Spain to import 492,000 tons of oil a year which represented about 60 per cent of previous Spanish consumption. In the same month an Anglo-American economic agreement was concluded with Spain in the form of a joint supply–purchase programme which enabled the Allies to buy Spanish commodities, including pre-emptive purchases of materials, such as wolfram, mercury and woollen goods to deny them to the German war economy.[62]

Apart from the strategy of controlled economic assistance, the British had another option available to keep Spain out of the war and strengthen her will to resist German demands by making some concession to Franco's North African ambitions, notably in French Morocco. Hoare was a strong advocate of this course of action. However, just as Hitler refused to seriously complicate his relations with Vichy France by making such concessions to Franco, the British Government wished to avoid alienating potential military allies in the form of French North African forces or at least avoid undermining the French will to resist German penetration of North Africa. While a public statement issued in October 1940 emphasised Britain's recognition of Spain's 'direct and legitimate' interests in North Africa, particularly Morocco, it also stressed that Moroccan questions should be decided exclusively between France and Spain.[63] In February 1941 the Foreign Office ruled out any deal over Morocco with the Franco regime and even the full-scale fighting in Syria in June 1941 between Free French and Vichy French forces – a contest won by the former – encouraged no change in policy. It is true that in October 1941 Eden, prompted by Churchill, instructed senior Foreign Office officials, such as Cadogan and William Strang, to review the subject of concessions to Spain in French Morocco. The outcome, however, was a decisive rejection of such a policy for the same reasons as previously and because Roosevelt would have to be consulted before making such a commitment to Spain.[64] The American President would certainly not have endorsed such a commitment. On the contrary, his Government had no intention whatsoever of going down that path. Indeed, Sumner Welles advised the Spanish Ambassador, Juan Franciso de Cárdenas, on 19 November 1941, that should Germany undertake measures towards expansion in North Africa, Spain should not be tempted by German offers to extend her own sphere of occupation there. If Spain were so tempted, Welles warned, his Government would regard her action as 'an overt and definite indication that Spain was definitely pursuing Hitler's strategy and was thereby greatly endangering [the] legitimate interests of the United States'.[65]

Should Spain be drawn into the war as the result of a German invasion of the Iberian Peninsula, the question arose as to whether the British would be able to provide military assistance to the Spanish forces in the event that they were prepared to resist.

Unfortunately, the prospects for a British landing in either Spain or Portugal were extremely bleak during 1940–1941. The Joint Planning Staff in October 1940, for example, argued that even with Spanish support the most British forces could do would be to hold a bridgehead in southern Spain and this would require the concentration of considerable naval and air support in the Peninsula and the Straits of Gibraltar.[66] When the meeting between Eden, Hoare and Dill at Gibraltar on 17 February 1941 concluded that, in the event of a German invasion, Britain must provide help on the Spanish mainland in the form of military and air support based on Cádiz, comprising two divisions, an army tank brigade and four fighter and four bomber squadrons, the Joint Planning Staff quickly disabused the Government of any such action. Their advice, delivered on 21 February, was that the proposed force could do no more than stiffen Spanish resistance and 'in the event of a Spanish collapse would be inadequate to hold the Cape Tarifa Peninsula and Gibraltar or even to defend itself'. With Britain heavily involved in the eastern Mediterranean the Chiefs of Staff in March 1941 insisted that for the time being Britain could not 'contemplate operations, even on a limited scale, in Spain or Spanish Morocco'.[67]

While there was nothing the British could do militarily to prevent a German invasion of the Iberian Peninsula during 1940–1941 and beyond, with the prospect of a forced evacuation of Gibraltar, the denial to Germany of Spain's and Portugal's Atlantic possessions was entirely feasible. Accordingly, British military planners prepared contingency plans to seize the Spanish Canary Islands and the Portuguese Cape Verde Islands and the Azores in the event of a German invasion of the Peninsula.

Even before the collapse of France the Allies did not regard the capture of the Balearic Islands in the western Mediterranean as practicable.[68] However, encouraged by Churchill, British military and strategic planners for a short period towards the end of 1940 explored the possibility of capturing Ceuta in Spanish Morocco, as an alternative site to Gibraltar from which to maintain control of the Straits. In the event, Operation 'Challenger' for the capture of Ceuta never got off the ground. The Joint Planning Staff concluded that, apart from provoking Spanish resistance, Ceuta and the surrounding region were too vulnerable to air and artillery attack from the Spanish mainland to provide a feasible alternative base to Gibraltar.[69] The capture of one or more of the Canaries was regarded as being more feasible and desirable. Towards the end of March 1941 the Chiefs of Staff, prompted by Churchill who was concerned about recent losses at sea at the hands of German U-boats and aware of Foreign Office concerns at the growing likelihood of German action in the Iberian Peninsula, advised that it was essential to prevent the Germans from utilising the Canaries as a base for surface ships, submarines and long distance aircraft. German control of the Canaries would enable them to attack Britain's South Atlantic convoys, render Freetown in Sierra Leone far less effective and force a rerouting of all maritime traffic via the western Atlantic. The Chiefs of Staff strongly counselled against taking precipitate action which would enable the Germans to take control of the Canaries, including the seizure of the Portuguese Atlantic Islands.[70]

In late April 1941 the Chiefs of Staff, believing that Germany's position was greatly strengthened as a result of her recent victories in the eastern Mediterranean and Balkans, anticipated increased German pressure on Spain which would deprive Britain of Gibraltar. Churchill agreed and told Roosevelt that he regarded the Spanish situation as 'most critical' and shared his fear that 'Hitler may easily be able to get control of the batteries which could deny us the use of Gibraltar harbour or even the batteries on the African shore'.[71] In these circumstances, the Chiefs of Staff advised that the only substitute for Gibraltar as a base for big ships was the Canaries. The necessary assault craft and aircraft for capturing and holding the islands had only just become available and they recommended the assembling of a force to carry out this operation codenamed 'Puma'.[72] While the forces for Operation 'Puma' were made ready in May, they remained on stand by. Internal developments within Spain itself seemed to ease the pressure on Gibraltar. Changes in the Spanish Government in early May, most notably the replacement of Serrano Suñer as Minister of the Interior, though he remained as Foreign Minister, and the appointment of the staunchly pro-Franco Colonel Valentín Galarza Morante as his successor, weakened the Falangist position within the regime and further strengthened that of the Caudillo. Galarza's appointment persuaded Churchill that it would be inopportune to invade the Canaries and drag Spain into the war.[73]

The decision not to execute 'Puma' yet was taken by the Defence Committee, Churchill's special body for authorising military operations, on 9 May and reaffirmed on 10 June because 'the political situation was unfavourable for it'.[74] At the same time, the grand 'Strategic Review' of 14 June, circulated by the Joint Planning Staff, reiterated the rationale for Operation 'Puma'. The joint planners emphasised that at any time that Germany chose and whatever line Spain took, the naval base at Gibraltar would be denied to Britain and, sooner or later, Germany would take this action. They advised that in order to maintain an effective blockade as well as to restrict the egress of Italian or even French naval units into the Atlantic an alternative base must be acquired. Occupying the Canaries, which would also provide a refuelling point between the United Kingdom and Freetown, would counter the Axis threat, as would a British occupation of the Azores. The joint planners warned that once the Germans were installed in the Canaries it was doubtful that they could be ejected.[75]

Hitler's invasion of the Soviet Union and the despatch of the Blue Division did nothing to alter the decision to hold back Operation 'Puma'. But then Franco's hostile speech of 17 July momentarily forced a review of the position. The Defence Committee on 21 July decided that 'Puma' should be launched against the Canaries at Britain's 'own chosen time and that all preparations for carrying it out in August should proceed'. Churchill told the Chiefs of Staff two days later that he was in favour of carrying out 'Puma' at the earliest opportunity because the political position in Spain had 'hardened' and Spain might at any moment 'go over to the German camp'. On 24 July the Prime Minister emphasised that it was necessary to secure the Canaries in order to forestall a German occupation there and that it would not be easy to do so in view of the large Spanish forces on the Islands.[76] The Foreign Office shared Churchill's view that capturing the Canary Islands would be no easy task. Even before Franco's speech, Eden and his senior officials had revealed their concern that the military authorities were seriously underestimating the danger of German aerial attacks on the proposed British landing force in view of the short distance between the Canary Islands and the African mainland, particularly Rio de Oro, a similar distance between that of Crete and mainland Greece; the scene of a decisive victory by German aircraft and airborne troops only weeks before.[77]

In the event, to improve the prospects for success the forces so far earmarked for operations to capture and occupy the Azores and Cape Verde Islands were incorporated with those destined for the Canaries and the entire operation was renamed 'Pilgrim'. The intention was for 24,000 troops to be sent to the Canaries to be escorted by one battleship, three aircraft carriers, three cruisers and 19 destroyers and to include almost the entire existing British fleet of assault-shipping and landing-craft.[78] Although President Roosevelt's reaction to Operation 'Pilgrim' was favourable when it was disclosed to him by Churchill at Placentia Bay on 11 August 1941, doubts about activating it became rapidly apparent in official British circles. It was recognised that 'Pilgrim' would impose a considerable strain on Britain's overstretched destroyer force. In addition, Churchill's reassessment of Franco's speech during August 1941, the advice of the military and naval attachés in Spain, respectively Brigadier William Torr and Captain Alan Hillgarth, both of whom counselled against a premature move on the Canaries which they believed would alienate the entire Spanish population, and the Chiefs of Staff acceptance of this advice resulted in a further postponement of operations. Since no other grounds emerged for activating 'Pilgrim' the expedition was eventually disbanded in February 1942. Thereafter, there was no further contingency planning to capture the Atlantic Islands.[79]

9 The Axis Powers and Portugal, 1939–1941

Despite Portugal's declaration of neutrality at the outset of the Second World War, every attempt by the Axis powers to wean her away from the British alliance was severely hampered by the Nazi–Soviet Pact and the invasion of Catholic Poland and the resulting deterioration in Luso-German relations, signified by German silence on the plight of Finland in the Russo-Finnish War which contrasted with Portugal's fervent support for the Finns' struggle against Soviet communism. And, while Portugal's relations with Italy remained friendly, particularly before the latter's entry into the war in June 1940, it was Germany who, as in the case of Spain, would play the primary role in Axis relations with the Iberian Peninsula's lesser power. Moreover, the Allies were able during the Phoney War to disrupt Portugal's communications, including her trade links with Germany although very limited exports, notably wolfram and tin continued via Spain and Italy.[1]

To offset the impact of the Nazi–Soviet Pact, German propaganda in Portugal, conducted mainly through the DNB news service, emphasised British duplicity by claiming that the authorities in London were dissatisfied with Portugal's neutrality and were planning the overthrow of the *Estado Novo* and Salazar himself. Later, German propaganda was insistent that if they won the war the British intended to substitute a democratic regime in Portugal; that the British blockade was doing untold harm to the Portuguese economy; that British forces intended to attack and occupy Portugal's Atlantic Islands; or that the British authorities had promised the Union of South Africa part of Mozambique and Angola.[2] These charges, some of which contained elements of truth, could be, and were refuted by the British but the impact of Germany's stunning victories between April 1940 and May 1941 on the Portuguese mind and policies could not be dismissed. Germany's military prowess provided the German propaganda machine with its most formidable weapon and the presence of German military forces along the Pyrenees frontier after June 1940 constantly reminded the Salazar regime of its precarious and vulnerable position which could be exploited not only by Germany but also by Spain. In this connection, Hitler told Mussolini in January 1941, on the occasion of the Duce's' visit to the Berghof, that he had to keep a certain number of troops in readiness in southwest France on account of the Portuguese, in case 'the English should attempt a landing in Portugal'.[3] In these circumstances, the Treaty of Friendship and Non-Aggression with Spain and the subsequent Protocol of July 1940 offered no real guarantee of Portugal's territorial integrity and independence; not least, because her British ally was unable to offer credible military assistance.

It was hardly surprising, therefore, that Salazar remained determined not to antagonise the Third Reich. It was because of Germany's military power that while the Portuguese authorities tolerated the presence of both allied and Axis agents in their country it was the Germans who, according to Jerold Packard, most outrageously offended Portuguese neutrality and hospitality. The German Legation, swelled by spies, housed 40 personnel, exactly four times that of the British Embassy. In addition, the German owned *Sitmar* travel agency employed 20 young Nazis among its staff of agents.[4] Moreover, in March 1941 the *Gestapo* secured the appointment of Erich Emil Schroeder to the German Legation as liason officer with the Portuguese international police. Schroeder was actively involved in persuading the police to take steps against suspected British agents and in spreading disinformation and forgeries amongst the Portuguese authorities.[5] Germany's growing influence with the Portuguese police authorities was clearly demonstrated in late 1941 at a time when Salazar's regime was confronted for the first time since the early 1930s by civil disturbances orchestrated by the clandestine Portuguese Communist Party. The Germans deliberately sought to implicate members of the British business community in Portugal in the communist agitation at a time when Britain and Soviet Russia had become wartime allies. The police carried out a campaign of arrests and intimidation which eventually resulted in the arrest of British SOE (Special Operations Executive) operatives in Oporto and Lisbon.[6]

Although Salazar had no intention of joining the Axis powers and abandoning the British alliance, pressure was exerted on him to do just that in the summer of 1940 while negotiations for the Protocol were proceeding. At the beginning of July, while still Minister of the Interior, Serrano Suñer advised Pereira that Portugal should align herself more closely with Spain. When the Ambassador reported back that Salazar was 'firmly determined to repel most sharply any encroachment on the part of England', Serrano Suñer stated that even closer political collaboration between Spain and Portugal, possibly even a military alliance, seemed desirable because after it was concluded Britain would 'no longer dare to undertake anything at all against Portugal'.[7] He also warned Pereira that a German attack on Portugal across Spain was only conceivable because of Portuguese ties to Britain and he stressed that it was in Portugal's interest to detach herself from Britain and the first step in that direction would be the conclusion of a military alliance with Spain.

The making of such an alliance was welcomed in Berlin. Ribbentrop believed that it would entail the detachment of Portugal from Britain and possibly the formal denunciation of the Anglo-Portuguese alliance, and this would definitely be in Germany's interest. Stohrer was, accordingly, instructed to promote the plan for a Luso-Spanish alliance in a manner which seemed suitable to him and to discuss the matter with Beigbeder as well as Serrano Suñer. Meanwhile, in Lisbon, Hoyningen-Huene was instructed to refrain from a special *démarche* with Salazar but when the opportunity arose in conversation with the Portuguese dictator he was to advise that a Luso-Spanish alliance and Portugal's detachment from her alliance with Britain would negate any German action against his country since the British would not dare in that case take forcible action against her.[8] In the event, there was no Luso-Spanish alliance, only the Protocol. Hoyningen-Huene was convinced that the signing of the Protocol amounted to 'a forward step and to encouragement for Portugal to continue on the path of separation from England' and Franco himself believed that while it gave maximum security to Spain it simultaneously strengthened Portugal's position with regard to Britain. According to the Caudillo, Portugal was undertaking 'a departure from English policy and an entrance into the Spanish sphere of influence'.[9] In this connection, according to Beigbeder, a secret oral agreement was made at the conclusion of the Protocol which would give Spain an entirely free hand for an attack on Gibraltar.[10]

None the less, and unfortunately for the Axis powers and Spain, the Protocol proved compatible with the continuation of the Anglo-Portuguese alliance and, in September 1940 in Berlin, Serrano Suñer was left to lament to Ribbentrop a missed opportunity at the time of the Protocol negotiations 'to draw Portugal entirely over to the side of the authoritarian states'.[11] Hitler himself was convinced that it was not possible to destroy the Anglo-Portuguese alliance by diplomatic means. As he told Serrano Suñer in late September 1940, Britain at the slightest suspicion of Portugal's defection would undoubtedly occupy the Portuguese Islands at once. The Spanish Foreign Minister agreed that the Portuguese problem would not be solved by diplomatic negotiations, but only by a military operation.[12] Later, at the meeting between Mussolini and Franco at Bordighera in February 1941, Serrano Suñer was forced to concede that: 'Last June she [Portugal] was much further from England than she is at present. It must be admitted, however, that the Press, the army and the ruling class in Portugal are Anglophiles and Masons.'[13]

The only time during the Second World War when there was even a remote possibility of Portugal abandoning her neutrality in favour of the Axis powers was in the summer of 1941 after the German invasion of the Soviet Union. For the Salazar regime Soviet Russia was quite literally the anti-Christ and it viewed Hitler's invasion as a crusade against the evils of communism. Even before the invasion, on 11 June 1941, the Portuguese Legion had issued an order in which it announced its solidarity with Hitler's crusade.[14] The raising of the Blue Division in Spain naturally created some expectation on the German side that the Portuguese would also raise a volunteer force to fight on the eastern front. When Hoyningen-Huene saw Salazar on 2 July the Portuguese dictator diplomatically sidestepped the issue by alluding to the reserved character of the Portuguese people and promising to consider the organisation of a demonstration by the Portuguese Legion to express sympathy with Germany's fight against Bolshevism. On 6 July the German Minister reported that while pro-German Portuguese officers were advocating a special Portuguese formation to be sent to the eastern front, the Portuguese Ministry of War favoured a strengthening of the garrisons in Portugal and on the Atlantic islands.[15] According to the British Embassy at Lisbon, when the German Military Attaché asked the Portuguese authorities for help in raising a corps of volunteers from the Portuguese Legion to fight against Soviet Russia, he was declared *persona non grata*.[16] Salazar continued to prevaricate on the issue of volunteers. At the end of October Hoyningen-Huene reported that he had again brought up the matter of a Portuguese volunteer force with Salazar who listened to the arguments in favour of sending such a force for the fight against Soviet Russia. The Portuguese leader, however, told the German Minister not to expect an immediate reply.[17] In the event, a Portuguese volunteer force was never sent to the eastern front but the future first President of the Portuguese Republic, following the coup which overthrew the *Estado Novo* in April 1974, General António Sebastião Ribeiro de Spinola, was sent as a young officer to the Russian front as an observer with the German forces. Spinola's reports were rumoured to have convinced Salazar that Hitler's cause was lost, thereby strengthening Portugal's commitment to neutrality.[18]

Apart from the volunteers issue, the possibility of Portugal joining the revised Anti-Comintern Pact was explored by the German Foreign Ministry in late 1941. There were some grounds for optimism in view of Spain's adhesion to the pact and Portugal's unremitting anti-communism. In 1934 she had been one of a tiny minority of countries, the others were Holland and Switzerland, who had voted against the entry of Soviet Russia into the League of Nations; the Salazar regime continued to refuse to recognise the Soviets and formal diplomatic relations did not exist and no agreement had been made between the two countries; no Soviet Russian had received permission to enter Portugal; and thousands of Portuguese volunteers had given their lives fighting Bolshevism during the Spanish Civil War. Hoyningen-Huene, however, advised against an approach to Salazar because the assumption would have to be that in the present circumstances Portugal would decline any formal invitation to join the Anti-Comintern Pact. The Minister was convinced that Britain would immediately brand Portugal's accession to the Pact as a demonstration directed against herself, and 'Portugal would then be confronted with economic consequences difficult to calculate'.[19] As a result, when the Anti-Comintern Pact was formally extended by a further five years on 29 November 1941 Portugal remained outside.

As Christian Leitz has noted, Germanophilia existed during the Second World War among the officer corps in the Portuguese Army, the Portuguese Legion, the secret police, the international police and the youth movement but their pro-German activities were confined to Portugal, notably in ensuring Germany's access to Portuguese wolfram supplies.[20] Indeed, it was in the economic sphere that the Salazar regime provided significant support for the Third Reich which admittedly was offset by more considerable support for the western allies. In 1941, 19 per cent of Portuguese exports went to Germany rising to almost 25 per cent in 1942 when Germany also became the primary importer of Portuguese products. The mainstay of Portuguese exports to Germany were tin, tinned sardines and above all wolfram (tungsten).[21] When it came to supplying wolfram to Germany, Portugal made an even greater contribution than Franco's Spain. In 1941 the Third Reich imported almost 2000 metric tons of Portuguese wolfram and a further 3000 metric tons during 1942–1943.[22] The German authorities had applied considerable pressure during 1941 to persuade the Portuguese to increase their wolfram exports to the Third Reich to 250 metric tons per month or 3000 tons per year at a total annual fixed price of 45 million reichmarks. In return the Germans undertook to provide a range of products, including 60,000 metric tons of iron material (railway material, shipbuilding material, structural iron) per year, up to 15,000 tons of ammonium sulphate annually, mining machinery and other mining installations.[23] As a result of tremendous price inflation which was causing a serious dislocation in the Portuguese economy – the price per ton of wolfram had risen from 2500 reichmarks in May 1941 to over 60,000 reichmarks in the first two months of 1942 – and also of Anglo-American pressure, Salazar decided in February 1942 to institute a system of government control over the sale of wolfram with specific allocations for each of the belligerents. While Germany received nothing like the 3000 tons of wolfram per year as proposed in 1941, she continued to receive considerable amounts to the consternation of the western Allies. It was not until 1944 with the clear decline of German military fortunes that the Portuguese imposed a complete embargo on all wolfram exports, but by that time the Third Reich had stockpiles adequate for another two years.[24]

Aware that their Italian allies were already supplying arms to Portugal, the German authorities also engaged in competition with Britain to supply war material to the Portuguese armed forces during 1941 and after. Previously, in November 1940, the Economic Policy Department of the German Foreign Ministry had reached the conclusion that German imports of strategic raw materials from Portugal – tungsten, tin, sardines in oil, oil – were threatened by insufficient means to pay through normal exports and that, accordingly, it would be necessary to deliver arms to the Portuguese. Apart from acquiring important raw materials for the German war economy, such purchases would also disrupt British imports of the same raw materials from Portugal. Field Marshal Wilhelm Keitel, head of the OKW, having objected previously now approved negotiations for armaments deliveries.[25] The value of actual German arms exports to Portugal amounted to 14.6 million reichmarks in 1941 and almost 10 million in 1942 and arms contracts amounting to more than 36 million reichmarks were exchanged during 1943. The provision of arms, including field artillery, anti-aircraft guns and machine guns, partly offset the cost of wolfram imports and eased the pressure on supplying hard currency or gold as payment for these imports.[26] Nevertheless, according to an allied postwar investigation it was estimated that the Bank of Portugal had received between 38 and 47 metric tons of gold from the Third Reich with a value of between $43 million and $53 million, more than any other neutral country.[27]

While the Germans sought to cooperate with the Salazar regime in the economic and political sphere, even to the point of providing scarce war material, beginning in the autumn of 1940 they also made contingency plans to invade Portugal and her island possessions which had become significant in terms of Hitler's evolving world policy. The question of an occupation of the Azores and Portugal's other Atlantic islands by Germany was first raised between Grand Admiral Raeder and Hitler on 20 June 1940 in an exchange of views on the acquisition of bases after the end of the war when, as they mistakenly anticipated, Britain had surrendered.[28] The Führer's attention during July and August was directed towards Gibraltar and the Spanish Canary Islands but his interest and that of his military advisers in the Azores and Cape Verde Islands was awakened by awareness of the developing destroyers-bases deal between Britain and the United States, which was eventually announced on 3 September 1940. The

German Embassy in Washington, on 21 August, reported that the Americans were displaying a keen interest in Morocco and the Spanish and Portuguese island groups. The German Naval Command shared similar concerns.[29] So too did leading German military figures, such as General Walter Warlimont, Chief of the National Defence Branch of the OKW, who observed to his immediate superior, General Alfred Jodl, Chief of Operations Staff of the OKW, on 20 August, that it was essential for Spain to strengthen its ties with Portugal to avoid the possibility of a British naval base in that country.[30] In this connection, General Franz Halder, Chief of the General Staff of the OKH, recorded in his diary on 23 August his belief, mistakenly, that Britain and the United States were engaged in negotiations with Portugal about the Azores which were being considered for a base for joint Anglo-American naval forces.[31]

During early September the Naval Command drew the implications of the destroyers-bases deal for Germany's strategic position in the Atlantic, including the possibility of an American occupation of the Spanish and Portuguese islands. In this connection, it was essential, they argued, to recognise the special dangers which lay in the occupation of the Azores and Canary Islands by the United States or Britain.[32] Hitler was quick to recognise the dangers and stated for the first time that the Azores, the Canary and Cape Verde Islands would have to be taken 'in timely fashion by German and Italian forces to prevent such seizure by the British or Americans'.[33] For the first time, Raeder revealed to Hitler his *Mittelmeer* concept to counter the Anglo-American 'destroyer for bases deal'. His plan envisaged a major naval initiative by the Axis powers, designed to gain control not only of Gibraltar but also Suez, French possessions in North Africa and the Spanish and Portuguese Atlantic Islands.[34] The Führer took little convincing. As he explained to Serrano Suñer on 17 September in Berlin, it was not out of the question that Britain and France would try to entice the United States to the Azores and in these efforts 'find support in certain imperialistic tendencies of America now already coming to the fore'. In this way Britain could 'gain a foothold in the islands stretching out in front of Africa – whereby, in time, a very unpleasant situation would arise'. This 'unpleasant situation', he explained, would be one in which 'the Continent [Africa] would be dependent upon that power which kept the outlying islands occupied, especially if it concerned a power with naval superiority'. In these circumstances, the control of the seas could be exercised 'neither by Italy, nor by Germany, nor by Spain'. The Führer stressed that it was a matter not only of the Azores but of the other island groups in order to defend Europe and Africa, which he designated as the Eastern Hemisphere, against the Western Hemisphere. To achieve this defence, bases were needed in the islands and on the African coast.[35]

When he saw Raeder on 26 September, shortly after the postponement of Operation 'Sealion', Hitler insisted that Britain and the United States must be excluded from West Africa. In the event of Spanish cooperation in this venture the Canary Islands and possibly also the Azores and Cape Verde Islands would have to be seized beforehand by the Luftwaffe. Raeder, however, advised the Führer that the lack of an adequate fleet constituted a continued drawback for 'the further extension of warfare' with regard to 'the Canary Islands, the Cape Verde Islands, the Azores, Dakar [and] Iceland'. At a further meeting, on 14 October, Hitler queried whether the Navy could help in transporting troops and material in case it should be necessary to occupy the Canary Islands, the Azores or the Cape Verde Islands. Raeder replied in the affirmative but warned that it would not be possible to occupy the islands from the air before bringing up reinforcements by sea, because all the approaches would then be patrolled by the enemy. Undeterred, Hitler then ordered an investigation of the occupation of the Azores and Cape Verde Islands and that necessary preparations be made.[36]

The Operations Division of the German Naval Staff, however, revealed little enthusiasm for an occupation of the Portuguese islands. A better alternative was to use political pressure and the threat of military action to stop Portuguese assistance to the British, and if the latter should attempt to land in Portugal it would not be difficult, so the Naval Staff believed, to force them to evacuate the country. Moreover, any German military action against Portugal itself would afford Britain the opportunity to occupy Madeira, the Cape Verde Islands and the Azores.[37] A memorandum prepared by Rear Admiral Kurt Fricke, the OKM Operations Chief, entitled 'Reflections on the Question of Occupation of the Atlantic Islands by Forces of the Wehrmacht', which was endorsed by Raeder on 31 October, emphasised the problems which would confront any landing force once they had occupied the Azores. According to Fricke, because of Britain's naval superiority, the German Navy could do no more than disembark the troops at the main islands of Fayal and São Miguel and leave them there, where they would remain for the rest of the war with only the slightest possibility of support from Europe. In short, it was feared that the capture of the islands would saddle the Wehrmacht with a 'permanent Narvik'. In addition, there was a distinct possibility that the occupation of the islands would provoke anti-German political measures both in the United States and Latin America at a time when these would be undesirable.[38]

Despite these reservations, Hitler was determined to press ahead. As he explained to Franco, when he saw him at Hendaye on 23 October 1940, the United States posed no immediate military threat – at least 18 months to 2 years would pass before its military power was fully armed – but there would be considerable danger if the Americans and British established themselves on the islands lying off Africa in the Atlantic Ocean. For Hitler the danger was all the greater because it was not certain that French troops in the colonies would always remain loyal to Vichy and 'the greatest threat existing at the moment was that a part of the colonial empire would, with abundant material and military resources, desert [Vichy] France and go over to De Gaulle, England, or the United States'.[39] In conference with his principal advisers from the three armed services on 4 November the Führer stressed the importance of improving the position in the western Mediterranean and in the Atlantic. Once Spain had entered the war the operation against Gibraltar would be launched and, at the same time, the Canary Islands and the Cape Verde Islands were to be occupied by German troops. The measures would be justified to the Portuguese Government as preventive, to forestall a British occupation of the islands and Lisbon was to be threatened with invasion by German armed forces if it supported Britain in any way whatever.[40] Soon after this conference, on 12 November, he issued his directive which officially sanctioned Operation 'Felix', whose objective was German intervention in the Iberian Peninsula to drive the British from the western Mediterranean. To this end, Gibraltar was to be captured and the Straits closed and Britain was to be prevented from gaining a foothold at any other point on the Iberian Peninsula or in the Atlantic Islands. Troops, based on mobile units, were to be assembled to march into Portugal in case the British should gain a foothold there and the Commanders in Chief of the Navy and the Luftwaffe were instructed to study how the Spanish defence of the Canaries could be supported and how the Cape Verde Islands could be occupied. Hitler also ordered an examination of the question of occupation of Madeira and of the Azores and insisted special measures were taken to restrict the number of staff involved in planning in order to ensure secrecy.[41]

The same day that he signed the directive for Operation 'Felix', Hitler saw the Soviet Foreign Minister, Vyacheslav Molotov, in Berlin, and warned him about America's imperialistic tendencies and the growth of Anglo-Saxon power so that 'the Continent of Europe had to adjust itself now to this development and had to act jointly against the Anglo-Saxons and against any of their attempts to acquire dangerous bases'.[42] Two days later, in conversation with Raeder, the Führer brushed aside the objections of the Naval Staff to an occupation of the islands. Hitler was convinced that Britain would occupy the Azores immediately upon Germany's entry into Spain, with or without a breach of Portuguese neutrality, and that she would later cede the Azores to the United States. Moreover, he believed the Azores would afford him the only facility for attacking America should it enter the war; with a modern plane of the Messerschmidt type which had a range of 12,600 km[43] and which had the additional virtue of forcing the United States to build up her own anti-aircraft defences, which were completely lacking, instead of assisting Britain. Raeder was less convinced. While he accepted, 'with luck', that it was possible for German forces to occupy the Azores, the defensive requirements thereafter, in face of British and probably American counter-offensives, would have a definite detrimental effect on naval operations, particularly sub-marine warfare since German submarines would have to be used for defence. Ironically, in view of British endeavours in 1940 and 1941, the Grand Admiral wished Portugal to be influenced to strongly fortify the Azores and to defend them. At the same time, he considered an occupation of the Cape Verde Islands and Madeira unnecessary since they would offer a useful base neither to Germany nor to Britain.[44]

From a conversation with Serrano Suñer on 29 November Stohrer reported that while the Spaniards feared British retaliation, in response to an attack on Gibraltar, against the Galician coast,

Bilbao, Cádiz, the Canary Islands and Spanish possessions in West Africa, they had little fear of British action against Portugal because the Portuguese Government was determined not to permit any landing and would immediately request Spanish, and hence German assistance. This view was confirmed by Nicolás Franco, the Spanish Ambassador at Lisbon, who told Stohrer personally that Portugal had promised 'full information on any English designs against Portugal or Spain that came to light'. At the same time, he advised that Portugal would do everything possible to maintain its neutrality.[45] Later, however, towards the end of January 1941, Generalísimo Franco himself advised Stohrer that 'at the present moment one could no longer reckon with certainty that Portugal would resist an English landing'.[46]

Uncertainty concerning Portugal did not affect matters because, as a result of Hitler's failure to persuade Franco to enter the war immediately, and to the highest priority being given to Operation 'Barbarossa' for the invasion of Soviet Russia, Operation 'Felix' had been postponed in December 1940. Even before Franco's refusal to enter the war on 7 December and the subsequent postponement of Operation 'Felix', Hitler had concluded that a British landing in Portugal was unlikely, and Jodl had confirmed that the islands operation would have to be postponed owing to the impossibility of gathering the necessary intelligence in time for the assault on Gibraltar.[47]

While both Hitler and Mussolini failed to change Franco's mind in January and February 1941, forward operational planning concerning the Iberian Peninsula was set in motion. Operation 'Felix-Heinrich' was to proceed once the defeat of Soviet Russia was assured, which was expected to occur within a matter of weeks. Later, this was modified in Hitler's directive of 11 June 1941 to include preparations to 'the fullest extent' even during the course of operations in the East.[48] In early March the Portuguese Under Secretary for War, the pro-Axis Captain Fernando dos Santos Costa, expressed his concern to the German Military Attaché, Colonel Freiherr von Esebeck, that the Azores would become greatly threatened if the United States actively entered the war. He also revealed that for the past three months the British had proposed occupying the Azores as a protective measure against any threat from Germany but that the Portuguese authorities had consistently turned this down.[49] However, on

23 March the Secretary General of the Ministry for Foreign Affairs, Luís Teixeira de Sampaio, categorically denied that either Britain or the United States 'had made demands for the granting of bases or leasing of the islands or permitting any kind of control in the ports'.[50] On 20 April Salazar himself told the Italian Minister, Renato Bova Scoppa, that at no time had the British or the Americans made territorial demands affecting the territorial integrity of Portugal, but he did not rule out the possibility that the Portuguese islands could be threatened in the future by the United States.[51] At the same time, the German Embassy in Washington reported disturbing rumours of an imminent occupation of the Azores.[52]

It is certain that Hitler was disturbed by these reports and rumours because he openly expressed his fear at this time of British measures against the Iberian Peninsula. He revealed his concern to the Spanish Ambassador at Berlin, Espinosa de los Monteros, when he told him on 28 April that the British intended 'to establish themselves in North Africa, to occupy the Portuguese Islands, and to overthrow Franco'.[53] More significantly, the Führer insisted to Jodl that the Army should find a way to release eight to ten divisions for possible use in Spain and Portugal, to buttress the defence of the two countries and drive any landing force back into the sea. Consequently, Operation 'Isabella' was conceived in the expectation that Britain would take advantage of the concentration of German forces on the eastern front in the summer of 1941 to create for herself a new continental position on the Iberian Peninsula with the aim of preventing Spain from joining the Axis powers, restoring British prestige and improving conditions for an eventual American entry into the war, seizing strategic bases to strengthen her naval and aerial position, and strengthening the defences of Gibraltar. It was anticipated that a British landing would take place in Portuguese ports rather than those in northern Spain and that Portugal would resign herself to this, under protest. Operation 'Isabella', therefore, aimed to destroy the invading British forces or at least to drive them out, while in the process capturing the most important ports on the Spanish and Portuguese Atlantic coasts to create favourable conditions for a subsequent German attack on Gibraltar.[54]

Considerable and detailed planning for Operation 'Isabella' was undertaken during May and June 1941. Charged with carrying out the operation, Seventh Army worked out a precise study of the plan during August which was based primarily on the assumption that the United States would occupy the Azores, Canaries and Cape Verde Islands as well as Madeira, and that Britain might land troops in Portugal and southern Spain.[55] Meanwhile, on 22 May, in conference with Raeder at the Berghof, Hitler raised the subject of the occupation of the Azores with his naval chief for the first time since December 1940. Raeder, reiterating his reservations of the previous autumn, advised that it was extremely unlikely that the islands could be held and supplies brought up in the face of British and possibly also American attacks. Moreover, all of the Navy's combat forces, including submarines, would be required to achieve a successful occupation and they would have to be withdrawn from all other offensive activities in the Battle of the Atlantic which would be intolerable. Despite the Grand Admiral's reservations, the Führer still favoured occupying the Azores in order to operate long range bombers against the United States and he considered that the occasion for this might arise by autumn. In the meantime, the main task of the German Navy during the summer of 1941 was the disruption of British supply lines.[56] Hitler had persisted with his intention to occupy the Azores despite confirmation in May 1941 by Santos Costa to Esebeck that the Portuguese were determined to defend the Azores and that their best troops were garrisoned there. German intelligence reports in late May and July reported considerable reinforcement of the Azores garrisons to 10,000 and then 17,000 men.[57]

It was during the summer of 1941 that the Germans became increasingly concerned with American moves in the Atlantic, notably the arrival in Iceland of United States troops on 7 July which they linked with earlier declarations by politicians, such as Senator Claude Pepper, who had spoken openly in favour of an American occupation of the Azores.[58] On 22 July the Condé de Tovar, former head of the Economics Section of the Portuguese Foreign Ministry and newly appointed Minister at Berlin, told Under State Secretary Ernst Woermann that Portugal had not been calmed by the public reassurances of Sumner Welles that 'the United States hoped that Portugal would remain in control of the Azores and Cape Verde Islands and that this country [the United States] had no intention of acting against them'.[59] He also told Woermann that Portugal was not willing to make any compromises whether open or covert with regard to the Azores but would rather fight if the occasion arose. He advised that Portugal had greatly increased the defensive strength of the islands.[60] As it happened, the German Foreign Ministry had been informed two days earlier that all indications showed that Roosevelt had postponed his intention to occupy the Cape Verde Islands, the Azores and Dakar. This change was, according to the German Embassy in Washington, decisively influenced by 'the grave misgivings of the Army and the Navy' and by reports of the strengthening of the Portuguese garrisons on the Azores and Cape Verde Islands and French preparations for the defence of Dakar. Uncertainty as to Japan's intentions also accounted for Roosevelt's hesitation to push further into the Atlantic[61] Whether the American threat in the Atlantic had receded did not trouble Hitler. He was determined, as he told Raeder in conference at the *Wolfsschanze* on 25 July, that an American occupation of the Spanish or Portuguese islands would be countered by the German occupation of the Iberian Peninsula, as well as the deployment of German armoured and infantry divisions in Northwest Africa.[62]

Hitler still continued to show an interest in the Azores towards the close of 1941. He asked Serrano Suñer, on the occasion of his visit to Berlin to sign the extension to the Anti-Comintern Pact, what Spain would do if the Azores were attacked. When the Spanish Foreign Minister replied that Spain would defend the Azores, Hitler countered that 'offence was the best defence'.[63] In the event, however, the failure to achieve a blitzkrieg victory in the vast expanses of Soviet Russia, America's entry into the war and Franco's continuing non-belligerency forced a further postponement of the Führer's plans for the Iberian Peninsula and the Atlantic Islands. At the same time, the prospects of an allied landing on the Atlantic islands, even to recover prestige lost as a result of the developing disaster in the Pacific and Indian Oceans, were considered to be remote, as Raeder told Hitler in Berlin, on 12 December 1941, the day after Germany's declaration of war on the United States. The Grand Admiral believed that the Allies were too preoccupied with the Pacific and Indian Oceans to launch operations against the islands; a view shared by the Army High Command.[64] From 1942 onwards, Hitler's instructions regarding the Iberian Peninsula were concerned with measures to counter allied actions rather than to initiate German offensive actions. Further references to the occupation of the Atlantic Islands were merely academic.[65]

10 The Allies and Portugal, 1939–1941

The British and French Governments both welcomed Portugal's decision to remain neutral in September 1939 and accepted Salazar's assurances that his neutrality would be benevolent towards the Allies. It is true that there was some irritation in early 1940 when the Portuguese dictator refused to provide assistance to suppress meteorological broadcasts, to intercept German cable messages and to permit the passage of British arms through Mozambique, and when he made difficulties over the signing of a war trade agreement.[1] However, as long as the Phoney War continued the British recognised that they could not expect any appreciable cooperation from Lisbon until the Portuguese could be sure of British protection by land, sea, and especially by air. Unfortunately, the British authorities could not provide such protection. Towards the end of May, with the Battle of France going so badly for the Allied forces, the British Chiefs of Staff reported that there were no trained and fully equipped troops available for action in Portugal and they were unable to provide the Portuguese with artillery and anti-aircraft equipment. Selby was made aware of the situation but the Ambassador was firmly instructed not to say anything to the Portuguese authorities.[2]

The collapse of France, the entry of Italy into the war and Franco's declaration of non-belligerency brought into question Britain's commitment to the continued neutrality of the Salazar regime, but Churchill and Halifax were encouraged by the negotiations between Portugal and Spain which concluded with the Protocol at the end of July. It will be recalled that the British Government enthusiastically welcomed the Protocol as a contribution to the maintenance of peace and neutrality in the Iberian Peninsula.[3] This was hardly surprising in view of the imperative need to confine the struggle to as few military theatres as possible. By the summer of 1940 Britain was confronting the Axis powers alone in the Atlantic, Home waters, the Mediterranean, North and

North East Africa; and an extension of the war into the Iberian Peninsula, especially if Spain became an active belligerent, would be intolerable. While every endeavour would be made to keep Spain non-belligerent and to preserve the peace of the Iberian Peninsula, the need to counter Axis influence in Portugal, and to maintain her benevolent neutrality, was recognised as a significant priority by Churchill's Government; not least in view of Salazar's genuine support in helping to prevent Spain's entry into the war, as witness his part in the making of the Protocol. By encouraging and strengthening Portugal and undermining Axis influence Britain would contribute towards the preservation of Portuguese independence and their benevolent attitude. At the same time, there was no guarantee that Germany would desist from military action in the Peninsula even if Spain remained firmly opposed to entering the war and in such a case Portugal would probably be drawn into the conflict. The result was that from the summer of 1940 the British authorities decided to pursue a dual strategy in their relations with Portugal. While they intended to strengthen their position in Portugal by countering Axis activity and by insisting on the maintenance of Portuguese benevolent neutrality, they also set in motion contingency planning which envisaged, in the event of a clearly perceived German military threat to the Peninsula, the occupation of the Portuguese Islands – the Azores, the Cape Verde Islands and Madeira – the strengthening of Portuguese defences on the islands and the establishment there of a Portuguese government-in-exile.

In 1940 and 1941, as in the pre-war period, British efforts to counter Axis influence were concentrated in the fields of propaganda, trade (economic warfare) and Portuguese rearmament, but also in intelligence and special operations activity. With regard to the latter, the SIS had established a station in Lisbon before the war but its effectiveness was severely weakened by acrimonious relations with Embassy staff so that by 1940 its existence was called into question. Fortunately, relations improved and in 1941 its position was consolidated within the Embassy. The significance of Lisbon as a port on the Atlantic serving shipping bound for South America and the United States was recognised by the SIS which regarded it as a vital link in their counter-espionage effort. As Neville Wylie emphasises, 'if SIS needed reminding of what was at stake in Portugal in early 1942 it needed to look no further than to Juan Pujol Garcia, alias *Garbo*, who contacted Lisbon in early 1942 and provided Britain with one of its most successful double-cross agents of the war'.[4] *Garbo* was closely involved in the deception which persuaded Hitler to dismiss Normandy as the main location for the cross Channel invasion in favour of the Pas de Calais.[5]

With the fall of France and the stationing of German armed forces on the Pyrenees frontier the British authorities were naturally concerned that Portugal might become a target for a German occupation and as one means of counteracting this they set up an SOE station in Lisbon in January 1941. These operatives established and equipped several underground networks capable of performing a number of tasks under a German occupation, including information gathering and small-scale acts of sabotage. The head of the station, John Beevor, acting as an Assistant Military Attaché, and Commander Alex Glen, former Assistant Naval Attaché and SOE officer in Belgrade, also drew up a list of targets for immediate destruction in the event of a German invasion, including oil refineries on the River Tagus, various road and rail bridges and viaducts, and some of Portugal's main industrial and mining facilities. Unfortunately, the Portuguese police authorities became aware of the SOE's presence in Portugal during the winter of 1941–1942 and Beevor was withdrawn in June 1942 following Salazar's personal intervention with the British Ambassador, Sir Ronald Campbell, who had succeeded Selby in late 1940. Salazar, went so far as to accuse Beevor of abusing his diplomatic privileges and undermining Portuguese confidence in Britain's good faith.[6]

The pre-war reorganisation of Britain's propaganda service in Portugal – the appointment of a Press Attaché, the inauguration of a Portuguese news bulletin by the BBC and the utilisation of a regular British news service – provided the British Embassy in Lisbon with the means to challenge Germany's strident anti-British propaganda during the war. Although the Germans spent more on propaganda through their considerable subsidy of the DNB, they did not dominate the Portuguese press in the way that Spanish newspapers were overwhelmingly pro-Axis. It was often the case that press opinion would shift in line with developments in the war so that the Fall of France led to considerable criticism of French and British democracy while Britain's victory in the Battle of Britain was greeted with many leading articles which revealed a growing confidence in Britain's will to resist. During the period 16–26 September, for example, as Britain's air triumph became clear there was widespread coverage of her victories in all Portuguese newspapers and virtually all DNB messages were excluded from the front pages of every newspaper, including the Government backed *Diário de Notícias* (referred to as the Portuguese *Times*) which was unprecedented.[7]

It seems that the British handled their propaganda efforts in a more subtle way than the Germans who had a tendency to antagonise the Portuguese authorities. According to 'well documented records held at the *Pálacio das Necessidades* of the [Portuguese] Foreign Ministry' a Luso-German press debate began with a heated exchange in the summer of 1940 and lasted well into 1942, souring relations between the two countries. The Germans complained frequently about the pro-allied tone and content of much of the Portuguese press. Between June 1940 and June 1944 Nazi Germany apparently lodged more than a hundred protests about offensive items in the press while Britain lodged only nine.[8] The British also achieved one or two notable propaganda successes with the visit of the Duke of Kent in June 1940, on the occasion of the celebrations of the eight hundredth anniversary of the foundation of Portugal and the tercentary of Portugal's independence from Spain, and the visit of a delegation from Oxford University to Coimbra University in April 1941, where the former professor, Salazar, was presented with an honorary Oxford degree. The Portuguese dictator had previously hesitated to accept the honour because of fear of jeopardising Portuguese neutrality and because he had already refused honorary degrees from several German universities. The event received abundant publicity in the Portuguese press. It was, according to Campbell, 'first class propaganda. The Germans are livid'.[9]

Despite these propaganda successes and heavy-handed German diplomacy, Portuguese opinion was not prepared to throw its entire support behind the Allied cause. There remained a considerable residue of respect, if not admiration, for Germany's military prowess, no doubt reinforced by the German military presence on the Pyrenees frontier. Unquestionably, this was the greatest challenge confronting the British in Portugal. During the summer of 1941, for example, German propaganda in Portugal naturally stressed the series of German victories over Soviet forces, and in particular the capture of Smolensk. Salazar was obviously impressed and, according to Campbell, took an unduly exaggerated view of German industrial and military strength.[10] As the Ambassador lacked sufficient information to make an effective impression, he was provided, in an unprecedented move, with a Joint Intelligence Committee memorandum which contained information about German losses in Russia and an assessment of the drain on German resources resulting from the Russian campaign. The memorandum also covered recent progress in British military reorganisation and rearmament, the improvement in Britain's strategic position in the Middle East and the eastern Mediterranean, the extent of American military and economic support and the successes of the Royal Navy and Royal Air Force against German forces.[11] Campbell made good use of this material in his subsequent interviews with Salazar.

Britain's developing relationship with the United States was a crucial factor in persuading Portuguese opinion because it strengthened the credibility of those in Portugal, both British and Portuguese, who argued ceaselessly that Britain would emerge from the struggle victorious.[12] When America entered the war in December 1941 Portuguese confidence in an ultimate victory for the Allies was greater than at any time since May 1940. Moreover, and despite their deep-seated hatred of communism, Salazar's regime was not blind to the significance of the Russian factor in the military balance of the war.[13] Despite German propaganda, the Portuguese authorities, like the Spanish generals, realised that Britain had allied herself to Soviet Russia for purely military reasons and that it was not a step towards communism. As a precaution, the British took care to tone down support for their Soviet ally in BBC broadcasts to Portugal.[14] None of these developments, however, convinced the Portuguese to abandon their neutrality. Fear of German retribution should they actively and openly back the Allied cause lingered for a considerable time after 1941. According to António Telo, at the end of 1941 Salazar remained convinced that Germany had established a dominant position on the European continent; that the British did not have the power to win the war and should reach an accommodation with Hitler before it was too late; and that, in view of Germany's dominance, United States involvement would endlessly prolong the war.[15] Clearly, the Portuguese dictator was greatly concerned about the spread of communism should the Soviets succeed in throwing back the German armed forces on the eastern front. In this connection, Campbell reported in April 1942 that Salazar was convinced that unless the Wehrmacht succeeded in breaking the Soviets that summer 'Europe would be engulfed in a wave of communism such as no other power on earth could stop'.[16] It was this concern coupled with Germany's ability to strike at the Iberian Peninsula that convinced Salazar to cooperate with the Germans, not least by supplying wolfram to the Third Reich, albeit at an advantageous price.

The considerable importance of wolfram (tungsten) as a raw material for weapons production and other war uses meant that the allies could not ignore the significance of Portuguese (and Spanish) exports to Germany. Even before the German invasion of Soviet Russia there had been growing competition in Portugal between German and British buyers of wolfram which resulted in a price explosion during 1940 and 1941. The British then copied the Americans and substituted molybdenum which could be obtained from the United States at a relatively stable cost. The emphasis, therefore, shifted in late 1941 towards preemptive purchases of wolfram in the Iberian Peninsula. Deliberate efforts were made by Britain to raise the price of wolfram in both Spain and Portugal with the intention that higher prices would attract supplies already committed to the Germans as well as exhaust their funds. By the end of 1941 the price of wolfram in Portugal was nearly £6000 per ton compared to £300 per ton in August 1940.[17] The regulation of the wolfram trade imposed by Salazar in February 1942 with its division between Germany and the Allies was not well received in London or Washington even if they accepted the reasons why Salazar felt compelled to continue supplies to the Third Reich. More generally, trade issues between Portugal and Britain created some problems in their relationship with the former expressing criticism of the navicert system which limited the reexport of Portuguese colonial produce to Germany, Italy and enemy-occupied countries, the main recipients of such trade before the war. While, following considerable discussion during 1940, Salazar was eventually prepared in early 1941 to acquiesce in British quotas by means of 'an agreement in principle' he would not provide a written guarantee and insisted that the British trust him in the matter and he ruled that materials already stored in Portugal were not subject to the 'agreement in principle'.[18]

Economic issues were a source of continuing friction for the rest of 1941 with the Ministry of Economic Warfare suspecting the Portuguese of breaking the spirit of the 'agreement in principle'. At the beginning of 1942 they learned that goods which required export licences were being disguised as indigenous products, for example, palm oil as turpentine, despite a regulation of September 1941 which required that everything except wool and coal be verified at the place of loading. The Ministry was also compelled to recognise the growth of Portuguese trade in commodities, such as sugar, sardines and tin with the occupied countries of western Europe, notably France and Belgium, and with French North Africa.[19] Throughout 1940 and 1941 the British authorities recognised the problems which economic warfare created for them in Portugal and they suspected that the Germans were exercising strong and continuous pressure in Lisbon to secure some modification in the operation of the British blockade which, in Salazar's view, threatened Portugal's neutrality. However, Eden rejected any modification, insisting that German policy was guided by strategic rather than commercial considerations.[20] The British were also aware that Portuguese infractions of the blockade were not, apart from wolfram, on a large scale and this awareness was tempered by their knowledge of the important part Portugal was playing in helping to preserve Spanish non-belligerency, notably through the strategy of controlled economic assistance to the Franco regime.

It will be recalled that before the war Britain was engaged in a competition with Germany and Italy to supply war material to the Portuguese armed forces and this continued during the war. The British military authorities realised that it was essential to provide Portugal's arms requirements while recognising that the French were unable to do anything substantial in support. At the beginning of the war the Deputy Chiefs of Staff advised that Portugal's naval requirements were considered as being of first importance while her military and air requirements were regarded as having some importance. The Foreign Office emphasised that, as an ally, Portugal had a special relationship with Britain and it was important to retain her goodwill and support. It was essential that Portugal's requirements should be met as far as possible and it was particularly important that existing contracts should be fulfilled.[21] At this time, Portugal's main arms requirements from Britain consisted of anti-aircraft guns, submarines and motor torpedo boats, fighter aircraft and a coast defence system which included heavy Bofors guns and anti-aircraft equipment. The enormous demands of Britain's own rearmament programme made it virtually impossible to provide any of these items. Although the various service ministries intimated their willingness to help, in recognition of Foreign Office concerns that the Axis powers were actively seeking to undermine the British position in Portugal, very little had been achieved by the end of 1940. The only area in Anglo-Portuguese military relations where real progress had been made was in the supply of anti-aircraft guns and equipments. No firm date had been set for the Bofors guns, the earliest date which could be offered for the delivery of six motor torpedo boats was June 1943 and Portuguese requests for certain equipment for the construction of a destroyer in Portugal had been refused. In addition, despite a promise from the Air Ministry to supply 12 Spitfires by August not one of these aircraft had actually been delivered.[22]

This extremely limited response did not prove fatal to the Anglo-Portuguese relationship because after 1940 the issue of supplying Portugal's arms requirements became caught up in British and American strategic planning with regard to the Portuguese Atlantic Islands. Even before the fall of France, the British Chiefs of Staff had examined the strategic implications of Portuguese intervention on the side of Britain's enemies. Assuming Spanish ports and airfields would be available to the Axis powers in view of Spain's hostility, it was considered that bases in Portugal would not be of much additional value and the Chiefs, accordingly, recommended no action against the Portuguese mainland. The Azores and Cape Verde Islands were a different matter because they occupied important strategic positions on the Atlantic trade routes between the South Atlantic and the United Kingdom and if enemy naval and air forces were established on the islands they would be in a position to seriously threaten Britain's communications. The Chiefs of Staff recommended that operations should be undertaken 'to deny the facilities of the Cape Verde Islands and the Azores to the enemy'. They also advised that plans should be made to capture the railway from the frontier of Southern Rhodesia to the coast of Mozambique and the port of Beira. At the end of May the Cabinet endorsed these recommendations and acknowledged that contingency planning would be necessary.[23]

As a result, the preparation of an operations report by the Joint Planning Staff during June 1940 was incorporated into planning initiatives involving the Spanish Atlantic Islands and the Balearic Islands. In addition, on 17 June, the Chiefs of Staff agreed that as long as Spain and Portugal remained genuinely neutral, no action would be taken against their islands. However, if Spain were to enter the war on the side of the Axis powers, or show signs of so doing, Britain should seize the Azores and Cape Verde Islands whether or not Portugal had entered the war against her or had been attacked. At a meeting of the Defence Committee four days later Churchill emphasised that irrespective of any decision on priorities between the Spanish and Portuguese islands there should be no delay in getting troops trained and making arrangements for embarkation at short notice.[24] Separate operations were envisaged codenamed 'Accordion' for the seizure of the Azores and 'Sackbut' for the Cape Verde Islands. The Chiefs of Staff also continued to insist that the seizure of the islands remained the only option. The alternative of sending an expeditionary force to the Portuguese mainland while shortages of troops and equipment continued and higher priorities existed elsewhere was untenable.[25]

Towards the end of July 1940 Churchill became very exercised about the prospect of seizing the islands. According to intelligence reports which the Prime Minister had ordered, the coastal defences of the Azores were still under construction while in the Cape Verde Islands they were non-existent and there was absolutely no air cover since almost all the aircraft of the Portuguese air force were concentrated in and around Lisbon.[26] It was probably Churchill's awareness of the weak condition of Portuguese defences which prompted him on 24 July 1940 to suggest to Halifax an early occupation of the Azores. He told the Foreign Secretary that all of his reflections about the danger to British ships 'lying under the Spanish howitzers in Gibraltar' led him continually to the Azores and he did not believe that it followed that a temporary occupation of the islands, to forestall the enemy, 'would necessarily precipitate German intervention in Spain and Portugal' and, that indeed, it 'might have the reverse effect'. The Prime Minister added candidly that 'once we have an alternative base to Gibraltar, how much do we care whether the Peninsula is overrun or not?' and he admitted that he was 'increasingly attracted by the idea of simply taking the Azores one fine morning out of the blue, and explaining everything to Portugal afterwards'.[27] Halifax and his senior officials – Cadogan, William Strang and Vansittart – were appalled because they believed that the action Churchill proposed would precipitate German intervention in Spain and Portugal. The Foreign Secretary therefore advised Churchill to wait 'yet a while before taking action'.[28] In the absence of overt Spanish or Portuguese hostility or of any tangible sign that either intended to intervene on the Axis side, the forces earmarked for 'Accordion' and 'Sackbut' remained on standby throughout the late summer and autumn of 1940. Meanwhile, planning for the seizure of the railways and the ports of Beira and Lourenço Marques in Mozambique, respectively operations 'DHQY' and 'DHQZ', were completed.[29]

By October 1940 the British authorities could not discount the possibility of a sudden German move against the Azores. The Chiefs of Staff felt that a close naval patrol should be instituted despite the greater risk of submarine attack, the additional demand on the Navy's attenuated destroyer strength and the opportunity it presented for Axis propaganda in Portugal and Spain.[30] A continuous naval patrol close to the Azores seemed to offer a possible solution to the strategic problem since it would deny the islands to Germany while not permitting British use of their facilities. Unfortunately, because the Royal Navy was unable to maintain a continuous patrol even this limited aim could not be achieved. As a result, the only realistic course was to occupy the islands at the critical moment provided Britain was not responsible for precipitating it and the Foreign Office was adamant on this point. At the end of October it advised the Chiefs of Staff that if Britain seized the Azores in anticipation of German aggression in Spain, the political effect would be Spanish and Portuguese hostility. It would be regarded in both countries as an attack upon the neutrality of the Peninsula. It would almost certainly bring Spain into the war, and lead to German occupation of bases for operations in both Spain and Portugal. Apart from creating lasting and bitter resentment among the Portuguese, it was likely to arouse American criticism.[31]

This advice was pertinent and the Chiefs of Staff were aware of the risks, including German control of Lisbon as a result of Portugal following Spain and joining the Axis. The Portuguese capital would provide the Germans with a naval base which could accommodate all classes of ships, including capital ships, and from which they could directly threaten the Western Patrol. The Chiefs did not overlook the possibility that the Germans could use Lisbon as a base for 'fast surface craft, including possibly a battle cruiser' to raid British communications down the northern Atlantic to the Middle East; and such raiding forces would be extremely difficult to deal with since they would be operating outside the cover of Britain's main fleet in home waters.[32] When asked by the Defence Committee whether it would be advisable to carry out operations 'Brisk' (previously 'Accordion') and 'Shrapnel' (previously 'Sackbut') so as 'to make certain of forestalling the Germans in the Azores and Cape Verde Islands' the Chiefs of Staff agreed on the importance of seizing the Azores should Gibraltar become untenable, but they recognised that if the operation were carried out immediately a German advance into Spain and Portugal could be precipitated, and Gibraltar lost earlier than might otherwise happen.

When it met on 25 November the Defence Committee discussed the matter at some length. Halifax stressed the risk of precipitating an Iberian crisis while others queried whether Lisbon or Cueta could be taken by British forces at the same time as the occupation of the Azores, only to be met by the objection of the Chief of the Imperial General Staff, Sir John Dill, who advised that there were insufficient resources to hold Lisbon or even Ceuta, and if the Azores were not seized in good time, Britain would be left with nothing. The First Sea Lord, Admiral Sir Dudley Pound, warned that if the Germans occupied Portugal, Spain and the Canary Islands, the Navy would have to run their transatlantic convoys across the South Atlantic to Trinidad and thence north to Halifax in Nova Scotia. He also stressed that enemy occupation of the Canary Islands would negate any material advantage in Britain holding the Azores. It was clear from the discussion that the arguments in favour of carrying out 'Brisk' and 'Shrapnel' immediately were not overwhelming and that it would be better 'to wait and see whether a suitable moment would arise before long', though everything should be ready for when that moment came.[33]

The threat of a German descent on Spain without Spanish connivance remained a real one. Italy's disastrous intervention in Greece in late October 1940 had been followed by the opening of General Archibald Wavell's offensive in North Africa and Churchill was convinced that Hitler would retaliate and that he would do so in Spain. The Joint Intelligence Committee agreed but ruled out any German assault on the Azores since photographic reconnaissance had revealed there were no naval forces in the Biscay ports, and the chief of the Secret Service believed Germany would 'do a Norway' on the west coast of the Iberian Peninsula.[34] By mid-December 1940 Churchill was therefore inclined to favour occupation of the Cape Verde Islands and the Azores as a precaution but he was opposed by the Chiefs of Staff because available forces were insufficient for the operation.[35] Although the Prime Minister still believed that a German descent on Spain was more likely than an attack on the Balkans, the decision concerning 'Brisk' and 'Shrapnel' was deferred, though he told Jan Smuts, the South African Prime Minister, on 17 December that the matter would be kept under review.[36]

All this time, the British authorities had not seriously considered helping the Portuguese to fortify the Cape Verde Islands and the Azores as a deterrent to German action other than to encourage the Salazar regime to strengthen the defences on the islands. On 17 December this changed when Monteiro, acting on personal instructions from Salazar, raised the question of Anglo-Portuguese military collaboration with regard to preserving the integrity and independence of Portugal. What Salazar intended were staff talks between the British and Portuguese armed forces in London. Apparently, the Portuguese dictator did not wish to be taken by surprise, to see events in Portugal follow the pattern of Belgium and Holland.[37] Following consultation with the Foreign Office and the Chiefs of Staff, Churchill authorised Anglo-Portuguese staff talks in London.[38]

The talks did not start until the beginning of March 1941. Meanwhile, as a result of an optimistic assessment by the Chiefs of Staff of the likelihood of Spanish military resistance to a German invasion and Churchill's own strategic appreciation of the war, there was a relaxation of 'Brisk' and 'Shrapnel' early in the New Year. Moreover, Salazar made it clear that he did not anticipate a German attempt to take the Azores because they did not have superiority at sea and the problem of holding the islands in the face of a hostile population would be too great. He reassured the British that the Azores garrison had been strengthened, the Portuguese would send more troops if it were thought necessary and the German colony on the islands was being watched.[39] In connection with this last point, the Joint Planning Staff recommended that the Portuguese be persuaded to accept a small number of technical advisers in the guise of civilians and some defensive material in order to improve the defences of the Islands and the Joint Intelligence Committee suggested that if the Portuguese did not agree a small number of men should be infiltrated into the islands before the outbreak of hostilities or alternatively a 'trojan horse' expedition might be attempted by a force kept on reserve in ships in the South Atlantic. The question of infiltration was, however, remitted to the staff conversations.[40]

The Portuguese delegation, ostensibly visiting the United Kingdom to study aspects of London's defences, was deliberately composed of junior officers as more senior personnel would have aroused suspicions that the Portuguese were breaking their neutrality. It was led by Colonel J. F. de Barros Rodrigues of the Portuguese General Staff, who had the personal confidence of Salazar and who alone was empowered to engage in the conversations, and also included Lieutenant Colonel Higino Craveiro Lopes who would later be Commander-in-Chief of the Army and President of the Portuguese Republic from 1951 to 1958.[41] The British delegation was headed by the former Military Attaché at Lisbon, Lieutenant Colonel G. A. Fenton. Although the Chiefs of Staff had stressed that no impression should be given that Britain might be prepared to support the Portuguese mainland, Rodrigues immediately asked what help Portugal could expect if a German attack came. To avoid an immediate breakdown of the talks which could result, it was argued, in 'a moral deterioration which would render Portugal vulnerable to German infiltration on the Roumanian model' and a serious reduction in Britain's 'chances of securing the Atlantic Islands', the Chiefs of Staff recommended that outline contingency plans be drawn up provided no promise was made to send an expeditionary force to Portugal. Churchill agreed but emphasised the importance of the proviso.[42]

Within a few days of the Prime Minister's sanction an outline plan was drawn up which involved all three fighting services. The Army was to contribute a force headquarters, one corps of two divisions, one heavy tank brigade, anti-aircraft troops, base and lines of communication units; the Navy, naval base staff, and the Royal Air Force, a force headquarters, two fighter squadrons, two medium bomber squadrons and ancillary units. Altogether the force would consist of approximately 80,000 personnel and 12,000 vehicles and guns requiring 24 liners, 70 motor transport and five petrol ships. Approximately one million tons of shipping would be involved and it was estimated that 64 days would elapse between the appeal from Lisbon and the arrival of the last convoy in Portugal.[43] In view of the absence of a prior commitment to send an expeditionary force the plan was merely academic, which was just as well since a joint intelligence estimation of a timetable for a German attack on Portugal, using four divisions with air support, estimated that the German attack would be launched long before the British expeditionary force was fully established in Portugal.[44]

In the talks with the Portuguese staff it was stressed that in view of Britain's worldwide commitments no promises could be made and that any assistance which could be given to Portugal would be conditional on the Portuguese Islands, particularly the Azores, being denied to the Germans. The Portuguese were left with no illusions that the defence of the islands was the first priority of the British military authorities.[45] Despite the talks, there was no discernible stiffening of Portuguese resolve to resist an invasion and the Foreign Office, worried that a German setback in the Balkans might result in a drive against the Iberian Peninsula, advised an approach to the Americans. The Chiefs of Staff agreed that the best deterrent to a German occupation of the Atlantic Islands was an increase in American interest which might be achieved by taking them into full confidence. Churchill wondered how it would be for the United States to be asked to send a few ships to Madeira, or to cruise among the islands. As a result Halifax, now Ambassador at Washington, informed the State Department of British concerns at German fifth-column activities in Portugal and increased German activity in the Cape Verde Islands and requested that the United States naval squadron, withdrawn early in the war, should return to the Tagus and Lisbon. As a further deterrent, he also recommended an American naval visit to the Atlantic Islands.[46]

Pressure was also exerted in Lisbon on the Portuguese authorities to reinforce the islands and thus reduce the danger of an internal coup and of fifth-column activities. At the same time, it remained clear that without rapid and effective assistance from Britain there was little prospect of viable resistance from within Portugal itself to a German attack. According to Campbell, without a strong preventive British occupation of Portugal, there would be no repeat of the Peninsular War. Since a British occupation of Portugal was out of the question, there was no alternative other than to persuade the Portuguese Government to acquiesce in a German occupation, resist overseas and accept British help in defending their islands and colonial possessions.[47] Before this stark position could be put it was essential to know Salazar's precise intentions and this proved exceedingly difficult to obtain for several weeks but then on 21 May 1941 he preempted any further discussion by presenting his British ally with a formidable list of arms requirements, sufficient to equip five full divisions by August that year. The intention was to resist a German invasion and if Britain provided such war material, as Monteiro told Eden, the Portuguese would fight hard but without it they could offer no more than token resistance. Smaller quantities of material – 24 anti-aircraft guns and 36 Bofors guns – were also required for the defence of the Cape Verde Islands and the Azores.[48] There was no question of encouraging Portugal to resist a German invasion and at the end of May the Defence Committee agreed that British support would be confined to assisting the Portuguese Government to transfer to the Azores and the full re-equipping of the defences of the Azores and Cape Verde Islands.[49]

By this time the Americans had become more involved in Portuguese affairs having shown little interest previously. Roosevelt first raised the subject of the Azores in September 1940, and his intervention prompted the British to inform him of their contingency plans concerning the Azores and Cape Verde Islands and to canvass his support, but there was no positive American response.[50] Later, the President was reluctant to provide naval visits to Portugal and the islands following the British request of 28 March 1941. Churchill made a further effort to solicit American support towards the end of April when he appealed to Roosevelt to send 'at the earliest moment' a squadron for a 'friendly visit' to the Azores and Cape Verde Islands in order to 'warn Nazi raiders off' and to 'keep the place warm for us as well as giving us valuable information'.[51] Roosevelt's reaction was not encouraging. The Portuguese had protested strongly against America's offer of a 'friendly visit' to the Azores and Cape Verde Islands and this had now been deferred. The President was convinced that no expedition should be sent to 'either place' unless Portugal was attacked or definite word of an immediate German attack on the islands was received, and he insisted that in the event of a British occupation of the Azores it would be made very clear to the American people that it was for the purpose of British defence and was not permanent, that Britain would restore the islands to Portuguese sovereignty at the end of the war.

Early in May, after consulting Eden, Churchill advised Roosevelt that because of German infiltration his conditions made it almost certain that Britain would be forestalled by the Germans in the islands. He assured the President that the islands would be restored to Portuguese sovereignty at the close of the war: 'We are far from wishing to add to our territory, but only to preserve our life and perhaps yours'.[52] At the same time, the forces earmarked for the Azores operation were absorbed into the larger force required for the Canaries under operation 'Puma'. The joint planners justified this move because in their view the Canaries were strategically more important and any German occupation of the Azores would only be temporary since British forces ought to be able to recapture them, particularly if American help were available. They were aware that American interest in the Azores was growing and believed this was likely to act as a deterrent to any German action against them.[53]

Indeed, Roosevelt's initial reticence began to fade during the first half of May to a point where he considered sending a confidential emisary to Lisbon to ask Salazar whether in the event of a retreat to the Azores he would agree to anti-Axis forces joining in the defence of these islands. Churchill and the Foreign Office were convinced that Salazar would only approve a British intervention and in view of the Portuguese request for armaments of 21 May they concluded that it would be a tactical error to send a United States emissary to Lisbon and that American influence should be held in reserve.[54] Roosevelt was not deterred and on 29 May he told Halifax that he was anxious to reach a complete understanding with Churchill with regard to the islands in the event of a German occupation of Spain and Portugal. The President wished to agree a common plan which could function 'on the pressing of a button', and revealed that an American expeditionary force of 25,000 men – Plan 'Gray' – was being prepared.[55] He envisaged a situation where Britain would take immediate action perhaps with the help of a token American force but that eventually the Americans would take over, thus releasing British forces for use elsewhere. Roosevelt attached considerable importance to receiving Salazar's assent to intervention and was considering sending someone like Sumner Welles to see the Portuguese leader.[56] Plan Gray was approved by Roosevelt on 4 June.

Even before the war United States military planners had considered the possibility of a challenge by the Fascist powers in the Atlantic. In November 1938, after Munich, the Joint Planning Committee predicted that Germany and Italy would seek to obtain bases from Spain and Portugal in the Azores, Canaries and Cape Verde Islands as well as bases in Spanish and Portuguese West Africa. In response to German and Italian aggression, the planners had advised that the United States should concentrate a battlefleet off the Azores to challenge Axis control of the sea while the Army should organise an expeditionary force of 30,000 to 50,000 men to seize Bissau if Portugal cooperated with Germany and Italy.[57] During the recent talks between 29 January and 29 March 1941, known as the ABC-1 Conference, a war plan had been produced – United States–British-Commonwealth Joint Basic War Plan – which dealt with the initial stages of a conflict and focused on defensive tasks and force deployments. Under the plan the United States Navy would operate in the western Atlantic protecting the Western Hemisphere and preparing to occupy the Azores and Cape Verde Islands if they were threatened by the Axis powers.[58]

The decision of the British Defence Committee to offer to help the Portuguese to reinforce the islands while continuing to persuade Salazar to relocate his Government there in the event of a German invasion of the Iberian Peninsula meant the temporary exclusion of the Americans from the island project though this was offset by Churchill's request that they relieve the British garrison in Iceland. At the same time, Churchill assured Roosevelt that whatever Salazar's decision 'we should in the event have to obtain control of the islands for which United States cooperation would be invaluable' and the British Government would also 'welcome collaboration with an American token force, before, during or after occupation of [the] Atlantic Islands and if you wish would turn them over to you as a matter of mutual war convenience'.[59] Roosevelt realised that the United States could not play a prominent part with regard to the islands because of the uproar created in Portugal by his references in his fireside chat to the American people of 27 May, to the dangers which German control of any of the Atlantic islands posed to the security of the Western Hemisphere and the need for the American Navy to extend its naval patrols in the Atlantic. Lisbon had interpreted this as implying that Portuguese sovereignty over the islands would not be respected which was understandable in view of the alarm created in Portugal earlier in May by a speech in which Senator Claude Pepper had publicly invited American forces to occupy the Azores and Cape Verde Islands. Previously in April, the influential American columnist, Walter Lippman, writing for the *New York Herald Tribune*, had argued that Germany would have to be beaten to the Azores with or without Portuguese permission or cooperation. As Monteiro told Eden on 30 May, things had reached a point where 'a not unimportant section of the Portuguese public was more afraid of the United States than of any other country'.[60] The failure of the Roosevelt Administration to provide precise assurances compounded the rift in Luso-American relations which continued, despite British attempts to mediate, until mid-July when Roosevelt provided Salazar with a personal assurance concerning the Azores and all Portuguese colonies.[61]

In mid-June the President agreed to leave the business of handling Salazar to the British. Having previously withheld his final approval for Plan 'Gray' owing to changes in the war situation – notably the destruction of the pocket battleship *Bismarck* and the German invasion of Crete which together reduced Germany's naval and air strength and eased the threat to the Azores and Cape Verde Islands – and to increased speculation concerning the likelihood of a German invasion of Soviet Russia, Roosevelt suspended the Azores operation. His interest, however, remained undiminished and he wrote to President Getulio Vargas of Brazil on 10 July to solicit support in the form of a token Brazilian force should an occupation of the Azores prove necessary. The Brazilians would not commit themselves until the operation was more definite but they agreed to approach the Portuguese Government on behalf of the United States at 'the opportune time'.[62]

In July Salazar finally agreed to relocate his Government to the Azores in the event of an attack on the mainland, but it was evident that he had not given up on defending Portugal itself because he expected that the programme to equip five divisions, as well as reinforcing the islands, would not be altered or postponed.[63] The British Chiefs of Staff, however, were adamant that no war material should be supplied to the Portuguese unless they offered a *quid pro quo*, such as an undertaking to grant naval and air facilities in the islands immediately if Spain or Portugal were attacked by the Axis powers. They were also dissatisfied with the Portuguese intention to repair to the Azores only in the event of an actual rather than a threatened attack. The Chiefs were concerned that if the German action in the Peninsula were confined to Spain, including rendering Gibraltar untenable, there would be no certainty of Britain securing alternative bases in the Atlantic islands.[64] Eden, on the advice of Campbell, recognised that it was essential to convince Salazar of the indivisibility of Peninsula security and to disabuse him of any illusion that if Spain became belligerent and Portugal remained inviolate Britain would continue to supply arms and other assistance without reciprocal use of air and naval facilities in the islands.[65]

The process of disillusioning the Portuguese had begun during the first half of August 1941, in separate conversations between Campbell and Salazar in Lisbon and Eden and Monteiro in London, when it was interrupted by Churchill who revealed that during their conversations at Placentia Bay between 9 and 12 August Roosevelt had indicated his desire to occupy the Azores but only if invited by Salazar. The Portuguese dictator had written to the President and had referred to the provision of war material by the United States should Britain prove unable to supply. The President had interpreted this as implying a request for armed assistance from the United States in the event of a German move into the Iberian Peninsula. Churchill told the War Cabinet on 19 August that in view of Roosevelt's interest in the Azores a 'slight' change in British policy ought to be considered: the Portuguese should be actively encouraged to apply to the United States for assistance.[66] But there was widespread agreement in the Foreign Office that Salazar wanted nothing other than the provision of war material from the United States and that he would not in any circumstances issue an invitation to the United States to occupy the islands. From sources in Lisbon they were aware that the Portuguese dictator continued to express his suspicions and fears of American influence. The view was also expressed that the Americans were motivated in their interest in the islands by imperialist expansion rather than a desire to assist the Allied war effort.[67] Accordingly, Churchill was informed on 28 August that his proposal involved a 'radical' rather than a 'slight' change in the existing policy. Eden disillusioned Churchill as to the advisability of armed American intervention in the Azores, not least because it would threaten the prospects of Anglo-Portuguese cooperation with regard to the islands. Pending a decision on operation 'Pilgrim', the replacement code for 'Puma', and without prejudice to it, the Foreign Secretary advised the continuation of negotiations with Salazar. Churchill concurred and the American Government was so informed on 3 September.[68]

Three days later the Portuguese were presented with a clear and unambiguous statement of Britain's position. The British authorities rejected any prospect of Portugal maintaining her neutrality and escaping occupation once Spain had been drawn into the war and they stressed that Spanish belligerency would compel the abandonment of Gibraltar which would gravely handicap the allied war effort if it were not counter-balanced by the use of some alternative base between the United Kingdom and her African colonies, since 'the defence of Atlantic sea routes against submarines and air attack would in such circumstances become a matter of very great difficulty'. It was made absolutely clear that notwithstanding Portuguese defences, the defence of the Atlantic islands depended above all on the maintenance of British sea power which in turn depended on the use of facilities on the islands once Gibraltar had become untenable as a naval base. It was also expected that the Portuguese Government would relocate to the Azores in the event of a threat to Portugal itself.[69]

It took a further six weeks to persuade the Portuguese to engage in a second round of staff talks in London which began on 20 October and ended on 7 November 1941, with Colonel Rodrigues again the key figure on the Portuguese side. The talks focused on the ways and means of withdrawing the Portuguese Government from Portugal with the aid of their British allies. A plan for joint action 'from the moment when the Portuguese Government decides to abandon their neutrality' was drawn up and it was made clear that the successful execution of the plan depended on the Portuguese abandoning their neutrality well before they were actually attacked. The plan was divided into two phases: first, advanced preparations by the Portuguese, including the laying in of supplies and the improvement of the defence of the Azores and the construction of buildings by the Portuguese to accommodate British personnel on the islands once the Portuguese Government had relocated there; and second, joint action which would commence as soon as Salazar decided it was no longer desirable to maintain Portugal's neutrality. As part of the plan it was agreed that Britain would train officers of the Portuguese armed forces while a Portuguese air force officer would visit London to discuss the development of air facilities in the Azores with the Air Ministry.[70] Although it was still difficult to pin Salazar down on the question of the timing and circumstances of a Portuguese retreat, progress was made during 1942 concerning defence preparations for the Azores, particularly on improving air facilities following further talks in London between the ill-fated future presidential candidate, Staff Major Humberto Delgado, and the British air staff.[71]

While Anglo-Portuguese staff talks would continue after 1941 it was also the case that by the end of that year the Chiefs of Staff had come to the conclusion that responsibility for Operation 'Pilgrim' should be undertaken by the United States owing to British shortage of aircraft carriers, since all available carriers, then based on Mombassa, were required for operations against the Japanese in the Indian Ocean.[72] However, the likelihood of operation 'Pilgrim' being activated was growing more remote. A joint intelligence report at the end of 1941 concluded that Spain was anxious to remain non-belligerent, to avoid the risk of being at war with the United States and of alienating the Latin American republics and, in any case, there was no sign of any military movement by Germany towards the Iberian Peninsula.[73] The setbacks suffered by the German armies in Soviet Russia and North Africa during 1942 and the continuation of the policy of controlled economic assistance sufficed to keep Franco's regime non-belligerent and made any German threat to Spain and Portugal extremely remote.

Conclusion

In retrospect, the entry of the United States into the Second World War at the end of 1941 ensured that the Iberian Peninsula would eventually be located fully within the orbit of the western Allies even though Franco and Salazar would remain guarded for some time yet about American and British prospects for ultimate victory against the Third Reich. In contrast, the preceding decade had witnessed, with varying degrees of attention and interest, the involvement of all the great powers in Iberian affairs, with the exception of Imperial Japan; though the Japanese took a considerable interest in the Portuguese far eastern colonies of Macao and Timor and the former Spanish colony, the Philippines.[1]

The Soviets had no formal diplomatic relations with Portugal for the whole of the period under review and with Spain only for the duration of the Spanish Civil War. Despite the interest shown by the Comintern during the period of the Second Spanish Republic, there was no conspiracy to sovietise Spain, or Portugal for that matter. Soviet Russia only became involved in the civil war in Spain when Stalin realised that Britain and France would not intervene on the side of the Republic despite its democratic credentials. Soviet aid was intended to keep the Republicans fighting until such time as London and Paris had a change of heart and abandoned non-intervention, and was motivated by the need to make the policy of collective security effective in countering the fascist challenge which threatened Soviet security at a time when their industrialisation and rearmament programme remained incomplete. For Moscow, the establishment of a Right-wing regime in Spain to complement that in Portugal would weaken France strategically and render her less credible as a potential ally. In endeavouring to influence Britain and France to intervene in Spain, Stalin recognised that the revolutionary process occurring within Republican Spain would have to be ended and the cause of a bourgeois parliamentary republic emphasised in its place. It must be stressed, however, that the centralising tendencies of the Republican Government from the autumn of 1936 onwards were not solely the result of a malign Soviet influence but were essential to the task of building a viable state and effective conventional military forces to combat Franco's war of annihilation. Moreover, if Soviet aid was bought and paid for by the deposits of Spanish gold in Moscow and while there were definitely examples of commercial sharp practice by the Russians, the fact remains that without Soviet Russia's intervention the Republicans would have succumbed much earlier in the face of the fascist onslaught.

After March 1939, however, the Soviets ceased to take an interest in Iberian affairs and even made a rapprochement, albeit a temporary one, with their German antagonists. It was only in late 1944, with the defeat of the Third Reich inevitable, that interest was revived in Moscow where Stalin advocated confrontation with his western Allies over their lack of enthusiasm for the removal of the Franco regime, including guerrilla warfare in the peninsula.[2] In the spring of 1945 the Soviet dictator changed his mind and decided that the future of Spain should serve as a 'test' of the Allies' commitment to post-war cooperation in international affairs. At the Potsdam Conference in July–August 1945 the Soviets advocated great power intervention in Spain to remove the Franco regime but were met by a blank refusal from their former wartime allies. As the Cold War developed in 1946 cooperation was replaced by confrontation involving PCE led guerrilla warfare and then in1948, with a final reversal, Spanish communists were advised to end the guerrilla struggle and instead concentrate on infiltrating the worker organisations tolerated by the Franco regime.[3]

The intervention of the Fascist powers in the civil war in Spain contributed significantly to their growing rapprochement in the form of the Rome–Berlin Axis and subsequent Pact of Steel. Prior to July 1936 Germany had shown little interest in the Iberian Peninsula other than in improving commercial relations, which included arms sales to the Spanish Republican Government. In no circumstances did the Germans conspire with the Spanish militarists to overthrow the Second Spanish Republic. Italy was concerned to weaken the Franco-Spanish entente in order to improve her strategic prospects in the western Mediterranean but even the advent of a Right-wing Government in Spain in 1933 did not produce a corresponding Italo-Spanish rapprochement. Moreover, while Mussolini provided financial assistance to various monarchist groups and to the *Falange*, the Italians played no part in the Generals' attempted *coup d'état* of 18 July 1936. Having decided independently to intervene in the ensuing civil war, in the expectation that it would be of short duration, the two Fascist powers made a decisive contribution to the total victory of Franco's regime. Their commitment remained absolute despite their irritation with what they perceived to be a too cautious military approach by Franco but which in reality was a consequence of the Generalísimo's resolve not only to defeat but also to annihilate his Republican enemies. The destruction of the Red Republic, and the setback which this entailed for international communism, fulfilled their initial objective for intervening and, because Britain and France could no longer rely on Spain's benevolent or even strict neutrality in the event of war, the strategic position of both Fascist powers was enhanced. Moreover, the estrangement of France and Soviet Russia after the ratification of the Franco-Soviet Pact in February 1936 owed much to the latter's intervention in Spain, which also created suspicion and hostility in British governing circles. Far from the encirclement of Germany, Hitler was able to draw satisfaction and confidence from the disarray of his perceived enemies and ultimately divided them with the infamous Nazi-Soviet Pact of August 1939. Unlike the Italians, the Germans also succeeded in deriving economic and military benefits through their intervention in Spain. In a cost–benefit analysis of the Spanish Civil War it is certain that of all the great powers it was Nazi Germany who benefited most from the conflict.

Notwithstanding the benefits that accrued from the civil war, Germany entered the Second World War without a Spanish or Italian ally though the latter rectified this by her intervention in June 1940. Before the fall of France, the Franco regime had been isolated from its civil war partners by the facts of geography and the British blockade but afterwards it still remained non-belligerent. Irrespective of its support for the Axis war effort – including economic assistance, notably in the provision of strategic minerals, such as iron ore and wolfram, intelligence on Allied activity and morale, consistently favourable propaganda, and refuelling and restocking bases for German submarines and surface craft – the regime continued to avoid taking the final step to intervention. Spain's considerable economic distress, which made her dependent on economic assistance from the Allies, partly accounted for this

but Hitler's refusal to concede all of Franco's imperial demands
in North Africa probably mattered more, and the Caudillo was
simply not prepared to take the risk of entering the war unless
Britain's complete defeat was certain.[4] The Führer's peripheral
strategy, which aimed at bringing about a British surrender or
at least a weakening of her strategic position after the cancellation
of Operation 'Sea Lion', required the occupation of Gibraltar
and bases in the Canary Islands and along the coast of Spanish
Morocco and Rio de Oro. Franco's refusal to cooperate and
Germany's subsequent invasion of Soviet Russia rendered the
Wehrmacht's operational and contingency planning – Operations
'Felix', 'Felix-Heinrich' and 'Isabella' – ultimately superfluous.

While Franco's refusal to enter the war in 1940 and 1941
caused Hitler considerable irritation and anger, Mussolini was
more philosophical despite the boost which Spain's entry and the
capture of Gibraltar would have provided to Italy's fortunes in the
war in the Mediterranean and North Africa. He consistently
advised his Axis partner not to expect too much from the Franco
regime because he appreciated the degree of economic distress in
Spain but also because Spain's participation in the war would have
created another rival for territorial acquisition in North Africa.

The relations of Germany and Italy with Portugal were of a
different order. Before the civil war in Spain it was assumed in
Berlin and Rome that the Anglo-Portuguese alliance was unbreak-
able and that Portugal was firmly located within Britain's orbit.
However, the Spanish conflict and Salazar's hostility towards the
non-intervention policy promoted by Britain and France offered
the opportunity to undermine the alliance with serious consequences for British strategy in the Atlantic, in the Indian Ocean
and the Far East. Between the summer of 1936 and the outbreak
of war in September 1939, the Germans and Italians waged
a deliberate campaign to woo Portugal and weaken the British
connection through propaganda, improved cultural relations,
increased commercial activity and by competing for contracts to
rearm the Portuguese armed forces. While some progress was
made Portugal, unlike Franco's Spain and out of deference to her
British ally, did not join the Anti-Comintern Pact nor did she leave
the League of Nations. When war came in 1939, and partly because
of the Nazi–Soviet Pact, Portugal appeared to be as firmly wedded
to the British connection as ever. But, as in the case of her Iberian

neighbour, the fall of France in June 1940 radically altered the position with German armed forces on the Pyrenees frontier threatening Portugal's independence.

In these more favourable circumstances, considerable German pressure was put on the Portuguese Government to relinquish the British connection. In Portugal the Germans waged an anti-Allied propaganda war, cultivated pro-Axis institutions, such as the Portuguese Legion and elements in the Portuguese secret police, engaged in espionage, exchanged war material and gold for Portuguese products, notably wolfram, all to little avail. Salazar would not emulate Franco and send a Portuguese division to the eastern front after June 1941 despite his unremitting hostility to Soviet communism and there remained no prospect of Portugal's adhesion to the Anti-Comintern Pact when it came up for renewal in November 1941. At the same time, Portugal was included in German operational and strategic planning. Hitler and his military planners showed a great interest in the Portuguese Atlantic Islands – the Azores, the Cape Verde Islands and Madeira – along with the Canary Islands. Logistical difficulties in the face of British and possibly American naval forces made a German assault on the islands unlikely but the Führer persisted and it is probable that had the German forces on the eastern front succeeded in forcing a Soviet surrender in the summer and autumn of 1941 the Atlantic Islands would have risen rapidly in the order of strategic priorities not least to consolidate Hitler's Eastern Hemisphere and provide forward bases for an ultimate confrontation with the Western Hemisphere.

Although German influence over Portugal waned after 1941, Salazar's respect for German military prowess and his empathy with the German-led anti-communist crusade in the East caused him to maintain cordial relations with Berlin, epitomised by the continuation of Portuguese exports, notably wolfram and tinned sardines, until the summer of 1944 when the Salazar regime finally succumbed to Allied pressure and ended the trade. Measured in pure wolfram yield, Portugal accounted for about 62.5 per cent of the Third Reich's total imports in 1942 and about 61 per cent in 1943. For their part, the Germans continued to provide gold and war material as payment for Portuguese products. In the summer of 1943 a contract was signed which guaranteed the Portuguese military war material valued at more than 27 million reichmarks and included the supply in installments of 129 field cannon, 200 anti-aircraft guns and 600 machine guns. Although the German authorities maintained supplies until the last possible moment, the contract remained incomplete when the land communications between the Third Reich and the Iberian Peninsula were cut for good in July 1944.[5] Formal diplomatic relations between Lisbon and Berlin were only severed two days before the end of the war in Europe but not before Salazar, on hearing of Hitler's death, had ordered three days of mourning which included the lowering of flags on official buildings.

After 1941 Germany's experience with Franco's Spain was similar to that with Portugal. The prospects of Spain's entry into the war continued to recede as the Franco regime remained completely neutral during the Allied invasion of North Africa in late 1942. The reverses suffered during 1943 by German forces on the eastern front and in North Africa, and the demise of Fascist Italy eventually persuaded Franco to replace the Blue Division with a much smaller force, the Blue Legion, which in turn was withdrawn in the early summer of 1944. Hitler was in no position to challenge these developments but he succeeded in maintaining strong commercial relations with Spain, the latter continuing to supply wolfram and other raw materials in exchange for war material. The Führer recognised the significance of Spanish exports when he emphasised in January 1944 that 'the greatest amounts of Spanish raw materials, above all wolfram, had to be secured' and he was even prepared 'to accommodate Spanish demands for aircraft as much as possible'.[6] In the event, the German authorities continued to send war material of various kinds, including tanks and machine guns, to Spain until virtually the end of the war, albeit in diminishing quantities. As in Portugal, the end of the Third Reich was mourned not celebrated by the Franco regime. Many major figures of the regime called at the German Embassy to express their condolences for the death of Hitler. The Caudillo himself appeared regularly in Falangist uniform and did not break off diplomatic relations with Germany until VE Day itself, 8 May 1945.[7]

From the inception of the Second Spanish Republic the democratic great powers sought to protect their commercial and economic interests with some success despite disagreements over tariff policies and legislation designed to benefit Spanish workers in foreign-owned concerns. Although the Americans suspected that an international communist conspiracy was underfoot from the early days of the Spanish Republic onwards, they came to accept the more considered British view that internal forces within Spain posed a greater threat to their mutual economic interests, including Spanish anarchism and Catalan and Basque national-ism. Apart from a trade war, which lasted several months during 1935, Franco-Spanish economic relations remained amicable until the outbreak of the civil war. The period between the elec-toral victory of the Spanish Popular Front in February 1936 and the July coup revived fears in Washington and London that the Spanish Prime Minister and then President, Azaña, was a Spanish Kerensky, presiding over a government which was about to be overwhelmed by revolutionary forces. In the event, the crisis of order in Spain in the months following the victory of the Left was seemingly resolved by an attempted military coup, which was wel-comed by business interests and others on both sides of the Atlantic. When the failed coup turned into a civil war such groups, and they included the British Prime Minister, Neville Chamberlain, and most of his Cabinet, continued to favour the cause of General Franco and the Nationalists. The Second Spanish Republic, which at no time had threatened the strategic interests of the United States, Britain and France in the Atlantic or Mediterranean and which had sought to cooperate with Britain and France within the framework of the League of Nations, received little sympathy and no real assistance from the demo-cratic powers in face of anti-democratic Right-wing forces aided and abetted by the Fascist powers. The non-intervention policy, pursued strictly and consistently by Britain and the United States, the latter through its moral and legal arms embargoes, and deviated from only occasionally by France, made the Republic's prospects of survival marginal in the extreme and dependent on the one thing that London, Paris and Washington feared most in 1936, namely the extension of international communist influence in the Iberian Peninsula.

Anti-Republican prejudices and ill-will apart, and these were considerable in the echelons of government in all three powers, the fear of the civil war in Spain escalating into a more general conflict, probably based on ideological divisions, greatly exercised the officials and their political leaders in the State Department, the

Foreign Office and the Quai d'Orsay, and persuaded them that non-intervention was the only viable alternative if general peace was to be preserved. In this connection, the London-based Non-Intervention Committee served its original purpose which was to confine the civil war to Spain and enable the British and French Governments to pursue the goal of a general European settlement by appeasing Nazi Germany, and in the British case at least, Fascist Italy. To achieve these ends the British and French author-ities, in particular the former, promoted a number of initiatives within the Committee to take the heat out of the confrontation taking place in Spain. To do this required turning a blind eye to the activities of the interventionist powers, which reached absurd levels in September 1937 when, as a result of the Nyon Conference, Italy, who had been responsible for attacking a large number of vessels in the Mediterranean during the previous month, was allo-cated a zone in that sea to patrol on behalf of the Non-Intervention Committee. For their part the United States Government, in par-ticular the State Department, went along with the non-intervention fiction as the best means of preserving peace and confining the war to Spain. Although the Non-Intervention Committee had served its purpose by the summer of 1938 when London and Paris concluded that the civil war was no longer a threat to international peace, it continued to pursue chimerical schemes for the with-drawal of foreign volunteers, the granting of belligerent rights and mediation in the conflict.

In Britain and France the military advisers endorsed non-intervention as the best means of preserving essential strate-gic interests in the Mediterranean and Atlantic, bearing in mind that senior officers in the Royal Navy and most of the High Command of the French Army favoured Franco and regarded his Republican enemies with considerable distaste. At the same time, the pursuit of non-intervention enabled the authorities in London, Paris and Washington to avoid exacerbating existing divisions in their respective societies, and this was particularly significant in the case of France.

The policy of non-intervention offered no guarantees that the economic interests of the democratic powers would be protected. As the three largest foreign investors in the Spanish economy before the civil war Britain, France and the United States grew increasingly concerned at the growing relationship between Franco and his German and Italian allies. As the largest investor, Britain felt compelled in late 1937 to exchange diplomatic agents with the Franco regime essentially to safeguard the investments of companies such as Rio Tinto. In addition, by refraining from intervention the three powers were unable to test weapons, develop battlefield tactics or practice aerial warfare. However, they were able closely, through their service attachés and other elements of military intelligence, to observe and scrutinise the conduct of the war on both the Republican and Nationalist sides.

While the three democratic powers lost little time in recognising the Franco regime in the last weeks of the civil war, they were unable during the following months, indeed up to the outbreak of the Second World War, to disturb the close relationship which existed between Franco's Spain and the Axis powers. Neither Britain nor France could prevent Franco from adhering to the Anti-Comintern Pact or from leaving the League of Nations and while the remaining German and Italian forces were withdrawn from Spain in May 1939 collaboration on military matters continued. The French refusal to fully implement the Bérard–Jordana Agreement until there was considerable progress on the Spanish refugee problem contrasted with British attempts to appease the Franco regime, which remained disinterested in their proposals for further economic cooperation. Even Spain's declaration of neutrality at the beginning of September 1939 offered little in the way of consolation to Britain and France. The British Chiefs of Staff had argued in August 1936 that it was in Britain's strategic interests in relation to the Mediterranean and eastern Atlantic that in the event of war a future Spain should be at least strictly neutral but preferably benevolently neutral and to achieve this they had concurred in the non-intervention policy. Unfortunately, Franco's neutrality in September 1939 was benevolently directed towards Nazi Germany.

Portugal's decision to adopt a neutralist position at the outbreak of the war was welcomed by Britain and France and they shared Salazar's wider aim of securing a neutral Iberian Peninsula. Moreover, Lisbon tended to lean more to the Allied than to the German side. The British connection still mattered in Portugal despite the strenuous efforts of the Axis powers to weaken and undermine the Anglo-Portuguese alliance prior to September 1939. By effectively countering German and Italian propaganda and engaging in active cultural diplomacy, and in aggressively competing for Portuguese arms contracts, which included financial inducements and the dispatch of a senior military mission to Lisbon accompanied by a large naval demonstration, the British Government largely succeeded in overcoming the Axis challenge to their predominant position in Portugal's foreign relations; this, despite Salazar's aversion to non-intervention in Spain and his distrust of the western powers whom he suspected, erroneously at least in the case of the British, of favouring the Republicans in Spain. For their part, the British recognised the continuing strategic significance of their alliance with Portugal, which enabled them to make use of military facilities on the Portuguese mainland or in the overseas territories, notably in the Azores and Cape Verde Islands which were important for Atlantic defence and the protection of British trade in time of war.

Driven by this strategic imperative, the British authorities worked vigorously to counter the fascist challenge in Portugal after September 1939. By utilising their improved news services, the British prevented the Germans from winning the propaganda war as they were doing in Spain. The Ambassadors, Selby and Campbell, consistently encouraged Salazar's regime to have faith in an ultimate British victory; an objective which was made credible by Britain's association with the United States and from the summer of 1941 with Soviet Russia. Despite the virulent anti-communism of the *Estado Novo* and Salazar's personal antipathy for American liberal capitalism, this association was a significant counterweight to Salazar's appreciation of German military power and compelled him eventually to revise his earlier view that Germany was too dominant in Europe to be defeated.[8] To keep Portugal on side, the British blockade was worked comparatively gently even if it did irritate Salazar occasionally and the United States were persuaded to take a less firm stand against Portuguese trading infringements than they did in the case of Spain. And while the Germans were able to sign contracts with Portugal for the provision of arms and munitions, the British were able to maintain others and to insist on specific Portuguese deployments which suited their purposes, including the defences of the Azores and Cape Verde Islands.

Until the fall of France, the pro-German tendencies of Franco's regime caused little concern in London and Paris, and the conclusion of trade agreements with Madrid by both powers demonstrated the limits of Spanish hostility. After June 1940 it was entirely a different matter as the Caudillo all but succumbed to the temptation of exploiting Britain's isolated and exposed position by entering the war in alliance with the Axis powers, and the reality of German armed forces poised along the Pyrenees frontier was a constant reminder to Britain that the war could be extended easily and quickly into the Iberian Peninsula. The last thing the British authorities needed in the summer and autumn of 1940 and beyond was an extension of the war into the Peninsula with or without Spanish approval. In the absence of available military forces to counter a German assault, especially if supported by Spain, Gibraltar would almost certainly be lost and Britain's position in the western Mediterranean rendered untenable. It was therefore in the British interest to keep the Iberian Peninsula neutral and out of the war; a view shared entirely by the Salazar regime in Portugal. To this end Churchill and his Ministers, with the exception of Hugh Dalton, willingly pursued a strategy of controlled economic assistance to take advantage of Spain's desperate need for wheat and oil, commodities that could not be supplied in sufficient quantities by the Third Reich or Fascist Italy. In pursuing this strategy the British Government tended to give the benefit of doubt to Franco's actions and intentions, such as the Spanish occupation of Tangier in late 1940 and the intensive anti-British propaganda of the Spanish press, though they would not go so far as to support the Caudillo's ambitions with regard to colonial acquisition in North Africa. The United States also became involved in providing economic assistance but took a firmer line than their erstwhile British allies, demanding reciprocal concessions from Franco's regime, such as an end to the promotion of anti-US propaganda in Latin America, and when these were not sufficiently forthcoming to eventually impose an oil embargo in late 1941, albeit temporarily. Geographically remote from the Iberian Peninsula and the war in the Mediterranean and North Africa, Washington could afford to take a stronger line with the Franco regime than London who, unfortunately, enjoyed no such luxury during 1940 and 1941.

The need to appease Franco's Spain did not, however, deter Churchill and his military advisers from planning contingency measures to seize the Canary Islands in the event of a German invasion of the Iberian Peninsula whether supported or not by

Madrid. Operation 'Pilgrim' and its predecessor Operation 'Puma', though never activated, were intended to forestall German action in the Peninsula on the assumption that Gibraltar would become untenable as a base. The plans to seize the Spanish islands were explicitly linked to those which envisaged the seizure of the Portuguese Atlantic Islands – the Azores and Cape Verde Islands – and in the late spring of 1941 these were amalgamated in Operation Puma' and then 'Pilgrim'. The Americans, whose support was solicited by Churchill during 1941, had their own contingency plans to occupy the Azores – Plan 'Gray' – but eventually they deferred to the British who worked assiduously in the summer and autumn of 1941 to persuade a reluctant Salazar to relocate his Government to the islands in the event of a German attack on the Iberian Peninsula. Conversations between the British and Portuguese staffs were held in March and November 1941 followed by further talks in 1942 which involved the reinforcement of the Azores and Cape Verde Islands by Portuguese forces equipped from British stocks.

While the threat of a German attack on the Iberian Peninsula receded in 1942 with the Wehrmacht heavily engaged in Soviet Russia and the successful 'Torch' landings by Anglo-American forces in North Africa later in that year, the Allied powers maintained a considerable interest in the Portuguese Atlantic Islands. The determination of the Allies, in particular the Americans, to launch a second front in western Europe as soon as it was feasible, made the acquisition of logistical bases on the Azores a high priority which was achieved by diplomacy and not by force; Salazar eventually agreeing to the Atlantic Bases Deal of October 1943 which included the presence of British forces and subsequently American ones on the islands.[9]

Portuguese cooperation in the matter of the islands did much to mitigate, in the minds of London and Washington, the continuation of supplies of wolfram to the Third Reich until the summer of 1944. There was less mitigation in the case of Spain yet the British Government, and in particular Churchill, continued to give the Franco regime the benefit of the doubt even after the successful conclusion of the North African campaign. Indeed, in the autumn of 1942 prior to the activation of Operation 'Torch', for the allied invasion of French North Africa, both the British and American Governments provided assurances to the Franco regime that they had no intention of intervening in the internal affairs of Spain during the war or its aftermath.[10]

It was only in 1944 with the United States applying greater pressure that Franco was compelled to end officially wolfram exports to the Third Reich and withdraw the Blue Legion. Franco, however, remained oblivious to British and American warnings that unless his regime discarded its pro-fascist tendencies it would be isolated in the new democratic order that was emerging in newly liberated western Europe. By the end of the war, Washington and London were in full agreement that Franco's Spain should be kept isolated but neither advocated intervening in its internal affairs and at the Potsdam Conference in the summer of 1945 Soviet demands for great power intervention were firmly rejected.[11] Eventually, as the Cold War intensified Franco's regime would be rehabilitated as its anti-communist credentials found favour with presidents Harry S. Truman and Dwight D. Eisenhower, and successive British Governments.[12] Salazar's Portugal was treated even more favourably being admitted into the United Nations and becoming a founder member of the North Atlantic Treaty Organisation (NATO). Apart from the ideological perspective, the Iberian Peninsula continued to maintain its strategic significance in the context of the Cold War confrontation.

Notes

INTRODUCTION

1. D. Birmingham, *A Concise History of Portugal*, Cambridge: Cambridge University Press, 2nd edn, 2003, pp. 155–7.
2. The smaller parties included the United Socialist Party of Catalonia (*Partido Socialista de Cataluña*) formed in July 1936 from the merger of four smaller parties and the POUM (*Partido Obrera de Unificación Marxista*) which was formed in September 1935 from the *Izquierda Comunista* (Left Communists) and the BOC (*Bloc Obrer i Camperol* – Workers and Peasants Bloc).
3. H. Graham, *The Spanish Republic at War, 1936–1939*, Cambridge: Cambridge University Press, 2002, pp. 23–78.
4. See H. Thomas, *The Spanish Civil War*, London: Penguin, 3rd edn, 1977, pp. 926–7 and A. Beevor, *The Spanish Civil War*, London: Cassell, 1999, pp. 266–8.
5. Thomas, *The Spanish Civil War*, pp. 939–40. R. L. Proctor, *Hitler's Luftwaffe in the Spanish Civil War*, Westport, CN.: Greenwood Press, 1983, pp. 3–37. J. F. Coverdale, *Italian Intervention in the Spanish Civil War*, Princeton, NJ: Princeton University Press, 1975, pp. 85–7. M. de Madriaga, 'The intervention of Moroccan troops in the Spanish Civil War', *European History Quarterly*, vol. 22, 1992, p. 77. B. R. Sullivan, 'Fascist Italy's military involvement in the Spanish Civil War', *Journal of Military History*, vol. 59, 1995, p. 719. E. Moradiellos, 'The gentle general: the official British perception of General Franco during the Spanish Civil War' in P. Preston and A. L. Mackenzie (eds), *The Republic Besieged: Civil War in Spain, 1936–1939*, Edinburgh: Edinburgh University Press, 1996, pp. 4, 38.
6. P. Preston, *Franco: A Biography*, London: HarperCollins, 1993, p. 294.
7. See W. C. Frank Jr., 'Politico military deception at sea in the Spanish Civil War, 1936–1939', *Intelligence and National Security*, vol. 5, 1990, pp. 90–105.
8. Ibid., pp. 93, 95. The first two German vessels were the *Kamerun* and the *Usaramo*.
9. For extensive detail on the arms black market see G. Howson, *Arms for Spain: The Untold Story of the Spanish Civil War*, London: John Murray, 1998.
10. Graham, *Spanish Republic at War*, p. 352. P. Preston, 'General Franco as military leader', *Transactions of the Royal Historical Society*, 6th series, vol. 4, 1994, pp. 21–41.
11. W. C. Frank Jr, 'The Spanish Civil War and the coming of the Second World War', *International History Review*, vol. 9, 1987, pp. 371–2, 408.

12. W. S. Churchill, *The Second World War, Vol. III: The Grand Alliance*, London: Cassell, 1950, pp. 539–40.

1. THE GREAT POWERS AND THE SECOND SPANISH REPUBLIC, 1931–1936

1. Lord Vansittart, *The Mist Procession: The Autobiography of Lord Vansittart*, London: Hutchinson, 1958, p. 416.

2. Minutes by Sir George Mounsey and Vansittart, 15–16 April 1931. FO371/15771 W4251/46/41. See also D. Little, *Malevolent Neutrality: The United States, Great Britain and the Origins of the Spanish Civil War*, Ithaca, NY and London: Cornell University Press, 1985, p. 64.

3. Vansittart to Sir Edward Harding, Dominions Office, 8 May 1931. FO371/15772 W5330/46/41.

4. See, for example, *Foreign Relations of the United States*, 1931, vol. II, pp. 987, 989, 994–5. Hereafter FRUS.

5. Ovey to Arthur Henderson, British Foreign Secretary, 21 April 1931. FO371/15772 W4789/46/41. T. Rees, 'The "Good Bolsheviks": the Spanish Communist Party in the third period' in M. Worley (ed.), *In Search of Revolution: International Communist Parties in the Third Period*, London: I. B. Taurus, 2004, pp. 175, 187.

6. J. Degras (ed.), *The Communist International, 1919–1943. Documents. Volume III 1929–1943*, London: Frank Cass, 1971, p. 156.

7. A. Elorza and M. Biscarrondo, *Queridos Camaradas: La Internacional Cominista y España, 1919–1939*, Barcelona: Planeta, 1999, pp. 147–52.

8. Degras (ed.), *The Communist International*, pp. 183–4. K. McDermott and J. Agnew, *The Comintern: A History of International Communism from Lenin to Stalin*, London: Macmillan, 1996, p. 107.

9. Sir George Grahame, British Ambassador at Madrid, to Sir John Simon, Foreign Secretary, 31 July 1933. William Strang, British Chargé d'Affaires at Moscow, to Simon, 31 July 1933. FO371/17260 N5869/N5886/605/38.

10. Jean Herbette, French Ambassador at Madrid, to François Piétri, interim Foreign Minister, 27 August 1934. *Documents Diplomatiques Français, 1932–1939*, 1st series, vol. VII, no. 159, pp. 253–4. Hereafter DDF.

11. A. Shubert, *The Road to Revolution in Spain: The Coal Miners of Asturias, 1860–1934*, Urbana/Chicago: University of Illinois Press, 1987, p. 163.

12. Noel Charles, British Chargé d'Affaires at Moscow, to Simon, 22 October 1934. FO371/18597 W9458/27/41.

13. J. Haslam, 'Soviet Russia and the Spanish problem' in R. Boyce and J. Maiolo (eds), *The Origins of World War Two: The Debate Continues*, London: Palgrave Macmillan, 2002, p. 75.

14. For Hitler's early indifference to Spain see A. Viñas, *Franco, Hitler y el Estallido de la Guerra Civil: Antecedentes y Consecuencias*, Madrid: Alianza Editorial, 2001, pp. 119–34. See also I. Saz, 'The Second Republic in the international arena' in S. Balfour and P. Preston (eds), *Spain and the Great Powers in the Twentieth Century*, London: Routledge, 1999, p. 91.

15. A. Viñas and C. C. Seidel, 'Franco's request to the Third Reich for military assistance', *Contemporary European History*, vol. 11, 2002, p. 196. See also R. H. Whealey, *Hitler and Spain: The Nazi Role in the Spanish Civil War, 1936–1939*, Lexington, KY: University of Kentucky Press, 1989, pp. 4, 32–3, 96.

16. Viñas and Seidel, 'Franco's request', pp. 196–8. A. Léon, 'La dimension internacional de la Segunda República: un proyecto en el crisol' in J. Tusell, J. Avilés and R. Pardo (eds), *La Política Exterior del España en el Siglo XX*, Madrid: Biblioteca Nueva, 2000, pp. 209–10.

17. Viñas and Seidel, 'Franco's request', p. 206.

18. The trade dispute was finally resolved in December 1935 but not before French exports to Spain had fallen from nearly 40 million francs a month at the beginning of 1935 to about 5 million from August onwards. See Sir George Clerk, British Ambassador at Paris, to Sir Samuel Hoare, Foreign Secretary, 23 December 1935. FO371/19742 W10986/192/41.

19. AGK to the German Foreign Ministry, 24 September 1935 enclosing a 'Report on Negotiations in Spain in respect of the Delivery of German War Material'. *Documents on German Foreign Policy, 1918–1945*, series C, vol. IV, no. 303, pp. 641–50. Hereafter DGFP.

20. AGK to the German Foreign Ministry, 6 December 1935. DGFP, series C, vol. IV, no. 450, p. 892. See also E. Moradiellos, *Neutralidad Benévola: El Gobierno Británico y la Insurrección Militar Española de 1936*, Oviedo: Pentalfa Ediciones, 1990, pp. 67–9.

21. C. Leitz, *Economic Relations between Nazi Germany and Franco's Spain, 1936–1945*, Oxford: Oxford University Press, 1996, p. 15.

22. See, for example, D. Puzzo, *Spain and the Great Powers, 1936–1941*, New York: Columbia University Press, 1962, p. 47.

23. Viñas, *Franco, Hitler y el Estallido de la Guerra Civil*, pp. 240–7.

24. Hans Hermann Völckers, German Chargé d'Affaires, to the German Foreign Ministry, 26 March 1936. DGFP, series C, vol. V, no. 221, p. 313.

25. Viñas and Seidel, 'Franco's request', pp. 197–8. Leitz, *Economic Relations*, pp. 13–15.

26. For the American decision to recognise the Spanish Republic see FRUS, 1931, vol. II, pp. 987, 994.

27. Little, *Malevolent Neutrality*, p. 114.

28. FRUS, 1932, vol. II, pp. 530–6, 545–6. FRUS, 1933, vol. II, 694–8. Little, *Malevolent Neutrality*, pp. 114–25.

29. FRUS, 1934, vol. II, pp. 687–708. FRUS, 1935, vol. II, pp. 694–7, 712–32. Little, *Malevolent Neutrality*, pp. 168–70, 172–5, 177–81.

30. Thomas, *The Spanish Civil War*, p. 148.
31. FRUS, 1932, vol. II, pp. 560–76. Little, *Malevolent Neutrality*, pp. 95–9, 101–7, 152–3.
32. Little, *Malevolent Neutrality*, pp. 152–5, 159–60.
33. Ibid., p. 195.
34. Ibid., p. 218.
35. Within a matter of weeks of the proclamation of the Spanish Republic Mussolini was moved to declare: 'The Spanish Republic is not a revolution but a plagiarism. A plagiarism that arrives a good one hundred and fifty years late. To found a parliamentary republic today means using an oil lamp in the era of electric lights.' J. F. Coverdale, *Italian Intervention in the Spanish Civil War*, Princeton, NJ: Princeton University Press, p. 38.
36. I. Saz, *Mussolini contra la II República: Hostilidad, Conspiraciones, Intervención (1931–1936)*, Valencia: Edicions Alfons el Magnànim – Institució Valenciana d'Estudis i Investigació, 1986, pp. 232–3. I. Saz, 'Fascism and empire: Fascist Italy against Republican Spain' in R. Rein (ed.), *Spain and the Mediterranean since 1898*, London: Frank Cass, 1999, pp. 116–17. N. T. Garcia, 'The Mediterranean in the foreign policy of the Second Spanish Republic' in ibid., p. 66.
37. Saz, 'Fascism and empire', pp. 118–19.
38. Ibid., pp. 119–20.
39. Ibid., pp. 121–3. Garcia, 'The Mediterranean in the foreign policy of the Second Spanish Republic', pp. 75–7. Coverdale, *Italian Intervention*, pp. 54–5.
40. Saz, 'Fascism and empire', p. 118. Coverdale, *Italian Intervention*, pp. 41–2.
41. Saz, *Mussolini contra la II República*, pp. 35–40.
42. Ibid., pp. 66–82. Saz, 'Fascism and empire', pp. 120–1. Coverdale, *Italian Intervention*, pp. 50–4. M. Alpert, *A New International History of the Spanish Civil War*, London: Macmillan, 1994, pp. 35–6. Payne, 'Fascist Italy and Spain, 1922–1945' in Rein (ed.), *Spain and the Mediterranean since 1898*, p. 103.
43. Alpert, *A New International History*, p. 36. Saz, 'Fascism and empire', p. 122. Payne, 'Fascist Italy and Spain', p. 106.
44. Saz, 'Fascism and empire', p. 124.
45. Herbette to Laval, 5 December 1934. DDF, 1st series, vol. VIII, no. 205, p. 305.
46. See, for example, Édouard Herriot, French Foreign Minister, to Herbette, 16 August 1932 and Herbette to Herriot, 14 September 1932. DDF, 1st series, vol. I, nos. 105, 179, pp. 186–7, 323–6.
47. R. H. Whealey, 'Economic influence of the great powers in the Spanish Civil War: from the Popular Front to the Second World War'. *International History Review*, vol. 5, 1983, p. 232.
48. Herbette to Herriot, 14 September 1932. DDF, 1st series, vol. I, no. 179, p. 323.
49. Herbette to Herriot, 9 November 1932. DDF, 1st series, vol. I, no. 311, p. 679. Garcia, 'The Mediterranean in the foreign policy of the Second Spanish Republic', pp. 69–70.

50. Saz, 'The Second Republic in the international arena'. p. 79.
51. Garcia, 'The Mediterranean in the foreign policy of the Second Spanish Republic', p. 70.
52. Léon, 'La dimensión internacional de la Segunda República', p. 205.
53. Herbette to Paul-Boncour, 22 July 1933. Paul-Boncour to Herbette, 31 July 1933. Herbette to Paul-Boncour, 6 August 1933. DDF, 1st series, vol. IV, nos. 32, 62, 87, pp. 57–8, 112, 161–3.
54. Garcia, 'The Mediterranean in the foreign policy of the Second Republic', p. 72–3.
55. Herbette to Laval, 30 September 1935. DDF, 1st series, vol. XII, no. 275, p. 390.
56. Herbette to Laval, 18 October 1935. DDF, 1st series, vol. XIII, no. 38, p. 50.
57. See G. Stone, 'From entente to alliance: Anglo-French relations 1935–1939' in A. Sharp and G. Stone (eds), *Anglo-French Relations in the Twentieth Century: Rivalry and Cooperation*, London: Routledge, 2000, pp. 182–4.
58. Herbette to Pierre-Etienne Flandin, Foreign Minister (caretaker Government), 14 May 1936. DDF, 2nd series, vol. II, no. 213, pp. 315–17.
59. Herbette to Yvon Delbos, French Foreign Minister, 6 June 1936. DDF, 2nd series, vol. II, no. 279, pp. 436–7.
60. Herbette to Delbos, 10 and 12 July 1936. DDF, 2nd series, vol. II, nos. 423, 435, pp. 651–3, 667–8.
61. Grahame to Vansittart, 29 March 1932. Vansittart to Grahame, 5 April 1932. FO371/16511 W3959/3959/41. Grahame surmised that the Spanish Government, led by Azaña, was largely composed of intellectuals who were inclined to be favourably disposed towards France for cultural and political reasons.
62. Grahame to Simon, 5 May 1933. FO371/17426 W5425/116/41.
63. Vansittart to Grahame, 2 June 1933. FO371/17426 W5425/116/41.
64. E. Moradiellos, 'The origins of British non-intervention in the Spanish Civil War: Anglo-Spanish relations in early 1936', *European History Quarterly*, vol. 21, 1991, pp. 341–4. See also Moradiellos, *Neutralidad Benévola*, pp. 95–103.
65. See Little, *Malevolent Neutrality*, pp. 99–110.
66. See minutes by Charles Stirling and Orme Sargent, 16, 19 October 1934. FO371/18596 W9132/27/41.
67. Herbette to Laval, 19 September 1935. DDF, 1st series, vol. XII, no. 193, pp. 282–3.
68. Sir Henry Chilton, British Ambassador at Madrid, to Anthony Eden, Foreign Secretary, 26 February 1936. FO371/20520 W1936//622/41.
69. Moradiellos, 'Origins of British non-intervention', pp. 347–58.
70. Foreign Office Memorandum, 23 June 1936. FO371/20522 W5693/62/41.
71. Minute by Vansittart, 24 June 1936. FO371/20522 W5693/62/41.
72. For details see Little, *Malevolent Neutrality*, pp. 215–16 and C. E. Harvey, *The Rio Tinto Company: An Economic History of a Leading International Mining Concern*, Penzance: Alison Hodge, 1984, pp. 264–6.

2. THE INTERVENTIONIST POWERS AND THE SPANISH CIVIL WAR, 1936–1939

1. P. Preston, 'Mussolini's Spanish adventure: from limited risk to war' in H. Graham and P. Preston (eds), *The Republic Besieged: Civil War in Spain, 1936–1939*, Edinburgh: Edinburgh University Press, 1996, pp. 21–51. P. Preston, 'Italy and Spain in civil war and world war, 1936–1943' in Balfour and Preston (eds), *Spain and the Great Powers*, pp. 152–5. See also Coverdale, *Italian Intervention*, pp. 69–74 and Alpert, *A New International History*, pp. 37–8.

2. Viñas and Seidel, 'Franco's request', p. 205.

3. For details of the Bayreuth meeting and Hitler's decision to intervene see Viñas, *Hitler, Franco y el Estallido de la Guerra Civil*, pp. 368–84.

4. Ibid., pp. 354–68. Viñas and Seidel, 'Franco's request', pp. 200–5. See also G. L. Weinberg, *The Foreign Policy of Hitler's Germany: Diplomatic Revolution in Europe, 1933–1936*, Chicago: Chicago University Press, 1970, pp. 288–9. H.-H. Abendroth, *Hitler in der Spanischen Arena: Die Deutsch–Spanischen Beziehungen im Spannungsfeld der Europäischen Interessenpolitik vom Ausbruch des Bürgerkrieges bis zum Ausbruch des Weltkrieges, 1936–1939*, Paderborn: Schöningh, 1973, pp. 23–39; M. Merkes, *Die Deutsches Politik gegenüber im Spanischen Bürgerkrieg, 1936–1939*, Bonn: 2nd edn, Ludwig Röhrscheid, 1969, pp. 23–30; and C. Leitz, 'Nazi Germany's intervention in the Spanish Civil war and the foundation of HISMA/ROWAK' in Graham and Preston (eds), *The Republic Besieged*, pp. 53–7.

5. For details see Proctor, *Hitler's Luftwaffe*, 1983, pp. 10–19.

6. Viñas and Seidel, 'Franco's request', pp. 208–9.

7. For details see Thomas, *The Spanish Civil War*, pp. 977–9; Coverdale, *Italian Intervention*, pp. 393, 418–19; Merkes, *Die Deutsche Politik*, ch. 3; and Preston, 'Italy and Spain', p. 173.

8. DGFP, series D, vol. III, no. 783, pp. 892–4. Coverdale, *Italian Intervention*, pp. 392–3. Harvey, *The Rio Tinto Company*, n. 59, p. 289. R. H. Whealey, 'Foreign intervention in the Spanish Civil War' in R. Carr (ed.), *The Republic and the Civil War in Spain*, London: Macmillan, 1971, p. 219. Preston, 'Italy and Spain', pp. 172–3. R. G. Pérez, *Franquismo y Tercer Reich: Las Relaciones Economicas Hispano-Alemanas durante la Segunda Guerra Mundial*, Madrid: Centro de Estudios Constucionales, 1994, pp. 59–89.

9. See P. Broué and E. Témime, *The Revolution and the Civil War in Spain*, London: Faber, 1972, p. 346 and D. Mack Smith, *Mussolini's Roman Empire*, London: Longman, 1976, p. 100.

10. Coverdale, *Italian Intervention*, pp. 78–83, 399–404. Thomas, *The Spanish Civil War*, p. 353. For the Farinacci mission see H. Fornari, *Mussolini's Gadfly: Roberto Farinacci*, Nashville, TN: Vanderbilt University Press, 1971, pp. 162–4.

11. Speech to Nazi Party officials, 29 April 1937. D. Smyth, 'Reflex reaction: Germany and the onset of the Spanish Civil War' in P. Preston (ed.),

NOTES 223

Revolution and War in Spain 1931–1939, London: Methuen, 1984, p. 244. See also G. L. Weinberg, *The Foreign Policy of Hitler's Germany: Starting World War II, 1937–1939*, Chicago: Chicago University Press, 1980, pp. 155–6.

12. See M. Blinkhorn, 'Conservatism, traditionalism and fascism in Spain, 1898–1937' in M. Blinkhorn (ed.), *Fascists and Conservatives: The Radical Right and the Establishment in Twentieth Century Europe*, London: Unwin Hyman, 1990, pp. 129–34.

13. Whealey, *Hitler and Spain*, p. 29.

14. Thomas, *The Spanish Civil War*, p. 356.

15. 'A Busman's Holiday', 10 September 1936. *Documents on British Foreign Policy, 1919–1939*, 2nd series, vol. XVII, app. I, p. 760. Hereafter DBFP. See also G. Stone, 'Sir Robert Vansittart and Spain, 1931–1941' in T. G. Otte and C. A. Pagedas (eds), *Personalities, War and Diplomacy: Essays in International History*, London: Frank Cass, 1997, pp. 133–4.

16. Thomas, *The Spanish Civil War*, p. 356. Smyth, 'Reflex reaction', pp. 253, 257. M. Muggeridge (ed.), *Ciano's Diplomatic Papers*, London: Odhams, 1948, p. 57.

17. For Hitler's extension of military conscription see DGFP, series D, vol. III, no. 55, pp. 56–7.

18. Whealey, *Hitler and Spain*, pp. 26–31.

19. Smyth, 'Reflex Reaction', p. 251.

20. DBFP, 2nd series, vol. XVII, app. I, p. 761. Stone, 'Sir Robert Vansittart and Spain', p. 134.

21. Smyth, 'Reflex reaction', p. 252. See also Viñas, *Hitler, Franco y el Estallido de la Guerra Civil*, pp. 393–4.

22. Smyth, 'Reflex Reaction', pp. 254–5.

23. Abendroth, *Hitler in der Spanischen Arena*, pp. 35–6. For the debate on Hitler's ultimate objectives including discussion of the so-called *Stufenplan* see K. Hildebrand, *The Foreign Policy of the Third Reich*, London: Batsford, 1973; M. Michaelis, 'World power status or world dominion? A survey of the literature on Hitler's plan of world dominion (1939–1970)', *Historical Journal*, vol. 15, 1972; A. Hillgruber, 'England's place in Hitler's plan for world dominion', *Journal of Contemporary History*, vol. 9, 1974; M. Hauner, 'Did Hitler want a world dominion?', *Journal of Contemporary History*, vol. 12, 1978; and E. M. Robertson, 'Hitler's planning for war and the response of the great powers (1938–early 1939)' in H. W. Koch (ed.), *Aspects of the Third Reich*, London: Macmillan, 1985.

24. R. M. Salerno, *Vital Crossroads: Mediterranean Origins of the Second World War, 1935–1940*, Ithaca, NY: Cornell University Press, 2002, p. 71.

25. CAB24/277, CP 163(38) 'German Attitudes towards Events in Spain and Portugal: Memorandum by Lord Halifax', 7 July 1938. G. Stone, *The Oldest Ally: Britain and the Portuguese Connection, 1936–1941*, Woodbridge: Boydell and Brewer, 1994, pp. 47–8. See also the *News Chronicle*, 12 July 1938. For strategic issues see D. C. Watt, 'German strategic planning and Spain 1938–1939', *Army Quarterly*, 1960, pp. 220–7. For the strategic significance of the Portuguese alliance for Britain at this time see G. A. Stone, 'The official

British attitude to the Anglo-Portuguese alliance, 1910–1945', *Journal of Contemporary History*, vol. 10, 1975, pp. 738–40. For German naval planning see J. Dülffer, *Weimar, Hitler und die Marine: Reichspolitik und Flottenbau, 1920 bis 1939*, Düsseldorf: Droste, 1973.

26. See chapter 6.

27. Coverdale, *Italian Intervention*, pp. 40–1, 339. It is Coverdale's contention that it was principally concern over Italy's position in the western Mediterranean *vis-à-vis* France which influenced Mussolini to provide arms and money to army and monarchist conspirators before 1936. Ibid., p. 65. See also, Salerno, *Vital Crossroads*, p. 17.

28. Coverdale, *Italian Intervention*, pp. 50–3, 76.

29. Ibid., 76–7. J. Edwards, *The British Government and the Spanish Civil War, 1936–1939*, London: Macmillan, 1979, pp. 138–42.

30. Coverdale, *Italian Intervention*, pp. 76–7. D. T. Cattell, *Soviet Diplomacy and the Spanish Civil War*, Berkeley, CA: University of California Press, 1957, pp. 2–3.

31. C. Leitz, 'Nazi Germany and Francoist Spain, 1936–1945' in Balfour and Preston (eds), *Spain and the Great Powers*, p. 130.

32. R. G. Colodny, *Spain: The Glory and the Tragedy*, New York: Humanities Press, 1970, p. 32 and Thomas, *The Spanish Civil War*, p. 951.

33. CAB24/277, CP 163(38). Weinberg, *The Foreign Policy of Hitler's Germany 1937–1939*, pp. 164–5. Thomas, *The Spanish Civil War*, pp. 940–1. Coverdale, *Italian Intervention*, pp. 394–8. Proctor, *Hitler's Luftwaffe*, pp. 253–65. M. Cooper, *The German Air Force 1933–1945: An Anatomy of Failure*, London: Jane's, 1981, pp. 58–60. Whealey, *Hitler and Spain*, pp. 104–8. J. S. Corum, 'From biplanes to blitzkrieg: the development of German air doctrine between the wars', *War in History*, vol. 3, 1996, p. 98. M. Alpert, ' The clash of Spanish armies: contrasting ways of war in Spain, 1936–1939', *War in History*, vol. 6, 1999, pp. 338–45.

34. Proctor, *Hitler's Luftwaffe*, pp. 258–9.

35. B. R. Sullivan, 'Fascist Italy's military involvement in the Spanish Civil War', *Journal of Military History*, vol. 59, 1995, pp. 711–21.

36. For the internal position in Italy in 1936 see Coverdale, *Italian Intervention*, pp. 408–10.

37. Ibid., p. 390. Weinberg, *The Foreign Policy of Hitler's Germany, 1933–1936*, pp. 295–6. Preston, 'Italy and Spain', pp. 169–70.

38. For the view that economic considerations were a by-product of German intervention see H.-H. Abendroth, 'Deutschlands Rolle im spanischen Bürgerkrieg' in M. Funke (ed.), *Hitler, Deutschland und die Mächte: Materialen zur Aussenpolitik des Dritten Reichs*, Düsseldorf: Droste, 1978, p. 480. Abendroth's view is shared to a large extent by Smyth, 'Reflex reaction', pp. 256–7.

39. C. Leitz, *Economic Relations between Nazi Germany and Franco's Spain, 1936–1945*, Oxford, 1996, pp. 17–52. Leitz, 'Nazi Germany's intervention', pp. 62–85. C. Leitz, 'Hermann Göring and Nazi Germany's economic exploitation of Nationalist Spain, 1936–1939', *German History*, vol. 14, 1996, pp. 24–6.

W. Deist, M. Messerschmidt, H-E. Volkmann, W. Wette, *Germany and the Second World War. Volume I: The Build-up of German Aggression*, Oxford: Oxford University Press, 1990, pp. 316–23. Pérez, *Franquismo y Tercer Reich*, pp. 59–89.

40. Weinberg, *The Foreign Policy of Hitler's Germany, 1937–1939*, pp. 146–9. Harvey, *The Rio Tinto Company*, pp. 271–3. Á Viñas, 'The financing of the Spanish Civil War' in Preston (ed.), *Revolution and War in Spain*, pp. 277–8. For the significance of German intervention for the second Four Year Plan see W. Schieder, 'Spanischen Bürgerkrieg und Vierjahresplan' in W. Schieder and C. Dipper (eds), *Der Spanischen Bürgerkrieg in der Internationalen Politik, 1936–1939*, München: Nymphenburger Verlagshandlung, 1976, pp. 162–90.

41. Leitz, *Economic Relations*, pp. 53–90. Leitz, 'Nazi Germany and Francoist Spain', pp. 134–5. Weinberg, *The Foreign Policy of Hitler's Germany, 1937–1939*, pp. 152–4, 158–69. Harvey, *The Rio Tinto Company*, pp. 275, 282–4.Viñas, 'Financing the Spanish Civil War', pp. 278–9.

42. Viñas, 'Financing the Spanish Civil War', pp. 273–7. DGFP, Series D, vol. VII, no. 329, p. 325.

43. M. Muggeridge (ed.), *Ciano's Hidden Diary, 1937–1938*, New York: Dutton, 1953, entry 29 October 1937, p. 26.

44. Robertson, 'Hitler's planning for war', p. 206.

45. Harvey, *The Rio Tinto Company*, pp. 285–6 and Weinberg, *The Foreign Policy of Hitler's Germany, 1937–1939*, pp. 153–4, 165–6.

46. For the origins of the Italo-German rapprochement see E. M. Robertson, *Mussolini as Empire Builder: Europe and Africa 1932–1936*, London: Macmillan, 1977, pp. 181–3, 186–8. For the impact of the Spanish Civil War on the development of an official anti-semitic policy in Italy see M. Michaelis, *Mussolini and the Jews: German–Italian Relations and the Jewish Question in Italy, 1922–1945*, Oxford: Oxford University Press, 1978, pp. 93, 102.

47. Weinberg, *The Foreign Policy of Hitler's Germany, 1937–1939*, pp. 143–4, 163.

48. For the Hossbach Conference see J. Noakes and G. Pridham (eds), *Nazism 1919–1945: 3: Foreign Policy, War and Racial Extermination*, Exeter: University of Exeter Press, 1988, no. 503, p. 686.

49. Frank Jr, 'The Spanish Civil War', p. 377. Smyth, 'Reflex reaction', pp. 258–60. Preston, 'Italy and Spain', pp. 163–4, 166.

50. H. J. Burgwyn, *Italian Foreign Policy in the Interwar Period, 1918–1940*, Westport, CN: Praeger, 1997, p. 153.

51. M. Knox, *Mussolini Unleashed, 1939–1941: Politics and Strategy in Fascist Italy's Last War*, Cambridge: Cambridge University Press, 1982, p. 40. M. Knox, 'The Fascist regime, its foreign policy and its wars: an "anti-anti-Fascist" orthodoxy?', *Contemporary European History*, vol. 4, 1995, p. 359. A. Cassels, 'Reluctant neutral: Italy and the strategic balance in 1939' in B. J. McKercher and R. Legault (eds), *Military Planning and the Origins of the Second World War in Europe*, Westport, CN: Praeger, 2001, p. 38.

52. Giral to V. M. Potemkine, Soviet Ambassador at Paris, 25 July 1936. R.Radosh, M. R. Habeck, G. Sevostianov (eds), *Spain Betrayed: The Soviet*

Union in the Spanish Civil War, New Haven and London: Yale University Press, 2001, no. 10, p. 21.

53. Ibid., nos. 1, 5, 6, pp. 7–8, 11–14. A. Dallin and F. I. Firsov (eds), *Dimitrov and Stalin, 1934–1943: Letters from the Soviet Archives*, New Haven: Yale University Press, 2000, no. 8, pp. 46–7.

54. J. Haslam, *The Soviet Union and the Struggle for Collective Security in Europe, 1933–1939*, London: Macmillan, 1984, pp. 108–11. E. H. Carr, *The Comintern and the Spanish Civil War*, London: Macmillan, 1984, p. 15. Thomas, *The Spanish Civil War*, pp. 360–1.

55. Stalin to Kaganovich, 18 August 1936. Kaganovich to Stalin, 18 August 1936. R. W. Davies, O. V. Khlevniuk, E. A. Rees, L. P. Kosheleva and L. A. Rogovaya (eds), *The Stalin–Kaganovich Correspondence, 1931–1936*, New Haven: Yale University Press, 2003, nos. 131, 132, p. 327.

56. Haslam, *The Soviet Union and the Struggle for Collective Security*, pp. 111–20. Carr, *Comintern and the Spanish Civil War*, pp. 23–5. Thomas, *The Spanish Civil War*, pp. 392–4, 440–3. Radosh *et al.*, *Spain Betrayed*, p. 22. W. G. Krivitsky, *Stalin's Secret Service: Memoirs of the First Soviet Master Spy to Defect*, New York: Enigma Books, 2000 edn, p. 70. D. Kowalsky, *La Unión Soviética y la Guerra Civil Española: una Revisión Crítica*, Barcelona: Crítica, 2003, pp. 195–8. G. Roberts, 'Soviet foreign policy and the Spanish Civil War, 1936–1939' in C. Leitz and D. J. Dunthorn (eds), *Spain in an International Context, 1936–1959*, Oxford: Berghahn Books, 1999, p. 87. On 6 September Stalin had told Kaganovich that 'it would be good to sell Mexico 50 high speed bombers, so that Mexico can immediately resell them to Spain' and he suggested sending them 20 Soviet pilots to perform combat functions in Spain and to train Spanish pilots to fly high-speed bombers. He also considered the sale via Mexico of 20,000 rifles, 1000 machine guns and about 20 million rounds of ammunition. Stalin to Kaganovich, 6 September 1936. Davies *et al.* (eds), *Stalin–Kaganovich Correspondence*, no. 159, p. 351.

57. R. Reese, *The Soviet Military Experience: A History of the Soviet Army, 1917–1991*, London, Routledge, 2000, p. 55.

58. Thomas, *The Spanish Civil War*, pp. 940–1, 943, 980–4. Broué and Témime, *Revolution and Civil War in Spain*, pp. 372–3. For NKVD activity in Spain see D. T. Cattell, *Communism and the Spanish Civil War*, Berkeley, CA: University of California Press, 1955, pp. 116–19; Haslam, *The Soviet Union and the Struggle for Collective Security*, pp. 116, 133–4; and Carr, *Comintern and the Spanish Civil War*, pp. 35–44.

59. Graham, *Spanish Republic at War*, p. 175. R. Miralles, *Juan Negrín: La República en Guerra*, Madrid: Ediciones Temas de Hoy, 2003, pp. 90–1.

60. Carr, *Comintern and the Spanish Civil War*, pp. 28–9. Cattell, *Communism and the Spanish Civil War*, pp. 98–115.

61. D. Smyth, 'We are with you: solidarity and self-interest in Soviet policy towards Republican Spain, 1936–1939' in Preston and Mackenzie (eds), *Republic Besieged*, p. 99.

62. Graham, *Spanish Republic at War*, pp. 210, 306–7.

63. Haslam, *The Soviet Union and the Struggle for Collective Security*, pp. 1–3. The Soviet collaboration with Weimar Germany under the Rapallo arrangements was certainly consistent with this approach since it sought to drive a wedge between the defeated and victorious imperialist powers of the First World War. Ibid., p. 3.

64. Ibid., pp. 6–51. See also J. A. Large, 'The origins of Soviet collective security policy 1930–1932', *Soviet Studies*, vol. 30, 1978.

65. For the origins and adoption of the popular front strategy of the Comintern see E. H. Carr, *Twilight of Comintern*, London: Macmillan, 1982, pp. 143–55, 405–17; Degras (ed.), *Communist International III*, pp. 355–65; and J. Haslam, 'The Comintern and the origins of the Popular Front, 1934–1935', *Historical Journal*, vol. 22, 1979.

66. Haslam, 'Soviet Russia and the Spanish problem', p. 77.

67. Haslam, *The Soviet Union and the Struggle for Collective security*, pp. 107–20. Carr, *Comintern and the Spanish Civil War*, pp. 12–28. Cattell, *Soviet Diplomacy*, 1957, pp. 14–52. Roberts, 'Soviet foreign policy', pp. 87–8. Smyth, 'We are with you', p. 99.

68. Smyth, 'We are with you', p. 100.

69. For the reorganisation of the Republican military forces in late 1936 and early 1937 see Carr, *Comintern and the Spanish Civil War*, pp. 29–30; Cattell, *Soviet Diplomacy*, pp. 111–15; and Thomas, *The Spanish Civil War*, pp. 542–50. For the need to neutralise bourgeois opposition and to end the revolutionary phase of the civil war see Joseph Stalin to Largo Caballero (Spanish Prime Minister), 21 December 1936 and Caballero to Stalin, 12 January 1937 in Carr, *Comintern and the Spanish Civil War*, pp. 86–88. See also Degras (ed.), *Communist International III*, pp. 396–400. For the destruction of the Spanish revolution see Cattell, *Communism and the Spanish Civil War*, pp. 120–63; Carr, *Comintern and the Spanish Civil War*, pp. 37–44; and Broué and Témime, *Revolution and War in Spain*, pp. 265–95.

70. Haslam, *The Soviet Union and the Struggle for Collective Security*, pp. 125–8, 142–57.

71. Soviet assistance to Nationalist China in 1937 was predicated on the same assumptions as those influencing their intervention in Spain. In this connection, *Le Journal de Moscou*, in an editorial during August 1937, re-emphasised the indivisibility of peace and referred to the close 'interdependence' of 'the events which are taking place in China and Spain'. Ibid., p. 143.

72. Carr, *Comintern and the Spanish Civil War*, p. 71.

73. Graham, *Spanish Republic at War*, pp. 393–4. The final consignment of Soviet aid reached Spain in January 1939 but it was already too late to make a difference.

74. Thomas, *The Spanish Civil War*, pp. 943–5, 952–3. J. Erickson, *The Soviet High Command: A Military-Political History*, London: Macmillan, 1962, pp. 429–31, 455–6. A. Boyd, *The Soviet Air Force since 1918*, London: MacDonald and Jane's, 1977, pp. 74–83. Colodny, *The Glory and the Tragedy*, pp. 32–3.

75. R. J. Jarymowycz, 'Jedi knights in the Kremlin: the Soviet military in the 1930s and the genesis of deep battle' in McKercher and Legault (eds), *Military Planning*, pp. 125–31. See also Reese, *The Soviet Military Experience*, p. 55.

76. D. M. Glantz, *Stumbling Colossus: The Red Army on the Eve of World War*, Lawrence, KS: University Press of Kansas, 1998, p. 185.

77. For an illuminating discussion of the issue of the Spanish gold see Á.Viñas, 'Gold, the Soviet Union and the Spanish Civil War', *European Studies Review*, vol. 9, 1979, pp. 105–28 and Whealey, 'Economic influence of the great powers', pp. 241–3.

78. Graham, *Spanish Republic at War*, pp. 150–1.

79. Howson, *Arms for Spain*, pp. 146–52.

80. Graham, *Spanish Republic at War*, p. 153.

81. See, for example, Frank Jr, 'The Spanish Civil War and the coming of the Second World War', pp. 396–7 and Salerno, *Vital Crossroads*, pp. 24–9. For the Spanish mercantile marine see Graham, *Spanish Republic at War*, p. 317.

82. Haslam, *The Soviet Union and the Struggle for Collective Security*, p. 146. See also Frank Jr, 'Politico-military deception', pp. 92–3.

83. Viñas, 'Gold', pp. 120–2. See also Graham, *Spanish Republic at War*, p. 369.

84. See Kowalsky, *La Unión Soviética y la Guerra Civil Española*, pp. 73–132.

85. T. G. Powell, *Mexico and the Spanish Civil War*, Albuquerque: University of New Mexico Press, 1981, pp. 58–105. F. E. Schuler, *Mexico between Hitler and Roosevelt: Mexican Foreign Relations in the Era of Lázaro Cardenas, 1934–1940*, Albuquerque: University of New Mexico Press, 1997, pp. 56–7.

86. Powell, *Mexico and the Spanish Civil War*, pp. 59–60.

3. THE NON-INTERVENTIONIST POWERS AND THE SPANISH CIVIL WAR, 1936–1939

1. Thomas, *The Spanish Civil War*. Viñas, 'Financing the Spanish Civil War', pp. 268–70.

2. For a discussion of the economic issues as they affected Britain see Harvey, *The Rio Tinto Company*, pp. 270–89 and Edwards, *The British Government and the Spanish Civil War*, pp. 64–100. See also C. E. Harvey, 'Politics and pyrites during the Spanish Civil War', *Economic History Review*, 2nd series, vol. 31, 1978.

3. For a discussion of the domestic considerations see R. J. Young, *In Command of France: French Foreign Policy and Military Planning, 1933–1940*, Cambridge MA: Harvard University Press, 1978, pp. 139–41; J. E. Dreifort, *Yvon Delbos at the Quai d'Orsay: French Foreign Policy during the Popular Front 1936–1938*, Lawrence, KS: University Press of Kansas, 1973, pp. 38–43; D. Carlton, 'Eden, Blum and the origins of non-intervention', *Journal of Contemporary History*, vol. 6, 1971, pp. 46–7; and N. Haywood Hunt, 'The French Radicals, Spain and the emergence of appeasement' in M. S. Alexander and

H. Graham (eds), *The French and Spanish Popular Fronts*, Cambridge: Cambridge University Press, 1989, pp. 38–49.

4. For a full discussion of Britain's role in the context of the French decision to adopt a policy of non-intervention see Edwards, *The British Government and the Spanish Civil War*, pp. 1–37; Dreifort, *Yvon Delbos*, pp. 35–8, 43–54; M. Thomas, *Britain, France and Appeasement: Anglo-French Relations in the Popular Front Era*, Oxford: Berg Press, 1996, pp. 89–93; Carlton, 'Eden Blum', pp. 40–55; G. A. Stone, 'Britain, non-intervention and the Spanish Civil War', *European Studies Review*, vol. 9, 1979, pp. 129–49; G. Warner, 'France and non-intervention in Spain, July–August 1936', *International Affairs*, vol. 38, 1962, pp. 204–5, 212–15, 218–20; and E. Moradiellos, 'British political strategy in the face of the military rising of 1936 in Spain', *Contemporary European History*, vol. 1, 1992, pp. 123–37.

5. J. Néré, *The Foreign Policy of France from 1914 to 1945*, London: Routledge and Kegan Paul, 1975, p. 215. N. Jordan, *The Popular Front and Central Europe: The Dilemmas of French Impotence, 1918–1940*, Cambridge: Cambridge University Press, 1992, pp. 203–4.

6. Stone, 'Britain, non-intervention', pp. 139–45.

7. T. Jones, *A Diary with Letters, 1931–1950*, London: Oxford University Press, 1954, diary entry, 27 July 1936, p. 231.

8. Ibid., pp. 136–7. Little, *Malevolent Neutrality*, pp. 222–45. Moradiellos, 'Origins of British non-intervention', pp. 347–61.

9. Chatfield Papers CHT/3/1, located at the Greenwich Naval Museum. Simon Papers MSS.7 diary entry, 5 February 1938, located at the Bodleian Library, Oxford. L. Pratt, *East of Malta, West of Suez: Britain's Mediterranean Crisis 1936–1939*, Cambridge: Cambridge University Press, 1975, n35, p. 43. S. Roskill, *Naval Policy Between the Wars II: The Period of Reluctant Rearmament 1930–1939*, London: Collins, 1976, p. 374. Thomas, *The Spanish Civil War*, p. 258.

10. For Vansittart's conversion see Stone, 'Sir Robert Vansittart and Spain', pp. 144–6.

11. CAB27/624 FP(36) 35th meeting, 23 January 1939. Smyth, 'We are with you', p. 105.

12. Stone, 'Britain, non-intervention', pp. 139–41. Little, *Malevolent Neutrality*, pp. 244–5.

13. See, for example, T. Buchanan, *The British Labour Movement and the Spanish Civil War*, Cambridge: Cambridge University Press, 1991. Buchanan has shown how the British labour movement itself was divided over the issue of intervention in Spain arguing convincingly that trade union leaders supported non-intervention to maintain the unity of their members.

14. Dreifort, *Yvon Delbos*, pp. 52–3. For the immediate impact of Blum's speech see *The Times*, 4, 5 and 7 September 1936. A month earlier, at Sarlat, Blum had declared to his constituents: 'At no cost must a new ideological crusade

materialise in Europe, a crusade which would inevitably lead to war'. Warner, 'France and non-intervention', p. 207.

15. For the Foreign Office view see minutes by Sir Orme Sargent, Cadogan and Mounsey, 12–13 August 1936. DBFP, 2nd series, vol. XVII, no. 84 and n1, pp. 90–1. For Eden's view see his conversation with Arthur Grenwood, Deputy Leader of the Labour Party, 19 August 1936. FO371/20534 W9331/62/41. See also Lord Avon, *The Eden Memoirs: Facing the Dictators*, London: Cassell, 1962, p. 463 and Lord Halifax, *Fulness of Days*, London: Collins, 1957, p. 192.

16. Franco-British efforts to reach a general settlement between March and August 1936 are well documented in W. N. Medlicott, *Britain and Germany: the Search for Agreement 1930–1937*, London: Athlone, 1969, pp. 25–30.

17. British efforts to appease Germany and Italy, and especially the latter, in the context of the Spanish Civil War provide the theme of the author's unpublished MA dissertation, *Britain and the Spanish Civil War 1936–1939: A Study in Appeasment*, University of Sussex, 1971.

18. CAB24/264 CP 234(36) CID 1259-B (COS 509) 'Western Mediterranean – Situation Arising from the Spanish Civil War', 24 August 1936. CA5/9 478-C (Also CID 1457-B and COS 750) 'The Spanish Civil War: Position in the Straits of Gibraltar', 20 July 1938. CAB 53/45 COS 843 'European Appreciation, 1939–1940', 20 February 1939.

19. See memorandum by Lord Cranborne and minutes by Eden and Sir George Mounsey, 21 July 1937. FO371/21298 W14857/1/41. See also Edwards, *The British Government and the Spanish Civil War*, pp. 190–1.

20. Young, *In Command of France*, pp. 136–9 and nn22 and 25, p. 286.

21. P. Jackson, 'French strategy and the Spanish Civil War' in Leitz and Dunthorn (eds), *Spain in an International Context*, pp. 60–1.

22. Jordan, *The Popular Front*, pp. 208–9.

23. Eleventh session of the Comité Permanent de la Défense Nationale, 15 March 1938. A. Adamthwaite (ed.), *The Making of the Second World War*, London: Allen and Unwin, 1977, no. 46, p. 182.

24. Stone, 'Britain, non-intervention', pp. 138, 144.

25. Ibid., p. 136.

26. For the Bérard–Jordana Agreement see A. Adamthwaite, *France and the Coming of the Second World War*, London: Frank Cass, 1977, pp. 261–2 and G. A. Stone, 'Britain, France and Franco's Spain in the aftermath of the Spanish Civil War', *Diplomacy and Statecraft*, vol. 6, 1995, pp. 377–9.

27. Edwards, *The British Government and the Spanish Civil War*, pp. 208–9. For the Labour and Liberal parties' attitudes towards the civil war in Spain and those of the smaller parties on the Left – the Communist Party and the Independent Labour Party – see T. Buchanan, *Britain and the Spanish Civil War*, Cambridge: Cambridge University Press, 1997, pp. 69–85.

28. CAB55/15 AFC(39)1 JP379 'Anglo-French Staff Conversations 1939: British Strategical Memorandum', 14 March 1939.

29. SHAT (Service Historique de l 'Armée de Terre) 7N2757. Le Général, Chef d'État-Major Général de la Défense Nationale: 'Extrait de la note au sujet des conséquences stratégiques d'un succès du Général Franco', 15 March 1938.

30. Jackson, 'French strategy and the Spanish Civil War', p. 55.

31. C. E. Harvey, 'Politics and pyrites during the Spanish Civil War', *Economic History Review*, 2nd series, vol. 31, 1978, pp. 99–100. See also, E. Moradiellos, *La Perfida de Albion: El Gobierno Británico y la Guerra Civil Española*, Madrid: Siglo XXI de España Editores, 1996, pp. 210–20 and J. L. N. Hernández, 'La sublevación y la improvisación de una política exterior de guerra, 1936–1939' in Tusell *et al.* (eds), *La Política Exterior de España*, pp. 292–3.

32. Harvey, *The Rio Tinto Company*, pp. 285–6.

33. SHAT 7N2758: 'Etudes: Espagne: Enseignements de la guerre d'Espagne', March 1938.

34. P. Jackson, *France and the Nazi Menace: Intelligence and Policy Making, 1933–1940*, Oxford: Oxford University Press, 2000, p. 344.

35. A. D. Harvey, 'The Spanish Civil War as seen by British officers', *RUSI Journal*, August 1996, pp. 65–7.

36. Sullivan, 'Fascist Italy's military involvement', p. 718.

37. Edwards, *The British Government and the Spanish Civil War*, pp. 15–39, 172–5. Thomas, *The Spanish Civil War*, pp. 344–5, 387–9, 825. Dreifort, *Yvon Delbos*, pp. 37–54. D. Smyth, *Diplomacy and Strategy of Survival: British Policy and Franco's Spain, 1940–1941*, Cambridge: Cambridge University Press, 1986, pp. 12–13.

38. A. Adamthwaite, 'France and the coming of the Second World War' in W. J. Mommsen and L. Kettenacker (eds), *The Fascist Challenge and the Policy of Appeasement*, London: Allen and Unwin, 1983, p. 250.

39. G. A. Stone, 'Britain, France and the Spanish problem, 1936–1939' in D. Richardson and G. Stone (eds), *Decisions and Diplomacy: Essays in Twentieth Century International History*, London: Routledge, 1995, pp. 131–2.

40. Phipps to Halifax, 16 July 1938. Phipps Papers, PHPP 1/20, located at the Churchill College Archive Centre, Cambridge. Note of interview with Lord Halifax at the Foreign Office, 29 July 1938. Cecil of Chelwood Papers MSS 51084, located at the British Library.

41. Minute by Orme Sargent of his meeting with Roger Cambon, French Chargé d'Affaires at London, 12 October 1937. Phipps Papers, PHPP 1/19. The idea of using Minorca as a *gage* was revived momentarily in January 1939. See P. Stafford, 'The Chamberlain–Halifax visit to Rome – a reappraisal', *English Historical Review*, vol. 97, 1983, p. 93.

42. Stone, 'Britain, non-intervention', p. 135.

43. Moradiellos, *El Reñidero de Europa*, p. 258.

44. Salerno, *Vital Crossroads*, pp. 46–7, 57–8. Jackson, 'French strategy and the Spanish Civil War', pp. 56, 69–71. Stafford, 'The Chamberlain–Halifax visit to Rome', p. 91. Frank Jr, 'The Spanish Civil War', p. 395.

45. D. C. Watt, 'Britain, France and the Italian problem, 1937–1939' in Colloques Franco-Britanniques, *Les Relations Franco-Britanniques de 1935 à 1939*, Paris: Éditions du Centre National de la Recherche Scientifique, 1975, pp. 287–90. R. Girault, 'La décision gouvernementale en politique extérieure' in R. Rémond and J. Bourdin (eds), *Edouard Daladier: Chef de Gouvernement, Avril 1938–Septembre 1939*, Paris: Presses de la Fondation des Sciences Politiques, 1977, pp. 213–14, 220.

46. Jackson, 'French strategy and the Spanish Civil War', pp. 67–8.

47. Stone, 'From entente to alliance', pp. 195–6.

48. See D. C. Watt, 'The initiation of the negotiations leading to the Nazi–Soviet Pact: a historical problem', in C. Abramsky (ed.), *Essays in Honour of E. H. Carr*, London: Macmillan, 1974, p. 155.

49. J. Degras (ed.), *Soviet Documents on Foreign Policy Volume III 1933–1941*, London: Oxford University Press, 1953, p. 322.

50. Roberts, 'Soviet foreign policy and the Spanish Civil War', p. 97.

51. CAB27/625 FP(36) 47th meeting, 16 May 1939.

52. FRUS, 1936, vol. II, pp. 471, 475–6. Little, *Malevolent Neutrality*, pp. 233–7. Puzzo, *Spain and the Great Powers*, pp. 150–3. R. P. Traina, *American Diplomacy and the Spanish Civil War*, Bloomington. IN: Indiana University Press, 1968, pp. 50–2, 54–6. R. A. Divine, *The Illusion of Neutrality*, Chicago: Chicago University Press, 1962, pp. 168–9. R. Dallek, *Franklin D. Roosevelt and American Foreign Policy, 1932–1945*, New York: Oxford University Press, 1979, p. 127. W. S. Cole, *Roosevelt and the Isolationists, 1932–1945*, Lincoln, NE: University of Nebraska Press, 1983, p. 224. C. Hull, *The Memoirs of Cordell Hull Vol. I*, London: Hodder and Stoughton, 1948, pp. 478–9.

53. H. Blumenthal, *Illusion and Reality in Franco-American Diplomacy, 1914–1945*, Baton Rouge, LA: Louisiana State University Press, 1986, p. 220.

54. Alpert, *A New International History*, p. 110. Howson, *Arms for Spain*, pp. 167–77.

55. Alpert, *A New International History*, p. 111. Howson, *Arms for Spain*, pp. 178–85. Traina, *American Diplomacy*, pp. 84–95. Puzzo, *Spain and the Great Powers*, pp. 154–9. Cole, *Roosevelt and the Isolationists*, pp. 225–7. Divine, *Illusion of Neutrality*, pp. 169–71.

56. FRUS, 1937, vol. I, pp. 344–6, 353–5. Cole, *Roosevelt and the Isolationists*, pp. 228–30. Divine, *Illusion of Neutrality*, p. 223. Dallek, *Roosevelt and American Foreign Policy*, pp. 140–3.

57. FRUS, 1938, Vol. I, pp. 194–5. Traina, *American Diplomacy*, pp. 131–6, 138–41. Cole, *Roosevelt and the Isolationists*, pp. 235–7. Dallek, *Roosevelt and American Foreign Policy*, pp. 160–1. Divine, *Illusion of Neutrality*, pp. 224–7.

58. D. Tierney, 'Franklin D. Roosevelt and covert aid to the Loyalists in the Spanish Civil War, 1936–1939', *Journal of Contemporary History*, vol. 39, 2004, p. 310.

59. Ibid., pp. 299–313. For Bullitt's opposition see O. H. Bullitt (ed.), *For the President Personal and Secret: Correspondence between Franklin D. Roosevelt and William C. Bullitt*, London: Andre Deutsch, 1973, pp. 274–6.

60. Dallek, *Roosevelt and American Foreign Policy*, pp. 177–8. Traina, *American Diplomacy*, pp. 150–6.
61. Dallek, *Roosevelt and American Foreign Policy*, pp. 179–80. Traina, *American Diplomacy*, pp. 205–13. Cole, *Roosevelt and the Isolationists*, pp. 237–8.
62. Dallek, *Roosevelt and American Foreign Policy*, p. 180. Cole, *Roosevelt and the Isolationists*, p. 238.
63. Little, *Malevolent Neutrality*, pp. 223–4. F. B. Pike, 'The background to the civil war in Spain and the U.S. response to the war' in M. Falcoff and F. B. Pike (eds), *The Spanish Civil War, 1936–1939: American Hemispheric Perspectives*, Lincoln, NE: University of Nebraska Press, 1982, p. 29.
64. Little, *Malevolent Neutrality*, p. 228.
65. Ibid., pp. 234–8.
66. Puzzo, *Spain and the Great Powers*, p. 35.
67. Little, *Malevolent Neutrality*, pp. 249–50. FRUS, 1936, vol. II, pp. 600–5.
68. Traina, *American Diplomacy*, p. 229.
69. Traina, *American Diplomacy*, pp. 179–85. Puzzo, *Spain and the Great Powers*, pp. 165–6. Dallek, *Roosevelt and American Foreign Policy*, p. 142. Pike, 'The Spanish background', p. 28. A. Guttmann, *The Wound in the Heart: America and the Spanish Civil War*, New York: Free Press of Glencoe, 1962, pp. 29–52.
70. Traina, *American Diplomacy*, pp. 227–8, 236. Divine, *Illusion of Neutrality*, p. 223. Dallek, *Roosevelt and American Foreign Policy*, pp. 143, 161.
71. Pike, 'The Spanish background', pp. 29–30.
72. C. B. Burdick, 'The American military attachés in the Spanish Civil War, 1936–1939', *Militärgeschichtliche Mitteilungen*, vol. 46, 1989.
73. Thomas, *The Spanish Civil War*, p. 576.
74. R. Whealey, 'How Franco financed his war – reconsidered', *Journal of Contemporary History*, vol. 12, 1977, pp. 133–152.

4. THE GREAT POWERS AND SPANISH CIVIL WAR DIPLOMACY, 1936–1939

1. For details of the League's greatly modified role in the Spanish Civil War see P. M. van der Esch, *Prelude to War: The International Repercussions of the Spanish Civil War 1936–1939*, The Hague: Martinus Nijhoff, 1951, pp. 62–71, 106–17 and R. Veatch, 'The League of Nations and the Spanish Civil War, 1936–1939', *European History Quarterly*, vol. 20, 1990. For British attitudes see, for example, Eden to Viscount Cecil, 17 September 1936. Cecil of Chelwood Papers, MSS 51083.
2. Edwards, *The British Government and the Spanish Civil War*, app. D, pp. 222–3.
3. Ibid., pp. 40–1. N. J. Padelford, *International Law and Diplomacy in the Spanish Civil Strife*, New York: Macmillan, 1939, p. 60.

4. One source for this view was Ivan Maiskii, the Soviet Ambassador in London during the 1930s, who continued to insist that the British Government invented non-intervention in Spain. He wrote later: 'the idea of non-intervention in Spanish affairs ... was born in the depths of the Britsh Foreign Office immediately after the start of Franco's rebellion'. I. Maisky, *Spanish Notebooks*, London: Hutchinson, 1966, p. 27.

5. Stone, 'Britain, France and the Spanish problem', pp. 130–2.

6. Eden to Sir George Clerk, British Ambassador at Paris, 24 August 1936. DBFP, 2nd series, vol. XVII, no. 128, p. 161.

7. Meeting of the British Cabinet Foreign Policy Committee, 25 August 1936. CAB27/622 FP(36) 5th meeting.

8. For Portuguese intransigence in refusing to join the Non-Intervention Committee and Franco–British pressure see Stone, *The Oldest Ally*, pp. 22–7.

9. Note by Roger Makins on the work of the Non-Intervention Committee, 10 September 1936. DBFP, 2nd series, vol. XVII, no. 182, pp. 252–3.

10. For details of these sub-committees see Edwards, *The British Government and the Spanish Civil War*, app. E, pp. 224–5.

11. Stenographic notes of the first meeting of the Non-Intervention Committee, 9 September 1936. DBFP, 2nd series, vol. XVII, no. 178, p. 233.

12. Note by Walter Roberts, Head of the League of Nations and Western Department, 3 October 1936. DBFP, 2nd series, vol. XVII, no. 265, p. 363.

13. Samuel Cahan, Soviet Chargé d'Affaires at London, to Plymouth, 7 October 1936. FO371/20579 W13242/9549/41. DDF, 2nd series, vol III, no. 321, pp. 479–80. Cattell, *Soviet Diplomacy*, p. 43.

14. NIS (36) 8th meeting, 28 October 1936. FO849/1 and the Hemming Papers, located at the Bodleian Library. The Hemming collection contains the stenographic minutes for all of the meetings of the Non-Intervention Committee and the Chairman's Sub-Committee. See also Stone, *The Oldest Ally*, pp. 29–32.

15. DBFP, 2nd series, vol. XVII, nos 308, 328, pp. 438–9, 465–7.

16. NIS (36) 7th meeting, 23 October 1936. FO849/1 and Hemming Papers. See also Maisky, *Spanish Notebooks*, p. 56 and J. Alvarez del Vayo, *Freedom's Battle*, London: Heinemann, 1940, pp. 75–6. Julio Alvarez del Vayo was the Spanish Republic's Foreign Minister during the civil war.

17. NIS (36) 9th and 10th meetings. FO849/1 and Hemming Papers.

18. NIS (C) (36) 6th meeting. FO849/27 and Hemming Papers.

19. NIS (C) (36) 8th meeting. NIS (36) 11th and 12th meetings. FO849/27, FO849/1 and Hemming Papers. See also DBFP, 2nd series, vol. XVII, nos 347, 427, pp. 493–4, 615–26.

20. For the Republican and Nationalist replies see DBFP, 2nd series, vol. XVII, nos 491, 492, pp. 706–8.

21. For details of the mediation proposal see DBFP, 2nd series, vol. XVII, nos 417, 434, 443, pp. 600–1, 636, 647–8. DDF, 2nd series, vol. IV, no. 39, pp. 53–4; and DGFP, series D, vol. III, nos 147, 150, 152, pp. 147–8, 163–6.

See also R. Miralles, 'Las iniciativas diplomáticas de la Segunda República durante la guerra civil, 1936–1939' in Tusell *et al.* (eds), *La Política Exterior de España*, pp. 251–2.

22. The Condor Legion, 'a well-led experimental tank and aircraft unit', consisted of about 100 fighters and bombers supported by anti-aircraft and anti-tank units and two armoured units, of four tank companies, of four tanks each. Thomas, *The Spanish Civil War*, pp. 469, 977. See also Whealey, *Hitler and Spain*, pp. 101–2. Thousands more Italian volunteers would be sent to Spain during January 1937. In this connection, Ciano told Ulrich von Hassell, the German Ambassador at Rome, on 13 January, that on the following day an additional 4000 men would be shipped to Spain and that a new division, or 9000 combat troops plus 4000 other personnel, would be ready to leave between 22 and 24 January 1937. DGFP, series D, vol. III, no. 198, p. 221. According to British intelligence sources, between 1 and 7 January 1937 two contingents of Italian troops, each 4000 strong, arrived in Spain. DBFP, 2nd series, vol. XVIII, no. 25, pp. 29–30.

23. NIS (36) 14th meeting. FO849/1 and Hemming Papers.

24. Memorandum by Eden on Spain, 8 January 1937. CAB24/267 CP 6(37).

25. DBFP, 2nd series, vol. XVIII, no. 33, pp. 42–51. See also the Templewood Papers IX: 3 located at Cambridge University Library; Roskill, *Naval Policy between the Wars II*, pp. 376–7; and Edwards, *The British Government and the Spanish Civil War*, pp. 110–12.

26. For detail of Portuguese intransigence see Stone, *The Oldest Ally*, pp. 35–9.

27. For full details of the Non-Intervention Land and Sea Control Scheme see *Parliamentary Papers 1936–1937*, vol. XXVIII, cmd. 5399.

28. Miralles, 'Las iniciativas diplomáticas', pp. 252–3. According to Miralles, the Republicans were prepared to accept non-intervention only if it was truly effective and when it was shown not to be so they sought to end non-intervention by denouncing Germany and Italy and working to obtain the diplomatic support of Britain and France, all to no avail. Ibid., p. 248.

29. Vansittart to Eden, 11 May 1937. Foreign Office Telegram to Paris, Berlin, Rome, Moscow and Lisbon. FO371/21333 W8913/7/41.

30. Foreign Office minute by Mounsey with marginal comments by Vansittart, 3 June 1937. FO371/21334 W10518/7/41. No international enquiry was ever held on the bombing of Guernica though the Basque government-in-exile in 1945 attempted to bring a case against Germany at the Nuremberg War Crimes Tribunal. The attempt was unsuccessful because no events which occurred before September 1939 were taken into account at Nuremberg. Thomas, *The Spanish Civil War*, pp. 624–9.

31. Minutes by Mounsey, Vansittart and Eden, 28 April–7 May 1937. Foreign Office telegram to Paris, Berlin, Rome, Lisbon and Moscow, 11 May 1937. FO371/21333 W9306/7/41. P. Preston, *¡Comrades!: Portraits from the Spanish Civil War*, London: HarperCollins, 1999, pp. 177–8. See also J. M. Reverte, *La Batalla del Ebro*, Barcelona: Crítica, 2003, p. 4. Eden apparently asked

Besteiro to keep their meeting unofficial and there is no record in the Foreign Office files at The National Archives.

32. DBFP, 2nd series, vol. XVIII, nos 486, 496, 544,. pp. 740–1, 750–1, 810–11.

33. Thomas, *The Spanish Civil War*, p. 685. Thomas claims that the aircraft were piloted by Russian airmen. A few days previously, the Italian auxiliary vessel *Barletta* had been hit during Spanish Republican bombing raids on Palma, Majorca; six Italian officers were killed. Earlier in May, a British destroyer, *Hunter*, had been damaged by a German-laid mine.

34. Ibid., pp. 685–6. J. L. Heinemann, *Hitler's First Foreign Minister: Constantin Freiherr von Neurath, Diplomat and Statesman*, Berkeley, CA: University of California Press, 1979, pp. 150–1. See also the unpublished Dalton Diaries, 1.18, diary entry, 24 June 1937, recording a conversation between Hugh Dalton of the Labour Party and Vansittart. According to Vansittart, Hitler had been keeping a vigil alone with the dead of the *Deutschland*. The Dalton Diaries are located at the Library of the London School of Economics and Political Science.

35. Neurath to the German Embassy at London, 30 May 1937. Memorandum by an Official of Neurath's Secretariat, 31 May 1937. DGFP, series D, vol. III, nos 268, 272, pp. 297, 299–300. Initially, the Germans had tried to persuade the Italians to remain in the Non-Intervention Committee but they refused on the grounds that it would be interpreted internationally as evidence of a divergence of views between Berlin and Rome which was not the case.

36. Wolfgang Krauel, German Consul at Geneva, to the German Foreign Ministry, 1 June 1937. DGFP, series D, vol. III, no. 275, p. 303.

37. Robert Bingham, United States Ambassador at London, to Cordell Hull, 1 June 1937. FRUS, 1937, vol. I, p. 318. Eden told Bingham that the Soviet Government 'wanted the British to pull its chestnuts out of the fire and would not be disturbed if Germany was at war with England and France leaving Russia with a comparatively free hand on the other side'.

38. Neurath to the German Embassies at London, Paris and Rome, 19 June 1937. DGFP, series D, vol. III, pp. 339, 354–6. Vansittart told Dalton on 24 June that he was extremely doubtful whether any torpedo had been fired at the *Leipzig* and the Admiralty shared his opinion. Dalton Diaries, 1.18, diary entry, 24 June 1937.

39. Joachim von Ribbentrop, German Ambassador at London, to the German Foreign Ministry, 19 June 1937. DGFP, series D, vol. III, no. 341, pp. 356–8.

40. *Hansard Parliamentary Debates*, 5th Series, HC, vol. 325, cc. 1548–9.

41. CAB23/88 CM 25(37) and CM 26(37).

42. DGFP, series D, vol. III, no. 354, p. 369. DBFP, 2nd series, vol. XVIII, nos 633, 636, 638, 641, pp. 917, 920–1, 924–5, 928–9. With regard to the proposed visit of Neurath to London, Eden had intended to raise 'several questions arising out of the Spanish problem' and also to carry out 'a *tour d'horizon* of the general European situation'. DBFP, 2nd series, vol. XVIII, no. 595, p. 871.

43. Eden to Sir Nevile Henderson, British Ambassador at Berlin, 30 June 1937. DBFP, 2nd series, vol. XVIII, no. 669, pp. 955–6.

44. DBFP, 2nd series, vol. XVIII, nos 655, 656, pp. 938–9. DDF, 2nd series, vol. VI, no. 136, p. 213. *Dez Anos de Política Externa, 1936–1947: A Nação Portuguesa e a Segunda Guerra Mundial*, vol. IV, no. 1124, pp. 453–4. Hereafter DAPE. See also F. Nogueira, *Salazar III: As Grandes Crises (1936–1945)*, Porto: Livraria Civilização, 1983, p. 106.

45. Memorandum by Prince Otto von Bismarck, Deputy Director of the Political Department of the German Foreign Ministry, 29 June 1937. DGFP, series D, vol. III, no. 367, pp. 380–1.

46. DGFP, series D, vol. III, nos 361, 362, pp. 374–5. FO371/21336 W13262/7/41. DAPE, vol. IV, nos 1134, 1140, pp. 460–2, 469–72.

47. Sir Eric Phipps, British Ambassador at Paris, to the Foreign Office, 1–3 July 1937. FO371/21339 W12645/W12652/W12735/7/41 and FO371/21340 W12787/7/41.

48. William Bullitt, United States Ambassador at Paris, to Secretary of State Cordell Hull, 15 July 1937. FRUS, 1937, vol. II, pp. 360–1.

49. NIS (36) 24th and 25th meetings, 9 July 1937. FO849/1 and Hemming Papers. See also FO371/21389 W13547/169/41 and FO371/21390 W16478/169/41.

50. Foreign Office to Sir Charles Wingfield, British Ambassador at Lisbon, 14 July 1937. FO371/23142 W13561/7/41.

51. Minute by Lord Cranborne, Parliamentary Under Secretary of State for Foreign Affairs, 17 July 1937. FO371/21341 W13250/7/41.

52. R. M. Salerno, 'Britain, France and the emerging Italian threat' in M. S. Alexander and W. J. Philpott (eds), *Anglo-French Defence Relations between the Wars*, London: Palgrave Macmillan, 2002, p. 78.

53. Eden to Phipps, 15 May 1937. DBFP, 2nd series, vol. XVIII, no. 499, p. 753. See also DAPE, vol. IV, nos 976, 980, pp. 294, 298.

54. See, for example, the German and Portuguese replies. DBFP, 2nd series, vol. XVIII, nos 522, 525, pp. 785–6, 791–2. See also Moradiellos, *La Perfidia Albión*, pp. 172–3.

55. See DGFP, series D, vol. III, nos 122, 123, 124, 125, 131, pp. 132–4, 140–1. Following recognition of Franco, Hitler ordered that henceforth the belligerents in the Spanish Civil War be designated as the 'Spanish Nationalist Government' and the 'Spanish Bolshevists' with the clear implication that the latter were illegitimate. Ibid., no. 127, pp. 136–7.

56. CAB23/86 CM 64(36). Edwards, *The British Government and the Spanish Civil War*, pp. 184–6. Thomas, *Britain, France and Appeasement*, pp. 101–2.

57. Minutes by Beckett (Foreign Office Legal Adviser), Mounsey, Vansittart and Eden, 7–10 April 1937. FO371/21352 W6481/23/41. CAB23/88 CM (37), 11 April 1937. See also J. Cable, *The Royal Navy and the Siege of Bilbao*, Cambridge: Cambridge University Press, 1979, pp. 58–61 and Alpert, *A New International History*, pp. 119–24.

58. Minutes by Cranborne, Plymouth, Vansittart and Eden, 30 June–1 July 1937. FO 371/21294 W11685/1/41. Roskill, *Navy Policy between the Wars, II*, pp. 380–1.

59. Sir Henry Chilton, British Ambassador at Hendaye, to Mounsey, 14 June 1937. FO371/21295 W11819/1/41. DBFP, 2nd series, vol. XVIII, no. 664, pp. 948–9. See also CAB27/622 FP(36) 15th meeting, 28 June 1937; DAPE, vol. IV, no. 1145, pp. 475–8; and FRUS, 1937, vol. I, p. 354.

60. For details of the Italian submarine attacks see Coverdale, *Italian Intervention in the Spanish Civil War*, pp. 306–8, 311–13 and Salerno, 'The emerging Italian threat', pp. 79–81. See also Muggeridge (ed.), *Ciano's Hidden Diary 1937–1938*, diary entries 23 and 31 August, 2 and 4 September, pp. 3, 6–9.

61. Ciano commented on the exclusion of Soviet Russia as follows: 'From suspected pirates to policemen of the Mediterranean and the Russians whose ships we were sinking, excluded'. Muggeridge (ed.), *Ciano's Hidden Diary 1937–1938*, diary entry, 21 September 1937, p. 17.

62. For details of the Nyon Conference and its aftermath see Roskill, *Naval Policy between the Wars, II*, pp. 383–7; P. Gretton, 'The Nyon Conference – the Naval aspect', *English Historical Review*, vol. 90, 1975, pp. 103–12; W. C. Mills, 'The Nyon Conference: Neville Chamberlain, Anthony Eden, and the appeasement of Italy in 1937', *International History Review*, vol. 16, 1993, pp. 1–22; and Salerno, *Vital Crossroads*, pp. 24–9. For Delbos' initiative see Dreifort, *Yvon Delbos*, pp. 62–4.

63. Salerno, *Vital Crossroads*, pp. 28–9. Salerno, 'The emerging Italian threat', pp. 80–1.

64. Alpert, *A New International History*, p. 145.

65. In his response to the victory at Santander Mussolini had stated: 'I am particularly glad that during ten days of hard fighting the Italian legionary troops have made a valiant contribution to the splendid victory of Santander. ... This comradeship of arms – now so close – is a guarantee of the final victory which will liberate Spain and the Mediterranean from all threats to the civilisation we share'. *The Times*, 29 August 1937.

66. CAB23/89 CM 35(37). By this time it was apparent that in British governing circles there was a growing divergence of opinion concerning relations with Italy. The weight of this opinion, in deference to the importance they attached to the Italian end of the general appeasement policy, tended towards giving Mussolini the benefit of the doubt over Spain and therefore the adoption of a more critical view of French policy. In this respect, Vansittart and Eden were in a small minority who showed a greater sympathy for the French on the Spanish issue. See Stone, 'Britain, France and the Spanish problem', pp. 137–9 and Stone, 'Sir Robert Vansittart and Spain', pp. 144–6.

67. CAB24/271 CP 234(37). See also *Parliamentary Papers 1936–1937*, vol. XXIX, cmd. 5570.

68. CAB23/89 CM 37 (37) 13 October 1937. Minute by Orme Sargent, 12 October 1937, Phipps Papers, PHPP1/19. J. Harvey (ed.), *The Diplomatic*

Diaries of Oliver Harvey, 1937–1940, London: Collins, 1970, diary entry, 5 October 1937, pp. 49–50. Oliver Harvey was Private Secretary to both Eden and his successor, Lord Halifax. Salerno, *Vital Crossroads*, p. 32.

69. NIS (C) (36) 64th meeting, 16 October 1937. FO849/28 and Hemming Papers.

70. NIS (C) (36) 65th meeting, 19 October 1937. FO849/29 and Hemming Papers. See also Harvey (ed.), *Diplomatic Diaries*, diary entry, 20 October 1937, pp. 52–3. The Soviets had no faith that the Italians would withdraw their troops in substantial numbers. See Edwards, *The British Government and the Spanish Civil War*, pp. 160–2.

71. Graham, *Spanish Republic at War*, p. 322. According to a Comintern report of 25 November 1937, Franco's Navy had more cruisers and more submarines in good repair while the Republican Navy had a much larger number of destroyers. Radosh *et al.*, *Spain Betrayed*, no. 80, p. 505.

72. NIS (C) (36) 70th meeting, 2 November 1937. FO849/29 and Hemming Papers. NIS (36) 28th meeting , 4 November 1937. FO849/1 and Hemming Papers.

73. CA23/90 CM 42(37) 17 November 1937. FO371/21349 W21300/7/41.

74. Eden to Sir Walford Selby, British Ambassador at Lisbon, 17 December 1937. FO371/21350 W22336/7/41.

75. NIC (C) (36) 77th meeting, 11 January 1938. FO849/29 and Hemming Papers.

76. For example, if the basic figure was 15,000 and the commissions reported that one side had 60,000 and the other side 40,000 then the latter would have to evacuate 15,000 while the former would have to evacuate 22,500.

77. NIS (C) (36) 83rd meeting, 31 March 1938. FO849/29 and Hemming Papers.

78. Foreign Office to Phipps, 4 March 1938. FO371/22638 W2827/83/41.

79. Salerno, *Vital Crossroads*, pp. 43–6. Graham, *Spanish Republic at War*, p. 351.

80. Graham, *Spanish Republic at War*, pp. 356–7.

81. Ibid., p. 43. Salerno, 'The emerging Italian threat', p. 84. Thomas, *The Spanish Civil War*, pp. 804–5, 832. Salerno, *Vital Crossroads*, p. 56.

82. CAB24/276 CP 109(38). Salerno, *Vital Crossroads*, p. 53.

83. Veatch, 'The League of Nations and the Spanish Civil War', p. 200.

84. Foreign Office to the British Embassies at Berlin, Lisbon, Moscow, Paris and Rome, 23 May 1938. FO371/22645 W6641/83/41. See also DAPE, vol. V, no. 1636, pp. 301–2.

85. See Stone, 'The European great powers and the Spanish Civil War', pp. 222–3; Graham, *Spanish Republic at War*, pp. 367–8; and Moradiellos, *El Reñidero de Europa*, pp. 203–19.

86. NIS (36) 29th meeting, 5 July 1938. FO849/1 and Hemming Papers. See also *Parliamentary Papers 1937–1938*, vol. XXX, cmd. 5793.

87. Salerno, *Vital Crossroads*, p. 58.

88. See FO371/22646 W6977/W7165/W7195/W7196/83/41 and FO371/22647 W7679/83/41.

89. Armindo Monteiro, Portuguese Ambassador at London to António Salazar, Portuguese Prime Minister, 21 July 1938. DAPE, vol. V, nos 1691, 1703, pp. 335–7, 373–5.

90. António de Faria, Portuguese Chargé d'Affaires at London, to Salazar, 1 September 1938. DAPE, vol. V, no. 1743, pp. 429–32.

91. Foreign Office to Sir Robert Hodgson, British Special Agent at Burgos, 27 September 1938. FO371/22654 W12897/83/41. For details of Soviet objections see DAPE, vol. V, no. 1748 annex, p. 436.

92. Reverte, *La Batalla del Ebro*, p. 345. Moradiellos, *El Reñidero de Europa*, p. 34.

93. P. Stafford, 'The Chamberlain–Halifax visit to Rome: a reappraisal', *English Historical Review*, vol. 98, January 1983, p. 67.

94. 'Hemming Report', 17 November 1938. Hemming Papers. See also Hemming Diaries, diary entries, 21 and 22 November 1938. See also DGFP, series D, vol. III, no. 701, pp. 803–4. For the Negrín–Alba talks see Graham, *Spanish Republic at War*, p. 384.

95. See DGFP, series D, vol. III, nos 682, 686, 691, 692, 693, 700, pp. 769–71, 777–9, 784–89, 802. At this time, Hitler personally ruled out the sending of extra units to replenish the Condor Legion. Ibid., no. 697, p. 795. According to Kim Philby, reporter for *The Times* and secretly a spy for Soviet Russia, there was a steady flow each week of a hundred or so recruits from Lisbon to Seville for eventual training in the Spanish Foreign Legion. Hodgson to W. St. C. Roberts, Foreign Office, 23 November 1938. FO371/22657/84/41.

96. During January 2035 army officers and troops were despatched to Spain and in February another 1857. At the same time, 920 members of the Fascist militia also left for Spain and during March close to 5500 men were sent; the army accounting for 3776 and the militia for 1090. Coverdale, *Italian Intervention*, pp. 374, 381.

97. Foreign Office Memorandum (unsigned), 2 January 1939. Halifax to Phipps, 5 January 1939. FO371/24114 W312/W475/5/41.

98. 'The Visit to Rome of the Prime Minister and the Secretary of State for Foreign Affairs from January 11 to January 14, 1939'. CAB24/282 CP 8(39). See also Stafford, 'The Chamberlain–Halifax visit', p. 93.

99. For French support for an armistice and pressure on the Republicans to accept see R. Miralles, 'The international policy of the Second Republic during the Spanish Civil War' in Rein (ed.), *Spain and the Mediterranean*, p. 147.

100. Minute by Cadogan to Halifax, 18 January 1939. FO371/24115 W1464/5/41. CAB27/624 FP (36) 35th meeting, 23 January 1939. During the first two months of 1939 France opened its frontier with Spain again to allow into Catalonia Russian war material but it arrived too late to save the Spanish Republic. See Thomas, *The Spanish Civil War*, pp. 869, 871 and Edwards, *The British Government and the Spanish Civil War*, pp. 206–7.

101. See J. Tusell, *Franco en la Guerra Civil: Una Biografía Política*, Barcelona: Tusquets Editores, 1992, pp. 341–3.

102. Record of Conversations between British and French Ministers, 29–30 November 1937. DBFP, 2nd series, vol. XIX, no. 354, p. 614.
103. Halifax, *Fulness of Days*, p. 192.
104. Alpert, *A New International History*, p. 172.
105. Memorandum by Karl Schwendemann, Head of Political Division IIIa (Spain and Portugal) of the German Foreign Ministry, 3 December 1938. DGFP, series D, vol. III, no. 701, pp. 803–4.
106. Leitz, 'Nazi Germany and Francoist Spain', p. 132.
107. Roberts, 'Soviet foreign policy and the Spanish Civil War', p. 90.
108. See Graham, *Spanish Republic at War*, p. 321.

5. THE GREAT POWERS AND THE AFTERMATH OF THE SPANISH CIVIL WAR, MARCH–AUGUST 1939

1. DGFP, series D, vol. II, nos 622, 638, 641, 659, pp. 950–1, 969–70, 972–3, 991. See also Merkes, *Die Deutsche Politik*, p. 328. It is worth noting that Franco was having difficulties at this time in persuading the Third Reich to send a further large consignment of war material to assist in countering the Republican offensive on the Ebro which had commenced in July. Hitler insisted on linking arms supplies with progress on the Montana negotiations. See Ch. 2.
2. C. Leitz, *Nazi Germany and Neutral Europe during the Second World War*, Manchester: Manchester University Press, 2000, p. 116.
3. Eberhard von Stohrer, German Ambassador at Madrid, to the German Foreign Ministry, 27 March 1939. Ernst Freiherr von Weizsäcker, State Secretary, German Foreign Ministry, to the Madrid Embassy, 29 March 1939. Stohrer to the Foreign Ministry, 3 April 1939. DGFP, series D, vol. III, nos 767, 770, 776, pp. 880, 882, 888–9. For the protocol of Spain's adhesion to the Anti-Comintern Pact see Ibid., no. 768, p. 881.
4. Abendroth, *Hitler in der Spanischen Arena*, p. 231.
5. Coverdale, *Italian Intervention*, pp. 324–5.
6. Baron Oswald von Hoyningen-Huene, German Minister at Lisbon, to the German Foreign Ministry, 21 April 1939. DGFP, series D, vol. VI, no. 241, p. 301. Nicolás Franco was Spain's Ambassador at Lisbon.
7. Preston, *Franco*, pp. 325–6.
8. For the full text of the treaty see DGFP, series D, vol. III, no. 773, pp. 884–6.
9. See Leitz, *Economic Relations*, pp. 108–9.
10. Ibid., pp. 108–10.
11. Ibid., pp. 99–100. See also Leitz, *Nazi Germany and Neutral Europe*, pp. 117–18.
12. DGFP, series D, vol. VII, no. 329, p. 325.
13. Coverdale, *Italian Intervention*, pp. 407–8.

14. Sullivan, 'Fascist Italy's military involvement', pp. 711–12. Preston, 'Italy and Spain', p. 173.
15. Hans Georg von Mackensen, German Ambassador at Rome, to the German Foreign Ministry, 24 February 1939. DGFP, series D, vol. III, no. 744, pp. 854–5. Preston, *Franco*, p. 325.
16. Record of a Conversation between Göring and Mussolini in the presence of Ciano in Rome, 16 April 1939. DGFP, series D, vol. VI, no. 211, p. 261. For the treaty see Coverdale, *Italian Intervention*, pp. 413–14. While the Balearics and other Spanish bases are not explicitly stated in the treaty, Franco's Government pledged to adopt an attitude of benevolent neutrality and to put at Italy's disposal 'all facilities, the use of ports, of air-lines, of railways and roads'.
17. Conversation between Ciano and Ribbentrop at Milan, 6–7 May 1939. Muggeridge (ed.), *Ciano's Diplomatic Papers*, p. 285. The German Foreign Minister was responding to a memorandum drawn up by Mussolini.
18. Stohrer to the German Foreign Ministry, 13 March 1939. DGFP, series D, vol. III, no. 755, p. 865.
19. Preston, *Franco*, pp. 329–30.
20. A. Randle-Elliott, 'Spain after civil war', *Foreign Policy Reports*, vol. 16, 1940, p. 67. K. Duff 'Italy' and 'Germany' in A. and V. Toynbee (eds), *Survey of International Affairs, 1939–1946: The Eve of War 1939*, London: Oxford University Press, 1958, pp. 292–3, 358.
21. Salerno, *Vital Crossroads*, p. 126.
22. Ibid., p. 132.
23. For Franco's colonial ambitions, which were dependent on Axis support, see Preston, *Franco*, p. 324.
24. Ibid., pp. 327, 333–4. S. G. Payne, *The Franco Regime, 1936–1975*, London: Phoenix Press, 2000, pp. 244–5.
25. Conversation between Ciano and Franco, 19 July 1939. Muggeridge (ed.), *Ciano's Diplomatic Papers*, pp. 291–2.
26. Payne, *The Franco Regime*, pp. 244–5.
27. Mussolini justified his failure to join his Axis ally in war in September 1939 on the grounds of insufficient economic and military resources. To save face he had presented Hitler with a formidable list of the resources the Italian armed forces and economy needed if Italy were to fight. See Knox, *Mussolini Unleashed*, pp. 42–3.
28. Leitz, *Economic Relations*, p. 129.
29. Serrano Suñer told Ciano on 5 June 1939 that if Spain could have two or preferably three years, she could 'reconstitute herself and complete her military preparations'. However, when Ciano met Franco at San Sebástian for a second time on 19 July the Caudillo was adamant that a period of five years at least was necessary. Muggeridge (ed.), *Ciano's Diary, 1939–1943*, diary entry, 5 June 1939, p. 100. Muggeridge (ed.), *Ciano's Diplomatic Papers*, p. 291.

30. Muggeridge (ed.), *Ciano's Diary, 1939–1943*, diary entry, 5 June 1939, p. 100. Duff, 'Italy', p. 292. When Serrano Suñer saw the German Ambassador at Rome, Hans Georg von Mackensen, on 10 June he strongly advised that 'any détente between the Reich and the Vatican … would in view of the foreign policy of Franco's Government, be exceedingly welcome'. Mackensen to the German Foreign Ministry, 11 June 1939. DGFP, series D, vol. VI, no. 507, p. 698.

31. Muggeridge (ed.), *Ciano's Diary, 1939–1943*, diary entry, 14 June 1939, p. 105. Earlier, in May 1939, the Italian Naval Staff, assuming that Franco's Spain would ally itself with the Axis powers in the event of a war against Britain and France, acknowledged that the Balearics offered an excellent base from which to menace French communications with North Africa and were crucial for safeguarding the transportation of goods from Spanish Atlantic ports to Italy. They advised that Franco should be approached to strengthen the defences on the islands as soon as possible. See R. Mallett, *The Italian Navy and Fascist Expansionism, 1935–1940*, London: Frank Cass, 1998, pp. 142–3, 148, 154–5.

32. C. Burdick and H-A. Jacobsen (eds), *The Halder War Diary, 1939–1942*, London: Greenhill Books, 1988, diary entries 14 and 22 August 1939, pp. 19, 29.

33. Mackensen to Weizsäcker, 11 July 1939. DGFP, series D, vol. VI, no. 654, pp. 902–3. Mussolini's warning was contained in a letter to Franco which Ciano delivered personally on his arrival in Spain.

34. Stohrer to the German Foreign Ministry, 13 July 1939. DGFP, series D, vol. VI, no. 663, p. 913.

35. Stohrer to the German Foreign Ministry, 2 July 1939. DGFP, series D, vol. VI, no. 605, p. 831.

36. Preston. *Franco*, pp. 336–8. See also H. Höhne, *Canaris*, London: Secker and Warburg, 1979, pp. 426–7.

37. Stohrer to the German Foreign Ministry, 28 August 1939. DGFP, series D, vol. VII, no. 392, pp. 888–9.

38. Hellmuth Dietmar, German Chargé d'Affaires at Lisbon, to the German Foreign Ministry, 25 August 1939. DGFP, series D, vol. VII, no. 278, p. 290. For German pressure on Portugal to maintain an 'impeccable neutrality' see Ch.6.

39. Preston, *Franco*, pp. 340–1.

40. Ibid., p. 341.

41. Stohrer to the German Foreign Ministry, 1 September 1939. DGFP, series D, vol. VII, no. 524, pp. 501–2.

42. Sir Robert Hodgson, Burgos, to the Foreign Office, 2 March 1939. FO 371/24151 W3759/1114/41. See also R. Griffiths, *Marshal Pétain*, London: Constable, 1970, p. 214 and J. Isorni, *Philippe Pétain, Tome I*, Paris: La Table Ronde, 1972, pp. 399–401.

43. The last thing the Foreign Office wished to see was the complete adhesion of Franco's Spain to the Rome–Berlin Axis when they were endeavouring to wean Italy away. Phipps to the Quai d'Orsay, 10 February 1939. Charles Corbin, Ambassador at London, to Bonnet, 20 February 1939. Phipps to the Quai d'Oray, 22 February 1939. DDF, 2nd series, vol. XIV, nos 92, 147, 174, pp. 166, 255–6, 278–9.

44. CAB53/45 COS 843 'European Appreciation, 1939–1940', 20 February 1939. CAB55/15 AFC(39)1 JP 379 'Anglo-French Staff Conversations 1939: British Strategic Memorandum', 14 March 1939.

45. P. N. Buckley, E. B. Haslam and W. B. R. Neave-Hill, 'Anglo-French staff conversations, 1938–1939 and P. Le Goyet, 'Les relations économiques Franco-Britanniques à la veille de la deuxième guerre mondiale' in Colloques Franco-Britanniques, Les Relations Franco-Britanniques de 1935 à 1939, pp. 114, 198–9.

46. According to the Foreign Office, it was because of Spain's economic difficulties, reflected in growing public dissatisfaction, that Franco made a number of ministerial changes in mid-August 1939, including the removal of Jordana and his replacement as Foreign Minister by Beigbeder. Serrano Suñer remained as Minister of the Interior. The changes had not resolved the rivalries between the Army and the fascist Falange Española, between the traditionalists and the totalitarians, but they had enhanced Franco's power. Corbin to Bonnet, 31 August 1939. DDF, 2nd series, vol. XIX, no. 290, pp. 297–8.

47. Corbin to Bonnet, 20 June 1939. DDF, 2nd series, vol. XVI, no. 487, pp. 919–21.

48. Preston, Franco, p. 330.

49. For Vansittart's opposition to providing loans to the Franco regime see Stone, 'Sir Robert Vansittart and Spain', pp. 149–50.

50. Corbin to Bonnet, 31 August 1939. DDF, 2nd series, vol. XIX, no. 290, pp. 297–8.

51. Note of a meeting between Neville Chamberlain, Robin Austen Butler, Parliamentary Under Secretary of State for Foreign Affairs, and a Parliamentary Deputation, 1 August 1939. PREM1/361.

52. Léon Bérard was a member of the French Senate and a friend of Pierre Laval; later he became Vichy Ambassador to the Vatican.

53. For the full text of the Bérard–Jordana Agreement see DDF, 2nd series, vol. XIV, no. 211, pp. 372–4.

54. Verbal assurances given by General Jordana on the refugee problem (undated). Papiers 1940 – Reconstitution Fouques-Duparc (Dossiers Bonnet), no. 21, located at the Quai d'Orsay archives in Paris. Hereafter Papiers 1940. Departmental notes, Quai d'Orsay, 25 February 1939: meetings on 23, 24 and 25 February. DDF, 2nd series, vol. XIV, no. 210, pp. 370–1. Bonnet told Phipps that Bérard had obtained definite assurances from

Jordana that Spain had not entered into any military commitments with Italy or Germany. Phipps to Halifax, 22 February 1939. Phipps Papers 1/22.

55. Foreign Office minutes by Cadogan and Mounsey, 17 March 1939. FO371/22944 C3140/312/17. See also Mounsey to Cadogan, 11 March 1939. FO371/24128 W4461//8/41.

56. Admiralty to Foreign Office, 23 March 1939. Ronald Campbell, British Minister at Paris, to the Foreign Office, 23 and 26 March 1939. FO371/24158 W4945/W4996/W5068/3719/41.

57. Phipps to Cadogan, 8 April 1939. DBFP, 3rd series, vol. V, no. 96, pp. 143–4.

58. CAB23/98 CM 20(39) 13 April 1939 and CM 21(39) 19 April 1939. Corbin to Bonnet, 12 April 1939. DDF, 2nd series, vol. XV, no. 353, p. 567. See also Neville Chamberlain's speech in the House of Commons, 13 April 1939. *Hansard Parliamentary Debates*, 5th series, HC, vol. 346, c. 14.

59. Pétain to Bonnet, 20 April 1939. Pétain to Bonnet, 22 April 1939. DDF, 2nd series, vol. XV, nos 451, 471, pp. 722, 771–2.

60. Noguès to Bonnet, 17 April 1939. DDF, 2nd series, vol. XV, no. 424, pp. 681–2.

61. Bonnet to French Diplomatic Representatives at London, Rabat and San Sebastian, 17 April 1939. DDF, 2nd series, vol. XV, no. 423, pp. 680–1.

62. For Noguès' objections see Noguès to Bonnet, 26 April 1939, DDF, 2nd series, vol. XV, no. 492, pp. 807–8.

63. For full details of the Spanish exodus and the strain it imposed on French society and politics, see L. Stein, *Beyond Death and Exile: The Spanish Republicans in France, 1939–1945*, Cambridge, MA: Harvard University Press, 1979.

64. Peterson to the Foreign Office, 18 and 27 April 1939. Foreign Office minute by Mounsey, 3 May 1939. FO371/24118 W6396/5/41. FO371/24129 W6926/8/41. FO371/24159 W7221/3719/41. See also DAPE, vol. V, nos 2036, 2037, pp. 732–3.

65. Halifax to Phipps, 4 May 1939. FO371/24129 W6929/8/41. Phipps to Foreign Office, 8 May 1939. FO 371/24159 W7361/3719/41.

66. Phipps to Foreign Office, 19 April 1939. FO371/24158 W6422/3719/41.

67. Extract from the Record of Conversations between the Secretary of State and M. M. Daladier and Bonnet at the Ministry of War, Paris, 20 May 1939. FO371/24159 W8295/3719/41. Foreign Office Note for the Secretary of State on Franco-Spanish Relations, 19 May 1939. FO371/24159 W8087/3719/41.

68. CA23/99 CM 31(39). The extent of Chamberlain's irritation with the French at this time is clearly revealed in a letter to his sister Hilda of 17 June: 'The French for their part continue to keep up a quarrel with everyone with whom they ought to make friends, Italy, Spain, Turkey. And we inevitably get tarred with their brush'. Neville Chamberlain Papers, NC 18/1/1103, located at the University of Birmingham Library.

69. Halifax to Sir Walford Selby, British Ambassador at Lisbon, 9 June 1939. FO371/24159 W9069/3719/41. See also Armindo Monteiro, Portuguese

Ambassador at London, to Salazar, 9 June 1939. DAPE, vol. V, no. 2056, pp. 769–71.

70. In his speech of 5 June 1939, delivered to the National Council of the *Falange Española*, Franco praised Italy, Germany and Portugal for their support of the Nationalist cause while criticising France for failing to fulfil the Bérard–Jordana Agreement and Britain for failing to release 'a great part of the wealth of our banks' which remained 'sequestrated and subject to litigation'. *Keesing's Contemporary Archives*, 1939, pp. 3607–8.

71. Foreign Office minutes: Mounsey, Cadogan, Halifax and Butler, 10–15 June 1939. FO371/24159 W9153/3719/41.

72. Quai d'Orsay to the Spanish Embassy, 10 June 1939. DDF, 2nd series, vol. XVI, no. 390, pp. 756–7.

73. Pétain to Bonnet, 27 June 1939. DDF, 2nd series, vol. XVII, no. 22, p. 60. Pétain to Bonnet, 28 June 1939. Papiers 1940, no. 23.

74. Pétain to Bonnet, 4 July 1939. Papiers 1940, no. 23.

75. Bonnet to Albert Sarraut, Minister of the Interior, 4 August 1939. DDF, 2nd series, vol. XVII, no. 430, pp. 717–19. Stein, *Beyond Death and Exile*, pp. 86, 92–3. For a detailed analysis of the integration of the refugees into the French economy see M. S. Alexander, 'France, the collapse of Republican Spain and the approach of general war: national security, war economics and the Spanish refugees, 1938–1940' in Leitz and Dunthorn (eds), *Spain in an International Context*, pp. 105–128.

76. Peterson to Halifax, 8 July 1939. FO371/24159 W10599/3719/41. See also M. Peterson, *Both Sides of the Curtain: An Autobiography*, London: Constable, 1950, p. 212 and Alexander, 'France, the collapse of Republican Spain', p. 111.

77. Peterson to Halifax, 23 August 1939. FO371/24159 W12555/3719/41. Bonnet to Pétain, 26 August 1939, Pétain to Bonnet, 31 August 1939. DDF, 2nd series, vol. XIX, nos 50, 272, pp. 51, 275.

78. Bonnet to Corbin, 2 September 1939. Bonnet to Pétain, 2 September 1939. Pétain to Bonnet, 3 September 1939. DDF, 2nd series, vol. XIX, nos 354, 355, 420, pp. 358–9, 421–2.

6. THE GREAT POWERS AND PORTUGAL, 1931–1939

1. Preston, *Franco*, p. 377.

2. For the early years of the military dictatorship see, T. Gallagher, 'The mystery train: Portugal's military dictatorship, 1926–1932', *European Studies Review*, vol. 11, 1981.

3. Portugal and Austria were two small agriculturally based countries possessing Catholic corporatist structures, each overshadowed by a much larger and powerful neighbour. T Gallagher, *Portugal: A Twentieth Century Interpretation*, Manchester: Manchester University Press, 1983, pp. 96–7.

4. Throughout the history of the *Estado Novo*, from 1933 until its demise in 1974, the head of state was a senior military figure. Carmona was succeeded by Marshal Higino Craveiro Lopes who was replaced in 1958 by Admiral Americo Tomás who was still President in 1974 when the *Estado Novo* was overthrown. See D. L. Wheeler, 'The military and the Portuguese dictatorship, 1926–1974: the "honor of the army" ' in L. S. Graham and H. M. Makler (eds), *Contemporary Portugal: The Revolution and Its Antecedents*, Austin, TX: University of Texas Press, 1979.

5. Leitz, *Nazi Germany and Neutral Europe*, p. 144. According to Hugh Kay, Salazar was deeply impressed by Mussolini's organising genius but he distrusted Hitler from the start, especially when 'the Führer cast a roving eye over Africa, and German influence gained ground in Portuguese business and intellectual circles'. *Salazar and Modern Portugal*, London: Eyre and Spottiswoode, 1970, p. 67.

6. Russian citizens were prohibited from entering Portugal or the Portuguese colonies. In 1934 the Portuguese vigorously opposed the Soviet Union's entry into the League of Nations. S. G. West, 'The present situation in Portugal', *International Affairs*, vol. 17, 1938.

7. See, for example, FRUS, 1933, vol. II, pp. 640–55 and FRUS, 1934, vol. II, pp. 677–83.

8. Stone, 'The official British attitude to the Anglo-Portuguese alliance', pp. 732–5.

9. Ibid., pp. 735–8. In reconstructing the Portuguese Navy over £1 million was spent in 1935 alone in British shipyards, notably Vickers Armstrong and Hawthorne Leslie. By 1937 the reconstructed navy consisted of six flotilla leaders, five destroyers and three submarines with an aggregate tonnage of 20,000 tons. Secretariado Nacional da Informação, *Portugal: the New State in Theory and Practice*, Lisbon, 1937, pp. 58–9. A. Telo, *Portugal na Segunda Guerra*, Lisboa: Perspectivas Realidades, 1987, pp. 96–7.

10. Russell to the Marquess of Reading, British Foreign Secretary, 31 August 1931. FO425/408 W10424/801/36.

11. Adam to Reading, 19 October 1931. FO425/408 W12510/801/36.

12. Saz, 'Second Republic in the international arena', p. 77.

13. Membership of the PCP (*Partido Comunista Português*) numbered only 500 in 1936 but it was well organised and considered to be the centre of the antifascist movement. Its influence was mainly among military arsenal, trolley and railway workers in the Lisbon area but it was organised in every region of Portugal. See C. A. Cunha, 'The Portuguese Communist party, its ancillary organisations, and the Communist International's third period' in Worley (ed.), *In Search of Revolution*, pp. 154, 171.

14. Eden to Sir Charles Wingfield, British Ambassador at Lisbon, 21 April 1936. FO425/413 W2540/478/36.

15. Eden to Wingfield, 30 April 1936. FO425/413 W3358/403/36.

16. Charles Dodd, British Chargé d'Affaires at Lisbon, to the Foreign Office, 7 August 1936. Foreign Office to Wingfield, 10 August 1936. FO371/20527 W7918/62/41. Reports of Conversations between the Foreign Minister and the English Chargé d'Affaires', 7 and 11 August 1936. DAPE, vol. III, nos 111, 141, pp. 88–93, 119–20.

17. Amé Leroy, French Minister at Lisbon, to Delbos, 6 August 1936. Delbos to Roger Cambon, French Chargé d'Affaires at London, 7 August 1936. DDF, 2nd series, vol. III, nos 96, 99, pp. 147, 151.

18. D. W. Pike, *Les Français et la Guerre d'Espagne, 1936–1939*, Paris: Presses Universitaires de France, 1975, p. 74, n. 23.

19. Charles Dodd, British Chargé d'Affaires at Lisbon, to the Foreign Office, 7 August 1936. FO371/20527 W7918/62/41. DAPE, vol. III, no. 111, pp. 90–1. DGFP, series D, vol. III, nos 53, 76, pp. 54, 77–8. See also G. C. Queipo de Llano, 'El impacto internacional de la Guerra Civil Española' in Tusell *et al.* (eds), *La Política Exterior de España*, pp. 225–6.

20. See Stone, *The Oldest Ally*, pp. 8–12 and C. Oliveira, *Salazar e a Guerra Civil de Espanha*, Lisboa: O Jornal, 1987, pp. 244–7.

21. Leitz, *Nazi Germany and Neutral Europe*, p. 145.

22. CAB24/277 CP 163(38). See also the *News Chronicle*, 12 July 1938.

23. The German Minister at Lisbon, Baron Oswald von Hoyningen-Huene, issued an immediate denial which Salazar accepted. According to Franco Nogueira, the Portuguese dictator had read the text of Reichenau's lecture very carefully before concluding that it was a forgery. However, he was impressed by the knowledge it revealed and the detailed argument. *Salazar, III*, p. 165.

24. For German and Italian exploitation of Portugal's exclusion from the Nyon Conference see FO371/21405 W16294/16618/41. Salazar was singularly unimpressed by the British explanation that Portugal was not included because it was not a Mediterranean power. See Nogueira, *Salazar, III*, p. 129.

25. Charles Bateman, British Chargé d'Affaires at Lisbon, to Eden, 4 November 1937. FO425/414 W20510/923/36 *Hansard Parliamentary Debates*, 5th series, HC, vol. 330, cc. 789–90, 2262–3.

26. Annual Report of the British Embassy in Lisbon, 1937. FO371/22601 W3407/3407/36.

27. Ibid. According to Bateman, the Portuguese increasingly regarded Geneva as Stalin's second capital. Bateman to Eden, 4 November 1937. FO425/414 W20510/923/36.

28. Memorandum by Lord Elibank, 19 October 1938. FO371/22597 W14363/153/36.

29. Italian centres of culture existed in Lisbon, Coimbra and Oporto but their activities were somewhat neutralised by their lack of continuity and because Italian was not a class-based subject in Portuguese lyceums.

30. British Embassy Report, 1937. FO371/22601 W3407/3407/36. West. 'The present situation in Portugal', pp. 217–18.

31. Hoyningen-Huene to the German Foreign Ministry, 4 September 1936. DGFP, series D, vol. III, no. 70, pp. 71–2.

32. Undated Memorandum. Dawson Papers, MSS Dawson 79, located at the Bodleian Library, Oxford.

33. 'The German Trade Offensive: Anglo-German Competition', *The Economist*, 5 November 1938. Sir Walford Selby, British Ambassador at Lisbon, to Halifax, 18 November 1938. FO425/415 W15733/152/36.

34. Leitz, *Nazi Germany and Neutral Europe*, p. 146.

35. T. Gallagher, 'Controlled repression in Salazar's Portugal', *Journal of Contemporary History*, vol. 14, 1979, p. 387. D. L. Wheeler, 'In the service of order: the Portuguese political police and the British, German and Spanish intelligence, 1932–1945', *Journal of Contemporary History*, vol. 18, 1983, pp. 9–15. H. A. Jacobson, *National Sozialistische Aussenpolitik, 1933–1938*, Frankfort am Main/Berlin: Alfred Metzner Verlag, 1968, p. 462.

36. British Embassy Report, 1937. FO371/22601 W3407/3407/36. *The Times*, 28 and 31 January 1938.

37. Bateman to Eden, 4 November 1937. FO425/414 W20510/923/36.

38. Bateman to Eden, 9 November 1937. FO371/21278 W21055/923/36. *The Times*, 6 November 1937.

39. Count Karl Max du Moulin-Eckart, German Chargé d'Affaires at Lisbon, to the German Foreign Ministry, 27 August 1936. DGFP, series D, vol. III, no. 53, p. 55.

40. Leitz, *Nazi Germany and Neutral Europe*, p. 145.

41. Ibid., pp. 146, 163. Stone, *The Oldest Ally*, pp. 75, 80.

42. On 29 June 1937, for example, Salazar told the retiring British Ambassador at Lisbon, Sir Charles Wingfield, that there was 'no real confidence in French or British impartiality' and that 'Germany, Italy and all Europe believed the British Government supported the Republicans'. He added that Britain's close collaboration with France 'whose sympathies with the "Reds" of Valencia and Barcelona were not concealed' simply confirmed this view. Wingfield to Eden, 29 June 1937. FO371/21341 W13250/7/41. See also DAPE, vol. IV, nos 1134, 1140, pp. 460–2, 469–72.

43. See Stone, *The Oldest Ally*, pp. 40–4.

44. Salazar expressed his personal pleasure at the first of *The Times*' articles, published on 14 September 1937. Wingfield to Eden, 17 September 1937. FO371/21269 W17905/25/36.

45. See, for example: West, 'The present position in Portugal'; W. F. Deedes, 'Portugal', *Quarterly Review*, 272, 1939; E. Wakenham, 'Portugal today', *Nineteenth Century and After*, September 1938; W. C. Atkinson, 'Portugal and her empire', *Fortnightly Review*, July 1939; and W. A. Hirst, 'Greater Portugal', *Contemporary Review*, September 1939. After the near bankruptcy of the

Parliamentary Republic Salazar had succeeded in stabilising Portuguese public finances.

46. *The Times*, 20 May 1938, 23 November 1938 and 6 June 1939. British Embassy Report, 1937. FO371/22601 W3407/3407/36. British Broadcasts to Portugal. FO371/24008 W7845/398/36.

47. Halifax to Selby, 10 August 1939 and Selby to Halifax, 17 August 1939. FO371/24064 W10614/W12374/160/36.

48. Stone, *The Oldest Ally*, pp. 56–9.

49. See Ch. 10.

50. B. Pimlott (ed.), *The Political Diary of Hugh Dalton, 1918–1940, 1945–1960*, London: Jonathan Cape, 1986, p. 212.

51. In their paper the Chiefs of Staff had stressed that since the previous reaffirmation of the alliance in 1927 German rearmament, the civil war in Spain and Italy's changed attitude had tended to increase the importance of the alliance in relation to naval strategy. CAB 24/270 CP 189(37) CID Paper 1336-B (also COS 602).

52. CAB 2/7 297th meeting Committee of Imperial Defence, 15 July 1937. CAB 23/88 CM 31(37), 21 July 1937. For details of the military mission to Portugal see Stone, *The Oldest Ally*, pp. 62–73.

53. *The Times*, 28 January and 2 February 1938. For details of the visit see also W. Selby, *Diplomatic Twilight*, London: John Murray, 1953, pp. 91–3.

54. Selby to Eden, 15 February 1938. FO371/22592 W2584/146/36. DDF, 2nd series, vol. VIII, no. 519, pp. 949–50. DDF, 2nd series, vol. IX, nos 100, 137, 153, 173, 219, pp. 191–4, 280–1, 315–17, 354–5, 459–61. DDF, 2nd series, vol. X, nos 3, 203, pp. 4, 371–2.

55. See, for example, General Sir Noel Birch, Vickers, to Vansittart, 20 May 1937 and Birch to Sir Charles Craven, Chairman of Vickers, 21 May 1937. Vickers' Papers, K611 (microfilm) located at Cambridge University Library.

56. The Foreign Office, urged on by the Lisbon Embassy, had been pressing for the appointment of permanent service attachés since 1936, partly to provide expert advice on the spot in relation to the various armaments contracts. See FO371/21269 W9033/W12160/W12233/25/36.

57. G. A. Stone, 'The British Government and the sale of arms to the lesser European powers, 1936–1939', *Diplomacy and Statecraft*, vol. 14, 2003, pp. 255–6.

58. Halifax to Selby, 18 March 1938. FO371/22639 W3547/7/41. Foreign Office minutes, Cadogan and Frank Roberts, 21–22 March 1938. FO371/22641 W4211/83/41. Armindo Monteiro, Portuguese Ambassador at London, to Salazar, 18 March 1938. DAPE, vol. V, no. 1574, pp. 226–8. Kay, *Salazar and Modern Portugal*, pp. 115–16. Nogueira, *Salazar III*, p. 155.

59. Selby to Halifax, 28 June 1938. FO371/22597 W8995/153/36.

60. Halifax to Oswald Scott, British Chargé d'Affaires at Lisbon, 29 September 1938. FO371/22594 W12807/146/36. See also DAPE, vol. II, no. 407, p. 14.

61. Selby to Halifax, 17 March 1939. Foreign Office to Selby, 18 March 1939. FO371/24150 W4589/W4671/1076/41. Cadogan to Monteiro, 17 March 1939. DAPE, vol. V, no. 1990, p. 685.

62. Oliveira, *Salazar e a Guerra Civil*, p. 356. E. O. Rosas, *O Salazarismo e a Aliança Luso-Britânica: Estudos Sobre a Política Externa do Estado Novos nos Anos 30 e 40*, Lisboa: Fragmentos, 1988, p. 113. According to António Telo, the treaty also checked the ambitions of those Spaniards who desired a united Iberia. For Franco it proved an important lever in his relations with the Axis powers and a bridge to a new relationship with Britain and France. *Portugal na Segunda Guerra*, p. 44.

63. Selby to Halifax, 8 April 1939. FO371/24068 W5745/658/36. Selby to Foreign Office, 13, 15, 17 April 1939. Sir Maurice Peterson, British Ambassador, San Sebastián, to Foreign Office, 18 April 1939. FO37124118 W6109/W6174/W6193/W6396/5/41. Nogueira, *Salazar III*, pp. 197–8.

64. Muggeridge (ed.), *Ciano's Diary, 1939–1943*, diary entry, 5 June 1939, pp. 100–1.

65. See, for example, Salazar to Monteiro, 11 August 1939. DAPE, vol. V, no. 2088, pp. 804–5.

66. Halifax to Selby, 15 August 1939. Selby to Halifax, 17 August 1939. FO425/416.

67. Foreign Office Minute, Mounsey, 31 August 1939. Selby to Foreign Office, 1 September 1939. FO371/24160 W13054/W13007/5056/41. For Spain's decision to remain neutral see Ch. 5.

68. Hellmuth Dietmar, Chargé d'Affaires, Lisbon, to the German Foreign Ministry, 25 August 1939. Ribbentrop to the German Legation in Portugal, 31 August 1939. Hoyningen-Huene to the German Foreign Ministry, 1 September 1939. DGFP, series D, vol. VII, nos 278, 487, 522, pp. 290, 473–4, 500. See also DAPE, vol. II, no. 897, pp. 523–4.

69. CAB53/54 COS 973. 'The Role of Portugal in the Event of War', 1 September 1939. Selby to Foreign Office, 1 September 1939. FO371/24064 W12998/160/36.

70. *Hansard Parliamentary Debates*, 5th series, HC, vol. 330, cc. 1880–1.

71. See Stone, 'The official British attitude to the Anglo-Portuguese alliance', pp. 730–1.

72. For full details of the colonial issue in Anglo-Portuguese relations see Stone, *The Oldest Ally*, pp. 82–113.

7. THE AXIS POWERS AND FRANCO'S SPAIN, 1939–1941

1. Sir L. Woodward, *British Foreign Policy in the Second World War, Vol. I*, London: HMSO, 1974, pp. 433–4.

2. Leitz, *Economic Relations*, p. 125.

3. Ibid., pp. 122–3. See also Memorandum by the Director of the Economics Department, 19 October 1939. DGFP, series D, vol. VIII, no. 282, p. 322.

4. Woodward, *British Foreign Policy I*, p. 434.

5. K. Benton, 'The ISOS years: Madrid, 1941–1943', *Journal of Contemporary History*, vol. 30, 1995, pp. 372–3. According to Benton, who served in British intelligence during the war, the *Abwehr* officers were a 'gentlemanly organisation' who accommodated their agents well at good hotels and provided first class travel which made it somewhat easier for British intelligence operatives to identify them. Ibid., p. 381.

6. Stohrer to the German Foreign Ministry, 10 September 1940. DGFP, series D, vol. XI, no. 39, p. 48.

7. Leitz, *Nazi Germany and Neutral Europe*, p. 120. J. M. Packard, *Neither Friend nor Foe: The European Neutrals in World War II*, New York: Charles Scribner, 1992, p. 280.

8. Leitz, *Nazi Germany and Neutral Europe*, p. 120. Packard, *Neither Friend nor Foe*, p. 119. Preston, *Franco*, pp. 360–1. C. Burdick, ' "Moro": the re-supply of German submarines in Spain, 1939–1942', *Central European History*, vol. 3, 1970, pp, 256–83. D. W. Pike, 'Franco and the Axis stigma', *Journal of Contemporary History*, vol. 17, 1982, p. 387.

9. G. Schreiber, B. Stegemann, D. Vogel, *Germany and the Second World War. Volume III: The Mediterranean, South-east Europe, and North Africa, 1939–1941*, Oxford: Oxford University Press, 1995, pp. 147–8.

10. Leitz, *Nazi Germany and Neutral Europe*, p. 132.

11. Ibid., pp. 130–7. Stone, *The Oldest Ally*, pp. 142–3.

12. C. Leitz, 'Programm Bär: the supply of German war material to Spain, 1943–1944' in Leitz and Dunthorn (eds), *Spain in an International Context*, pp. 171–87. See also Pérez, *Franquismo y Tercer Reich*, pp. 393–403.

13. Stohrer to the German Foreign Ministry, 16 April 1940. DGFP, series D, vol. VIII, no. 129, p. 191.

14. Memorandum by an Official of the Dienstelle Ribbentrop, 10 May 1940. Stohrer to Weizsäcker, 27 May 1940. DGFP, series D, vol. IX, nos 230, 330, pp. 318, 450.

15. Stohrer to the German Foreign Ministry, 20 May 1940. DGFP, series D, vol. IX, no. 285, p. 396.

16. Stohrer to the German Foreign Ministry, 4 June 1940. DGFP, series D, vol. IX, no. 380, p. 511.

17. Preston, *Franco*, p. 358.

18. Stohrer to the German Foreign Ministry, 14 June 1940. DGFP, series D, vol. IX, no. 429, p. 565. Preston, *Franco*, pp. 361–2. N. Goda, *Tomorrow the World: Hitler, Northwest Africa and the Path toward North America*, College Station, Tx: Texas A and M University Press, 1998, pp. 58–9.

19. Unsigned memorandum: Conversation between Hitler and Vigón in the presence of Ribbentrop, 16 June 1940. DGFP, series D, vol. IX, no. 584, pp. 585–6.

20. Weiszäcker to Ribbentrop, 19 June 1940. DGFP, series D, vol. IX, no. 488, pp. 620–1.

21. N. Rich, *Hitler's War Aims: Ideology, the Nazi State and the Course of Expansion, Vol. I*, London: Andre Deutsch, 1973, p. 167.

22. Muggeridge (ed.), *Ciano's Diplomatic Papers*, pp. 373–4.

23. Muggeridge (ed.), *Ciano's Diary, 1939–1943*, diary entry, 18–19 June 1940, pp. 266–7.

24. For a discussion see Goda, *Tomorrow the World*, pp. xvi–xxvi; Schreiber *et al.*, *Germany and the Second World War, III*, pp. 278–301; and K. Maier, H. Rohde, B. Stegemann, H. Umbreit, *Germany and the Second World War. Vol. II: Germany's Initial Conquests in Europe*, Oxford: Oxford University Press, 1991, pp. 60–6.

25. C. Burdick and Jacobsen (eds), *The Halder War Diary*, diary entry, 13 July 1940, p. 227.

26. Woodward, *British Foreign Policy I*, pp. 436–7.

27. M. Gallo, *Spain under Franco: A History*, London: Allen and Unwin, 1973, p. 95.

28. See Burdick and Jacobsen (eds), *The Halder War Diary*, diary entry, 31 July 1940, pp. 244–5.

29. Ribbentrop to the German Embassy at Madrid, 2 August 1940. Stohrer to Ribbentrop, 8 August 1940. DGFP, series D, vol. X, nos 274, 313, pp. 396, 442–5.

30. Note of the High Command of the Army, 10 August 1940. DGFP, series D, vol. X, no. 326, pp. 461–4.

31. The Foreign Ministry to the Embassy at Madrid, 12 August 1940. Erich Heberlein, Chargé d'Affaires at Madrid, to the German Foreign Ministry, 16 August 1940. DGFP, series D, vol. X, nos 329, 355, pp. 466–7, 499–500. See also Pérez, *Franquismo y Tercer Reich*, p. 173.

32. Stohrer to the German Foreign Ministry, 20–21 August 1940. DGFP, series D, vol. X, nos 369, 373, pp. 514–15, 521.

33. Mussolini to Franco, 25 August 1940. DGFP, series D, vol. X, no. 392, p. 542.

34. Burdick and Jacobsen (eds), *The Halder War Diary*, diary entry, 27 September 1940, p. 252.

35. Goda, *Tomorrow the World*, p. 69.

36. Hitler to Mussolini, 17 September 1940. DGFP, series D, vol. XI, no. 68, p. 104.

37. Hitler to Franco, 18 September 1940. DGFP, series D, vol. XI, no. 70, pp. 106–8.

38. Memorandum by an Official of Ribbentrop's Secretariat, 20 September 1940. DGFP, series D, vol. XI, no. 73, p. 121.

39. Franco's letter to Hitler, dated 22 September 1940, was handed to the Führer personally by Serrano Suñer on 25 September 1940. DGFP, series D, vol. XI, no. 88, pp. 153–5.

40. See DGFP, series D, vol. XI, nos 63, 66, 67, 97, 104, 117, pp. 83–91, 93–8, 98–102, 166–74, 183–4, 201–4. Ciano recorded in his diary on 28 September 1940 that: 'Generally speaking, Serrano Suñer's mission was not successful, and the man himself did not and could not please the Germans'. Muggeridge (ed.), *Ciano's Diary, 1939–1943*, p. 294.

41. Muggeridge (ed.), *Ciano's Diplomatic Papers*, pp. 393–4.

42. Unsigned Memorandum, 27 September 1940. DGFP, series D, vol. XI, no. 116, pp. 199–200.

43. Muggeridge (ed.), *Ciano's Diary, 1939–1943*, diary entry, 27 September 1940, p. 294. According to the German record of his meeting with Ciano, of 28 September, Hitler summarised the Spanish proposals, 'somewhat crassly expressed', as: (1) Germany is to deliver for the coming year 400,000–700,000 tons of grain; (2) Germany is to deliver all the fuel; (3) Germany is to deliver the equipment which the [Spanish] Army lacks; (4) Germany is to supply artillery, airplanes, as well as special weapons and special troops for the conquest of Gibraltar; (5) Germany is to hand over to Spain all of Morocco and besides that, Oran, and is to help her get a border revision west [south?] of Rio de Oro; (6) Spain is to promise to Germany, in return, her friendship. Memorandum by an Official of Ribbentrop's Secretariat, 29 September 1940. DGFP, series D, vol. XI, no. 211, p. 212.

44. For the impact of the attack on Dakar see M. Thomas, *The French Empire at War, 1940–1945*, Manchester: Manchester University Press, 1998, pp. 75–81.

45. Memorandum by an Official of Ribbentrop's Secretariat, 4 October 1940. DGFP, series D, vol. XI, no. 149, pp. 245–59. Muggeridge (ed.), *Ciano's Diary, 1939–1943*, diary entry, 4 October 1940, p. 296. On the following day Ciano recorded: 'I informed Serrano [Suñer] of the results of the meeting in so far as they concern Spain, and he is only half satisfied. Why hasn't he yet seen that the Germans have had an eye on Morocco for a long time?'. Ibid., p. 296.

46. In his meeting with Mussolini in Florence on 28 October, Hitler argued that it would be best for the Axis powers if the North African territories were defended by the French themselves and that 'some inducement therefore had to be held out to the French to defend the territory themselves'. Memorandum by an Official of Ribbentrop's Secretariat, 28 October 1940. DGFP, series D, vol. XI, no. 246, pp. 411–12.

47. N. Goda, 'Germany's conception of Spain's strategic importance, 1940–1941' in Leitz and Dunthorn (eds), *Spain in an International Context*, p. 138. For the record of Hitler's meetings with Franco and Pétain see DGFP, series D, vol. XI, nos 220, 227, pp. 371–9, 385–92.

48. P. Preston, 'Franco and Hitler: the myth of Hendaye, 1940', *Contemporary European History*, vol. 1, 1992, p. 9.

49. Schreiber *et al.*, *Germany and the Second World War, III*, p. 187.

50. Muggeridge (ed.), *Ciano's Diplomatic Papers*, p. 402. Burdick and Jacobsen (eds.), *The Halder War Diary*, diary entry, 1 November 1940, p. 272. Schreiber *et al.*, *Germany and the Second World War, III*, p. 195.

51. DGFP, series D, vol. XI, nos 221, 224, 235, 287, 294, pp. 377, 383, 402, 466–7, 478–9. Muggeridge (ed.), *Ciano's Diplomatic Papers*, pp. 405–6. Goda, *Tomorrow the World*, pp. 104–6. Schreiber *et al.*, *Germany and the Second World War, III*, pp. 192–4.

52. Memorandum by an Official of Ribbentrop's Secretariat, 28 October 1940. DGFP, series D, vol. XI, no. 246, p. 421.

53. Directive No.18, Führer Headquarters, 12 November 1940. H. R. Trevor-Roper (ed.), *Blitzkrieg to Defeat: Hitler's War Directives, 1939–1945*, New York: Holt, Rinehart, Winston, 1971, pp. 39–41.

54. Hitler to Mussolini, 5 December 1940. DGFP, series D, vol. XI, no. 452, pp. 790–1.

55. Memorandum by an Official of Ribbentrop's Secretariat, 19 November 1940. DGFP, series D, vol. XI, no. 352, pp. 602–3, 605. Serrano Suñer later recalled that he had been summoned to the Berghof on three days notice but, as he explained to Franco, he had no choice but to go because to do otherwise would probably have resulted in the conference being held in Vitoria, that is, on Spanish soil after the Germans had crossed the Pyrenees. D. S. Detwiler, 'Spain and the Axis during World War II', *Review of Politics*, vol. 33, 1971, p. 46.

56. On 9 December Stohrer reported that 'remonstrances by a number of influential generals' had aroused in Franco the fear that a clash of personalities and issues between Serrano Suñer and the military could become 'an acute danger for the regime if the grave misgivings of these generals toward immediate entry into the war, mainly on economic though also on military grounds, are not given heed'. DGFP, series D, vol. XI, no. 479, pp. 824–5.

57. Stohrer to the German Foreign Ministry, 12 December 1940. DGFP, series D, vol. XI, no. 500, pp. 852–3. See also the draft entries by Helmuth Greiner in the War Diary of the Wehrmacht Operations Staff (1 December 1940–24 March 1941). Ibid., no. 476, n.2, pp. 816–17.

58. Goda, *Tomorrow the World*, p. 135.

59. Führer conference with the Commander-in-Chief of the Navy, 27 December 1940. *Brassey's Naval Annual*, London: HMSO, 1948, p. 161. Schreiber *et al.*, *Germany and the Second World War III*, p. 242.

60. Hitler to Mussolini, 31 December 1940. DGFP, series D, vol. XI, no. 586, pp. 991–2.

61. Führer Conference, 8–9 January 1941. *Brassey's Naval Annual*, p. 171. Editors note: draft entries by Helmuth Greiner in the War Diary of the Wehrmacht Operations Staff (1December 1940–24 March 1941). DGFP, series D, vol. XI, p. 1058.

62. Memoranda by an Official of Ribbentrop's Secretariat, 21 January 1941. DGFP, series D, vol. XI, nos 672, 679, pp. 1127–33, 1145–51. See also Muggeridge (ed.), *Ciano's Diplomatic Papers*, pp. 419–20.

63. Hitler to Franco, 6 February 1941. DGFP, series D, vol. XII, no. 22, pp. 37–42. For Stohrer's interventions and Ribbentrop's instructions see DGFP, series D, vol. XI, nos 677, 682, 692, 695, 702, 718, 725, 728, pp. 1140–3, 1157–8, 1170–1, 1173–5, 1183–4, 1188–91, 1208–10, 1217–18, 1222–3. The German Ambassador consistently warned Franco

and Serrano Suñer that Britain's objective was to try to weaken and bring down their regime and restore the Spanish Republic.

64. Muggeridge (ed.), *Ciano's Diplomatic Papers*, pp. 421–30.
65. Preston, 'Italy and Spain', p. 175.
66. Memorandum by Weizsäcker, 14 February 1941. DGFP, series D, vol. XII, no. 49, pp. 96–8.
67. Schreiber *et al.*, *Germany and the Second World War III*, pp. 244–5.
68. Hitler confided in Mussolini on 28 February 1941 that 'he could only evaluate Franco's statement that Spanish troops would lead the attack on Gibraltar as a naïve overestimate of the ability and striking power of the Spanish armed forces'. DGFP, series D, vol. XII, no. 110, p. 197.
69. Ribbentrop to the Embassy in Spain, 22 February 1941. DGFP, series D, vol. XII, no. 73, pp. 131–2.
70. Franco to Hitler, 26 February 1941. DGFP, series D, vol. XII, no. 95, pp. 176–7.
71. Leitz, *Nazi Germany and Neutral Europe*, pp. 125–6.
72. Stohrer to the German Foreign Ministry, 22 April 1941. DGFP, series D, vol. XII, no. 386, pp. 611–15.
73. Memorandum by an Official of Ribbentrop's Secretariat, 28 April 1941. DGFP, series D, vol. XII, no. 422, pp. 664–5.
74. Directive of the High Command of the Army, 7 May 1941. DGFP, series D, vol. XII, pp. 731–3. See also Burdick and Jacobsen (eds), *The Halder War Diary*, entries 1, 3 and 4 May 1941, pp. 380–2 and G. P. Megargee, *Inside Hitler's High Command*, Lawrence KA: University Press of Kansas, 2000, p. 91.
75. Memorandum by an Official of Ribbentrop's Secretariat, 3 June 1941. DGFP, series D, vol. XII, no. 584, pp. 949–50.
76. Muggeridge (ed.), *Ciano's Diplomatic Papers*, pp. 443–4. Stohrer to the German Foreign Ministry, 11 June 1941. DGFP, series D, vol. XII, no. 615, pp. 1007–8.
77. Draft Directive No. 32: Preparations for the Time after Barbarossa, Führer's Headquarters, 11 June 1941. DGFP, series D, vol. XII, no. 617, pp. 1012–16. See also, Trevor Roper (ed.), *Blitzkrieg to Defeat*, pp. 78–82.
78. Stohrer to Ribbentrop, 25 June 1941. DGFP, series D, vol. XIII, no. 12, pp. 16–17.
79. S. Ellwood, *Franco*, London: Longman, 1994, pp. 130–1.
80. DGFP, series D, vol. XIII, nos 12, 34, 70, pp. 16–17, 38–9, 81. See also D. Smyth, 'The despatch of the Spanish Blue Division to the Russian Front: reasons and repercussions', *European History Quarterly*, vol. 24, 1994, pp. 537–53 and E. Hernández-Sandoica and E. Moradiellos. 'Spain and the Second World War, 1939–1945' in N. Wylie (ed.), *European Neutrals and Non-Belligerents during the Second World War*, Cambridge, 2002, pp. 259–60. According to Rafael Pérez, the total financial cost of the Blue Division, 1941–1945, amounted to 613.5 million pesetas. *Franquismo y Tercer Reich*, p. 269.
81. For Franco's speech see Pike, 'Franco and the Axis stigma', pp. 381–2.

82. Heberlein to the German Foreign Ministry, 18 July 1941. DGFP, series D, vol. XIII, n. 2, p. 223.

83. Hitler to Mussolini, 20 July 1941. Mackensen to the German Foreign Ministry, 26 July 1941 (translation of a letter of 24 July 1941 from Mussolini to Hitler). DGFP, series D, vol. XIII, nos 134, 156, pp. 192, 221.

84. Record of Mussolini's conversation with Hitler, 25 August 1941. DGFP, series D, vol. XIII, no. 242, p. 385. See also Muggeridge (ed.), *Ciano's Diplomatic Papers*, p. 450.

85. Memorandum of the High Command of the Wehrmacht, Führer Headquarters, 27 August 1941. DGFP, series D, vol. XIII, no. 265, pp. 422–33.

86. General Walter Warlimont, OKW, to the German Foreign Ministry, 13 September 1941. DGFP, series D, vol. XIII, no. 314, pp. 498–9. A further reinforcement of this order was sent to the Spanish Embassy on 13 November. See ibid., no. 467, p. 774.

87. Memorandum by an Official of Ribbentrop's Secretariat, 30 November 1941. DGFP, series D, vol. XIII, no. 523, pp. 904–6. See also Muggeridge (ed.), *Ciano's Diplomatic Papers*, p. 461.

88. Memorandum by an Official of the Protocol Department, Berlin, 9 December 1941. DGFP, series D, vol. XIII, no. 555, p. 971. Moscardó conveyed Franco's 'most cordial greetings and congratulations' and told Hitler that the Caudillo believed in the absolute final victory of Germany which was inevitable owing to the victorious campaigns of the Wehrmacht which he followed step by step.

89. P. Preston, 'Franco and the Axis temptation' in P. Preston (ed.), *The Politics of Revenge: Fascism and the Military in Twentieth Century Spain*, London: Unwin Hyman, 1990, p. 78.

8. THE ALLIES AND FRANCO'S SPAIN, 1939–1941

1. Pétain to Daladier, 27 September 1939. *Documents Diplomatiques Français 1939 (3 Septembre–31 Décembre)*, no. 161, p. 256. Hereafter DDF.

2. See, for example, Pétain to Daladier, 2 and 7 October 1939. DDF, 1939, nos 178, 204, pp. 293–6, 356–7.

3. Jackson, 'French strategy and the Spanish Civil War', pp. 65–6.

4. N. Wylie, 'An amateur learns his job? Special Operations Executive in Portugal, 1940–1942', *Journal of Contemporary History*, vol. 36, 2001, p. 451. C. Andrew, 'Introduction to the ISOS Years: Madrid, 1941–1943', *Journal of Contemporary History*, vol. 30, 1995, pp. 355–6.

5. Lord Halifax to Sir Maurice Peterson at Madrid, 19 April 1940. FO425/417 C5983/30/41. C. Leitz, 'More carrot than stick: British economic warfare and Spain, 1941–1944', *Twentieth Century British History*,

vol. 9, 1998, pp. 250–1. Hernández-Sandoica and Moradiellos, 'Spain and the Second World War', p. 247.

6. See *Keesing's Contemporary Archives, 1937–1940*, p. 3883. J-C. Allain, 'La France et les neutralités Helvétique et Espagnole en 1939–1940' in Colloque International des Universités de Neuchâtel et de Berne, *Les États Neutres Européens et la Seconde Guerre Mondiale*, Neuchâtel: Éditions de la Baconnière, 1985, pp. 350–1.

7. Peterson to Halifax, 20 April 1940. FO425/417 C6032/75/41.

8. Allain, 'La France et les neutralités Helvétique et Espagnole', p. 349.

9. R. G. Pérez, 'España y la Segunda Guerra Mundial' in Tusell, *et al.* (eds), *La Política Exterior de España*, p. 307.

10. See DDF, 1940 (Les Armistices de Juin 1940), nos 26, 27, 34, 45, 47, 96, pp. 43–4, 52, 65–7, 179–80.

11. For Britain's reluctance to cooperate with the Spanish opposition to Franco during the period 1940–1944 see D. J. Dunthorn, *Britain and the Spanish Anti-Franco Opposition, 1940–1950*, London: Palgrave, 2000, pp. 28–44.

12. Hoare to Halifax, 22 June 1940. FO371/24515 C7281/113/41.

13. *Hansard Parliamentary Debates*, 5th series, HC, vol. 365, c. 302.

14. Smyth, *Diplomacy and Strategy of Survival*, pp. 52–3.

15. As an indication of the continuing anxiety concerning anti-Franco press opinion, when Franco made a number of ministerial changes in May 1941, which appeared to be to Britain's advantage, Anthony Eden, Halifax's successor as Foreign Secretary, felt compelled to warn his colleagues that 'it was still most necessary that the Press should not comment on these changes'. CAB65/18 WM 49(41), 12 May 1941.

16. For a full discussion of the Negrín case see FO371/24510–13 File 75; D. Smyth, 'The politics of asylum, Juan Negrín and the British Government in 1940' in R. T. B. Langhorne (ed.), *Diplomacy and Intelligence during the Second World War: Essays in Honour of F. S. Hinsley*, Cambridge: Cambridge University Press, 1984; G. A. Stone, 'The degree of British commitment to the restoration of democracy in Spain, 1939–1946' in Leitz and Dunthorn (eds), *Spain in an International Context*, pp. 195–7. It is interesting to note that shortly before the fall of France the French authorities had promised to arrest Negrín, who was in France at the time, and to dissolve all Spanish Republican associations in France. See Stohrer to the German Foreign Ministry, 30 May 1940. DGFP, series D, vol. IX, no. 352, p. 474.

17. Eden to Hoare, 2 February 1941. FO371/26904 C986/46/41.

18. Hoare to the Foreign Office, 22 June 1941. FO371/26939 C6810/222/41.

19. Hoare to Eden, 23 July 1941. FO371/26940 C8416/222/41.

20. Minute by Cadogan, 18 July 1941. FO371/26906 C8104/46/41.

21. 'Our Policy in Spain: Memorandum by the Secretary of State for Foreign Affairs', 20 July 1941. CAB66/17 WP (41) 174. CAB65/19 WM 72(41), 21 July 1941. *Hansard Parliamentary Debates*, HC, 5th series, vol. 373, cc. 1074–5.

22. Churchill to Eden, 16 August 1941. FO371/26907 C9813/47/41.

23. 'Situation in Spain: Memorandum by the Secretary of State for Foreign Affairs', 10 November 1941. CAB66/19 WP (41) 266.

24. Eden to Hoare, 3 December 1941. FO371/26899 C13225/33/41. While Eden remained sceptical about the prospects of a coup he personally wished for a change at the top in Spain. He minuted on 1 December 1941: 'The Generals may be broken reeds but I would dearly love to see Suñer go and may be Franco too, and I am certainly not prepared to pretend otherwise'. FO371/26899 C13225/33/41.

25. Meeting of an interdepartmental meeting held at the Foreign Office, 18 May 1940. FO371/24490 C6527/379/36. Selby to Halifax, 23 May 1940. FO371/24501 C6938/30/41. See also DAPE, vol. VII, pp. 68–9; D. Eccles, *By Safe Hand: Letters of Sybil and David Eccles, 1939–1942*, London: Bodley Head, 1983, pp. 111–13; Telo, *Portugal na Segunda Guerra*, p. 162; Leitz, 'More carrot than stick', p. 253.

26. Hoare to Halifax, 1 August 1940. FO371/24526 C8051/6006/41. Hoare to Halifax, 15 August 1940. FO371/24503 C8761/40/41. Hoare to Neville Chamberlain, 30 July 1940. Neville Chamberlain Papers, NC 7/11/33/102 and Templewood Papers, XIII: 2, located at Cambridge University Library. C. R. Halstead, 'Consistent and total peril from every side: Portugal and its 1940 Protocol with Spain', *Iberian Studies*, vol. 3, 1974, p. 20.

27. Telo, *Portugal na Segunda Guerra*, pp. 212–14. See also Nogueira, *Salazar III*, pp. 285–6.

28. Secretary of State Cordell Hull to Alexander Weddell, Ambassador to Spain, 28 May 1940 and 5 June 1940. FRUS, 1940, vol. II, pp. 803–5.

29. Weddell to Hull, 7 September 1940. FRUS, 1940, vol. II, pp. 805–7.

30. Hull to Weddell, 26 September 1940. FRUS, 1940, vol. II, pp. 809–10.

31. Dalton to Eccles, 27 August 1940. Churchill to Halifax, 29 September 1940. FO800/323. Halifax to Churchill, 28 September 1940. PREM4/21/1. Dalton Diaries, XXIII, diary entry, 31 August 1940. Eccles, *By Safe Hand*, pp. 141–2. See also Smyth, *Diplomacy and Strategy of Survival*, pp. 60–4, 97 and Leitz, 'More carrot than stick', pp. 251–2.

32. For a detailed treatment of the Tangier crisis see Smyth, *Diplomacy and Strategy of Survival*, pp. 133–72. See also C. R. and C. J. Halstead, 'Aborted imperialism: Spain's occupation of Tangier, 1940–1945', *Iberian Studies*, vol. 7, 1978. For Beigbeder's dismissal see Preston, *Franco*, p. 391.

33. Weddell to Hull, 31 October 1940. FRUS, 1940, vol. II, p. 824.

34. Hull to Weddell, 8 November 1940. FRUS, 1940, vol. II, pp. 829–31.

35. Hoare to Foreign Office, 2 November 1940. FO371/24508 C11573/40/41. Hoare to Foreign Office, 19 November 1940. FO371/24513 C12249/75/41. Halifax to Cranborne, 5 December 1940. FO800/323. Hoare to R. A. Butler, Parliamentary Under Secretary of State for Foreign Affairs, 21 November 1940. Butler Papers RAB E3/8–127, located at Trinity College, Cambridge.

36. Aide Mémoire from British Embassy to State Department, 9 November 1940. Memorandum by Under Secretary of State, Sumner Welles,

19 November 1940. Herschel Johnson, American Chargé d'Affaires at London to Hull, 20 November 1940. FRUS, 1940, vol. II, pp. 831–2, 836, 839. W. F. Kimball (ed.), *Churchill and Roosevelt: The Complete Correspondence. Vol. I: Alliance Emerging*, Princeton, NJ: Princeton University Press, 1984, pp. 86–7.

37. Weddell to Hull, 29 November 1940. FRUS, 1940, vol. II, pp. 839–41.

38. Hull to Weddell, 10 December 1940. FRUS, 1940, vol. II, pp. 845–7. For Franco's interest in Latin America (Hispanidad) see Pérez, 'España y la Segunda Guerra Mundial', pp. 309–10.

39. Hull to Weddell, 19 December 1940. FRUS, 1940, vol. II, pp. 848–50.

40. Foreign Office to Lord Lothian, British Ambassador at Washington, 2 December 1940. FO371/24505 C12495/30/41. W. N. Medlicott, *The Economic Blockade Vol. I*, London: HMSO, 1952, pp. 541–2. Woodward, *British Foreign Policy I*, p. 442.

41. Butler to Hoare, 6 December 1940. Butler Papers RAB E3/8–131. Woodward, *British Foreign Policy I*, p. 446. Medlicott, *Economic Blockade I*, p. 542. Smyth, *Diplomacy and Strategy of Survival*, pp. 138–9.

42. D. Smyth, 'Franco and the Allies in the Second World War' in Balfour and Preston (eds), *Spain and the Great Powers*, p. 196.

43. Hull to Weddell, 27 December 1940. FRUS, 1940, vol. II, pp. 851–3.

44. Woodward, *British Foreign Policy I*, p. 447. See also Halstead and Halstead, 'Aborted imperialism', p. 58 who claim the Anglo-Spanish entente of February 1941 constituted a *de facto* retreat from the assertion of full sovereignty by Spain in Tangier. For Portuguese support see Stone, *The Oldest Ally*, pp. 145–7.

45. Woodward, *British Foreign Policy I*, pp. 447–8.

46. Hoare to Foreign Office, 24 January 1941. FO371/26957 C802/802/41. Hoare to Foreign Office, 31 January 1941. FO371/26904 C986/46/41.

47. Eden to Sir Alexander Cadogan, Permanent Under Secretary at the Foreign Office, 17 February 1941. FO371/26904 C1651/46/41. Smyth, *Diplomacy and Strategy of Survival*, pp. 176–8. Medlicott, *Economic Blockade I*, pp. 542–3. Apart from Eden and Dalton, Lord Cranborne, the Dominions Secretary, Alfred Duff Cooper, the Minister of Information, and Sir Auckland Geddes and J. N. Buchanan, respectively chairman and financial director of the Rio Tinto Company which was the largest British owned company operating in Spain, had reservations about the policy of continuing economic assistance to Spain. FO800/323. The Eden Diaries, diary entries, 2, 3, 21 January 1941. Unpublished [Oliver] Harvey Diaries, diary entries, 17 October 1940, 13 November 1940, 15 January 1940, located at the British Library.

48. Memorandum of Conversation with Lord Halifax, British Ambassador at Washington, by Sumner Welles, 20 March 1941. FRUS, 1941, vol. II, pp. 886–7.

49. Weddell to Hull, 1 March 1941. FRUS, 1941, vol. II, pp. 881–5.

50. Hull to Weddell, 10 April 1941. FRUS, 1941, vol. II, pp. 887–8.

51. Weddell to Hull, 19 and 20 April 1940. FRUS, 1941, vol. II, pp. 888–90.

52. Hull to Weddell, 30 April 1941. FRUS, 1941, vol. II, pp. 893–5.

53. Smyth, *Diplomacy and Strategy of Survival*, pp. 181–3. See also C. R. Halstead, 'The dispute between Ramon Serrano Suñer and Alexander Weddell', *Rivista di Studi Politica Internazionali*, 1974, pp. 445–74.

54. Smyth, *Diplomacy and Strategy of Survival*, pp. 183–5. Hoare to Foreign Office, 28 June 1941. FO371/26906 C7752/46/41.

55. Foreign Office to Halifax, 4 October 1941. FO371/26926 C10496/108/41.

56. Weddell to Hull, 16 September 1941. Hull to Weddell, 18 September 1941. FRUS, 1941, vol. II, pp. 915–17.

57. Weddell to Hull, 30 September 1941 and 6 October 1941. FRUS, 1941, vol. II, pp. 924–6, 928–9.

58. Hull to Weddell, 6 October 1941. Weddell to Hull, 7 October 1941. FRUS, 1941, vol. II, pp. 929–31. Smyth, *Diplomacy and Strategy of Survival*, pp. 190–1. According to Smyth, the Germans, with official Spanish connivance, arranged the replenishment at Spanish ports of fuel and other stocks of 16 German U boats between March and December 1941.

59. Smyth, *Diplomacy and Strategy of Survival*, pp. 191–3.

60. Foreign Office to the British Embassy in Washington, 19 December 1941. FO371/26926 C14052/108/41. See also Woodward, *British Foreign Policy in the Second World War, Vol. IV*, London: HMSO, 1975, pp. 4–5.

61. Foreign Office to British Embassy in Washington, 1 January 1942. FO371/26926 C14052/108/41. Kimball (ed.), *Churchill and Roosevelt I*, p. 313.

62. Smyth, *Diplomacy and Strategy of Survival*, pp. 194–6. C. Hull, *The Memoirs of Cordell Hull, Vol. II*, London: Hodder and Stoughton, 1948, pp. 1189–90. W. N. Medlicott, *The Economic Blockade II*, London: HMSO, 1959, pp. 303–8.

63. Smyth, *Diplomacy and Strategy of Survival*, pp. 96–8.

64. Ibid., pp. 163, 201–5. Churchill's intervention was a result of speculation should British forces break through in North Africa and require the support of General Maxim Weygand's French forces. The General could be offered the restoration of France to her former greatness but in return the French would have to make concessions in Morocco to the Spaniards and thus fortify them in their resistance to a German advance through their country.

65. Memorandum by Sumner Welles, 19 November 1941. FRUS, 1941, vol. II, pp. 931–2.

66. Smyth, *Diplomacy and Strategy of Survival*, pp. 106–7.

67. CAB79/9 JP(41)142. CAB80/57 COS(41)57 (0). Smyth, *Diplomacy and Strategy of Survival*, pp. 177, 206–7.

68. Woodward, *British Foreign Policy I*, p. 44.

69. CAB84/24 JP (40)733. Smyth, *Diplomacy and Strategy of Survival*, pp. 144–6, 150.

70. Chiefs of Staff Minute to Churchill, 23 March 1941. PREM3/361/1. CAB79/10 COS(41) 105th meeting. See also Smyth, *Diplomacy and Strategy of Survival*, pp. 220–2.

71. Kimball (ed.), *Churchill and Roosevelt I*, p. 176.

72. J. R. M. Butler, *Grand Strategy, Vol. II*, London: HMSO, 1957, pp. 432–3.

73. Smyth, *Diplomacy and Strategy of Survival*, pp. 215, 225–7. Preston, *Franco*, pp. 432–5. According to Serrano Suñer himself, 'from that moment the "F. E. T. de las J.O.N.S." was above all Franco's party'.

74. CAB69/2 DO(41) 27th and 40th meetings.

75. J. M. A. Gwyer, *Grand Strategy, Vol. III (part I)*, London: HMSO, 1964, pp. 6–7.

76. CAB69/3 DO(41) 52nd meeting. CAB79/86 COS(41) 259th meeting. CAB65/23 WM74(41). It seems that the British had no firm intelligence concerning the strength of Spanish defences on the Islands. On 27 August 1941 the Director of Combined Operations, Admiral Lord Keyes, seemingly oblivious of Spain's reluctance to allow German forces anywhere near the Canaries, expressed his opinion, in a memorandum for the Chiefs of Staff Committee, that the delay in utilising the Puma force had presented the Germans with 'practically a free hand to organise and strengthen the Spanish defences'. P. Halperin (ed.), *The Keyes Papers: Selections from the Private and Official Correspondence of Admiral of the Fleet Lord Keyes: Vol. III, 1939–1945*, London: Allen and Unwin: 1981, p. 185.

77. Smyth, *Diplomacy and Strategy of Survival*, pp. 232–3. See also Dilks (ed.), *Diaries of Sir Alexander Cadogan*, diary entry, 21 July 1941, p. 393.

78. Smyth, *Diplomacy and Strategy of Survival*, pp. 233–4. Gwyer, *Grand Strategy III (part I)*, p. 8.

79. Smyth, *Diplomacy and Strategy of Survival*, pp. 234–7.

9. THE AXIS POWERS AND PORTUGAL, 1939–1941

1. Leitz, *Nazi Germany and Neutral Europe*, pp. 148–9.

2. Circular telegram Ministry of Information, 17 October 1939. DAPE, vol. VI, annex to no. 199, pp. 169–70. Sir Ronald Campbell, British Ambassador at Lisbon, to Strang, 4 January 1941, Campbell to the Foreign Office, 25 January 1941 and 7 May 1941. FO371/26818 C369/C5053/214/36.

3. Memorandum by an Official of Ribbentrop's Secretariat, 21 January 1941. DGFP, series D, vol. XI, no. 672, p. 1130.

4. Packard, *Neither Friend nor Foe*, p. 217

5. Wheeler, 'In the service of order', pp. 12–13. Wylie, 'An amateur learns his job?', p. 449. Telo, *Portugal na Segunda Guerra*, pp. 437–8.

6. Wylie, 'An amateur learns his job?', pp. 449–50. Gallagher, 'Controlled repression in Salazar's Portugal', pp. 388–92.

7. Stohrer to the German Foreign Ministry, 3 July 1940. DGFP, series D, vol. X, no. 95, pp. 105–6.

8. Ribbentrop to the German Legation in Portugal, 16 July 1940. DGFP, series D, vol. X, no. 176, pp. 224–5.

9. Hoyningen-Huene to the German Foreign Ministry, 30 July 1940. Stohrer to the German Foreign Ministry, 21 August 1940. DGFP, series D, vol. X, nos 255, 374, pp. 364, 521–2.

10. Stohrer to the German Foreign Ministry, 20 August 1940. DGFP, series D, vol. X, no. 369, p. 515.

11. Unsigned Memorandum, 17 September 1940. DGFP, series D, vol. XI, no. 63, p. 86.

12. Memorandum by an Official of Ribbentrop's Secretariat, 28 September 1940. DGFP, series D, vol. XI, no. 117, pp. 302–4.

13. Muggeridge (ed.), *Ciano's Diplomatic Papers*, p. 429.

14. Leitz, *Nazi Germany and Neutral Europe*, pp. 151–2. F. Rosas, 'Portuguese neutrality in the Second World War' in Wylie (ed.), *European Belligerents and Non-Belligerents*, p. 275.

15. Hoyningen-Huene to the German Foreign Ministry, 2 July 1941. DGFP, series D, vol. XIII, no. 60 and n2, pp. 69–70.

16. Campbell to the Foreign Office, 9 July 1941. FO371/26835 C7748/900/36.

17. Hoyningen-Huene to the German Foreign Ministry, 31 October 1941. DGFP, series D, vol. XIII, n2, p. 70.

18. Gallagher, *Portugal*, p. 194.

19. Memorandum by Hoyningen-Huene, 15 November 1941. DGFP, series D, vol. XIII, no. 476, pp. 787–8.

20. Leitz, *Germany and Neutral Europe*, p. 153.

21. Ibid., p. 159.

22. Leitz, *Economic Relations*, n3, p. 171.

23. Head of Division W II Economic Policy Department to the German Legation in Portugal, 22 November 1941. DGFP, series D, vol. XIII, no. 489, pp. 808–10.

24. Medlicott, *Economic Blockade II*, pp. 323–6, 598–607. D. L. Wheeler, 'The price of neutrality: Portugal, the wolfram question and World War II', *Luso-Brazilian Review*, vol. 23, 1986, pt. 2, pp. 102–4.

25. Memorandum by the Director of the Economic Policy Department of the German Foreign Ministry, 23 November 1940. DGFP, series D, vol. XI, no. 390, pp. 690–1. Telo, *Portugal na Segunda Guerra*, pp. 440–1.

26. Leitz, *Germany and Neutral Europe*, pp. 161–3.

27. Ibid., p. 161.

28. Schreiber *et al.*, *Germany and the Second World War, III*, p. 211.

29. Hans Thomsen, German Chargé d'Affaires at Washington, to the German Foreign Ministry, 18 August 1940. DGFP, series D, vol. X, no. 362, pp. 507–8. Goda, *Tomorrow the World*, p. 66.

30. C. B. Burdick, *Germany's Military Strategy and Spain in World War II*, Syracuse, NY: Syracuse University Press, 1968, pp. 38–9.

31. Burdick and Jacobsen (eds), *The Halder War Diary*, diary entry, 23 August 1940, p. 250.

32. Goda, *Tomorrow the World*, pp. 66–7.

33. Ibid., p. 68.

34. H. H. Herwig, 'Prelude to *Weltblitzkrieg*: Germany's naval policy toward the United States of America, 1939–1941', *Journal of Modern History*, vol. 43, 1971, p. 657.

35. Memorandum by an Official of Ribbentrop's Secretariat, 17 September 1940. DGFP, series D, vol. XI, no. 66, pp. 96–7.

36. Führer Conferences with the Commander in Chief of the Navy, 26 September 1940 and 14 October 1940. *Brassey's Naval Annual*, pp. 142, 145. Schreiber *et al.*, *Germany and the Second World War, III*, pp. 222, 224.

37. Conference of Chief, Operations Division, Naval Staff, with Chief Operations Staff, OKW, General Jodl, 4 November 1940. Führer Conference with Commander in Chief of the Navy, 14 November 1940. *Brassey's Naval Annual*, pp. 147–8, 152.

38. Goda, *Tomorrow the World*, pp. 118–19. Schreiber *et al.*, *Germany and the Second World War, III*, pp. 214–15.

39. Unsigned Memorandum, n.d. DGFP, series D, vol. XI, no. 220, pp. 372–3.

40. Schreiber *et al.*, *Germany and the Second World War, III*, pp. 228–9.

41. Führer's Directive No. 18, 12 November 1940. DGFP, series D, vol. XI, no. 323, pp. 527–31. See also Trevor-Roper (ed.), *Blitzkrieg to Defeat*, pp. 39–43.

42. Memorandum by an Official of Ribbentrop's Secretariat, 16 November 1940. DGFP, series D, vol. XI, no. 326, p. 546.

43. This German aircraft never got beyond the planning stage. Regular production of the long range bomber, HE177, did not begin until the second half of 1943 by which time the British had succeeded in persuading the Portuguese to lease them bases on the Azores. See Herwig, 'Prelude to *Weltblitkrieg*', n43, p. 658.

44. Führer Conference with Commander in Chief of the Navy, 14 November 1940. *Brassey's Naval Annual*, pp. 152–3. See also Burdick, *Germany's Military Strategy*, p. 75; Schreiber *et al.*, *Germany and the Second World War, III*, p. 233; and Herwig, 'Prelude to *Weltblitzkrieg*', p. 658, who claims wrongly that Raeder raised no objection to Hitler's scheme for the Azores.

45. Stohrer to the German Foreign Ministry, 29 November 1940. DGFP, series D, vol. XI, no. 420, pp. 739–40.

46. Stohrer to the German Foreign Ministry, 27 January 1941. DGFP, series D, vol. XI, no. 718, p. 1209.

47. Goda, *Tomorrow the World*, pp. 121–2.

48. Burdick, *Germany's Military Strategy*, pp. 122–4. Trevor-Roper (ed.), *Blitzkrieg to Defeat*, p. 81.

49. German Legation in Portugal to the German Foreign Ministry, 3 March 1941. DGFP, series D, vol. XII, no. 120, p. 212.

50. Hoyningen-Huene to the German Foreign Ministry, 23 March 1941. DGFP, series D, vol. XII, no. 196, p. 343.

51. Hoyningen-Huene to the German Foreign Ministry, 20 April 1941. DGFP, series D, vol. XII, no. 374, pp. 589–90.

52. S. Friedländer, *Prelude to Downfall: Hitler and the United States, 1939–1941*, London: Chatto and Windus, 1967, p. 141.

53. Memorandum by an Official of Ribbentrop's Secretariat, 28 April 1941. DGFP, series D, vol. XII, no. 422, p. 665.

54. Directive of the High Command of the Army, 7 May 1941. DGFP, series D, vol. XII, no. 469, pp. 731–2.

55. Burdick, *Germany's Military Strategy*, pp. 133–49.

56. Führer Conference with the Commander in Chief of the Navy, 22 May 1941. *Brassey's Naval Annual*, pp. 198–9. At his meeting with Mussolini at the Brenner on 2 June 1941, Hitler revealed that new long-ranged bombers with an enormous radius were being mass-produced in Germany, but would not be ready until the end of the year. Memorandum by an Official of Ribbentrop's Secretariat, 3 June 1941. DGFP, series D, vol. XII, no. 584, p. 950.

57. Goda, *Tomorrow the World*, pp. 177–8.

58. Ribbentrop to the German Legation in Portugal, 13 July 1941. DGFP, series D, vol. XIII, no. 103, p. 130.

59. See the *New York Times*, 14 July 1941.

60. Memorandum by Woermann, 22 July 1941. DGFP, series D, vol. XIII, no. 141, pp. 202–3.

61. Thomsen to the German Foreign Ministry, 20 July 1941. DGFP, series D, vol. XIII, no. 133, pp. 189–90.

62. Goda, *Tomorrow the World*, p. 177.

63. Memorandum by an Official of Ribbentrop's Secretariat, 30 November 1941. DGFP, series D, vol. XIII, no. 523, pp. 905–6.

64. Goda, *Tomorrow the World*, p. 190. See also Führer Conference with Raeder, 12 December 1941. *Brassey's Naval Annual*, p. 245.

65. See in this connection Hitler's Directive of 29 May 1942. The Atlantic Islands were not even mentioned. Trevor-Roper (ed.), *Blitzkrieg to Defeat*, pp. 121–3.

10. THE ALLIES AND PORTUGAL, 1939–1941

1. Halifax to Selby, 24 February 1940. FO371/24489 C2886/379/36.

2. CAB80/11 COS(40)369 'Spain and Portugal – Neutrality: Note by the Secretary', 20 May 1940. CAB79/4 COS(40) 147th meeting, 24 May 1940. Halifax to Selby, 27 May 1940. FO371/24490 C6527/379/36.

3. See Ch. 8 of this book.

4. Wylie, 'An amateur learns his job?', p. 453. According to António Telo, Wilhelm Leissner of the *Abwehr* used Lisbon to infiltrate *Garbo* into the United Kingdom during 1941. *Portugal na Segunda Guerra*, p. 439.

5. See M. Howard, *British Intelligence in the Second World War, Vol. V*, London: HMSO, 1990, pp. 231–41.

6. Wylie, 'An amateur learns his job?', pp. 441–2. See also Telo, *Portugal na Segunda Guerra*, pp. 436–7.

7. 'Observations on the Portuguese Press for June, July, August and September 1940'. FO371/24494 C6574/4597/36.

8. D. L. Wheeler, 'Review of António Telo's *Portugal na Segunda Guerra*', *Luso-Brazilian Review*, vol. 27, 1990, pp. 135–6.

9. Selby to Halifax, 3 July 1940. FO371/24491 C7649/379/36. Campbell to Eden, 26 April 1941. FO371/26811 C4658/149/36.

10. Campbell to the Foreign Office, 30 August, 13 September, 7 October 1941. FO371/26795 C9773/C10275/C11211/41/36.

11. 'Information for Dr Salazar', 30 September 1941. JIC(41)390 (Final). FO371/26795 C11055/41/36.

12. 'Observations on the Portuguese Press, October–November 1940'. FO371/24494 C10958/C13281/4597/36. Campbell to the Foreign Office, 30 January 1941. FO371/26811 C1006/149/36. Campbell to the Foreign Office, 31 July 1941. FO371/26795 C8759/41/36.

13. Campbell to Eden, 6 August 1941. FO371/26795 C8917/41/36.

14. 'Guiding line for Broadcasts to Portugal', 11 October 1941. FO371/26819 C12584/214/36.

15. Telo, *Portugal na Segunda Guerra*, pp. 416–17.

16. T. Gallagher, 'Conservatism, dictatorship and fascism in Portugal, 1941–1945' in Blinkhorn (ed.), *Fascists and Conservatives*, pp. 165–6.

17. Medlicott, *Economic Blockade I*, pp. 527–9. Medlicott, *Economic Blockade II*, pp. 319–20.

18. Campbell to Eden, 1 February 1941. FO425/418. 'Economic Warfare during February 1941'. CAB68/8 WP 19(R)41.

19. Medlicott, *Economic Blockade II*, pp. 317–19. Eccles (ed.), *By Safe Hand*, pp. 351–5.

20. Eden to Campbell, 25 April 1941. FO425/418. DAPE, vol. VIII, no. 1610, pp. 210–13.

21. CAB92/18 AD(39)42 'Note by Secretary: Relative Strategical Importance of Countries requiring Arms from the United Kingdom (DCOS)', 7 November 1939. 'Note by Secretary: Foreign Office Memorandum', 17 November 1939.

22. 'Foreign Office Memorandum: Portuguese Arms Requirements', 20 December 1940. FO371/24485 C13740/22/36.

23. CAB66/8 WP(40)180 COS(40)408 'Report Chiefs of Staff Committee: Portugal', 29 May 1940. CAB65/7 WM149(40), 31 May 1940.

24. CAB80/13 COS(40)465(JP) 'Western Mediterranean and Atlantic Islands Project', 14 June 1940. CAB79/5 COS(40) 184th meeting, 17 June 1940. CAB69/1 DO(40) 18th meeting, 21 June 1940.

25. William Strang, Superintending Assistant Under Secretary to the Central Department of the Foreign Office, to Colonel Hollis, Secretary of the Chiefs

of Staff Committee, 30 June 1940. Hollis to Strang, 1 July 1940. FO371/24515 C7429/113/41.

26. 'Portuguese Armed Forces: Note by Secretary', 22 July 1940. JIC(40)187. FO371/24490 C7174/379/36.

27. Churchill to Halifax, 24 July 1940. PREM3/361/1.

28. Minutes Cadogan, Vansittart and Strang, 24–30 July 1940. Halifax to Churchill, 31 July 1941. FO371/24515/C7429/113/41 and PREM3/361/1. For a brief reference to the Foreign Office debate see E. Barker, *Churchill and Eden at War*, London: Macmillan, 1978, pp. 148–9.

29. See FO371/24495 C7171/C11261/7171/36 and PREM3/361/4.

30. CAB80/19 COS(40)798 'Naval Operations in the Atlantic', 4 October 1940. CAB79/55 COS(40) 11th meeting (0) part of COS(40) 335th meeting, 4 October 1940.

31. Hollis to Strang, 31 October 1941. Strang to Hollis, 9 November 1940. FO371/24404 C10637/4066/36.

32. CA66/13 WP(40)460 COS(40)968 'Spain: Report by the Chiefs of Staff', 23 November 1940.

33. CAB69/1 DO(40) 46th meeting, 25 November 1940. See also PREM3/361/6A.

34. F. H. Hinsley, *British Intelligence and the Second World War. Vol. I*, London: HMSO, 1979, pp. 256–7.

35. CAB79/55 COS(40) 32nd and 33rd meetings, 14 December 1940.

36. Churchill to Smuts, 17 December 1940. PREM3/361/4.

37. Halifax to Noel Charles, British Chargé d'Affaires at Lisbon, 17 December 1940. FO371/24491 C13546/379/36. Monteiro to Salazar, 19 September 1940. DAPE, vol. VII, no. 1376 and annex, pp. 677–83.

38. Halifax to Charles, 18 December 1940. FO371/24491 C13546/379/36. CAB79/8 COS(40) 432nd meeting, 18 December 1940.

39. Eden to Campbell, 3 January 1941. FO371/26793 C237/41/36.

40. CAB79/9 JP(41)100 COS(41)23|(0) 'Future Combined Operations', 6 February 1941. CAB79/9 COS(41) 50th meeting, 12 February 1941.

41. Strang to Hollis, 26 February 1941. FO371/26813 C1790/152/36. Monteiro to Salazar, 25 February 1941. DAPE, vol. VIII, no. 1535, pp. 134–7. See also Telo, *Portugal na Segunda Guerra*, p. 325.

42. CAB99/11. Major General Sir Hastings Ismay, Deputy Secretary to the War Cabinet and Chief of Staff to the Minister of Defence, to Churchill, 8 March 1941. Minute by Churchill, 9 March 1941.

43. CAB99/10 AP(41)3 'Notes on British Assistance to Portugal', 11 March 1941.

44. CAB99/10 AP(41)1 'Memorandum for the British Delegation on the Subject of Scale of Attack on Portugal', 10 March 1941.

45. CAB99/10 COS(41)181 also AP(41)4. Telo, *Portugal na Segunda Guerra*, p. 327. See also Churchill to Hoare, 15 April 1941. M. Gilbert (ed.), *The Churchill War Papers. Vol. III: The Ever Widening War 1941*, London: Heinemann, 2000, p. 501.

46. The Foreign Office to Halifax, 28 March 1941. FO371/26834 C3052/900/36. Minutes by Churchill, 22 and 24 March 1941 and Chiefs of Staff to Churchill, 23 March 1941. PREM3/361/1. Churchill to General Ismay, 24 March 1941. Gilbert (ed.), *The Churchill War Papers III*, pp. 391–2.

47. Campbell to Eden, 18 April 1941. FO371/26793 C047/41/36. Hollis to Makins, 29 April 1941. Foreign Office to Campbell, 1 May 1941. FO371/26794 C4794/41/36.

48. Eden to Campbell, 21 May 1941. FO371/26794 C5460/41/36. Monteiro to Salazar, 21 May 1941. DAPE, vol. VIII, no. 1832, pp. 425–9.

49. CAB69/2 DO(41) 36th meeting, 29 May 1941.

50. Lord Lothian, British Ambassador at Washington, to the Foreign Office, 25 September 1940. FO371/24511 C8361/75/41. CAB65/9 WM(40) 260th meeting, 27 September 1940. Foreign Office to Lothian, 9 October 1940 and Neville Butler, British Chargé d'Affaires at Washington, to the Foreign Office, 15 October 1940. FO371/24494 C10637/4066/36.

51. Kimball (ed.), *Churchill and Roosevelt I*, pp. 173–4. Churchill, *The Second World War III*, p. 125. See also J. P. Lash, *Roosevelt and Churchill, 1939–1941: The Partnership that Saved the West*, London: Andre Deutsch, 1977, p. 308.

52. Kimball (ed.), *Churchill and Roosevelt I*, pp. 178, 181. See also PREM3/469.

53. CAB84/29 JP(41)313 'The Atlantic Islands', 23 April 1941. See also Ch. 8 of this book.

54. Halifax to the Foreign Office, 17 May 1941. Campbell to the Foreign Office, 20 May 1941. Foreign Office to Halifax, 23 May 1941. FO371/26809 C5297/C5415/115/36.

55. For details of Plan 'Gray' see S. Conn and B. Fairchild, *The United States Army in World War II: The Western Hemisphere: The Framework of National Defence*, Washington DC: Office of the Chief of (Army) Defense Department, 1960, pp. 116–19, 121–5.

56. Halifax to the Foreign Office, 29 May 1941. PREM3/469.

57. S. Ross, 'American war plans' in McKercher and Legault (eds), *Military Planning*, pp. 152–3.

58. Ibid., p. 158.

59. Johnson to Hull, 29 May 1941. FRUS, vol. II, 1941, pp. 843–4. Kimball (ed.), *Churchill and Roosevelt I*, p. 201.

60. Campbell to Eden, 10 May and 7 June 1941. FO371/26809 C5052/C6701/115/36. Eden to Campbell, 30 May 1941. FO371/26848 C5883/3519/36. See also J. K. Sweeney, 'The Luso-American connection: the courtship, 1940–1941', *Iberian Studies*, vol. 6, 1977, pp. 4–5 and Packard, *Neither Friend nor Foe*, pp. 220–1. According to João de Bianchi, the Portuguese Minister at Washington, Pepper's speech had the prior approval of Roosevelt and his Cabinet. Telo, *Portugal na Segunda Guerra*, p. 368.

61. Roosevelt to Salazar, 14 July 1941. FRUS, 1941, vol. II, pp. 851–3. For a brief discussion of the Luso-American rift see Sweeney, 'The Luso-American

connection', pp. 5–6 and A. H. D'Araújo Stott-Howarth, *A Aliança Luso-Britânica e a Segunda Guerra Mundial: Tenrava de Intrepretação do seu Funcionamento*, Lisbon: ENP, 1956, pp. 27–30.

62. Conn and Fairchild, *United States Army*, pp. 125–6. Sweeney, 'The Luso-American connection', p. 5. W. L. Langer and S. E. Gleason, *The Undeclared War, 1940–1941*, New York: Harper, 1953, pp. 588–9.

63. Monteiro to Eden, 10 July 1941. DAPE, vol. IX, no. 2049, pp. 49–54.

64. CAB80/29 COS(41)425 'Portugal: Assistance in the Defence of the Atlantic Islands', 11 July 1941. CAB79/12 COS (41) 246th meeting, 15 July 1941 and 257th meeting, 23 July 1941.

65. Campbell to the Foreign Office, 6 August 1941. Minute by Orme Sargent, 6 August 1941. FO371/26849 C8709/C8763/3519/36.

66. CAB65/23 WM84(41) 19 August 1941.

67. British Embassy Lisbon to the Ministry of Economic Warfare, 20 August 1941. Minute by Roger Makins and marginal comment by Eden, 21 August 1941 and minute by Cadogan, 22 August 1941. FO371/26794 C4727/41/36.

68. Eden to Churchill, 28 August 1941. FO371/26794 C4727/41/36. Foreign Office to Washington Embassy, 3 September 1941. FO371/26849 C9734/3519/36. See also J. Harvey (ed.), *The War Diaries of Oliver Harvey, 1941–1945*, London: Collins, 1978, pp. 38–9.

69. Minute by Cadogan and memorandum handed to the Portuguese Ambassador, 6 September 1941. FO371/26849 C9734/C10096/3519/36. See also DAPE, vol. IX, nos 2263, 2268, pp. 220–4, 234–42.

70. CAB99/12 AP2(41). Also COS(41) 663 'Liaison with Portuguese: Plans for Anglo-Portuguese Collaboration in an Emergency', 11 November 1941.

71. For details of the staff conversations during 1942 see CAB99/14. See also H.Delgado, *The Memoirs of General Delgado*, London: Cassell, 1964, pp. 62–7. For Salazar's reluctance with regard to the timing and circumstances of Portugal's *casus belli* see Eden to Campbell, 13 February 1942. Eden Papers, PORT/42/6, located at Birmingham University Library.

72. CAB79/19 432nd meeting, 23 December 1941.

73. Foreign Office to the Embassies in Madrid and Lisbon, 2 January 1942. FO371/26946 C14322/300/41.

CONCLUSION

1. For Japanese attempts to infiltrate and eventually occupy Portuguese Timor see Stone, *The Oldest Ally*, pp. 182–99.

2. For the guerrilla war against Franco which reached its peak during 1945–1947 see A. Cowan, 'The guerrilla war against Franco', *European History Quarterly*, vol. 20, 1990 and Beevor, *The Spanish Civil War*, pp. 272–8.

3. For Soviet interest in Spain during the last months of the Second World War and the early Cold War see G. Swain, 'Stalin and Spain, 1944–1948' in Leitz and Dunthorn (eds), *Spain in an International Context*, pp. 245–64. See also E. Moradiellos, 'The Potsdam Conference and the Spanish problem', *Contemporary European History*, vol. 10, 2001, pp. 82–6.

4. Serrano Suñer candidly told a French reporter in 1945 that it had been the intention of the Franco regime 'to enter the war at the moment of German victory, at the hour of the last cartridge'. Detwiler, 'Spain and the Axis', p. 50.

5. Leitz, *Nazi Germany and Neutral Europe*, pp. 160–3.

6. Leitz, 'Programm Bär', p. 184.

7. Preston, *Franco*, p. 530.

8. For Salazar's earlier view of German dominance see Telo, *Portugal na Segunda Guerra*, pp. *416–17*. For his anti-American attitude see Rosas, 'Portuguese neutrality in the Second World War', pp. 274–5.

9. For the bases deal see Stone, 'The official British attitude to the Anglo-Portuguese alliance', pp. 741–3.

10. Stone, 'The degree of British commitment to the restoration of democracy in Spain', pp. 200–1. For Operation 'Torch' see D. Smyth, 'Screening "Torch": allied counter intelligence and the Spanish threat to the secrecy of the allied invasion of French North Africa in November, 1942', *Intelligence and National Security*, vol. 4, 1989.

11. Stone 'The degree of British commitment to the restoration of democracy in Spain', pp. 204–7, 210.

12. See Dunthorn, *Britain and the Spanish Anti-Franco Opposition*; Q. Ahmad, *Britain, Franco Spain and the Cold War, 1945–1959*, Kuala Lumpur: Noordeen, 1995; and J. Edwards, *Anglo-American Relations and the Franco Question, 1945–1955*, Oxford: Oxford University Press, 1999.

Selected Bibliography

UNPUBLISHED PRIMARY SOURCES

At The National Archives (UK): CAB2 Committee of Imperial Defence Minutes; CAB4 Committee of Imperial Defence Memoranda; CAB16 Ad Hoc Sub-Committees of Enquiry: Proceedings and Memoranda; CAB23 Cabinet Minutes; CAB24 Cabinet Memoranda; CAB27 Cabinet Foreign Policy Committee, 1936–1939; CAB62 International Committee for the Application of the Agreement Regarding Non-Intervention in Spain, 1936–1939; CAB65 War Cabinet Minutes; CAB66 War Cabinet Memoranda; CAB69 Defence Committee (Operations); CAB79 Chiefs of Staff Committee Minutes; CAB80 Chiefs of Staff Committee Memoranda; CAB99 Commonwealth and International Conferences (Anglo-Portuguese Military Conversations 1941); PREM1 Prime Minister Files (Chamberlain); PREM3 Prime Minister Operational Files (Churchill); PREM4 Prime Minister Confidential Papers (Churchill); FO371 Political Correspondence Foreign Office; FO425 Confidential Print (Portugal and Spain) Foreign Office; FO849 International Committee for the Application of the Agreement Regarding Non-Intervention in Spain 1936–1939.

At the Quai d'Orsay: Papiers 1940 – Reconstitution Fouques-Duparc (Dossiers Bonnet).

At the Vincennes Military Archives: SHAT (Service Historique de l'Armée de Terre) Papers.

PUBLISHED PRIMARY SOURCES

i. Official Documents and Publications

Documents on British Foreign Policy, 1919–1939, HMSO: 2nd series: vol. XVII, London, 1979; vol. XVIII, London, 1980; vol. XIX, London, 1982; vol. XX, London, 1984. 3rd series: vol. III, London, 1951; vol. V, London, 1952.

Dez Anos de Política Externa, 1936–1947: A Nação Portuguesa e a Segunda Guerra Mundial, Imprensa Nacional: vol. I, Lisboa, 1961; vol. II, Lisboa, 1962; vol. III, Lisboa, 1962; vol. IV, Lisboa, 1965; vol. V, Lisboa, 1967; vol. VI, Lisboa, 1971; vol. VII, Lisboa, 1972; vol. VIII, Lisboa, 1973; vol. IX, Lisboa, 1974; vol. X, Lisboa, 1974.

Documents Diplomatiques Français, 1932–1939, Imprimerie National: 1st series: vol. I, Paris, 1964; vol. III, Paris, 1967; vol. IV, Paris, 1968; vol. V, Paris, 1970; vol. VI, Paris, 1972, vol. VII, Paris 1979; vol. VIII, Paris, 1979; vol. IX, Paris, 1980; vol. XII, Paris, 1984; vol. XIII, Paris, 1984. 2nd series: vol. I, Paris, 1963; vol. II, Paris, 1964, vol. III, Paris, 1966; vol. IV, Paris, 1967; vol. V, Paris, 1968; vol. VI, Paris 1970; vol. VII, Paris, 1972; vol. IX, Paris, 1974; vol. XII, Paris, 1978; vol. XV, Paris, 1981; vol. XVI, Paris, 1983; vol. XVII, Paris, 1984; vol. XVIII, Paris, 1985; vol. XIX, Paris, 1986.

Documents Diplomatiques Français, P. I. E. (Presses Interuniversitaires Européenes) – Peter Lang: Septembre–Décembre, 1939, Paris, 2002; Juin, 1940, Paris, 2003.

Documents on German Foreign Policy, 1918–1945, HMSO: series C: vol. IV, London, 1962; vol. V, London, 1966. Series D: vol. II, London, 1950; vol. III, London, 1951; vol. VI, London, 1956; vol. VII, London 1956; vol. IX, London, 1956; vol. X, London, 1957; vol. XI, London, 1961; vol. XII, London, 1962; vol. XIII, London, 1964.

Foreign Relations of the United States, United States Government Printing Office: 1931, vol. II, Washington, 1946; 1932, vol. II, Washington, 1947; 1933, vol. II, Washington, 1949; 1934, vol. II, Washington, 1950; 1935, vol. II, Washington, 1952; 1936, vol. II, Washington, 1954; 1937, vol. I, Washington, 1954; 1938, vol. IV, Washington, 1955; 1940, vol. II, Washington, 1957; 1941, vol. I, Washington, 1958; 1941, vol. II, Washington, 1959.

Hansard Parliamentary Debates, 5th series, House of Commons.

Parliamentary Papers, 1936–1938.

Führer Conferences on Naval Affairs in *Brassey's Naval Annual*, London: HMSO, 1948.

Keesing's Contemporary Archives, 1937–1940.

The Making of the Second World War, ed. A. Adamthwaite, London: Allen and Unwin, 1977.

The Communist International, 1919–1943. Documents. Vol. III 1929–1943, ed. J. Degras, London: Frank Cass, 1971.

Soviet Documents on Foreign Policy Volume III, 1933–1941, ed. J. Degras, London: Oxford University Press, 1953.

Ciano's Diplomatic Papers, ed. M. Muggeridge, London: Odhams, 1948.

Spain Betrayed: The Soviet Union in the Spanish Civil War, eds, R. Radosh, M. R. Habeck and G. Sevostianov, New Haven, CT and London: Yale University Press, 2001.

Blitzkrieg to Defeat: Hitler's War Directives, 1939–1945, ed. H. R. Trevor Roper, New York: Holt, Rinehart, Winston, 1971.

ii. Memoirs, Diaries, Letters, Collected Papers

Alvarez del Vayo, J., *Freedom's Battle*, London, Heinemann, 1940.

Avon, Lord., *The Eden Memoirs: Facing the Dictators*, London: Cassell, 1962.

Bond, B. (ed.), *Chief of Staff: The Diaries of Lieutenant General Sir Henry Pownall, Volume II, 1940–1944*, London: Leo Cooper, 1974.

Bullitt, O. H. (ed.), *For the President Personal and Secret: Correspondence between Franklin D. Roosevelt and William C. Bullitt*, London: Andre Deutsch, 1973.

Burdick, C. and Jacobsen, H.-A. (eds), *The Halder War Diary, 1939–1942*, London: Greenhill Books, 1982.

Churchill, W. S., *The Second World War, Vols II and III*, London: Cassell, 1949–1950.

Dallin, A. and Firsov, F. I. (eds), *Dimitrov and Stalin, 1934–1943: Letters from the Soviet Archives*, New Haven: Yale University Press, 2000.

Davies, R. W., Khlevniuk, O. V., Rees, E. A., Kosheleva, P. and Rogovaya, L. A. (eds), *The Stalin–Kaganovich Correspondence, 1931–1936*, New Haven, CT: Yale University Press, 2003.

Delgado, H., *The Memoirs of General Delgado*, London: Cassell, 1964.

Dilks, D. (ed.), *The Diaries of Sir Alexander Cadogan, 1938–1945*, London: Cassell, 1971.

Eccles, D. (ed.), *By Safe Hand: Letters of Sybil and David Eccles, 1939–1942*, London: Bodley Head, 1983.

Gilbert, M. (ed.), *The Churchill War Papers. Vol. III: The Ever Widening War, 1941*, London: Heinemann, 2000.

Halifax, Lord, *Fulness of Days*, London: Collins, 1957.

Halperin, P. (ed.), *The Keyes Papers: Selections from the Private and Official Correspondence of Admiral; of the Fleet Lord Keyes: Vol. III, 1939–1945*, London: Allen and Unwin, 1981.

Harvey, J. (ed.), *The Diplomatic Diaries of Oliver Harvey, 1937–1940*, London: Collins, 1970.

Harvey, J. (ed.), *The War Diaries of Oliver Harvey, 1941–1945*, London: Collins, 1978.

Hoare, Sir S., *Ambassador on Special Mission*, London: Collins, 1946.

Hull, C., *The Memoirs of Cordell Hull*, 2 vols, London: Hodder and Stoughton, 1948.

Jones, T., *A Diary with Letters, 1931–1950*, London: Oxford University Press, 1954.

Kimball, W. F. (ed.), *Churchill and Roosevelt: The Complete Correspondence. Vol. I: Alliance Emerging*, Princeton, NJ: Princeton University Press, 1984.

Krivitsky, W. G., *In Stalin's Secret Service: Memoirs of the First Soviet Master Spy to Defect*, New York: Enigma Books, 2000 edition.

Muggeridge, M. (ed.), *Ciano's Hidden Diary, 1937–1938*, New York: Dutton, 1953.

Muggeridge, M. (ed.), *Ciano's Diary, 1939–1943*, London: Heinemann, 1947.

Peterson, Sir M., *Both Sides of the Curtain: An Autobiography*, London: Constable, 1950.

Pimlott, B. (ed.), *The Political Diaries of Hugh Dalton, 1918–1940, 1945–1960*, London: Jonathan Cape, 1986.

Selby, W., *Diplomatic Twilight*, London: John Murray, 1953.

Vansittart, Lord, *The Mist Procession*, London: Hutchinson, 1957.

Vintras, R. E., *The Portuguese Connection*, London: Bachman and Turner, 1974.

SECONDARY WORKS

Abendroth, H.-H., *Hitler in der Spanischen Arena: Die Deutsch–Spanischen Beziehungen im Spannungsfeld der Europäischen Interessenpolitik vom Ausbruch des Bürgerkrieges bis zum Ausbruch des Weltkrieges, 1936–1939*, Paderborn: Schöningh, 1973.

Adamthwaite, A., *France and the Coming of the Second World War, 1936–1939*, London: Frank Cass, 1977.

Ahmad, Q., *Britain, Franco Spain and the Cold War, 1945–1950*, Kuala Lumpur: Noordeen, 1995.

Alba, V., *Transition in Spain: From Franco to Democracy*, New Jersey: Transaction Books, 1978.

Alexander, M. S., *The Republic in Danger: General Maurice Gamelin and the Politics of French Defence, 1933–1940*, Cambridge: Cambridge University Press, 1992.

Alpert, M., *A New International History of the Spanish Civil War*, London: Macmillan, 1994.

Barker, E., *Churchill and Eden at War*, London: Macmillan, 1978.

Beevor, A., *The Spanish Civil War*, London: Cassell, 1999.

Blumenthal, H., *Illusion and Reality in Franco-American Diplomacy, 1914–1945*, Baton Rouge, LA: Louisiana State University Press, 1986.

Bolleton, B., *The Spanish Civil War: Revolution and Counter Revolution*, New York: Harvester Wheatsheaf, 1991.

Broué, P. and Témime, E., *The Revolution and the Civil War in Spain*, London: Faber, 1972.

Buchanan, T., *The British Labour Movement and the Spanish Civil War*, Cambridge: Cambridge University Press, 1991.

Buchanan, T., *Britain and the Spanish Civil War*, Cambridge: Cambridge University Press, 1997.

Burdick, C. B., *Germany's Military Strategy and Spain in World War II*, Syracuse, NY: Syracuse University Press, 1968.

Burgwyn, H. J., *Italian Foreign Policy in the Interwar Period, 1918–1940*, Westport, CT: Praeger, 1997.

Butler, J. R. M., *Grand Strategy, II: 1939–1941*, London: HMSO, 1957.

Cable, J., *The Royal Navy and the Siege of Bilbao*, Cambridge: Cambridge University Press, 1979.

Carr, E. H., *The Twilight of Comintern, 1930–1935*, London: Macmillan, 1982.

Carr, E. H., *Comintern and the Spanish Civil War*, London: Macmillan, 1984.

Cattell, D. T., *Communism and the Spanish Civil War*, Berkeley, CA: University of California Press, 1955.

Cattell, D. T., *Soviet Diplomacy and the Spanish Civil War*, Berkeley, CA: University of California Press, 1957.

Cole, W. S., *Roosevelt and the Isolationists, 1932–1945*, Lincoln, NE: University of Nebraska Press, 1983.

Colodny, R. G., *Spain: The Glory and the Tragedy*, New York: Humanities Press, 1970.

Conn S. and Fairchild, B., *The United States Army in World War II. The Western Hemisphere: The Framework of Hemisphere Defence*, Washington, DC: Office of the Chief of (Army) Defense Department, 1960.

Cooper, M., *The German Air Force, 1933–1945: An Anatomy of Failure*, London: Jane's, 1981.

Cortada, J. W., *United States–Spanish Relations: Wolfram and World War II*, Barcelona: Manuel Pareja, 1971.

Coverdale, J. F., *Italian Intervention in the Spanish Civil War*, Princeton, NJ: Princeton University Press, 1975.

Dallek, R., *Franklin D. Roosevelt and American Foreign Policy, 1932–1945*, New York: Oxford University Press, 1979.

Deist., W., Messerschmidt, M., Volkmann, H.-E. and Wette, W., *Germany and the Second World War. Volume I: The Build-up of German Aggression*, Oxford: Oxford University Press: 1990.

Delgado, I., *Portugal e a Guerra Civil de Espanha*, Lisboa: Publicaçoes Europa-América, 1980.

Divine, R. A., *The Illusion of Neutrality*, Chicago: Chicago University Press, 1962.

Dreifort, J. E., *Yvon Delbos and the Quai d'Orsay: French Foreign Policy during the Popular Front, 1936–1938*, Lawrence, KS: University Press of Kansas, 1973.

Dülffer, J., *Weimar, Hitler und die Marine: Reichspolitik und Flottenbau, 1920 bis 1939*, Düsseldorf: Droste, 1973.

Dunthorn, D. J., *Britain and the Spanish Anti-Franco Opposition, 1940–1950*, London: Palgrave, 2000.

Duroselle, J. B., *La Politique Étrangère de la France: La Décadence (1932–1939)*, Paris: Imprimerie National, 1979.

Edwards, J., *The British Government and the Spanish Civil War, 1936–1939*, London: Macmillan, 1979.

Edwards, J., *Anglo-American Relations and the Franco Question, 1945–1955*, Oxford: Oxford University Press, 1999.

Ellwood, S., *Franco*, London: Longman, 1994.

Elorza, A. and Bizcarrondo, M., *Queridos Camaradas: La Internacional Comunista y España, 1919–1939*, Barcelona: Planeta, 1999.

Esch, P. M. van der, *Prelude to War: The International Repercussions of the Spanish Civil War, 1936–1939*, The Hague: Martinus Nijhoff, 1951.

Figueiredo, A. de, *Portugal: Fifty Years of Dictatorship*, London: Penguin, 1976.

Fornari, H., *Mussolini's Gadfly: Roberto Farinacci*, Nashville, TN: Vanderbilt University Press, 1971.

Friedländer, S., *Prelude to Downfall: Hitler and the United States, 1939–1941*, London: Chatto and Windus, 1967.

Fryer P. and McGowan Pinheiro, P., *Oldest Ally: A Portrait of Salazar's Portugal*, London: Dobson, 1961.

Gallagher, T., *Portugal: A Twentieth Century Interpretation*, Manchester: Manchester University Press, 1983.

Gallo, M., *Spain under Franco: A History*, London: Allen and Unwin, 1978.

Goda, N. J. W., *Tomorrow the World: Hitler, Northwest Africa and the Path toward North America*, College Station, TX: Texas A and M University Press, 1998.

Graham, H., *The Spanish Republic at War, 1936–1939*, Cambridge: Cambridge University Press, 2002.

Graham, L. S., *Portugal: The Decline and Collapse of an Authoritarian Order*, London/ Beverley Hills: Sage, 1975.

Griffiths, R., *Marshal Pétain*, London: Constable, 1970.

Guttmann, A., *The Wound in the Heart: America and the Spanish Civil War*, New York: Free Press of Glencoe, 1962.

Gwyer, J. M. A., *Grand Strategy Vol. III (part I)*, London: HMSO, 1964.

Harper, G. T., *German Economic Policy in Spain during the Civil War*, The Hague: Mouton, 1967.

Harvey, C. E., *The Rio Tinto Company: An Economic History of a Leading International Mining Concern*, Penzance: Alison Hodge, 1981.

Haslam, J., *The Soviet Union and the Struggle for Collective Security in Europe, 1933–1939*, London: Macmillan, 1984.

Henke, J., *England in Hitler's Politischen Kalkül, 1935–1939*, Boppard Am Rhein: Harald Boldt, 1973.

Hildebrand, K., *The Foreign Policy of the Third Reich*, London: Batsford, 1973.

Hildebrand, K., *The Third Reich*, London: Allen and Unwin, 1984.

Hillgruber, A., *Germany and the Two World Wars*, Cambridge, MA: Harvard University Press, 1981.

Hinsley, F. H., *British Intelligence in the Second World War, Volume I*, London: HMSO, 1979.

Hodgson, Sir R., *Spain Resurgent*, London: Hutchinson, 1953.

Höhne, H., *Canaris*, London: Secker and Warburg, 1979.

Howson, G., *Arms for Spain: The Untold Story of the Spanish Civil War*, London: John Murray, 1998.

Isorni, J., *Philippe Pétain*, Paris: La Table Ronde, 1972.

Jackson, J., *The Popular Front in France: Defending Democracy, 1934–1938*, Cambridge: Cambridge University Press, 1988.

Jackson, P., *France and the Nazi Menace: Intelligence and Policy-Making, 1933–1939*, Oxford: Oxford University Press, 2000.

Jacobsen, H. A. *Nationalsozialistische Aussenpolitik, 1933–1938*, Frankfurt am-Main/Berlin: Alfred Metzner Verlag, 1968.

Jordan, N., *The Popular Front and Central Europe: The Dilemmas of French Impotence, 1918–1940*, Cambridge: Cambridge University Press, 1992.

Kay, H., *Salazar and Modern Portugal*, London: Eyre and Spottiswoode, 1970.

Kleine-Albrandt, W., *The Policy of Simmering: A Study of British Policy during the Spanish Civil War, 1936–1939*, The Hague: Martinus Nijhoff, 1962.

Knox, M., *Mussolini Unleashed, 1939–1941: Politics and Strategy in Fascist Italy's Last War*, Cambridge: Cambridge University Press, 1982.

Kowalsky, D., *La Unión Soviética y la Guerra Civil España: Una Revisión Crítica*, Barcelona: Crítica, 2003.

Langer, W. L. and Gleason, S. E., *The Undeclared War, 1940–1941*, New York, Harper, 1953.

Lash, J. P., *Roosevelt and Churchill, 1939–1941: The Partnership that Saved the West*, London: Andre Deutsch, 1977.

Leitz, C., *Economic Relations between Nazi Germany and Franco's Spain, 1936–1945*, Oxford: Oxford University Press, 1996.

Leitz, C., *Nazi Germany and Neutral Europe during the Second World War*, Manchester: Manchester University Press, 2000.

Leutze, J. R., *Bargaining for Supremacy: Anglo-American Naval Collaboration, 1937–1941*, Chapel Hill, NC: University of North Carolina Press, 1977.

Little, D., *Malevolent Neutrality: The United States, Great Britain and the Origins of the Spanish Civil War*, Ithaca, NY and London: Cornell University Press, 1985.

McDermott, K. and Agnew, J., *The Comintern: A History of International Communism from Lenin to Stalin*, London: Macmillan, 1996.

Mack Smith, D., *Mussolini's Roman Empire*, London: Longman, 1976.

Maier, K., Rohde, H., Stegemann, B. and Umbreit, H., *Germany and the Second World War. Volume II: Germany's Initial Conquests in Europe*, Oxford: Oxford University Press, 1991.

Maisky, I., *Spanish Notebooks*, London: Hutchinson, 1966.

Mallett, R., *The Italian Navy and Fascist Expansionism, 1935–1940*, London: Frank Cass, 1998.

Marques, A. H. De Oliveira, *A History of Portugal, II: From Empire to Corporate State*, New York: Columbia University Press, 1972.

Medlicott, W. N., *The Economic Blockade*, 2 vols, London: HMSO, 1952, 1959.

Medlicott, W. N., *Britain and Germany: The Search for Agreement, 1930–1937*, London: Athlone, 1969.

Megargee, G. P., *Inside Hitler's High Command*, Lawrence, KS: University Press of Kansas, 2000.

Merkes, M., *Die Deutsche Politik gegenüber dem Spanischen Bürgerkrieg, 1936–1939*, Bonn: Ludwig Röhrscheid, 1969.

Miralles, R., *Juan Negrín: La República en Guerra*, Madrid: Ediciones Temas de Hoy, 2003.

Moradiellos, E., *Neutralidad Benévola: el Gobierno Británico y la Insurrección Militar Española de 1936*, Oviedo: Pentalfa, 1990.

Moradiellos, E., *La Perfidia de Albión: El Gobierno Británico y la Guerra Civil Española*, Madrid: Siglo Veintiuno de España Editores, 1996.

Moradiellos, E., *El Reñidero de Europa: Las Dimensiones Internacionales de la Guerra Civil Española*, Barcelona: Ediciones Península, 2001.

Néré, J., *The Foreign Policy of France from 1914 to 1945*, London: Routledge and Kegan Paul, 1975.

Nogueira, F., *Salazar III: As Grandes Crises (1936–1945)*, Porto: Livraria Civilização, 1983.

Nowell, C. E., *A History of Portugal*, Princeton, NJ: Van Nostrand, 1952.

Oliveira, C., *Salazar e a Guerra Civil de Espanha*, Lisboa: O Jornal, 1987.

Packard, J. M., *Neither Friend nor Foe: The European Neutrals in World War II*, New York: Charles Scribner, 1992.

Payne, S. G., *A History of Spain and Portugal, Vol. II*, Madison, WI: University of Wisconsin Press, 1973.

Payne, S. G., *Spain's First Democracy: The Second Spanish Republic, 1931–1936*, Madison, WI: University of Wisconsin Press, 1993.

Payne, S. G., *The Franco Regime, 1936–1975*, London: Phoenix Press, 2000.

Pérez, R. G., *Franquismo y Tercer Reich: Las Relaciones Economicas Hispano–Alemanas durante la Segunda Guerra Mundial*, Madrid: Centro do Estudios Constitucionales, 1994.

Pike, D. W., *Les Français et la Guerre d'Espagne, 1936–1939*, Paris: Presses Universitaires de France, 1975.

Powell, T. G., *Mexico and the Spanish Civil War*, Albuquerque: University of New Mexico Press, 1981.

Pratt, L. R., *East of Malta, West of Suez: Britain's Mediterranean Crisis, 1936–1939*, Cambridge: Cambridge University Press, 1975.

Preston, P., *Franco: A Biography*, London: HarperCollins, 1993.

Preston, P., *¡Comrades!: Portraits from the Spanish Civil War*, London: HarperCollins, 1999.

Proctor, R. L., *Hitler's Luftwaffe in the Spanish Civil War*, Westport, CT: Greenwood Press, 1983.

Puzzo, D., *Spain and the Great Powers, 1936–1941*, New York: Columbia University Press, 1962.

Raby, D. L., *Fascism and Resistance in Portugal: Communists, Liberals and Military Dissidents in the Opposition to Salazar, 1941–1974*, Manchester: Manchester University Press, 1988.

Reese, R., *The Soviet Military Experience: A History of the Soviet Army, 1917–1991*, London: Routledge, 2000.

Reverte, J. M., *La Batalla del Ebro*, Barcelona: Crítica, 2003.

Reynolds, D., *The Creation of the Anglo-American Alliance, 1937–1941: A Study in Competitive Cooperation*, London: Europa Publications, 1981.

Rich, N., *Hitler's Aims: Ideology, the Nazi State and the Course of Expansion, Vol. I*, London: Andre Deutsch, 1973.

Robinson, R. A. H., *Contemporary Portugal: A History*, London: Allen and Unwin, 1979.

Rosas, F., *O Salazarismo e a Aliança Luso-Britânica: Estudos Sobre a Política Externa do Estado Novo nos Anos 30 e 40*, Lisboa: Fragmentos, 1988.

Roskill, S., *Naval Policy Between the Wars II: The Period of Reluctant Rearmament, 1930–1939*, London: Collins, 1976.

Salerno, R. M., *Vital Crossroads: Mediterranean Origins of the Second World War, 1935–1940*, Ithaca, NY: Cornell University Press, 2002.

Saz, I., *Mussolini contra la II República: Hostilidad, Conspiraciones, Intervación (1931–1936)*, Valencia: Edicions Magnànim, Institució Valenciana d'Estudis i Investigació, 1986.

Schreiber, G., Stegemann, D., Vogel, D., *Germany and the Second World War. Volume III: The Mediterranean, South-east Europe, and North Africa, 1939–1941*, Oxford: Oxford University Press, 1995.

Schuler, F. E., *Mexico between Hitler and Roosevelt: Mexican Foreign Relations in the Age of Lázaro Cárdenas, 1934–1940*, Albuquerque, University of New Mexico Press, 1998.

Shorrock, W. I., *From Ally to Enemy: The Enigma of Fascist Italy in French Diplomacy, 1922–1940*, Kent, OH: Kent State University Press, 1988.

Smyth, D., *Diplomacy and Strategy of Survival: British Policy and Franco's Spain, 1940–1941*, Cambridge: Cambridge University Press, 1986.

Stein, L., *Beyond Death and Exile: The Spanish Republicans in France, 1939–1945*, Cambridge, MA: Harvard University Press, 1979.

Stone, G. A., *The Oldest Ally: Britain and the Portuguese Connection, 1936–1941*, Woodbridge: Boydell and Brewer, 1994.

Stott-Howarth, A. H. d'Araújo, *A Aliança Luso-Britânica e a Segunda Guerra Mundial: Tenrava de Interpretação do seu Funcionamento*, Lisboa: ENP, 1956.

Telo, A., *Portugal na Segunda Guerra*, Lisboa: Perspectivas Realidades, 1987.

Thomas, H., *The Spanish Civil War*, 3rd edn. London: Penguin, 1977.

Thomas, M., *Britain, France and Appeasement: Anglo-French Relations in the Popular Front Era*, Oxford: Berg Press, 1996.

Thomas, M., *The French Empire at War, 1940–1945*, Manchester: Manchester University Press, 1998.

Toynbee, A. J., *Survey of International Affairs 1937, II: The International Repercussions of the War in Spain (1936–1937)*, London: Oxford University Press, 1938.

Traina, R. P., *American Diplomacy and the Spanish Civil War*, Bloomington, IN: Indiana University Press, 1968.

Tusell, J., *Franco en la Guerra Civil: Una Biografía Política*, Barcelona: Tusquets Editores, 1992.

Viñas, Á., *Franco, Hitler y el Estallido de la Guerra Civil: Antecedentes y Consecuencias*, Madrid: Alianza Editorial, 2001.

Watt, D. C., *How War Came: The Immediate Origins of the Second World War, 1938–1939*, London: Heinemann, 1989.

Weinberg, G. L., *The Foreign Policy of Hitler's Germany: Diplomatic Revolution in Europe, 1933–1936*, Chicago: Chicago University Press, 1970.

Weinberg, G. L, *The Foreign Policy of Hitler's Germany: Starting World War II, 1937–1939*, Chicago: Chicago University Press, 1980.

Whealey, R. H., *Hitler and Spain: The Nazi Role in the Spanish Civil War*, Lexington, KY: University of Kentucky Press, 1989.

Woodward, Sir L., *British Foreign Policy in the Second World War*, vols. I and IV, London: HMSO, 1970, 1975.

Young, R. J., *In Command of France: French Foreign Policy and Military Planning, 1933–1940*, Cambridge, MA: Harvard University Press, 1978.

Young, R. J., *France and the Origins of the Second World War*, London: Macmillan, 1996.

ARTICLES, ESSAYS

Abendroth, H-H., 'Deutschlands rolle im spanischen Bürgerkrieg' in M. Funke (ed.), *Hitler, Deutschland und die Mächte: Materialen zur Aussenpolitik des Dritten Reichs*, Düsseldorf: Droste, 1978.

Abendroth, H-H., 'Die deutsche intervention im spanische Bürgerkrieg: ein discussionbeitrag', *Vierteljahrshefte für Zeitgeschichte*, vol. 30, 1982.

Adamthwaite, A., 'France and the coming of war', in W. J. Mommsen and L. Kettenacker (eds), *The Fascist Challenge and the Policy of Appeasement*, London: Allen and Unwin, 1983.

Alexander, M. S., 'France, the collapse of Republican Spain and the approach of general war: national security, war economics and the Spanish refugees, 1938–1940' in C. Leitz and D. J. Dunthorn (eds), *Spain in an International Context, 1936–1959*, Oxford: Berghahn Books, 1999.

Allain, J-C., 'La France et les neutralités Helvétique et Espagnole en 1939–1940' in Colloque International des Universités de Neuchâtel et de Berne, *Les États Neutres Européens et la Seconde Guerre Mondiale*, Neuchâtel: Éditions de la Baconnière, 1985.

Alpert, M., 'The clash of Spanish armies: contrasting ways of war in Spain, 1936–1939', *War in History*, vol. 6., 1999.

Alpert, M., 'The Spanish Civil War and the Mediterranean' in R. Rein (ed.), *Spain and the Mediterranean since 1898*, London: Frank Cass, 1999.

Andrew, C., 'Introduction to "The ISOS years: Madrid, 1941–1943" ', *Journal of Contemporary History*, vol. 30, 1995.

Benton, K., 'The ISOS years: Madrid, 1941–1943', *Journal of Contemporary History*, vol. 30, 1995.

Blinkhorn, M., 'Conservatism, traditionalism and fascism in Spain, 1898–1937', in M. Blinkhorn (ed.), *Fascists and Conservatives: The Radical Right and the Establishment in Twentieth Century Europe*, London: Unwin Hyman, 1990.

Buchanan, T., 'A far away country of which we know nothing? Perceptions of Spain and its civil war in Britain, 1931–1939', *Twentieth Century British History*, vol. 4, 1993.

Buchanan, T., 'Edge of darkness: British "front-line" diplomacy in the Spanish Civil War, 1936–1937', *Contemporary European History*, vol. 12, 2003.

Burdick, C. B., ' "Moro": the resupply of German submarines in Spain, 1939–1942', *Central European History*, vol. 3, 1972.

Burdick, C. B., 'The American military attachés and the Spanish Civil War, 1936–1939', *Militärgeschichtliche Mitteilungen*, vol. 46, 1989.

Cardozo, M., 'England's fated ally', *Luso-Brazilian Review*, vol. 7, 1970.

Cassels, A., 'Reluctant neutral: Italy and the strategic balance in 1939' in B. J. McKercher and R. Legault (eds.), *Military Planning and the Origins of the Second World War in Europe*, Westport, CT: Praeger, 2001.

Carlton, D., 'Eden, Blum and the origins of non-intervention', *Journal of Contemporary History*, vol. 6, 1971.

Cierva, R. de la, 'The Nationalist army in the Spanish Civil War' in R. Carr (ed.), *The Republic and the Civil War in Spain*, London, Macmillan, 1971.

Cowan, A., 'The guerrilla war against Franco', *European History Quarterly*, vol. 20, 1990.

Cunha, C. A., 'The Portuguese Communist Party, its ancillary organisations, and the Communist International's third period' in M. Worley (ed.), *In Search of Revolution: International Communist Parties in the Third Period*, London: I. B. Taurus, 2004.

De Madriaga, M., 'The intervention of Moroccan troops in the Spanish Civil War', *European History Quarterly*, vol. 22, 1992.

Detwiler, D. S., 'Spain and the Axis during World War II', *Review of Politics*, vol. 33, 1971.

Duff, K., 'Portugal', in A. J. Toynbee and V. Toynbee (eds), *Survey of International Affairs, 1939–1946: The War and the Neutrals*, London: Oxford University Press, 1956.

Duff, K., 'Italy' and 'Germany' in A. J. Toynbee and V. Toynbee (eds), *Survey of International Affairs: The Eve of War, 1939*, London: Oxford University Press, 1958.

Frank Jr, W. C., 'The Spanish Civil War and the coming of the Second World War', *International History Review*, vol. 9, 1987.

Frank Jr, W. C., 'Politico-military deception at sea in the Spanish Civil War, 1936–1939', *Intelligence and National Security*, vol. 5, 1990.

Gallagher, M. D., 'Léon Blum and the Spanish Civil War', *Journal of Contemporary History*, vol. 6, 1971.

Gallagher, T., 'Controlled repression in Salazar's Portugal', *Journal of Contemporary History*, vol. 14, 1979.

Gallagher, T., 'The mystery train: Portugal's military dictatorship, 1926–1932', *European Studies Review*, vol. 11, 1981.

Gallagher, T., 'Salazar's Portugal: the "Black Book" on fascism', *European History Quarterly*, vol. 14, 1984.

Gallagher, T., 'Conservatism, dictatorship and fascism in Portugal, 1914–1945', in M. Blinkhorn (ed.), *Fascists and Conservatives: The Radical Right and the Establishment in Twentieth Century Europe*, London: Unwin Hyman, 1990.

García, N. T., 'The Mediterranean in the foreign policy of the Second Spanish Republic' in R. Rein (ed.), *Spain and the Mediterranean since 1898*, London: Frank Cass, 1999.

Girault, R., 'La décision gouvernementale en politique extérieure', in R. Rémond and J. Bourdin (eds), *Edouard Daladier: Chef de Gouvernement, Avril 1938–Septembre 1939*, Paris: Presses de la Fondation des Sciences Politiques, 1977.

Goda, N. J. W., 'Germany's conception of Spain's strategic importance, 1940–1941' in C. Leitz and D. J. Dunthorn (eds), *Spain in an International Context, 1936–1959*, Oxford: Berghahn Books, 1999.

Goda, N. J. W., 'Franco's bid for empire: Spain, Germany, and the western Mediterranean in World War II' in R. Rein (ed.), *Spain and the Mediterranean since 1898*, London: Frank Cass, 1999.

Halstead, C. R., 'Consistent and total peril from every side: Portugal and its 1940 Protocol with Spain', *Iberian Studies*, vol. 3, 1974.

Halstead, C .R., 'The dispute between Ramon Serrano Suñer and Alexander Weddell', *Rivista di Studi Politica Internazionali*, vol. 3, 1974.

Halstead, C. R. and C. J. Halstead, 'Aborted imperialism: Spain's occupation of Tangier, 1940–1945', *Iberian Studies*, vol. 7, 1978.

Halstead, C. R., 'Spanish foreign policy, 1936–1978', in J. W. Cortada (ed.), *Spain in the Twentieth Century: Essays on Spanish Diplomacy, 1898–1978*, London, Aldwych Press, 1980.

Harvey, A. D., 'The Spanish Civil War as seen by British officers', *RUSI Journal*, August 1996.

Harvey, C. E., 'Politics and pyrites during the Spanish Civil War', *Economic History Review*, 2nd ser., vol. 31, 1978.

Hartley, J., 'Recent Soviet publications on the Spanish Civil War', *European History Quarterly*, vol. 18, 1988.

Haslam, J., 'The Comintern and the origins of the Popular Front, 1934–1935', *Historical Journal*, vol. 22, 1979.

Haslam, J., 'Soviet Russia and the Spanish problem' in R. Boyce and J. Maiolo (eds), *The Origins of World War Two: The Debate Continues*, London: Palgrave Macmillan, 2002.

Haywood Hunt, N., 'The French Radicals, Spain and the emergence of appeasement' in M. S. Alexander and H. Graham (eds), *The French and Spanish Popular Fronts*, Cambridge: Cambridge University Press, 1989.

Hernández, J. L. N., 'La sublevación y la improvisación de una política exterior de guerra, 1936–1939' in J. Tusell, J. Avilés and R. Pardo (eds), *La Política Exterior de España en el Siglo XX*, Madrid: Biblioteca Nueva, 2000.

Hernández-Sandoica, E. and Moradiellos, E., 'Spain and the Second World War' in N. Wylie (ed.), *European Neutrals and Non-Belligents during the Second World War*, Cambridge: Cambridge University Press, 2002.

Herwig, H. H., 'Prelude to *Weltblitzkrieg*: Germany's naval policy towards the United States of America, 1939–1941', *Journal of Modern History*, vol. 43, 1971.

Hillgruber, A., 'England's place in Hitler's plans for world dominion', *Journal of Contemporary History*, vol. 9, 1974.

Jackson, P., 'French strategy and the Spanish Civil War' in C. Leitz and D. J. Dunthorn (eds), *Spain in an International Context, 1936–1959*, Oxford: Berghahn Books, 1999.

Jarymowycz, R. J., 'Jedi knights in the Kremlin: the Soviet military in the 1930s and the genesis of deep battle' in B. J. McKercher and R. Legault (eds), *Military Planning and the Origins of the Second World War in Europe*, Westport, CN: Praeger, 2001.

Kiernan, V. G., 'The old alliance: England and Portugal', *The Socialist Register*, 1973.

Knox, M., 'The Fascist regime, its foreign policy and its wars: an 'anti-Fascist' orthodoxy?', *Contemporary European History*, vol. 4, 1995.

Leitz, C., 'Nazi Germany's intervention in the Spanish Civil War and the foundation of HISMA/ROWAK' in P. Preston and A. L. Mackenzie (eds), *The Republic Besieged: Civil War in Spain, 1936–1939*, Edinburgh: Edinburgh University Press, 1996.

Leitz, C., 'Hermann Göring and Nazi Germany's economic exploitation of Nationalist Spain, 1936–1939', *German History*, vol. 14, 1996.

Leitz, C., 'More carrot than stick: British economic warfare and Spain, 1941–1944', *Twentieth Century British History*, vol. 9, 1998.

Leitz, C., 'Programm Bär: the supply of German war material to Spain, 1943–1944' in C. Leitz and D. J. Dunthorn (eds), *Spain in an International Context, 1936–1959*, Oxford: Berghahn Books, 1999.

Leitz, C., 'Nazi Germany and Francoist Spain, 1936–1945' in S. Balfour and P. Preston (eds), *Spain and the Great Powers in the Twentieth Century*, London: Routledge, 1999.

Léon, A. E., 'La dimensión internacional de la Segunda República: un proyecto en el crisol' in J. Tusell, J. Avilés and R. Pardo (eds), *La Política Exterior de España en el Siglo XX*, Madrid: Biblioteca Nueva, 2000.

Levy, D. A. L., 'The French Popular Front, 1936–1937' in H. Graham and P. Preston (eds), *The Popular Front in Europe*, London: Macmillan, 1987.

Little, D., 'Red scare 1936: anti-Bolshevism and the origins of British non-intervention in the Spanish Civil War, *Journal of Contemporary History*, vol. 23, 1988.

MacDonald, C., 'Deterrent diplomacy: Roosevelt and the containment of Germany, 1938–1940' in R. Boyce and E. M. Robertson (eds), *Paths to War: New Essays on the Origins of the Second World War*, London: Macmillan, 1988.

Manne, R., 'Some British light on the Nazi–Soviet pact', *European Studies Review*, vol. 11, 1981.

Manne, R., 'The Foreign Office and the failure of Anglo-Soviet rapprochement', *Journal of Contemporary History*, vol. 16, 1981.

Mills, W. C., 'The Nyon Conference: Neville Chamberlain, Anthony Eden and the appeasement of Italy in 1937', *International History Review*, vol. 15, 1993.

Miralles, R., 'The international policy of the Second Republic during the Spanish Civil War' in R. Rein (ed.), *Spain and the Mediterranean since 1898*, London: Frank Cass, 1999.

Miralles, R., 'Las iniciativas diplomáticas de la Segunda República durante la guerra civil, 1936–1939' in J. Tusell, J. Avilés and R. Pardo (eds.), *La Política Exterior de España en el Siglo XX*, Madrid: Biblioteca Nueva, 2000.

Monteath, P., 'German historiography and the Spanish Civil War: a critical survey', *European History Quarterly*, vol. 20, 1990.

Moradiellos, E., 'The origins of British non-intervention in the Spanish Civil War: Anglo-Spanish relations in early 1936', *European History Quarterly*, vol. 30, 1991.

Moradiellos, E., 'British political strategy in the face of the military uprising of 1936 in Spain', *Contemporary European History*, vol. 1, 1992.

Moradiellos, E., 'Appeasement and non-intervention: British policy during the Spanish Civil War' in P. Catterall and J. Morris (eds), *Britain and the Threat to Stability in Europe 1918–1945*, Leicester: Leicester University Press, 1993.

Moradiellos, E., 'The gentle general: the official British perception of General Franco during the Spanish Civil War' in P. Preston and A. L. Mackenzie (eds), *The Republic Besieged: Civil War in Spain, 1936–1939*, Edinburgh: Edinburgh University Press, 1996.

Moradiellos, E., 'The Allies and the Spanish Civil War' in S. Balfour and P. Preston (eds), *Spain and the Great Powers in the Twentieth Century*, London: Routledge, 1999.

Moradiellos, E., 'The Potsdam Conference and the Spanish problem', *Contemporary European History*, vol. 10, 2001.

Payne, S. G., 'Fascist Italy and Spain, 1922–1945' in R. Rein (ed.), *Spain and the Mediterranean since 1898*, London: Frank Cass, 1999.

Pérez, R.G., 'España y la Segunda Guerra Mundial' in J. Tusell, J. Avilés and R. Pardo (eds.), *La Política Exterior de España en el Siglo XX*, Madrid: Biblioteca Nueva, 2000.

Pike, D. W., 'Franco and the Axis stigma', *Journal of Contemporary History*, vol. 17, 1982.

Pike, F. B., 'The background to the civil war in Spain and the U.S. response to the war' in M. Falcoff and F. B. Pike (eds), *The Spanish Civil War, 1936–1939: American Hemisphere Perspectives*, Lincoln, NE: University of Nebraska Press, 1982.

Preston, P., 'Franco and the Axis temptation' in P. Preston (ed), *The Politics of Revenge: Fascism and the Military in Twentieth Century Spain*, London, Unwin Hyman, 1990.

Preston, P., 'Franco and Hitler: the myth of Hendaye 1940', *Contemporary European History*, vol. 1, 1992.

Preston, P., 'General Franco as military leader', *Transactions of the Royal Historical Society*, 6th series, vol. 4, 1994.

Preston, P., 'Mussolini's Spanish adventure: from limited risk to war' in P. Preston and A. L. Mackenzie (eds), *The Republic Besieged: Civil War in Spain, 1936–1939*, Edinburgh: Edinburgh University Press, 1996.

Preston, P., 'Italy and Spain in civil war and world war' in S. Balfour and P. Preston (eds), *Spain and the Great Powers in the Twentieth Century*, London: Routledge, 1999.

Queipo de Llano, G. G., 'El impacto internacional de la Guerra Civil Española' in J. Tusell, J. Avilés and R. Pardo (eds), *La Política Exterior de España en el Siglo XX*, Madrid: Biblioteca Nueva, 2000.

Raby, D. L., 'Controlled, limited and manipulated opposition under a dictatorial regime: Portugal, 1945–1949', *European History Quarterly*, vol. 19, 1989.

Rees, T., 'The "Good Bolsheviks": the Spanish Communist Party in the third period' in M. Worley (ed.), *In Search of Revolution: International Communist Parties in the Third Period*, London: I. B. Taurus, 2004.

Roberts, G., 'Soviet foreign policy and the Spanish Civil War, 1936–1939' in C. Leitz and D. J. Dunthorn (eds), *Spain in an International Context, 1936–1959*, Oxford: Berghahn Books, 1999.

Robertson, E. M., 'Hitler's planning for war and the response of the Great Powers (1938–early 1939)', in H. W. Koch (ed.), *Aspects of the Third Reich*, London: Macmillan, 1985.

Rosas, F., 'Portuguese neutrality in the Second World War' in N. Wylie (ed.), *European Neutrals and Non-Belligents during the Second World War*, Cambridge: Cambridge University Press, 2002.

Ross, S., 'American war plans' in B. J. McKercher and R. Legault (eds), *Military Planning and the Origins of the Second World War in Europe*, Westport, CT: Praeger, 2001.

Salerno, R. M., 'Britain, France and the emerging Italian threat' in M. S. Alexander and W. J. Philpott (eds), *Anglo-French Defence Relations between the Wars*, London: Palgrave Macmillan, 2002.

Saz, I., 'The Second Republic in the international arena' in S. Balfour and P. Preston (eds), *Spain and the Great Powers in the Twentieth Century*, London: Routledge, 1999.

Saz, I., 'Fascism and empire: Fascist Italy against Republican Spain' in R. Rein (ed.), *Spain and the Mediterranean since 1898*, London: Frank Cass, 1999.

Schieder, W., 'Spanischen Bürgerkrieg und Vierjahresplan', in W. Scheider and C. Dipper (eds), *Der Spanische Bürgerkrieg in der Internationalen Politik, 1936–1939*, München: Nymphenburger Verlagshandlung, 1976.

Smyth, D., 'Reflex reaction: Germany and the onset of the Spanish Civil War' in P. Preston (ed.), *Revolution and War in Spain, 1931–1939*, London: Methuen, 1984.

Smyth, D., 'The politics of asylum, Juan Negrín and the British Government in 1940' in R. T. B. Langhorne (ed.), *Diplomacy and Intelligence during the Second World War: Essays in Honour of F. S. Hinsley*, Cambridge: Cambridge University Press, 1984.

Smyth, D., 'Screening "Torch": allied counter intelligence and the Spanish threat to the secrecy of the allied invasion of French North Africa in November, 1942, *Intelligence and National Security*, vol. 4, 1989.

Smyth, D., 'The despatch of the Spanish Blue Division to the Russian Front: reasons and repercussions', *European History Quarterly*, vol. 24, 1994.

Smyth, D., ' "We are with you": solidarity and self-interest in Soviet policy towards Republican Spain, 1936–1939' in P. Preston and A. L. Mackenzie (eds), *The Republic Besieged: Civil War in Spain, 1936–1939*, Edinburgh: Edinburgh University Press, 1996.

Smyth, D., 'Franco and the Allies in the Second World War' in S. Balfour and P. Preston (eds), *Spain and the Great Powers in the Twentieth Century*, London: Routledge, 1999.

Stafford, P., 'The Chamberlain–Halifax visit to Rome: a reappraisal', *English Historical Review*, vol. 98, 1983.

Stone, G. A., 'The official British attitude to the Anglo-Portuguese alliance, 1910–1945', *Journal of Contemporary History*, vol. 10, 1975.

Stone, G. A., 'Britain, non-intervention and the Spanish Civil War', *European Studies Review*, vol. 9, 1979.

Stone, G. A., 'The European great powers and the Spanish Civil War' in R. Boyce and E. M. Robertson (eds), *Paths to War: New Essays on the Origins of the Second World War*, London: Macmillan, 1988.

Stone, G. A., 'Britain, France and the Spanish problem, 1936–1939' in R. C. Richardson and G. Stone (eds), *Decisions and Diplomacy: Essays in Twentieth Century International History*, London: Routledge, 1994.

Stone, G. A., 'Inglaterra, Portugal e a Não Beligerância Espanhola, 1940–1941', *Ler História*, vol. 25, 1994.

Stone, G. A., 'Britain, France and Franco's Spain in the aftermath of the Spanish Civil War', *Diplomacy and Statecraft*, vol. 6, 1995.

Stone, G. A., 'Sir Robert Vansittart and Spain, 1931–1941' in T. G. Otte and C. Pagedas (eds), *Personalities, War and Diplomacy: Essays in International History*, London: Frank Cass, 1997.

Stone, G. A., 'The degree of British commitment to the restoration of democracy in Spain, 1939–1947' in C. Leitz and D. J. Dunthorn (eds), *Spain in an International Context, 1936–1959*, Oxford: Berghahn Books, 1999.

Stone, G. A., 'From entente to alliance: Anglo-French relations, 1935–1939' in A. Sharp and G. Stone (eds), *Anglo-French Relations in the Twentieth Century: Rivalry and Cooperation*, London: Routlege, 2000.

Stone, G. A., 'The British Government and the sale or arms to the lesser European powers, 1936–1939', *Diplomacy and Statecraft*, vol. 14, 2003.

Sullivan, B. R., 'Fascist Italy's military involvement in the Spanish Civil War', *Journal of Military History*, vol. 59, 1995.

Swain, G., 'Stalin and Spain, 1944–1948' in C. Leitz and D. J. Dunthorn (eds), *Spain in an International Context, 1936–1959*, Oxford: Berghahn Books, 1999.

Sweeney, J. K., 'The Portuguese wolfram embargo: a case study in economic warfare', *Military Affairs*, vol. 38, 1974.

Sweeney, J. K., 'The Luso-American connection: the courtship, 1940–1941', *Iberian Studies*, vol. 6, 1977.

Tierney, D., 'Franklin D. Roosevelt and covert aid to the Loyalists in the Spanish Civil war, 1936–1939', *Journal of Contemporary History*, vol. 39, 2004.

Veatch, R., 'The League of Nations and the Spanish Civil War, 1936–1939', *European History Quarterly*, vol. 20, 1990.

Viñas, Á., 'Gold, the Soviet Union and the Spanish Civil War', *European Studies Review*, vol. 9, 1979.

Viñas, Á., 'The financing of the Spanish Civil War' in P. Preston (ed.), *Revolution and War in Spain, 1931–1939*, London: Methuen, 1984.

Viñas, Á. and Seidel, C. C., 'Franco's request to the Third Reich for military assistance', *Contemporary European History*, vol. 11, 2002.

Warner, G., 'France and non-intervention in Spain, July–August 1936', *International Affairs*, vol. 38, 1962.

Watt, D. C., 'German strategic planning and Spain, 1938–1939', *Army Quarterly*, 1960.

Watt, D. C., 'The initiation of the negotiations leading to the Nazi–Soviet Pact: a historical puzzle' in C. Abramsky (ed.), *Essays in Honour of E. H. Carr*, London: Macmillan, 1974.

Watt, D. C., 'Britain, France and the Italian problem, 1937–1939', in Colloques Franco-Britanniques, *Les Relations Franco-Britanniques de 1935 à1939*, Paris: Éditions du Centre de la Recherche Scientifique, 1975.

Whealey, R. H., 'Foreign intervention in the Spanish Civil War' in R. Carr (ed.), *The Republic and the Civil War in Spain*, London: Macmillan, 1971.

Whealey, R. H., 'How Franco financed his war – reconsidered', *Journal of Contemporary History*, vol. 12, 1979.

Whealey, R. H., 'Economic influence of the great powers in the Spanish Civil War: from the Popular Front to the Second World War', *International History Review*, vol. 5, 1983.

Wheeler, D. L., 'The military and the Portuguese dictatorship, 1926–1974: "the honor of the army" ', in L. S. Graham and H. M. Makler (eds), *Contemporary Portugal: the Revolution and its Antecedents*, Austin, TX: University of Texas Press, 1979.

Wheeler, D. L., 'In the service of order: the Portuguese political police and the British, German and Spanish intelligence, 1932–1945', *Journal of Contemporary History*, vol. 18, 1983.

Wheeler, D. L., 'The price of neutrality: Portugal, the wolfram question, and World War II', pts 1, 2, *Luso-Brazilian Review*, vol. 33, 1986.

Wheeler, D. L., 'And who is my neighbor? a World War II hero of conscience for Portugal', *Luso-Brazilian Review*, vol. 36, 1989.

Wylie, N., 'An amateur learns his job? Special Operations Executive in Portugal, 1940–1942', *Journal of Contemporary History*, vol. 36, 2001.

Index